# Education Reform in the American States

# Education Reform in the American States

*by*
**Jerry McBeath, Maria Elena Reyes,
and Mary Ehrlander**

**Information Age Publishing, Inc.**
Charlotte, North Carolina • www.infoagepub.com

**Library of Congress Cataloging-in-Publication Data**


McBeath, Jerry.
  Education reform in the American states / by Jerry McBeath, Maria Elena
Reyes & Mary Ehrlander.
    p. cm.
  Includes bibliographical references.
  ISBN-13: 978-1-59311-775-7 (paperback)
  ISBN-13: 978-1-59311-776-4 (hardcover)
  1. School improvement programs—United States—Case studies.
  2. Educational change—United States—Case studies.
  3. Education—Standards—United States—Case studies. I. Reyes, Marma Elena,
  1947- II. Ehrlander, Mary F. III. Title.
  LB2822.82.M377 2007
  371.2—dc22

                                                                    2007023802



ISBN 13: 978-1-59311-775-7 (paperback)
ISBN 13: 978-1-59311-776-4 (hardcover)

Printed in the United States of America

# CONTENTS

# ACKNOWLEDGMENTS

We began this project in 2000, as a study of the development and implementation of standards-based education reform in the state of Alaska. As the project matured, we examined the impacts of the federal No Child Left Behind act on Alaska education, and then expanded our research into the stories of education reform in the other states. For support of our early research, we thank the University of Alaska President's Special Project Fund, the Natural Resources Fund, and the Alaska Schools Research Fund and express our gratitude to UA President Mark Hamilton, Assistant to the Vice President for Academic Affairs Dave Veazey, and UAF School of Education Deans Roger Norris-Tull and Eric Madsen.

We are grateful for the assistance we have received in project management from Patti Carey and Jamie Caikoski in the School of Education and Tracie Cogdill in the College of Liberal Arts, from Julia Parzick in the Department of History & Northern Studies, Courtney Pagh in the Department of Political Science, and Celine Gonon, student assistant in political science. Eric Bauer provided essential research assistance.

For their constructive criticism of earlier versions of the manuscript, we thank Dr. Nicholas Stayrook, former consultant to the Alaska Department of Education and Early Development; Dr. Judith Kleinfeld, codirector of Northern Studies and Professor of Psychology; and John Korey, professor of political science, California Polytechnic University. Finally, we thank George Johnson of Information Age Publishing for advice and suggestions on style and formatting of the manuscript, and for preparing it for publication. Of course, we remain responsible for errors and omissions in the volume.

CHAPTER 1

# INTRODUCTION

## OVERVIEW

Publication of *A Nation at Risk* in 1983 alerted Americans to the serious problems in K-12 education, and the extent to which they impaired national and global competitiveness. By no means was this the first call for education reform in the American states, yet one can argue that the standards-based movement of the late 1980s and 1990s, and the federal No Child Left Behind (NCLB) legislation of 2002, have had a larger impact on schooling than any previous reform effort in American history. Schools and districts that had invested immense resources of money, time, and energy into meeting state standards and accountability systems were then required to implement new federal mandates (and bear much of the cost). NCLB was a new phase of educational federalism in the United States. Could states have ignored the federal mandate? Would resistance be effective? In the early twenty-first century neither course seemed feasible. Almost all states recognized national support for assessment and accountability, and instead they adapted while negotiating for the best terms possible. In this volume we examine state responses to federal education reform mandates, as a demonstration of the resilience of federalism in America.

By education reform we mean changes in the process of schooling directed toward improvement of student achievement. Because the governance, finance, and organization of public education in the United States

*Education Reform in the American States*
pp. 1–22
Copyright © 2008 by Information Age Publishing
All rights of reproduction in any form reserved.

are complex, systemic reform always is difficult, sometimes torturously so, and time consuming. The chief contribution to the complexity of the education reform process is variety among the American states and local governments, once wholly responsible for public schooling and now compromised by federal rules.

In this chapter we first outline the elements of complexity in the context of American federalism. We examine the idea of local control, bourgeoning state power, and the rapidly growing federal role in education. At each level we introduce the primary actors and agencies of educational change. Then we turn to education reform movements. We consider reforms to the inputs of the educational process, focusing on changes in school finance and development of programs to assist special student populations. We review major recent experiments of education change, such as charter schools and school vouchers, and then discuss in greater detail the focus on school outputs represented in the assessment and accountability movement. We analyze the education reform processes, treating models of policy diffusion, entrepreneurship, and general policy change.

This is the background to the most recent federal legislation, NCLB, which has had dissimilar effects on the states because of variety in their accountability systems before 2002. The chapter concludes with an introduction to the nine states forming case studies of educational change in the early twenty-first century.

## AMERICAN FEDERALISM AND PUBLIC K-12 EDUCATION

Most nations have unitary systems of government and a high degree of uniformity in educational finance, curricula and academic programs, and in the training and recruitment of teachers. Even among the small number (about 25) of federal systems, the United States historically has had the most decentralized K-12 public school system, as we see in a review of the relationships of local, state, and federal governments to the public school enterprise.

### The Idea of Local Control

Until the 1840s and the development of the "common school" movement, there was immense variety in the number, type, curriculum, and quality of schools in the American states. Typically, schools were under "local control," meaning they were responsible to a town council; a city, township, or country government; or in a small number of cases, to an independent school district. As Tocqueville observed in *Democracy in America*, administrative decentralization was one of the strengths of the American polity that incorporated views of ordinary people in government decisions "so that the maximum possible number of people has some concern with public affairs" (1969, p. 69).

Framers of the federal constitution spoke for most eighteenth and early nineteenth century Americans when they expressed distrust of government and fear of concentrated power. This explains the separation of powers systems adopted for both state and federal governments, and the reluctance to assign important functions such as education to distant powers. Although each state constitution listed education among the important state functions, the constitutions did not expressly delegate education powers to local governments. Instead, local control was the prevailing original condition, and it strengthened as provision of educational services expanded into the industrial era after the Civil War.

By the early twentieth century, school boards had become established in most states to exercise accountability over schools, a product of the Progressive movement and its interest in reducing the corruption of urban machines and buffering important activities from the political process. Working very loosely under the control of state boards of education, the local boards authorized development of school curricula, hired teachers and principals, set graduation requirements and student behavior standards, and built school facilities. They either went directly to taxpayers to raise revenues for schools, or called upon local town, city, township, or county governments to fund schooling (Hill, 2004).

Up to the end of World War II, local governments (usually through the property tax) and voters (through votes on school bonds and appropriation measures) supplied nearly two thirds of total K-12 education spending in the United States. Because of this tax burden, the politics of education attracted a large number of participants. In nearly all of the states, voters elected local school boards, and school board members became tireless advocates of local control. Local business groups, and particularly chambers of commerce, paid attention to school board elections, as did school and districtwide Parents and Teachers Associations (PTAs) (see Cibulka, 2001). Too, school administrators had direct stakes in electoral outcomes, and the organization of teachers into unions especially gave them bargaining advantages at the local level.

Both the professionalization and rationalization of public education in the post-WWII era changed the complexion of school politics. Increasingly, principals and superintendents, as well as other school administrators, earned specialized administrative credentials. This professional certification gave them a basis of independence from the school boards that had hired them, although the interests of boards and administrators (collectively, schools' managers) usually were consonant. Then, in the 1950s and 1960s, the school consolidation movement sought to achieve economies of scale in the operations of schooling, making them more rational and efficient economically. This reduced the large number of school districts, from nearly 100,000 nationwide to just over 16,000 by the 1980s. The increased focus of large numbers of school participants in fewer arenas gave relationships among local school actors an organizational cast.

## The Changing State Role in Public Education

Although each state includes education among its express constitutional powers, only half of the states mention a state school board or superintendent of public instruction in basic law. In 2006, all states have state-level boards of education. Each state has a superintendent of public instruction or commissioner of education, and in one-third of the states, these are elected officials. The state superintendent of public instruction directs the department of education, which is a large bureaucracy in most American states. These are developments of the last 60 years.

The growth of an education bureaucracy in most of the states is a product of increased state centralization of educational functions as well as their finance. In the last generation, states have established uniform criteria for credentialing of teachers and administrators; they have crafted attendance requirements, set the number of days in the school year and minimum credit requirements for high school graduation; they have made uniform the heating, safety, and building requirements for school facilities.

The increased centralization of public school education at the state level has been matched by an increase in state funding of schooling. From less than one third of total school expenditures in the late 1940s, in 2006 state governments spend about 48%, as compared to 44% by local governments. Most states allocate at least one third of their general fund budgets to K-12 school expenses, and this makes education a prominent issue for governors as well as members of the state legislature. Indeed, few state governors have not included education themes in election contests, and most aspire to be called an "education governor." (Mazzoni [1994, pp. 53-75] summarizes state activism in education reform. Focusing on the "reformist South," he treats gubernatorial activism, business alliances as well as national organizations.)

The number of state education actors exceeds that at the local levels. In addition to governor and legislators (as well as state courts, which periodically hear education issues), there is the state superintendent of public instruction and the state board of education (most members of which are appointed by governors). Then, school principals and superintendents have organized into statewide units, as have teachers, school boards, paraprofessionals, and PTAs. Many states also have statewide alliances of business groups, and the business sector closely follows politics of education in state capitals (see Goldberg & Traiman, 2001).

## The Growing Federal Role in Public Education

Although the state role in education is now more important than that of local governments, it increasingly is challenged by the federal government. Until the post-WWII era, the federal government adopted a laissez-faire stance toward K-12 education. After all, the U.S. Constitution contains no mention of education. The limited amount of federal spending on K-12 schooling (about 1% of total educational expenditures until the 1950s) was justified under the spending clause of the Constitution, for enhancement of the "general welfare."

By the 1960s, however, in an era of civil rights and other social protests, pressures for greater federal involvement in K-12 education led to action on the part of president, Congress, and the courts. We discuss the first large-scale federal effort—the Elementary and Secondary Education Act (ESEA) of 1965—below. It gave both president and Congress a permanent interest in federal funding of education, as well as issues of educational inequity. The Supreme Court and lower federal courts became involved in both school desegregation and special education issues (Viteritti, 2005).

In the Carter Administration, the Congress authorized establishment of the U.S. Department of Education (USDOE), and this significantly strengthened the representation of K-12 education issues in federal government, for the Secretary of Education became a cabinet member (the previous Office of Education had been headed by a director). In addition to president, Congress, courts, and a national education bureaucracy, in the intensified lobbying environment of the last generation, national education interest groups have figured in education policymaking. These include the two national teachers' unions, the National Education Association (NEA) and the American Federation of Teachers (AFT), the National School Boards Association, the Education Commission of the States, and the Council of Chief State School Officers (CCSSO). Too, the National Conference of State Legislatures (NCSL) and the National Governors' Association (NGA) regularly chime in on education issues, as do subject-area associations such as the National Council of Teachers of Mathematics.

Altogether, the cast of actors and agencies at the federal level is larger than that in any of the states (Manna, 2006). This is explained not only by the currency of education issues but also by the increase in federal contributions to K-12 education, from 1% in the 1940s to about 7-8% in 2006. Notwithstanding the smallest overall share in education funding as compared to the states and local governments collectively, national influence has grown dramatically. And the federal role to the present has been supported by the public.

The overall system of K-12 education, including its control, financing and the tangled web of local, state, and federal laws and authorities, developed incrementally, even accidentally. It followed no rational design or pattern of objectives. The very complexity of the system has made educational reform at the state as well as national level cumbersome and difficult.

## CURRENTS OF EDUCATIONAL REFORM

The episodic pattern of reform to improve educational quality in the American states is unlike that in any other nation. In the 100 year period from the start of the twentieth to the beginning of the twenty-first centuries, a number of major reform movements have influenced the conduct of schooling. Moreover, there is a substantial critical literature arguing that the reform process is problematic. For example, Tyack and Cuban (1995) comment on the difficulty in determining efficacy of reform efforts, because of: "the time lag between advocacy and implementation; the uneven penetration of reforms in the different sectors of public education; and the different impact of reforms on various social groups" (p. 55). We focus on the post-WWII era and consider educational reforms in three categories: inputs to the system of schooling, formation of incentives to improve school performance, and student outcomes. Then we analyze the processes of reforms in the American states.

### Inputs

When attempting to improve the quality of schooling, it is perhaps natural for advocates of change to turn to the input side of the educational process: the qualifications and experience of teachers, the number of pupils per teacher (the average class size, especially in lower grades), the special programs available to assist students with learning problems or those who are disadvantaged because of socioeconomic or ethnic/racial status, even the quality of school facilities and student amenities. All of these improvements may add value to the educational process; each, however, costs money and requires an increase in the economic resources allocated to education.

A broad and undifferentiated reform process in the post-WWII era has led to significant increases in the funding of K-12 education, and changes in values of inputs to the educational process. For example, as Hanushek notes, in the period from 1960 to 2000, the pupil-teacher ratios in the United States fell almost 40%. The number of teachers having a master's degree (or more graduate education) doubled, and by the early twenty-first century a majority of teachers in the United States had at least a master's degree. And the experience of teachers increased greatly, with the median level of experience nearly doubling from 1970 to 2000 (Hanushek, 2003).

An increase in the number of teachers reduced class size, while these teachers (mostly unionized) were better paid, and this brought about an increase in per-pupil expenditures. During the 100 year period from 1890 to 1990, Hanushek and Rivkin calculate that spending per student increased at a rate of 3.5% annually, well above the average rate of inflation. Estimating the cost adjusted for inflation (based on 1990 dollars), they calculated that in 1890 the per student spending was $164 compared to $771 in 1940 and $4,622 in 1990 (1997, p. 42).

The question is what this significant increase in inputs produced in terms of student achievement. Measuring student performance on the only national examination, the National Assessment of Educational Progress (NAEP), Hanushek (2003) found that student performance in reading and mathematics was just a bit higher in 1999 than 30 years previously when spending was much lower. Then, Hanushek compared student scores over the years on the Scholastic Aptitude Test (SAT), which is less good a measure of performance because the test is voluntary and taken by a select set of the national student population. SAT scores plunged from the mid-1960s until the end of the 1970s, which seemed to reflect little value to students taking it of the changes to inputs. (However, Hanushek does not emphasize that increased numbers of students taking SATs likely had an impact on the scores.)

The debate on educational inputs continues, and some scholars contradict Hanushek's findings, largely because of changes in composition of the student population in the last generation (see Mayer, 1997, p. 32). The issue of educational inputs is also heavily politicized, because supporters of increasing educational resources (for example, teachers' unions) will personally benefit from more funding to education, which gives them a very strong incentive to be organized.

## School Incentives

This second reform category is intermediate between inputs and outcomes. It considers the changes that can be made in the structure of school incentives. Essentially, reformers in this area ask how individual schools can be made more competitive, to the advantage of student learning. While a large number of incentives have been discussed and applied in the context of school reform, five bear mention: contracting arrangements for school functions, merit pay for teachers, open enrollment, charter schools, and school vouchers. We define each and give examples of states engaged in this type of educational reform.

Contracting is a form of privatization of school functions typically provided by the school itself. In the usual case, the school, district, or state permits private sector bidding on contracts for school services. For example, a study in 1996 found that among school districts in the United States, transportation was contracted out about 30%, food services by 7%, custodial work by 10%, and building operations and maintenance by 8% (Lambdin, 1996). The least controversial service is the custodial/maintenance function for individual schools or on a district-wide basis. The objective of this reform is to lower educational costs, and perhaps steer greater resources toward services directly benefiting students. Because most custodial/maintenance services in schools and school districts are performed by unionized employees, this cost-reducing alternative has been successful only in right-to-work states.

The logic of merit pay is that teachers will respond to market-based incentives. If they know that they will receive higher pay based on better student performance, then they will adjust and focus their teaching methods to help students excel. This reform proposal encounters an extreme reaction from teachers' unions, which are pledged to improving the salaries and working conditions of all teachers, not just those deemed by administrators to be excellent. Moreover, teachers emphasize that given wide disparity in students' abilities, socio-economic levels, and support received from home, it is fundamentally unfair to link teachers' performance to that of students.

The "open enrollment" reform refers to a change in either state or school district policy to allow parents to transfer their children from unsatisfactory, low-performing neighborhood schools to better schools out of their attendance area. This reform began in East Harlem in 1973, but the most pronounced reform has been in the state of Minnesota. In 1987 this state introduced a statewide open-enrollment plan, which permitted students to attend any public school appropriate for their age, but dependent on availability of space and adherence to desegregation rules (Mintrom & Vergari, 1997).

Charter schools are a relatively recent innovation in American education. These are schools that are exempt from most (but not all) school district and state regulations, in order to develop an innovative plan for school improvement. The objective of the charter school movement is to provide greater choice in public education, to increase competition among schools and improve accountability, and to enhance innovations in school management and pedagogy (Mintrom & Vergari, 1997). Minnesota was the first state to develop a charter school program, and it remains a national leader today. In the early twenty-first century, some 1,700 schools nationwide were labeled as charter schools, and they enrolled more than 350,000 students. State regulations on charter schools vary, from tight to very loose, which influences the number of such schools. They are most numerous in Washington, DC and in Arizona (see Fusarelli, 2001; Irons & Harris, 2007).

The final innovation is also the most controversial: school choice or voucher plans (see Macedo, 2003). It was University of Chicago economist (later Nobel prize winner) Milton Friedman who introduced the idea of school vouchers in 1955. His complaint about American K-12 education was its uncompetitive nature. Most schools were "government schools," and because they had a guaranteed enrollment (and captive audience) of students as well as full taxpayer support, they lacked any incentive to improve educational performance of their students (Friedman, 1962). He argued that if parents had the option of transferring their children to other public—even private—schools, that the competitive environment of education would be improved. Teachers and other school staff would work harder to improve educational outcomes. If they did not, their schools would fall under competitive pressure and they would lose their jobs. Teachers' unions uniformly have opposed voucher experiments. Ostensibly because they would drain from public school systems critically needed funding as well as the most capable students (along with the most efficacious parents who are essential to the high quality of public schools), vouchers would, in their view, leave public schools as a dumping grounds for those children whose families were the least able to advocate for them (see Irons & Harris, 2007; Metcalf & Tait, 1999).

## Output

The final category of school reform focuses on outcomes, and in particular, the improvement of students' academic performance through the systematic administration of student assessments and the development of accountability systems—at the local, state, and national level. This is the most recent era of educational change, and for this reason we devote more attention to it than to the other types of school reform.

Using tests and assessments to improve accountability of students and schools is not a new practice in American education. Linn (2000) identified five waves of educational reform that used tests and assessments as key elements:

- Using tests for tracking and selection emphasized in the 1950s;
- Using tests for program accountability in the 1960s;
- Minimum competency testing programs of the 1970s;
- School and district accountability in the 1980s; and
- The standards-based accountability systems of the 1990s (pp. 4-16).

The popularity of assessment for policymakers lies in its relative inexpensiveness, the fact that it can be externally managed, its ease of implementation, and its visibility. The most recent movement in assessments and accountability began in the late 1980s and continues to the present. It has featured three new elements or emphases: content standards, high performance standards and testing of all students, and high-stakes accountability (Linn, 2000).

As we note below, content standards were part of the Clinton Administration's Goals 2000: Educate America Act, but their use started at the state level, and states have been the leaders in this reform effort. Kentucky and Maryland were among the first states to use standards-based assessments. States did not assess the same content areas, but over time most developed content standards in English-language arts, mathematics, and science.

In addition to content standards, most reform states also established performance standards, which determined proficiency of students in specified areas. Linn (2000) notes the four critical aspects of performance standards:

> First, they are intended to be absolute rather than normative. Second, they are expected to be set at high, "world-class" levels. Third, a relatively small number of levels (e.g., advanced, proficient) are typically identified. Finally, they are expected to apply to *all*, or essentially all, students rather than a selected subset such as college-bound students seeking advanced placement. (p. 10)

The states adopting content and performance standards also determined proficiency levels for students, which, as we shall see below, introduced a discrepancy between state proficiency standards and those of the National Assessment of Educational Performance (NAEP) scores. The latter typically have been stricter. For example, in the late 1990s, the state of Wisconsin reported that 88% of its students were proficient on the third grade reading test, while the NAEP result for Wisconsin students on the fourth grade reading test was 35% (Linn, 2000).

The final new aspect of the assessment and accountability reform was introduction of high-stakes accountability, for schools, teachers, and often administrators and students. Some states, such as Kentucky, gave cash incentives for performance improvements; others, such as Texas, required testing of teachers for competency. Whatever the accountability target, the broadly-shared perception was that a blend of sanctions, rewards, and assistance to schools would lead to higher levels of performance. As Elmore, Abelmann, and Fuhrman (1996) note, "focusing on student performance should move states away from input regulations ... toward a model of steering by results" (p. 65).

Altogether, the reform initiatives from various states were impressive in their variety of standards and tests and attempts to improve accountability (see Cross, Rebarber, & Torres, 2004).

## Reform Processes

This brief review describes a large number of reform efforts within the last 50 years, but says little about the nature of the reform process. Whether the change was initiated at the state or federal level, it required mobilization of supporters and formation of a majority coalition in order to convince legislatures or the Congress to adopt it. When introducing education in American federalism, we referred to the roles played by governors, presidents, legislators, courts, business alliances, and teachers unions in advancing (or in some cases retarding) educational change. Students of state and U.S. national politics have proposed several theories to explain changes in policy areas, such as education. We consider three: policy diffusion, policy entrepreneurs, and punctuated equilibrium and then discuss resistance to reform.

Jack Walker (1969) first developed policy diffusion analysis, in order to explain the transfer of reform ideas from one jurisdiction to another. He and other scholars tended to focus on *horizontal* diffusion, the migration of policy change ideas from one state to others (see Gray, 1973, 1994; and Berry & Berry, 1998). Often, states in the same region, such as the South, adopted reform proposals simultaneously or strongly influenced one another. For example, Timar and Kirp (1994) argue that "regional competition for high technology firms and recognition that the region's economic future depended on a skilled work force and good educational system" were primary factors explaining adoption of reform proposals in the 1980s (p. 56; also see Mazzoni, 1994).

Researchers also have examined *vertical* diffusion processes. These can occur within states, as developments in local governments influence the state as a whole (a bottom-up process), or as state-level change makes its way to local governments (a top-down process). The more typical example of vertical diffusion concerns state-federal relationships, when either the federal government adopts a change initiated at the state-level (such as the Texas education reforms that influenced development of NCLB) or when it imposes mandates on the states, as NCLB has done. This aspect of diffusion emphasizes an important rationale for federalism, that is the role states play as initiators of social change experiments and "laboratories for democracy." Vertical diffusion describes asymmetric relationships, while those of horizontal diffusion are symmetric, but these differences do not appear to have had an impact on the success of policy diffusion.

Policy entrepreneurship describes the role that political leaders play in policy change. The entrepreneur makes "political capital" out of an idea, which he/she sells to the broader public. Although the public is disposed to change, such as adopting a school voucher system, the benefits to change are highly dispersed and there is concentrated opposition from teachers (in the case of vouchers). The policy entrepreneur is then an important catalyst who may be able to place the reform proposal on the government's issue agenda. Mintrom (1997) discusses the key role of policy entrepreneurs in serving as catalysts for policy change regarding school choice. He notes their significance in providing high quality information to policymakers. They were convincing because they could inform decision makers of local-level experiments showing the workability of the innovation, which in itself is a form of vertical (local-state) diffusion.

A related process pertains to what is called the "opportunity structure" for education change. Kingdon (1984) has popularized the concept of "policy windows" to describe the way in which reform ideas, lying dormant for several years, are energized by political actors. The actors find conditions favorable to hooking "solutions to problems," and "proposals to political momentum" (p. 191). Baumgartner and Jones (1993) enlarge this concept by what they call a "punctuated equilibrium" theory. This argues that policymaking is best described as composed of long periods of incremental change punctuated by brief periods of major policy change. Again leadership takes advantage of favorable political conditions and initiates major changes.

Finally, the processes may be combined. One example is Manna's (2006) concept of "borrowing strength." Both federal and state actions are interrelated, as Manna notes: "Policy entrepreneurs at one level of government attempt to push their agenda by leveraging the justifications and capabilities that other governments elsewhere in the federal system possess" (p. 5). A second combined approach is McGuinn's (2006) model of policy regimes, defined as "a systematic framework for analyzing the role of ideas, interests, and institutions in generating major policy change in a specific issue area over time" (p. 17). This approach emphasizes historical analysis of policymaking in areas such as education over a long period of time. It stresses change within continuity as represented by McGuinn's title *No Child Left Behind and the Transformation of Federal Education Policy, 1965-2005.*

All three of these change processes and particularly the variants were involved in creation and implementation of standards-based education reform. Again, for proposals to gain legislative approval, reformers had to establish a majority coalition. In the case of the assessment and accountability movement, this was relatively easy, for it was apparent that increased measurement and responsibility would benefit nearly all students and society generally. However, costs of reform would be borne by a concentrated group—primarily teachers. Because they would need to alter routines and be subject to intense scrutiny, they had incentives to organize (Wilson, 1980). As we see in most of the case studies, resistance to education reform emerged from teachers' unions and some parent organizations (see Koppick, 2005). Although they did not express a majority view, they have an organizational advantage, making the reform process quite fragile.

## NATIONAL INITIATION OF EDUCATIONAL REFORM

The increased federal role in K-12 education has been driven by equity and quality concerns related to: (1) the lasting effects of segregation and poverty on achievement, and (2) concerns about vastly different standards of quality and achievement in the context of the need to improve American competitiveness in an increasingly economically integrated world. The most recent educational reform represented in NCLB is based on expanding federal involvement in K-12 education. We discuss the two previous federal efforts before examining the provisions of NCLB and consider the impacts on states.

### Early Federal Reforms

The first significant federal legislation on K-12 education was enacted in the Johnson Administration, the Elementary and Secondary Education Act (ESEA) of 1965. Initially, ESEA provided financial support for the education of socioeconomically disadvantaged children, under Title 1. This provision of ESEA has been studied intensively, with largely critical reviews of its failure to close the achievement gap between poor and affluent students (see Natriello & McDill, 1999).

In the judgment of scholars, ESEA has undergone three distinct phases. During the initial period of operation, it projected bold expectations, but was "unclear with respect to its objectives, imprecise in its expectations, and inept in its administrative actions" (Peterson, Rabe, & Wong, 1991, p. 79). In its second phase, policymakers attempted to fix the problems revealed in its implementation. The third stage brought about a greater recognition of the need for local diversity in approach and implementation style (Manna, 2006; McGuinn, 2006).

Emphases by presidents and periodic reauthorizations of ESEA increased federal involvement. For example, in the 1988 presidential election, George H.W. Bush said he wanted to be an "education president," and during his term introduced several reform proposals to the Congress, but failed to see major reform enacted (McGuinn, 2006). In 1994, Congress and the Clinton Administration enlarged ESEA in the Improving America's Schools Act (IASA). They required that state recipients of federal funding (all 50 states), develop content and performance standards in reading and mathematics. Furthermore, the legislation required states to administer standardized tests in reading and math at three points in the educational march—once during grades three to five, a second test during grades six to nine, and a third test in grades ten to twelve. This congressional legislation did not, however, make enforceable mandates on the states regarding educational outcomes, and only 17 states fully complied (Debray, McDermott, & Wohlstetter, 2005; McGuinn, 2006).

## NCLB

The No Child Left Behind Act is the clearest example of vertical diffusion of education reform. Prior to winning the presidency in 2000, George W. Bush had been governor of Texas; he became convinced that the assessment and accountability system developed in Texas was a model for the nation. Throughout the 2000 presidential election campaign, Bush championed education reform and particularly the benefits of reform to America's lowest-performing students, believing that these students suffered from the "soft bigotry of low expectations" (Hess & McGuinn, 2002). Yet as developed, NCLB contained various proposals made by members of the education policy community over time (Rudalevige, 2003).

Upon taking office, President Bush gathered bipartisan congressional support for his reform proposal (winning 90% of the votes from both House and Senate members in 2001), which has been called "the most sweeping plan to shake up public education in a generation, as well as the most intrusive federal intervention in local schools" (Dillon, 2004; also see Manna, 2006). Others, however, call NCLB "an evolution of the federal role rather than a radical redefinition" (McDonnell, 2005, p. 19).

NCLB amended ESEA in four important respects. First, NCLB requires the administration of standardized tests for reading and mathematics every year from the third to the eighth grades as well as the administration of tests at 1 year in Grades 10 to 12. It adds science to the assessment targets for the 2007-08 school year (Dwyer, 2004).

Second, NCLB requires that all schools achieve 100% proficiency in mathematics and English-language arts by 2014, with states establishing "challenging" performance standards. Beginning in 2002, states were required to demonstrate "adequate yearly progress" (AYP) toward the goals of 100% proficiency, and states could be penalized for failure to reach scheduled levels through withdrawal of federal Title I funding. An innovative part of this requirement was that school districts needed to report annual progress on AYP for a number of student subgroups: major racial and ethnic groups, economically disadvantaged students, students with disabilities, and students with limited English proficiency (LEP students). Failure of any subgroup to meet AYP targets required school district action. In other words, NCLB mandated that states, school districts, and schools "close the achievement gap."

Third, NCLB imposed penalties for failure of compliance with legislative mandates. If a school failed to demonstrate AYP for 2 years successively, state officials were required to act. States and districts had a range of options, from allowing parents to transfer students to other public schools, more directed attention to school progress, dismissal of staff or indeed the school board, or closing the school (Dwyer, 2004).

Fourth, NCLB required that states be able to certify that teachers in core areas (such as English-language arts and mathematics) were "highly qualified," by 2005-06. Teachers would be considered highly qualified if they were fully certified and had demonstrated competence in the subjects they taught. Similar language applied to school paraprofessionals.

Finally, NCLB required states to participate biennially in the NAEP testing program, as one means of nationalizing educational standards. The difficulty is that NAEP and state testing programs are not interchangeable. As a panel of the National Research Council commented: "(T)here is far too much variability in the tests used by different states to justify an attempt to equate them to each other or to NAEP for purposes of reporting scores of individual students" (Dwyer, 2004, p. 251; also see Feuer, Holland, Green, Beretenthal, & Hemphill, 1999; McGuinn, 2006).

## Impacts on the States

Well before NCLB went into effect, almost every state had implemented a type of testing program, with consequences for low performance affecting educators and/or students. The state testing programs already were having significant effects on choices educators made about use of classroom time and curriculum. An early positive review of NCLB impacts on states comments:

> Prior to the passage of the No Child Left Behind act, state accountability policies on average were only fair, bordering on poor. NCLB, if properly implemented, would increase the average accountability ranking significantly (Cross, 2004, p. 8).

Most early reviews of NCLB, however, have been critical. For example, Margaret Goertz (2005) considered state education policies in 2002-03, the year following adoption of NCLB. She identified four implementation challenges: assessment, accountability provisions, special needs students, and capacity problems. Goertz concluded that most states lack the human and financial resources to support school improvement, a finding repeated in most critical reviews (Irons & Harris, 2007).

A second and very popular stream of critical reviews deplores NCLB because of the belief that it undermines good teaching through an overemphasis on testing and measurement. One example of this critique is found in Poetter, Wegwert, and Haerr (2006) *No Child Left Behind and the Illusion of Reform*.

A third critical review of the impact of NCLB on the states by James Ryan (2004) points out the pragmatic blend of national mandates and states' responses. For instance, although strict in defining AYP, the legislation is "remarkably loose with regard to state standards and tests" (p. 941). States determine their own standards, select their own tests, and decide what scores qualify for the label "proficient." Ryan points to three adverse consequences for the states of the federal legislation (also see Linn, 2003).

Ryan's (2004) first critique is that NCLB, through its combination of "regulatory stringency and laxity," will encourage states to "lower their standards, make their tests easier, or lower the scores by class and race" (p. 924). As requirements under NCLB rachet upward, Ryan believes (confirmed by early evidence in implementation of NCLB) that states will postpone the need for large increases until later in the reform period (closer to 2014); alternatively, they will make tests easier or lower scores needed to succeed (Dillon, 2003). Ryan points to Louisiana, Colorado, Connecticut, and Texas, which have "tinkered with their scoring systems in order to increase the number of students who will be deemed proficient for purposes of the NCLB" (p. 925). This observation can be extended to most of the nine case studies we present.

Ryan's (2004) second critique is that NCLB "unintentionally promotes racial, ethnic, and socioeconomic segregation" (2004, p. 961). Because NCLB requires disaggregation of scores for subgroups only if they are sufficiently numerous to yield statistically reliable information, and because NCLB allows states to determine the minimum size of subgroups, the incentive for states is to under-report subgroups by setting high subgroup minima. Although NCLB requires that students in Title 1 schools be allowed to attend another school in their district if their home school is failing, a very small number of parents have exercised this option; only a "trickle of parents" in the 2002-03 school year did so (p. 967). Further, states, districts, and schools now have incentives to exclude students who fall under the subgroup analysis provisions, leading to an increase in dropouts from schools, particularly high schools. We include dropout rates for most of the states in our case studies, but these rates are not greatly revealing. As Ryan notes:

> [NCLB] does not say what the rate (of graduation) must be, nor does it demand that the rate increase over a certain period of time. Moreover, graduation rates can only be counted *against* a school when determining AYP . . . . States thus have little incentive to establish a demanding graduation rate. (p. 970; also see Fusarelli, 2004)

The final critique pertains to the negative incentives NCLB provides concerning teachers (see Wayne & Youngs, 2003). Ryan (2004) argues that NCLB will make teaching a less attractive profession for talented prospective teachers, and that it will "bolster the tendency of good teachers to choose wealthy, white, and high-achieving schools" (p. 971). Indeed, the requirement of having highly qualified teachers in every classroom has been one of the most challenging for states to meet. In the early twenty-first century, states are experiencing severe teacher shortages. The pay scale for teachers is not competitive, especially for those with math and science degrees, where shortages are among the greatest.

Furthermore, most teachers currently instructing outside their fields, which renders them unqualified under NCLB, are in the lower-performing school districts that find it most difficult to attract highly qualified teachers. NCLB's requirement is a laudable one, given that much research shows that the single most important determinant of student success is the quality of the teacher. However, fulfilling NCLB's requirements on teacher quality will require much ingenuity and much greater investment of resources in teacher pay and professional development. As is shown in the following chapters, states have used a variety of policies to attract strong candidates for teaching to the field and to improve the instructional skills of current teachers (and some of these policies predate NCLB).

Another problematical aspect of NCLB is that it requires extraordinary progress on the part of low-performing, often disadvantaged, students, with little recognition of their substantial deficits upon entering school, especially with regard to pre-literacy skills. Many states have called for amending NCLB to recognize progress made among these students, instead of continuing to label them and their schools "low-performing" year after year. Meanwhile, states are taking aggressive action to institute targeted and sometimes universal prekindergarten programs, in order to address these children's educational deficits early, so that they may enter school ready to succeed. Washington appears to be responding to this concern, as well.

Secretary of Education Margaret Spellings announced in fall 2005 that the USDOE would consider the applications of 10 states to amend their accountability plans under NCLB to include a value-added approach. However, John Boehner (R) and George Miler (D) representing a bipartisan consensus of the House Committee on Education and the Workforce announced that "the integrity of the law must be maintained ... [and implementation] must be based on the law as it is written, not on a smorgasbord of different waivers for different states and districts" (McGuinn, 2006, p. 189).

NCLB's purpose and central strength are that it holds schools accountable, that is, it requires that federal dollars directed at disadvantaged children *actually make a difference in their achievement*. The act's requirements have and will produce unintended consequences, such as exacerbating the teacher shortage in low-performing schools and threatening withdrawal of federal funds from the most needy schools and districts. As well, NCLB's requirements, especially in testing at each grade level from 3 to 8, produce boredom in many students, and a number of experts believe this lowers the school performance and engagement of boys (J. Kleinfeld, personal communication, February 3, 2007). If NCLB is to achieve its central aim, clearly it will require adjustments, and the trick for policymakers will be to fine tune the act (due for reauthorization by the Congress in 2007) without jeopardizing the principle of providing equal educational opportunity for all children.

## PLAN OF THE BOOK

Education reform begins and ends in the American states, as they have the constitutional authority and most of the resources needed to educate America's children. We have selected nine states to voice the narrative of education reform. We selected states based on those enrolling the largest number of students, and thus we include California, Texas, New York, Florida, and Michigan, but we also include states with fewer students but unique educational problems, such as Alaska. Too, we have focused on those states contributing to the diffusion of policy innovations in education, the leaders in education reform—Texas, Virginia, North Carolina, and Massachusetts.

For each state, we have asked a common set of questions. We introduce the state and the challenges in its educational environment. Then we take a snapshot of the state's assessment and accountability system before the enactment of NCLB in 2002. We examine the impact that NCLB had initially on the state's accountability system, and then explore major implementation issues. We display early results of NCLB reforms in the state, and then conjecture about whether the state will attain NCLB goals by 2014.

Our presentation of states begins with America's oldest: Massachusetts in New England, New York in the mid-Atlantic, and Virginia and North Carolina in the South. Then we treat two other southern states, which have been national leaders in education reform: Florida, and Texas. We take an excursion to the Mid-West by investigating Michigan, but our coverage of this region is slim indeed. We then visit America's most populous state with the largest student population, California, and our largest state in land area, Alaska.

Throughout, our objective is to explain what motivates the reform process in the American states, and what impact national-level reforms have had on state action. Also, we seek to portray the back-and-forth actions of states and federal government, as they negotiate a new contract of educational federalism.

## REFERENCES

Baumgartner, F. R., & Jones, B. D. (1993). *Agendas and instability in American politics.* Chicago: The University of Chicago Press.

Berry, F. S., & Berry, W. D. (1998). Innovation and diffusion models in policy research. In P. A. Sabatier (Ed.), *Theories of the policy process* (pp. 169-200). Boulder, CO: Westview.

Cibulka, J. G. (2001, January/March). The changing role of interest groups in education: Nationalization and the new politics of education productivity. *Education Policy, 15*(1), 12-40.

Cross, R. W., Rebarber, T., & Torres, J. (2004). *Grading the system: The guide to state standards, tests, and accountability.* Washington, DC: Thomas B. Fordham Foundation.

Debray, E. H., McDermott, K. A. & Wohlstetter, P. (2005). Introduction to the special issue on federalism reconsidered: The case of the No Child Left Behind Act. *Peabody Journal of Education, 80*(2), 1-18.

Dillon, S. (2003, May 22). States are relaxing education standards to avoid sanctions from federal law. *New York Times,* p. A29.

Dillon, S. (2004, January 2). Some school districts challenge Bush's signature education law. *New York Times,* A1.

Dwyer, J. G. (2004). School accountability and "high stakes" testing. *Theory and Research in Education, 2*(3), 211-53.

Elmore, R. F., Abelmann, C. H., & Fuhrman, S. H. (1996). The new accountability in state education reform: From process to performance. In H. F. Ladd (Ed.), *Holding schools accountable: Performance-based reform in education* (pp. 65-98). Washington, DC: The Brookings Institution.

Feuer, J. J., Holland, P. W., Green, B. F., Beretenthal, M. W., & Hemphill, F. C. (1999). *Uncommon measures: Equivalence and linkage among educational tests.* Washington, DC: National Academy Press.

Friedman, M. (1962). *Capitalism and freedom.* Chicago: University of Chicago Press.

Fusarelli, L. D. (2001, February). The political construction of accountability: Where rhetoric meets reality. *Education and Urban Society, 33*(2), 157-169.

Fusarelli, L. D. (2004). The potential impact of the No Child Left Behind act on equity and diversity in American education. *Educational Policy, 18*(1), 71-84.

Goertz, M. (2005). Implementing the No Child Left Behind act: Challenges for the states. *Peabody Journal of Education, 80*(2), 73-89.

Goldberg, M., & Traiman, S. L. (2001). Why business backs education standards. In D. Ravitch (Ed.), *Brookings papers on education policy, 2001* (pp. 75-130). Washington, DC: The Brookings Institution.

Gray, V. (1973, December). Innovation in the states: A diffusion study. *American Political Science Review, 67,* 1174-85.

Gray, V. (1994). Competition, emulation, and policy innovation. In L. C. Dodd & C. Jillson (Eds.), *New perspectives on American politics* (pp. 230-248). Washington, DC: Congressional Quarterly Press.

Hanushek, E. A. (2003, February). The failure of input-based schooling policies. *The Economic Journal, 113,* pp. F64-F98.

Hanushek, E. A., & Rivkin, S. G. (1997, Winter). Understanding the twentieth-century growth in U.S. school spending. *Journal of Human Resources, 32*(1), 35-68.

Hess, F. M., & McGuinn, P. J. (2002, January/March). Seeking the mantle of "opportunity": Presidential politics and the educational metaphor. *Educational Policy, 16*(1), 56-117.

Hill, P. T. (2004). Recovering from an accident: Repairing governance with comparative advantage. In N. Epstein (Ed.), *Who's in charge here?* (pp. 75-103) Washington, DC: The Brookings Institution.

Irons, E. J., & Harris, S. (2007). *The challenges of No Child Left Behind: Understanding the issues of excellence, accountability, and choice.* Lanham, MD: Rowman & Littlefield.

Kingdon, J. (1984). *Agendas, alternatives, and public policy.* Boston: Little, Brown.

Koppick, J. (2005). A tale of two approaches—the AFT, the NEA, and NCLB. *Peabody Journal of Education, 80*(2), 137-55.

Lamdin, D. J. (1996). *The contracting out of instructional services.* Baltimore: University of Maryland, Department of Economics.

Linn, R. L. (2000, March). Assessments and accountability. *Educational Researcher, 29*(2), 4-16.

Linn, R. L. (2003, October). Accountability: Responsibility and reasonable expectations. *Education Researcher, 32*(7), 3-131.

Macedo, S. (2003, December). School reform and equal opportunity in America's geography of inequality. *PS, 1*(4), 743-55.

Manna, P. (2006). *School's in: Federalism and the national education agenda.* Washington, DC: Georgetown University Press.

Mayer, S. E. (1997). *What money can't buy: Family income and children's life chances.* Cambridge, MA: Harvard University Press.

Mazzoni, T. L. (1994). State policy-making and school reform: Influences and influentials. *Policy of Education Association Yearbook*, pp. 53-75.

McDonnell, L. (2005). No Child Left Behind and the federal role in education: Evolution or revolution? *Peabody Journal of Education, 80*(2), 19-38.

McGuinn, P. J. (2006). *No Child Left Behind and the transformation of federal education policy, 1965-2005.* Lawrence, KS: University Press of Kansas.

Metcalf, K., & Tail, P. (1999, September). Free market policies and public education: What is the cost of choice? *Phi Delta Kappan, 81*(1), 65-75.

Mintrom, M. (1997, Summer). The state-local nexus in policy innovation diffusion. *Publius, 27*(3), 41-60.

Mintrom, M., & Vergari, S. (1997, Spring). Education reform and accountability issues in an intergovernmental context. *Publius, 27*(2), 143-66.

Natriello, G., & McDill, E. L. (1999). Title 1: From funding mechanism to educational program. In *Hard work for good schools: Facts not mechanism to educational program* (pp. 27-49). Cambridge, MA: Harvard University Press.

Peterson, P., Rabe, B,. & Wong, K. (1991). The maturation of redistributive programs. In A. R. Odden (Ed.), *Education policy implementation* (pp. 65-80). Albany: State University of New York Press.

Poetter, T. S., Wegwert, J. C., & Haerr, C. (2006). *No Child Left Behind and the illusion of reform.* Lanham, MD: University Press of America.

Rudalevige, A. (2003). No Child Left Behind: Forging a congressional compromise. In P. E. Peterson & M. R. West (Eds.), *No Child Left Behind: The politics and practice of school accountability* (pp. 23-54). Washington, DC: The Brookings Institution.

Ryan, J. E. (2004, July). The perverse incentives of the No Child Left Behind act. *New York University Law Review, 79*, 932-989.

Timar, T. B., & Kirp, D. L. (1988). *Managing educational excellence*. London: Falmer Press.

Tyack, D., & Cuban, L. (1995). *Tinkering toward utopia: A century of public school reform*. Cambridge, MA: Harvard University Press.

Tocqueville, A. de (Trans.) (1969). *Democracy in America*. Garden City, NJ: Doubleday Books.

Viteritti, J. P. (2005). School choice: How an abstract idea became a political reality. In D. Ravitch (Ed.), *Brookings papers on education policy* (pp. 137-156). Washington, DC: The Brookings Institution.

Walker, J. (1969, September). The diffusion of innovations among the American states. *American Political Science Review, 63*, 880-99.

Wayne, A. J., & Youngs, P. (2003, Spring). Teacher characteristics and student achievement gains: A review. *Review of Educational Research, 73 (1)*, 89-122.

Wilson, J. Q. (1980). *The politics of regulation*. New York: Basic Books.

CHAPTER 2

---

# MASSACHUSETTS

---

## INTRODUCTION

### State's Socioeconomic and Political Characteristics

Massachusetts values its seventeenth century Pilgrim roots, its eighteenth century role as the hotbed of revolutionary activism, and its nineteenth century role as a center of industrial and intellectual activity. Eventually Irish Catholic Democrats outnumbered Protestant Republicans, and Irish Catholic working class sentiments and liberal intellectual thought emanating from the numerous colleges and universities in the state combined to form the most solidly liberal Democratic political culture in the nation. The commonwealth prides itself on being at the cutting edge of educational reform, just as it has been a leader in political and social reform historically.

In the late 1980s, liberal Democrats had a setback when the state's economy fell into a deep recession. The state government faced immense economic challenges; residents voted for large tax cuts and a Republican governor, William Weld, an economic moderate-conservative and a social liberal. Weld cut government substantially and the economy rebounded. Republicans controlled the executive branch until January 2007 when Deval Patrick, Massachusetts' first Black governor, succeeded Mitt Romney.

---

*Education Reform in the American States*
pp. 23–53
Copyright © 2008 by Information Age Publishing

Working with an overwhelmingly Democratic legislature, Romney closed a budget gap and avoided a tax increase in his first years in office. He held close reins on government spending, though he argued for a basic health insurance plan to cover the uninsured. Romney strongly supported educational reforms begun in 1993, including the commonwealth's school accountability system; however, Patrick claimed that he had not done enough, noting that school funding had not kept pace with the costs.

The legislature (formally called the "General Court") has been overwhelmingly Democratic since 1996, and all 12 members of the state's Congressional delegation are Democrats. By gerrymandering to favor incumbents, the legislature has rendered the state's elections among the least competitive in the nation. Once in office, many legislators face no competition in subsequent elections. Common Cause Massachusetts is working to change state law so that a commission, rather than the state legislature, performs redistricting (Barone & Cohen, 2005).

Massachusetts is overwhelmingly (81.9%) White, with 9% Hispanic, 5% Black and nearly 4% Asian populations. It is also overwhelmingly (91.4%) urban, though much of what is defined urban is suburban (Barone & Cohen, 2005). In the last 2 decades of the twentieth century, income inequality rose in Massachusetts and was greater than in any other state in the nation. Although over 90% of Massachusetts' population is urban/suburban, most of the state's minorities and poor people live in 15 cities: Boston, Brockton, Chelsea, Chicopee, Fall River, Fitchburg, Holyoke, Lawrence, Lowell, Lynn, New Bedford, Revere, Somerville, Springfield, and Worcester. Residents of these cities, besides being disproportionately poor and minority, are often new immigrants with limited English skills; these demographic factors contribute to their children's struggling in school (Gaudet, 2002). The implications of these demographics on student achievement and on the challenges of education reform are discussed below.

## The State Educational System

Massachusetts' State Board of Education (BOE), whose nine members are appointed by the governor, is relatively insulated from public pressure, which helps to explain why education reform has withstood strong opposition from relatively narrow sectors of the population, especially the Massachusetts Teachers Association (MTA) and residents of wealthy communities. In 1996, Republican Governor William Weld led an effort to reduce the then unwieldy 17-member board to the more manageable size of nine. Weld appointed as Chairman of the BOE an outspoken proponent of high-stakes accountability, John Silber, former president of Boston University. The current Chairman of the Board is James Peyser, also a strong proponent of Massachusetts' accountability system. The chief state school officer is the commissioner of education, who is appointed by the BOE. The current commissioner, David P. Driscoll, is an outspoken proponent of the Massachusetts Comprehensive Assessment System (MCAS) program. The BOE has substantial influence over education policy by establishing regulations pursuant to law (Hess, 2002).

Throughout the 1990s and into the twenty-first century, Massachusetts had Republican governors who supported education reform, as have the members of the State BOE and the Department of Education. Furthermore, the Democratic Speaker of the House strongly supported the administration's education policy, and the Senate President in the 1990s and beyond was one of the sponsors of the Education Reform Act of 1993. Thus, the bipartisan support for accountability in education among elective officials, along with the relative insulation of other education policymakers, has been critical to the initiation and resilience of standards-based education reform in Massachusetts (Peyser, 2003).

Funding for public education is allocated based on a foundation formula established under the Massachusetts Education Reform Act (MERA) of 1993. Each school district has a unique funding level based on demographic characteristics of the students and their families. At the time MERA was enacted, two thirds of districts were funded below the foundation, many well below. MERA called for incremental increases to bring all districts up to the foundation level by 2000, and this was accomplished (Berger & McLynch, 2005). Among successful 2006 Democratic gubernatorial candidate Deval Patrick's campaign promises was to increase the state's share of school funding and reduce the burden borne by property tax payers (Patrick, 2005).

Massachusetts public schools enrolled about 1 million students in 2004-2005. Its public school population is somewhat more diverse than the general population, with more minorities being of school age. The public school demographics are 74.2% White, 11.8% Hispanic, 8.9% Black and 4.8% Asian/Pacific Islander. In 2004-2005, 16.6% of students were on Individualized Education Programs (IEPs), 5% had Limited English Proficiency (LEP) and 28% were eligible for free or reduced price lunch, an indicator of poverty.[1] Twenty-seven percent of the state's public school students live in the 15 cities mentioned above, but 70% of the state's minority population and 62% of students eligible for free or reduced lunch live in these cities. Significant numbers of these students failed the state's (MCAS) achievement tests and performed very poorly on the NAEP. Two thirds of students who did not pass the MCAS in 2001 lived in one of the fifteen cities or were special education students (Gaudet, 2002).

In 2003, Massachusetts spent $9,431 per student, which placed the state, after cost adjustments, at nineteenth in the nation on per-pupil expenditures. It had climbed from 33rd place since 1993. Furthermore, during that 10-year time span, the proportion of the public education funding provided by the state grew from 31.5 to 41.4%. Local governments still provided 52.4% of public school funding, nearly 10 percentage points above the national average. Following these increases in public school spending, however, owing to an economic recession in 2002-2004, real per pupil spending for public education declined more in Massachusetts than in any other state (Berger & McLynch, 2005).

Massachusetts is known for its emphasis on education, for its strong accountability system, and for the high performance of its students. A 2005 poll by Mass Insight Education and Research Institute revealed that respondents felt that education should be the top priority of state government in 2006. In 2003-04 and 2004-05, Massachusetts was named the "Smartest State" by Morgan Quitno Press in Lawrence, Kansas in its annual Education State Rankings publication, and it was ranked third and second respectively in the following two years. The evaluation is based on 21 factors, including per pupil expenditures, graduation rates, student proficiency in reading and math, and pupil-teacher ratios. The National Center for Public Policy and Higher Education, in its report "Measuring Up 2004," ranked Massachusetts as best overall in student preparedness for college.[2]

## THE MASSACHUSETTS ASSESSMENT AND ACCOUNTABILITY SYSTEM BEFORE 2002

### MERA and the MCAS

In Massachusetts in the 1980s, broad support developed for education reform, including accountability, from both political parties, the business sector, and education leadership, especially in higher education. The state began education reform with the mild, noncoercive, essentially diagnostic Massachusetts School Improvement Law of 1985, which established the Massachusetts Educational Assessment Program (MEAP), a biannual test to be administered to all students. The test did not provide results on individual students, but allowed for comparison of school and district performances, along with analysis of curriculum and instruction (Hess, 2002).

In 1988, members of Massachusetts' business community who were concerned that significant education reform was needed if the state's high school graduates were to meet the needs of the economy and the polity formed the Massachusetts Business Alliance for Education (MBAE). Led by Jack Rennie, then chairman and CEO of Pacer Systems, and Paul Reville, director of the Alliance for Education in Worcester, the group attracted business leaders from throughout the state. Organizations such as the Associated Industries of Massachusetts and the Massachusetts Business Roundtable, as well as education leaders, worked with the group. The MBAE felt that accountability was needed in education, and they began to take an active role in the state's education policymaking. In 1991, MBAE produced a comprehensive school reform proposal called "Every Child a Winner!" The conceptual framework in the proposal provided the basis for the Massachusetts Education Reform Act (MERA) of 1993. The bill, which represented a comprehensive overhaul of public education in Massachusetts, had three main components: (1) academic standards, (2) improvements to the education process, and (3) increased financial resources and progressive redistribution of resources.[3]

The MBAE drafted a public education finance plan for the state which provided school districts with adequate, equitable, and stable funding, with extra resources provided for at-risk students. Localities would contribute to public education at a rate of .94% of local property values, up to the foundation level. The formula also considered incomes of residents and the districts' historic spending on schools. Accordingly, some districts required significant state contributions to bring them up to the foundation level, whereas wealthy districts would not qualify for any state contribution. The funding formula in MERA was based on present (1993) needs, however, and did not reflect new costs associated with the reforms outlined in the bill (Berger & McLynch, 2005).

As the General Assembly was considering MERA, the Massachusetts high court, the Supreme Judicial Court, was considering a case that called into question the constitutionality of Massachusetts's funding of education. Clearly the legislators were aware of the possible implications of the case. The court ruled in *McDuffy v. Robertson* (1993) that students in lower income communities were not receiving an education in keeping with the state Constitution and ordered the state to provide an equal educational opportunity for all Massachusetts students. MERA's foundation formula remedied the inequity cited by the court, and would provide all schools with an "adequate level" of per pupil expenditures. The court said school districts were permitted to fund schools beyond the basic level.

Since 1880, Massachusetts had authorized more than 100 studies related to reforming aspects of the commonwealth's public education system. Some were rather narrowly focused and some were comprehensive in scope. None, however, resulted in the fundamental type of reform represented in the Massachusetts Education Reform Act of 1993 (Gaudet, 2003). MERA was broad in scope, affecting nearly every aspect of public education. Hours spent in the core academic subjects were increased; certification requirements for teachers were enhanced; provisions were made for charter schools; and a plan was devised for placing in receivership schools that failed to perform adequately.

The act increased school districts' policymaking authority, including budgeting within the constraints of state guidelines, hiring and firing of school superintendents and approving school improvement plans. Superintendents were given the authority to hire and fire principals, and principals were given the authority to hire teachers, oversee the development of school improvement plans (which school councils would develop) and purchase textbooks.

MERA also provided for more local control in authorizing the state to approve charter schools. These are publicly funded schools that are released from some of the administrative burdens of traditional public schools, in order to provide educators, parents and students with more flexibility to meet the academic needs of the students. Like other schools in Massachusetts, they would be held accountable for student performance.

The act called for the development of broad educational goals, clarified in specific curriculum frameworks that identified common academic objectives that could be assessed. The BOE established a Commission on the Common Core of Leaning with over 40 members who represented a broad spectrum of Massachusetts residents. The commission labored from September 1993 through June 1994, holding 16 hearings throughout the state to develop the Common Core. As many as 50,000 people contributed directly or indirectly to the process. In June 1994, the BOE unanimously adopted the Common Core of Learning, whose guiding principles were high expectations for all students, along with lifelong learning and contributing to society. From the Common Core of Learning, curriculum frameworks were established in the arts, English, foreign languages, health, history and social studies, math, and science and technology. The frameworks contained academic content standards, which would form the basis for the assessments.

The process for developing the tests was contentious and took several years. The Massachusetts Comprehensive Assessment System (MCAS) tests, which were custom designed for the state, were piloted in 1997 and administered officially first in 1998. The tests have been ranked the best in the nation, partly because they include multiple choice, short answer and extended response questions. In English language arts (ELA) the students write compositions based on writing prompts. Tenth graders were to be tested in English, math, history, and science, and beginning with the class of 2003, they would have to pass the tests to graduate. Later, the BOE reduced the required tests for graduation to ELA and math.

In 1997, a poll of Massachusetts residents showed that 61% supported the requirement that students pass a competency exam in order to receive a high school diploma. About half of those expressing an opinion estimated that no more than 10% of students in their communities would fail the exam. However, more than 60% said they would support the requirement, even if 25% of students in their communities failed (Hess, 2002).

The MCAS has four performance levels: *Advanced, Proficient, Needs Improvement* and *Warning* (Failing). Students are also scored on a scale between 200 and 280. In 2000, the BOE determined that beginning with the class of 2003, in order to receive a Competency Determination (to graduate from high school), students would have to achieve a score of Needs Improvement (220) or higher on the Grade 10 MCAS tests in ELA and math. This was a rather high cut score, given that about 50% of the state's tenth graders had failed to score 220 on the tests two months earlier (Hess, 2004). Nevertheless, there were critics who said the cut score was too low and that it equated with a low "D" grade (Hess, 2002). Students who did not earn the Competency Determination would be allowed multiple opportunities to do so. To receive a high school diploma, students had to meet local graduation requirements in addition to receiving the Competency Determination. Students were to take MCAS tests in various subjects at different grade levels. The tests were phased in over several years. In 2006 for the first time, Massachusetts tested all children in Grades 3-8, (and Grade 10) in both mathematics and ELA/reading.

MERA did not hold teachers directly responsible for student performances. However, the Act called for the development of new standards and accountability measures regarding teacher training that would enhance the quality of the teaching corps in the commonwealth. Beginning in 1994, to be licensed, teachers were required to have degrees in the arts and sciences in fields appropriate to their area of instruction.

In 1998, Massachusetts passed the Teacher Quality Enhancement Law; among its provisions was a signing bonus for new teachers that awarded $20,000 to qualified college seniors with arts and science majors (it prioritized math, science and foreign languages), and to working professionals who had never taught in public school full time before. Bonus recipients who were college students or new graduates had to be in the top 10% of their classes and have 3.5 grade point averages, overall and in their majors. Mid-career professionals were evaluated on their work experience and performance. In addition to the signing bonus, recruits received free admission to the intensive, 7-week Massachusetts Institute for New Teachers (MINT) summer training program, which prepared prospective teachers for the classroom. Those who successfully completed the MINT program were licensed to teach in the state. Officials recruited at major universities throughout the country, and apparently Massachusetts was the only state to offer such signing bonuses. A $70 million endowment funded the programs.

The Teacher Quality Enhancement Law also required that new teachers pass the Massachusetts Educator Certification Test, a test on reading and writing skills for all, along with tests in the respective subject areas. The first cohort of new teachers took the tests in 1998, and the high failure rate prompted the BOE to establish a policy of placing on probation any teacher-training program in the state whose graduating classes had a less than 80% pass rate on the teacher tests. This caused Massachusetts colleges and universities to strengthen their teacher training programs and raise their admission standards for prospective teachers (Stotsky, 2004).

MERA also ended lifetime certification for teachers and required that they reapply for certification every 5 years; to be recertified, teachers had to show that they had participated in professional development in accordance with the goals of their schools and districts (Garcia & Rothman, 2002). Using the curriculum frameworks as guidelines, the DOE provided professional development for districts (Stotsky, 2004). The state also paid for educators to become certified by the National Board for Professional Teaching Standards. For those who subsequently became master teachers and mentored new teachers, the state provided $5,000 annual bonuses for up to 10 years. However this initiative was phased out in 2002-2003 because of low earnings on the endowment. It was hoped that the program could be reinstated when the economy improved.

BOE policy later required teachers to have specific numbers of credit hours in the subjects they taught. Prospective elementary and special education teachers must now take 36 hours of arts and sciences coursework in the subjects they will teach and must pass general knowledge tests in the subjects, as well as tests in reading pedagogy. At least half of the coursework in the masters degree in education that middle school and secondary teachers may use for the second stage of licensure in Massachusetts must now be in the subject area of the license. According to Sandra Stotsky, who helped develop the state's accountability system, this requirement of subject area coursework in the masters in education programs remains the most contentious of the new regulations regarding teacher licensure, because teachers may no longer take classes for their own edification or enjoyment that are unrelated to their teaching fields and have them count for licensure purposes (2004).

## Initial Impact of the Massachusetts Accountability System

Massachusetts students stand out, both for their position among the highest achievers in the nation on the National Assessment of Educational Progress (NAEP) and for the gains they have made since the 1990s reforms. Massachusetts students made strong and steady progress on the NAEP following the introduction of the Massachusetts Education Reform Act of 1993. Fourth grade *math* scores rose from 227 in 1992 to 242 in 2003. In both 1992 and 2003, Massachusetts students scored 8 points higher than the national average. Eighth grade math scores rose from 273 in 1992 to 287 in 2003, and Massachusetts eighth graders increased their lead on their peers in the nation from 5 to 9 points during that time span.

While this progress was laudable and certainly Massachusetts' high NAEP scores were impressive, progress on narrowing the achievement gaps was mixed. For instance, the gap in math between White and Black fourth graders narrowed from 36 to 26 points between 1992 and 2003, and the gap in math between White and Hispanic students narrowed from 34 to 25 points during that time. However the 22 point gap in math between poor and nonpoor fourth graders did not change significantly between 1996 and 2003. And among eighth graders, the gaps in math between Whites and Blacks (34 points in 1992), between Whites and Hispanics (38 points in 1992) and between poor and nonpoor students (30 points in 1992) did not narrow significantly.

On the NAEP *reading* test, Massachusetts fourth and eighth graders improved their test scores slightly between 1992 and 2003, and they increased their lead on the nation's students just slightly, as well. However, the fourth grade reading gaps of 26 points between White and Black students, 34 points between White and Hispanic students, and 28 points between nonpoor and poor students had not changed significantly by 2003. Similarly, in eighth grade reading the gaps of 27 points between Whites and Blacks, 32 points between Whites and Hispanics, and 29 points between nonpoor and poor students had not changed significantly by 2003. Table 2.1 below shows the NAEP scores in math and reading for Massachusetts students, compared with the national averages.

Though scores on the initial MCAS tests in 1998 were disappointing across the board, and failure rates were shockingly high for 10th grade (54% failed in math and 34% failed in ELA on the first tests), students made significant gains between 1998 and 2002. The percentages of students in the Advanced and Proficient categories at each grade level grew, and the percentages in the Warning category at each level declined. In tenth grade the improvement was dramatic. In ELA, the percentage in the Advanced category nearly quadrupled from 5 to 19 between 1998 and

**Table 2.1.   Massachusetts Students' NAEP Scores in Math and Reading 1992-2003**

| | 4th Grade | | | | 8th Grade | | | |
|---|---|---|---|---|---|---|---|---|
| | Math | | Reading | | Math | | Reading | |
| Year | MA Average | National Average | MA Average | National Average | MA Average | National Average | MA Average | National Average |
| 1992 | 227 | 219 | 226 | 215 | 273 | 267 | | |
| 1994 | | | 223 | 212 | | | | |
| 1996 | 229 | 222 | | | 278 | 271 | | |
| 1998 | | | 223 | 213 | | | 269 | 261 |
| 2000 | 233 | 234 | | | 279 | 272 | | |
| 2002 | | | 234 | 217 | | | 271 | 263 |
| 2003 | 242 | 234 | 228 | 216 | 287 | 276 | 273 | 261 |

*Note:*   http://nces.ed.gov/nationsreportcard/states/profile.asp

2002, while the percent in the Proficient category rose from 33 to 40, and the failure rate dropped from 34% in 1998 to 18% in 2001. In 10th grade math, the percent of students in the Advanced category nearly tripled from 7 to 20% between 1998 and 2002, while the percent in the Proficient category rose from 17 to 24. The percent in the failing category (Warning in other grades) dropped from 52 in 1998 to 25 in 2001. Thus, during the first years of MCAS administration, student achievement improved in all grades, dramatically so in high school.[4]

As on the NAEP, there were significant achievement gaps between Whites and non-Whites on the MCAS, but they were narrowing. In 10th grade for instance, in 2001 there was a 40-point gap between Black and White students who earned a Competency Determination. By 2003, the gap was down to 32 points. The gap had been wider yet between Hispanic and White students, but it too was narrowing; it was 48 percentage points in 2001 and 40 in 2003. The Asian-White gap was much smaller, and also narrowing, from 9 points in 2001 to 4 points in 2003.

The charter schools that MERA had permitted (the state limits the number of charter schools to 120), many of which were in inner city districts with low performance, showed mixed results on the MCAS. The idea behind their inception was that the flexibility given their administrators and teachers would allow for more innovation, which would translate into more effective teaching and higher student performance. More than 60% of urban charters out performed comparable schools in their cities, but across the state, charter schools showed lower performance than traditional schools. Charter schools enjoyed the support of many parents who were convinced that their children received a better education. However, their detractors agued that they drew funds away from traditional schools that had much higher percentages of LEP and disabled children (Schworm, 2004). Thus, there was no clear evidence of charter schools' success, though individual schools appeared to be very effective.

SAT and AP scores rose in the first years of implementation of the MCAS, as well. In 2000, Massachusetts' SAT I average score for math and verbal combined was 1024, five points above the national average. Since 1998, scores had risen from 508 to 511 on the verbal test and from 508 to 513 on the math test. This was especially noteworthy, because 78% of Massachusetts students took the SAT, which meant that a broader spectrum of students took the test than in most other states. Only in Washinton, DC, Connecticut, and New Jersey did a higher percentage of students take the SAT I. On Advanced Placement (AP) tests, Massachusetts students vaulted over six states to first in the nation in the percentage of students who received a score of 3, 4 or 5 on the AP tests in 2000.

## Criticism of the MCAS

When the initial administration of the MCAS tests in 1998 and 1999 resulted in very high Warning and Failure rates, especially for minority students, criticism arose on numerous aspects of the tests, including their length, level of difficulty, superficiality, lack of accommodation of disabled and LEP students' needs, and inability to assess fully and fairly the abilities of students. Critics charged that the MCAS stifled creativity and reinforced racial and socioeconomic inequities (Hess, 2002). The strongest opposition from the general public came from liberal, wealthy communities and was led by activists in Cambridge and elite Boston suburbs. These critics argued that the tests diverted resources from advanced programs and forced teachers to reduce the rigor of the curriculum to help weaker students succeed on the tests. Several groups, including a Committee of 100 Massachusetts Parents, Students' Coalition for Alternatives to the MCAS (SCAM), and the Coalition for Authentic Reform in Education (CARE) held rallies, encouraged boycotts and lobbied for revising or abolishing the tests (Hess, 2004). The DOE responded by revising the curriculum frameworks, reducing the length of the fourth grade tests, and making some accommodations for disabled and LEP students.

There were allegations that the 10th grade MCAS was unfair, because it tested concepts taught in geometry and algebra II, which the majority of students had not taken by 10th grade. For instance, the majority of 10th graders in Boston's public schools, where the failure rate was very high on the math exam, took algebra I in 10th grade (Cancell, n.d.). However, a thoroughgoing assessment of Massachusetts' (and five other states') exams by Achieve, Inc., an independent, bipartisan, nonprofit educational support organization, found that most of the algebra questions tested prealgebra skills and of the questions on the test that required geometry skills (27%), most required knowledge of congruence, similarity, transformations, or at most two-dimensional geometry and measurement (2004). Given the low cut scores on the tests, a student could easily pass the test by having a command of prealgebra and general measurement skills. Thus, rather than being unfairly demanding, the tests were so lenient that they did not require students to demonstrate concepts of algebra and geometry that they would need to succeed in college or in many occupations. On the other hand, the concern that large percentages of math teachers in high-poverty districts did not have degrees in mathematics was a valid concern, and in September 2003, Commissioner Driscoll announced that Massachusetts had been allotted $1.6 million through NCLB to enable colleges to partner with public school districts to offer math teachers continuing education that would enhance their abilities to teach under the math curriculum frameworks.

Critics also charged that the BOE's graduation figures did not account for the many students who dropped out between 9th and 12th grades, and they suggested that the MCAS would result in greater attrition during this interim (Wheelock, n.d.). To this concern, the BOE responded with numerous programs to assist students in acquiring the skills they needed to pass the exams. For instance, in 2004 Governor Romney included an additional $20 million in his proposed budget for assistance to students in the state's lowest-performing districts, to raise performance on the 10th grade MCAS. Another $10 million had already been appropriated to help 11th and 12th graders pass the MCAS.

Teacher opposition to the MCAS has been especially vocal. In 2000-2001, the Massachusetts Teachers Association (MTA) directed a $600,000 advertising campaign against the "one-size-fits-all, high stakes, do-or-die MCAS test." Governor Paul Cellucci responded with a $500,000 radio and television campaign promoting the exam and with numerous policies providing both flexibility and assistance to students that are discussed below. Despite these modifications and the public information campaign, a 2001 poll of 300 Boston school teachers by the Boston Teacher Union showed that 85% opposed the use of the MCAS exam as a graduation requirement. Only 7% supported the requirement (Hess, 2004).

Throughout the nation, teachers have been among the most, if not *the* most, organized and vocal opponents of high-stakes accountability in education, regardless of whether the stakes included direct sanctions for teachers. Educators tend to object to the concept of high-stakes accountability, because it violates the culture of the professional, autonomous teacher who operates on a value system of commitment and duty (Hess, 2002). Moreover, numerous factors outside the control of school administrators and teachers influence achievement, including student and parent effort and socioeconomic factors. Teacher opposition to standardized testing and its implications was illustrated at the 2001 convention of the National Education Association (NEA), where delegates voted to oppose national testing, with or without consequences, and to support state legislation permitting parents to exclude their children from standardized testing (Hess, 2004).

The MTA enjoyed strong influence in the overwhelmingly Democratic state legislature; however, the strong support for the MCAS from the leadership in the legislature, governors, and the relatively insulated BOE members, as well as strong support within the business community, allowed the high-stakes standards-based tests to survive. Revisions were made in response to criticism of weaknesses, but the central components of the program have withstood opposition, even as public office holders have changed.

Chairman of the State BOE, James Peyser noted in a 2002 address at the Performance Measurement Association Conference that the state was meeting structural resistance in the attitude of "we can't change," philosophical resistance from those essentially saying "we don't want to change," along with political uncertainty which caused actors to say "let's wait and see," rather than forging ahead aggressively to implement reform. Peyser acknowledged the uncertainty of whether such a large and diffuse system as the Massachusetts public education system could be reformed to achieve widespread excellence; whether performance-based management could be imposed on unwilling, politically influential organizations; and whether the state would be able to maintain the reform in the face of this resistance long enough to achieve results. He urged the public to consider that the MCAS was not creating a problem, but identifying one of which many were long aware but could not quantify. He noted that the test was identifying schools that were not "working," and the program was both providing assistance to and calling for accountability from those schools (Potier, 2001).

Indeed, MERA and the MCAS were effective in changing instructional methods and curriculum. A report for the Massachusetts Education Reform Review Commission found that more than 90% of superintendents, principals and teachers said that they had made curriculum changes based on MCAT results and almost the same percentage had made instructional changes. In particular, they noted more emphasis on writing and more use of open-response questions, which required higher levels of thinking. Furthermore, resources had been redirected to help the most at-risk students, for instance by assigning especially strong teachers to after-school programs for low-performing students (Garcia & Rothman, 2002).

An audit of the impact of MERA on 18 of the state's 344 school districts done by the Educational Management Accountability Board and released in March 2000, revealed a number of positive outcomes, as well as concerns. Among the positive findings were:

- municipalities were spending more than the minimum required by the new foundation formula on their public schools;
- most school districts had reduced student/teacher ratios;
- the average teacher salary had increased more than inflation;
- funding for art, music and physical education programs, which had been reduced recently because of funding shortages, had been increased again, and programs that had been cut had been reinstated;
- school districts had spent significant amounts on professional development for educators, (though the effectiveness of the programs was often questionable); and
- some districts' test scores surpassed expectations, based on their demographics.

Among the concerns of the auditors were:

- rising special education costs had absorbed very disproportionate amounts of the new resources;
- most superintendents had not used their new authority to establish performance-based contracts for principals, so principals were not being held accountable as MERA had intended; and
- little correlation appeared to exist between increased per pupil spending and improvement in student test scores.

District superintendents identified the following barriers to improving student performance:

- costs of special education,
- increasing enrollments,
- difficulties in dismissing incompetent teachers, and
- the lack of stable and coherent leadership.

Superintendents noted that in some districts leadership turnover was so frequent that there was insufficient time to put plans of action into place.

The auditors identified the following qualities of effective schools:

- strong, positive leadership with a clear vision that was effectively communicated to staff;

- mission statements and strategic plans with clearly communicated specific goals;

- methods of measuring progress and practices that held managers accountable; and

- sustained efforts to improve curriculum and align it with the frameworks.

In summary, the auditors found the most significant factors in the schools showing the most improvement related to leadership and accountability, both of which relied on effective communication.

The audit was helpful in identifying which policies and strategies were most effective. And as noted above, the state was responding to criticism and concerns with flexibility and aggressive intervention to provide assistance while holding administrators and students accountable. In 2000, Governor Celluci announced that disabled students could receive Certificates of Completion without passing the MCAS. The same year, the BOE decided to delay including science and history MCAS tests in the graduation requirement, as mentioned above. In January of 2001, the BOE decided to allow students five opportunities to pass the 10th grade MCAS and to delete some of the most difficult questions from the retests (Hess, 2002).

In 2001, about 50 bills were introduced in the state legislature seeking to modify the MCAS in a variety of ways from allowing exemptions for certain groups of students to abolishing the tests. More than 150 people, most of them opposing the tests, testified in a day-long hearing on the program. The legislature was largely unswayed (Hess, 2002), however, the public's concerns were not ignored.

In September 2001 the DOE announced two initiatives designed to help members of the Class of 2003 who had failed the MCAS. The state planned to provide an online Web-based tutorial program that allowed students unlimited access during a 7-week period in late fall; the program would diagnose students' weaknesses and provide online tutoring in the areas in which they needed help. The state also planned to provide real-time human-interactive online tutoring in the spring for up to 1,000 high school students who failed the MCAS. It was hoped that students who were uncomfortable seeking tutoring at school would do so online.

In the fall of 2001, the state announced an appeals process for students who failed the MCAS by narrow margins and who could prove by other means that they had knowledge and skills equal to the passing rate on the MCAS. The appeals process was very complex, and to be eligible, students had to have made multiple attempts to pass the MCAS and had to have exemplary attendance records. The MCAS Appeals Board, consisting of 12 educators appointed by the commissioner of education, reviewed the appeals and made its recommendations to the commissioner. As noted above, in addition to receiving the Competency Determination, to receive a high school diploma, the appellants also must meet their local graduation requirements. By April 2003, of the 1,800 performance appeals that had been submitted for the class of 2003, 578 math appeals and 342 English appeals had been granted, which brought the graduation rate for the Class of 2003 to 91%.

The state also supported efforts such as that of Holyoke Community College to assist students who failed the graduation test by offering students intense preparation, career guidance and the opportunity to take college courses while preparing to retake the test. Such programs softened the blow of failure on the exams and permitted students to move forward (Hess, 2002).

Thus Massachusetts education policymakers approached the comprehensive 1993 reforms as an ongoing endeavor. Test scores, outcomes assessments, and stakeholders' comments provided feedback to which the state responded with interventions of various forms, as well as flexibility, in the name of fairness.

## Evaluations of Massachusetts' Standards-Based Accountability System

The steadfastness with which Massachusetts has approached education reform, as well as the progress it has made, is reflected in formal evaluations of the state's standards and accountability system. For instance, the Fordham Foundation, in its 2004 assessment of the states' standards, tests and accountability policies, deemed Massachusetts' standards Outstanding, the best the foundation had surveyed; "for the most part they are exceptionally clear, specific, and measurable;" the foundation noted that Massachusetts is one of only two states that included a recommended reading list, and it is "especially praiseworthy" (Cross, Rebarbar, & Torres, 2004). Fordham's 2005 "The State of State ENGLISH Standards" again gave Massachusetts the highest ranking on its English standards, noting the comprehensiveness and clarity of expectations, again mentioning the recommended reading lists (Stotsky, 2005). Fordham's 2005 "The State of State MATH Standards" awarded Massachusetts an A for its math standards; it was one of only three math standards to receive the highest rating. The state had rewritten its math standards in 2000 and improved them substantially (Klein, 2005).

*Education Week's Quality Counts 2005* awarded the state an overall grade of A on its standards and accountability system, noting that the tests were custom developed and that the standards were clear, specific and grounded in content at all grade levels, and that the tests required a variety of multiple choice, short answer and extended responses. Also noteworthy were the disaggregation of student scores by race and other characteristics, the state's providing assistance to low-performing schools and sanctioning schools that did not improve, and the fact that the system had student accountability components.

Massachusetts also received praise from Achieve, Inc. on its curriculum frameworks, especially those for English language arts, which Achieve used as benchmarks against which to evaluate other states' standards. Achieve found that the state's tests were tightly aligned with the curriculum frameworks, and said that the MCAS tests were among the best the organization had reviewed. Massachusetts received praise for making the tests transparent, as well. The state makes public the entire tests each year, which is an expensive undertaking, but one the administration apparently finds worth the cost in strengthening public support for the tests (Garcia & Rothman, 2002).

*Education Week's Quality Counts 2007*, ranked Massachusetts fifth in the nation on its Chance-for-Success index, which included indicators such as family income, preschool enrollment, test scores in math and reading, and postsecondary participation. The education journal ranked the state 11th in the degree to which its education policies are aligned with the economy and workforce opportunities. Massachusetts ranked first in academic achievement. Finally, *Quality Counts* ranked the state 14th on its standards, assessment, and accountability system.

Thus, Massachusetts was one of the leaders in the standards-based reform movement, raising expectations for students and schools in order to prepare the commonwealth's young people better for life beyond high school. Factors contributing to the resilience of the reforms in the face of sometimes strident opposition were strong bipartisan support within state government, a board of education that was committed to the reforms and fairly insulated from public pressure, and broad consensus among the populace that improving education was a priority. The state's self-image as a leader in education, along with its high rankings on national tests surely contributed to the public's continued support for reform, despite the high costs of raising achievement among disadvantaged groups. Support within higher education and the business sector sustained the effort as well. Given Massachusetts' reputation as a leader in public education, it was not surprising that the state's congressional delegation strongly supported NCLB.

## MASSACHUSETTS' RESPONSE TO THE NCLB

Massachusetts played a prominent role in the passage of NCLB. Senator Edward Kennedy was a strong proponent of the bill. The bill was signed in Boston's historic Latin School, the oldest public school in the nation, founded in 1635. Senator Kennedy introduced President Bush at the signing ceremony on January 8, 2002 and spoke of the bipartisan support that had guided the bill through Congress. Massachusetts' accountability program was one of the earliest to be approved under NCLB and was offered as a model to other states that had not yet developed accountability systems.

Massachusetts' initial proficiency targets for making Adequate Yearly Progress (AYP) under NCLB appear low at first glance. However closer examination reveals high state standards for proficiency, particularly in math. Massachusetts set its initial proficiency targets for purposes of measuring AYP in *math* at 28% for 2002-2004, followed by 38% in 2004-2006, 51% for 2006-2008, 63% for 2008-2010, 82% for 2010-2012, and the required 100% for 2012-2014. A comparison between MCAS and NAEP scores shows that the state's proficiency definition was quite high in math; 41% of Massachusetts fourth graders scored proficient on the NAEP, whereas only 40% scored proficient on the MCAS. Similarly in eighth grade, 38% scored proficient on the NAEP, whereas only 37% scored proficient on the MCAS. In the vast majority of states far greater percentages of students are considered proficient by state standards for the purposes of NCLB than are proficient on the NAEP. The most striking difference between state and national standards is revealed in a comparison of Mississippi's fourth grade reading scores with NAEP reading scores for the state's fourth graders. While 87% were proficient on the state's test, only 10% were proficient on the NAEP.

In Massachusetts between 34 and 44% of grade level aggregates of students were at proficiency on the MCAS in the baseline year of 2001-2002. However many subgroups were well below the 2002-2003 target of 28% at proficiency. Thus Massachusetts would have difficulty making AYP in all subgroups in math from the very first year under NCLB, despite the fact that its achievement in the aggregate was among the highest in the nation.

Massachusetts set its initial proficiency targets in *reading* at 48% in 2002-2004, at 56% in 2004-2006, at 64% in 2006-2008, at 76% in 2008-2010, at 86% in 2010-2012, and at 100% in 2012-2014. The higher initial target in reading than in math reflected the higher baseline scores among Massachusetts students in reading than in math. Grade level aggregates stood at between 51 and 64% at proficiency on the MCAS in the baseline year of 2001-2002, but here again, several subgroups were well below the

**Table 2.3.   Massachusetts Proficiency Targets for
Grades 3-8 and 10\* for NCLB**

| Years | Math | Reading/Language Arts |
|---|---|---|
| 2002-04 | 28% | 48 % |
| 2004-06 | 38 % | 56 % |
| 2006-08 | 51 % | 64 % |
| 2008-10 | 63 % | 76 % |
| 2010-12 | 82 % | 86 % |
| 2012-14 | 100 % | 100% |

\*Grade 5 beginning in 2006.
*Note*:   Massachusetts Department of Education Consolidated State Application May 1,
2003 Submission, 10-11, accessed at http://www.doe.mass.edu/nclb/stateapp/0503app.pdf

48% baseline target. However, the higher baseline scores in reading actually reflected more lenient standards than in math, as evidenced by the
gap between percentages of Massachusetts students scoring at proficiency
on the NAEP and on the MCAS. On the 2003 NAEP reading test, 40% of
Massachusetts fourth graders scored at proficient, whereas 56% scored
proficient on the MCAS. And while 43% of eighth graders scored proficient on the NAEP reading test, 65% scored proficient on the MCAS.
Despite this leniency in the state's definition of proficiency in reading,
Massachusetts, like all other states, would find it very difficult to meet the
2013-2014 NCLB goal of having all children at proficiency in math and
reading.

Following NCLB's implementation, Massachusetts students continued
to make academic progress, as measured by the NAEP. In fourth grade
*math*, Massachusetts' average score rose from 242 in 2003 to 247 in 2005.
The White-Black gap narrowed another 2 points to 24 points; however
the White-Hispanic gap widened by 2 points to 27, though it was still significantly lower than the 34 point gap of 1992. The gap of 21 points
between nonpoor and poor fourth graders in math did not change significantly. In eighth grade, the average score in math rose by 5 points, as
well, from 287 to 292 between 2003 and 2005. The White-Black gap of 33
points in 2003 did not change significantly, but the nonpoor–poor gap,
which had widened between 1996 and 2003 from 30 to 34 points, narrowed to 26 points by 2005.

Massachusetts' fourth grade NAEP *reading* score was the highest in the
nation in 2005 at 231, up 3 points from 2003. Massachusetts eighth graders were also first in the nation in reading on the NAEP, with an average
score of 274, up from 273 in 2003. (This rise was not statistically signifi-

**Table 2.3.   Massachusetts NAEP Scores 1992-2005**

| | 4th Grade | | | | 8th Grade | | | |
| | Math | | Reading | | Math | | Reading | |
| Year | MA Average | National Average | MA Average | National Average | MA Average | National Average | MA Average | National Average |
| --- | --- | --- | --- | --- | --- | --- | --- | --- |
| 1992 | 227 | 219 | 226 | 215 | 273 | 267 | | |
| 1994 | | | 223 | 212 | | | | |
| 1996 | 229 | 222 | | | 278 | 271 | | |
| 1998 | | | 223 | 213 | | | 269 | 261 |
| 2000 | 233 | 234 | | | 279 | 272 | | |
| 2002 | | | 234 | 217 | | | 271 | 263 |
| 2003 | 242 | 234 | 228 | 216 | 287 | 276 | 273 | 261 |
| 2005 | 247 | 237 | 231 | 217 | 292 | 278 | 274 | 260 |

*Note:*   http://nces.ed.gov/nationsreportcard/states/profile.asp

cant.) The reading achievement gaps persisted, however, with 26 points in both fourth and eighth grade between Whites and Blacks, 35 points in fourth grade and 32 points in eighth grade between Whites and Hispanics, and 28 points between nonpoor and poor fourth graders. Only in eighth grade reading had the gap narrowed between nonpoor and poor students from 29 points in 1998-2003 to 24 points in 2005.

Following implementation of NCLB, Massachusetts students continued to improve on the SAT, as well, though performance declined for the first time in 14 years in 2006. In 2006, with 85% of Massachusetts' public and private school students taking the test, the second highest rate in the nation, the average SAT reading score was 513, ten points above the national average, and the average SAT reading score was 524, six points above the national average. On the new writing exam, Massachusetts students scored an average of 510, thirteen points above the national average. The significant gap between Whites and other ethnicities persisted, though they narrowed somewhat. Blacks averaged 430 in reading, 430 in math and 426 in writing. Hispanic students averaged 444 in reading, 447 in math and 437 in writing. Asian students scored 506 in reading, 577 in math and 508 in writing; and White students scored 525 in reading, 534 in math and 523 in writing.

On the MCAS, indicators of achievement were much more mixed following the implementation of NCLB. Overall, scores appeared to have plateaued in elementary and middle school, and by 2006, slight but troubling declines showed up, particularly in Grade 3 reading, although the

**Table 2.4. Percent of MA Students Achieving Advanced or Proficient on Reading/ELA and Math Tests**

| | Grades and Subjects | | | | | | | | | | | | | |
| | 3 | | 4 | | 5 | | 6 | | 7 | | 8 | | 10 | |
| Year | Read-ing | Math | ELA | Math | ELA | Math | ELA | Math | ELA | Math | ELA | Math | ELA | Math |
|---|---|---|---|---|---|---|---|---|---|---|---|---|---|---|
| 1999 | | | | | | | | | | | | | 34 | 24 |
| 2000 | | | | | | | | | | | | | 36 | 33 |
| 2001 | 62 | | 51 | 34 | | | 36 | 55 | | | | 34 | 41 | 45 |
| 2002 | 67 | | 54 | 39 | | | 41 | 64 | | | | 34 | 44 | 59 |
| 2003 | 63 | | 56 | 40 | | | 42 | 66 | | | | 37 | 51 | 61 |
| 2004 | 63 | | 55 | 42 | | | 43 | 68 | | | | 39 | 62 | 57 |
| 2005 | 62 | | 50 | 40 | | | 46 | 66 | | | | 39 | 64 | 61 |
| 2006 | 58 | 52 | 50 | 40 | 59 | 43 | 64 | 46 | 65 | 40 | 74 | 40 | 70 | 67 |

achievement gap continued to narrow. However, the percent of tenth graders passing the Competency Determination (CD) in both math and ELA on their first tries increased from 68% for the Class of 2003 in 2001 to 81% for the Class of 2007 in 2005, to 84% for the class of 2008 in 2006. Furthermore, the race/ethnicity achievement gap was narrowing. Among African-American students 68% earned their CD's in 2006, up from 58% in 2005. Asian students jumped four percentage points from 84 to 88%. Among Hispanic students, 61% received their CD's on the first try, up from 53% in 2005. Among White 10th graders 89% received their CD's in 2006, up from 87% in 2006.

Table 2.4 shows MCAS results in reading/ELA and math before and after NCLB was implemented in Massachusetts.

The John and Abigail Adams Scholarship program, established in 2004, for students performing at the highest levels on the MCAS was thought to provide a strong incentive for students. The scholarship provided full tuition waivers for four years of study (eight traditional semesters) to eligible students who were accepted at the University of Massachusetts and other colleges in the state system.

Ninety-five percent of the class of 2006 earned Competency Determinations by the end of the school year. This percentage included all students, even those with severe special needs who attended residential schools, and other special education programs. Those who had not yet passed the test would have another chance at a retest during the summer. The gaps had narrowed significantly between the first time the class of 2005 took the test and the results after four retakes. In the end, 97% of

**Table 2.5.   Massachusetts Graduation Rates in 2006,
Disaggregated by Race**

| Group | 2004 Test* | By 2006 |
|---|---|---|
| Whites | 86% | 97% |
| Asians | 82% | 96% |
| Native Americans | 71% | 94% |
| Blacks | 59% | 86% |
| Hispanics | 51% | 86% |
| Total | | 95% |

*Note:*   *Percentages passing both competency tests on the first try.

Whites, 96% of Asians, 94% of Natives Americans, 86% of Blacks, and
86% of Hispanics passed both the ELA and math tests. In 2004, when this
class first took the 10th grade tests, 86% of White, 82% of Asian, 71% of
Native Americans, 59% of Blacks, and 51% of Hispanics had passed both
tests (Massachusetts Department of Education, 2006). Table 2.5 shows
graduation rates in 2006 disaggregated by race.

In May 2006 Commissioner David Driscoll and Attorney General Tom
Reilly announced that the state had reached a settlement regarding the
last of many legal challenges to the state's graduation requirements. The
settlement allowed the MCAS to remain as a graduation requirement, but
included several provisions aimed at assisting students in meeting the
requirements and in improving the quality of education throughout the
state.

As for achieving AYP under NCLB, in 2003, Massachusetts made AYP
in the aggregate in both English and math. All but LEP and Hispanic students made AYP in English and all but LEP, Hispanic and special needs
students made AYP in math. The state report card included a list of 208
schools that were "In Need of Improvement" for having failed to make
AYP for two consecutive years. The report card also noted that 94% of the
state's teachers were licensed in the subjects they taught and 94% were
considered "highly qualified" under NCLB. Like other states, Massachusetts had difficulty staffing its high poverty schools with highly qualified
teachers; in these schools only 88% were highly qualified.

Each year from 2004 through 2006, fewer districts and schools made
AYP, as did fewer subgroups. By 2005, 10 of the state's school districts
were now on the "In Need of Improvement" list, up from 6 in 2004. By
2006, 205 schools were "In Need of Improvement," 47 were identified for
corrective action and 57 were to be restructured. In addition, 171 schools
were identified for improvement and 137 for corrective action with regard

to subgroup performances. Stagnation on the MCAS, except among 10th graders, moved education officials to call on educators to redouble their efforts to reach lower-performing children. For Massachusetts and for all states, meeting AYP would be increasingly difficult with each year.

## PROSPECTS FOR ATTAINING NCLB OBJECTIVES BY 2013-2014

In 2005, Massachusetts students' achievement levels were among the highest in the nation in the aggregate. The commonwealth had made steady progress in achievement on the NAEP since the 1990s, though gains had leveled out on the MCAS, except, as noted, among 10th graders. As Robert Gaudet, senior research analyst at the Donahue Institute of the University of Massachusetts, concluded in his 2002 report on student achievement in Massachusetts, "There is no general achievement problem in Massachusetts; there are challenges unique to specific student populations." Students in the 15 Massachusetts cities with the highest poor and minority student populations, along with special education students, were the two groups that would require the most aggressive intervention (p. 5). As noted above, disproportionate resources were already being directed at special education students. It was clear that substantially greater resources would be required if these groups, given their socioeconomic disadvantages and/or special needs, were to meet the NCLB goal of proficiency by 2013-2014.

In early 2004, the Governor's Task Force on State Intervention in Underperforming Districts, led by Paul Grogan, president of the Boston Foundation, released its report that offered recommendations to the state for how it could partner more effectively with school districts to turn around low performing schools. The task force noted five major barriers to achievement in the underperforming districts: (1) a lack of focus on or commitment to excellence, (2) unacceptable constraints on leadership, (3) weak management systems, (4) inability to retain highly qualified personnel, and (5) inadequate professional development. Among its recommendations were: (1) contracting to have classroom assessments that were aligned with the MCAS, but which would give teachers timely diagnostic information that they could apply immediately, (2) identifying turnaround partners to work with the schools, (3) establishing leadership evaluation teams to assess the performances and needs of the districts, (4) engaging communities in open dialogue about the schools' problems, and (5) addressing contract issues that hindered the removal of ineffective teachers as well as hindering other innovations, such as longer time on task and professional development (Governor's Task Force, 2004). Governor Romney publicly endorsed the Task Force's findings, saying he would take immediate action to implement them and noting that they offered a much better alternative to state receivership (The Boston Foundation, 2004).

Meanwhile, the Supreme Judicial Court, Massachusetts' high court, in *Hancock v. Driscoll* (2005) upheld Massachusetts' school financing system, declaring that the 1993 overhaul of the state's funding formula in MERA met with the constitutional mandate in *McDuffy*. Nineteen plaintiffs from 19 school districts had argued in *Hancock v. Driscoll* that the state was not fulfilling its constitutional obligation, as articulated in *McDuffy*, to provide all children, regardless of the financial means of their communities or school districts, with a quality education. The high court acknowledged obvious inequities and shortcomings in the school districts of the plaintiffs, but said that the state was making significant progress under the reforms of 1993.

Since NCLB's passage, the commonwealth had received federal grants to enhance achievement, which suggested that its high aggregate level of achievement and its very highly regarded accountability system would allow it to continue to attract federal grants to meet the needs of lower-performing students. For instance, in fall 2002, Massachusetts was 1 of 12 states that received $100 million in federal funds for Reading First, the NCLB-endorsed research-based reading instruction program whose aim was to have children reading at grade level by Grade 3. The funds would be used to train master trainers who would conduct summer reading academies to give teachers in the neediest schools in-depth research-based training based on the five central components of reading: phonics, phonemic awareness, vocabulary, fluency, and text comprehension.

Massachusetts was 1 of 10 states to receive an up to $2 million "Redesigning the American High School" grant from the Bill & Melinda Gates Foundation in 2005. The grant would target the achievement gap, hold schools accountable, and raise the value of the diploma. Massachusetts proposed a program with a strong science and math emphasis. The BOE had recently approved Governor Romney's proposal to add the science requirement to the MCAS by 2010. The state would match the $2 million grant to develop the model high school curriculum over the next two years and to improve teacher quality in science and math.

The commonwealth targeted additional funds toward other programs for low-performing schools, as well. In late 2005, 16 school districts received grants from the state legislature to plan significantly expanding the school day and/or school year to raise achievement. The districts would explore both logistical and pedagogical challenges, including bus schedules, teacher compensation, and the integration of project-based and experiential learning that the longer time in school would permit. In 1995 the Massachusetts Time and Learning Commission had concluded that extending the time children spent in school was essential to reaching high academic standards, especially with at-risk students, and in 2004, Governor Romney had called for extending the school day. The awarding of these planning grants was the first concrete action the state would take in this direction, and Massachusetts would lead the nation in this endeavor (Gabrieli, 2005). In the fall of 2006, 10 schools in five districts, Boston, Cambridge, Fall River, Madden and Worcester, began Expanded Learning Time programs with a total of $6.5 million in grants from the state.

In addition to these grants from national foundations and allocations from the state, Massachusetts public schools enjoyed the support of several foundations and other organizations which provided funding and other resources for initiatives to strengthen public education. Especially notable was Massachusetts 2020, a foundation dedicated to expanding educational and economic opportunities in Massachusetts. Founded in 2000, it supported a number of initiatives including an initiative to expand the traditional school day and year to improve achievement, especially among at-risk children, and several after school initiatives to expand and enrich after-school and summer programs for children (Massachusetts 2020 Foundation, n.d.).

In June 2005, the state received a $700,000 grant from the Wallace Foundation to support the Massachusetts State Action for Education Leadership Project (SAELP), which was designed to strengthen leadership skills in superintendents, principals and other school leaders in order to improve student achievement in 15 of the state's poorest districts. Over the next 5 years, nearly 400 educators were expected to take part in the leadership program. The state would contribute substantially to the program as well, a projected $541,000 in the first year.

Yet despite the infusion of monies directed at low-performing schools and at-risk students, the Massachusetts school systems were working with smaller budgets than they had at the turn of the century. In FY2004, the DOE cut grant programs it administered by $100 million, completely eliminating some transportation programs and grants to reduce classroom sizes in the lower grades. Funds for early literacy programs, MCAS remediation, and breakfast pilot programs were cut by more than 50%. In the FY2004 budget, total education funding was cut by nearly $250 million, which was close to $332 million below the amount that would have accounted for inflation (Greenberg, 2004). The FY2007 budget of $3.506 billion increased from FY2006; however when corrected for inflation, it was $491 million less than the FY2002 allocation to education. Critics of the state's funding system faulted the state for contributing a relatively low percentage of the total funding for public education (39.8%, versus 53.6% contributed by localities in 2004) and for contributing a relatively low percentage of state personal income to education (4.2%); Massachusetts ranked 35th in the nation in 2004 in terms of the percentage of state personal income spent on public education (Berger & McLynch, 2006).

On the positive side, the public was supportive of continuing with education reforms and had responded in a poll conducted by Mass Insight that education should be the state's first priority in 2006. Respondents said that the three most important education reforms had been statewide standards in English and math (79%), a process for intervening in and turning around failing schools (76%) and removing principals from collective bargaining units and holding them accountable for school performance (68%). Respondents expressed less confidence in their public schools than they had the year before (53% graded the schools in their own communities A or B, down from 60% the year before), and only 37% felt schools were improving, down from 46% who thought so the year before. However, 55% said they felt high school graduates were better prepared than they had been a decade before. About two thirds felt that school reform was not yet complete, and an overwhelming majority felt that it was very important (72%) or somewhat important (15%) to turn around the lowest performing schools in the next three years. Fifty-five percent felt that failing schools needed both more money and reform to improve student achievement, 19% felt they only needed more money, and 17% felt they did not need more money to raise achievement (Mass Insight Education, 2005). Thus, the public was solidly behind the continuation of education reforms and expressed support for aggressive efforts, including more funding, to improve the lowest-performing schools. Increasing the budget for education would not be controversial. However respondents were not asked whether they were willing to pay higher taxes, if necessary, to provide more funding to public education in a state with a high rate of taxation already.

Nevertheless, it appeared that revising the funding formula would be necessary to raise achievement, because the seemingly generous programs mentioned above that targeted low-performing schools and at-risk students were overshadowed by recent cuts in the total education budget. A 2005 financial report authored by Noah Berger and Jeff McLynch of the Massachusetts Budget and Policy Center recommended that Massachusetts reassess its 1993 foundation formula, to account for the costs of undertaking the requirements of MERA and NCLB. As noted above, the foundation formula established within MERA was based not on the cost of fulfilling MERA's objectives, but the cost of educating Massachusetts' children under pre-MERA notions of equity and quality. The Budget and Policy Center's analysis suggested that the slowing, and in some cases halting, of the steady progress seen in the 1990s on the MCAS likely resulted from the early twenty-first century cuts in programs targeted at students at risk for failing the MCAS.

A report by the Rennie Center for Education Research & Policy entitled *Reaching Capacity: A Blueprint for the State Role in Improving Low Performing Schools and Districts*, published in spring 2005, concluded that improving state assistance to low-performing schools and districts was the "central challenge of the next phase of education reform"(p. 44). In order for the state to meet its obligations to the lowest performing schools and districts, it would have to expand substantially the curriculum and professional development that faculty and administrators in the lowest performing schools required to address the learning needs of at-risk students. Furthermore, enhanced use of diagnostic assessments was needed to help individual students immediately; this was not available from the MCAS because the results did not arrive until the following school year. The report stressed, as well, the urgent need for leadership development in low-performing districts and schools. The challenges in teaching disadvantaged children in these schools required the greatest expertise on the part of teachers and administrators. Yet these schools oftentimes suffered from high turnover, lack of experience and lack of expertise. Finally, the report noted that increased time on learning, including early childhood education, would be necessary to compensate for the disadvantages children in the low-performing schools experienced.

The report also stressed, as had the "Grogan" (Governor's) Task Force, that closer oversight was needed in the lowest performing schools and districts and noted that many districts were eager for more guidance, for instance in identifying effective curricular materials and professional development and in analyzing data. Moreover, standards-based accountability assumed a strong state role in guiding and assisting the most challenged school districts, with financial support and in providing direction. However, the report noted, "The state's heavy and sustained investment in the development of standards and assessments has not been paired with a commensurate investment in developing the capacity of teachers and educational leaders at the school, district and state levels, to meet the challenges of educating all students to a higher standard" (pp. 5-6).

Given all of the above-described circumstances, Massachusetts was perhaps better positioned than any other state to meet NCLB's goal of having all students proficient by 2013-2014. However, its progress toward that goal had slowed. In order to raise to proficiency students within the lowest performing groups, much more specific guidance, along with substantial increases in funding, would be necessary to support fundamental changes in leadership, instructional methods and time in school.

Thus Massachusetts illustrates the enormity of the challenge within NCLB. If any state could ensure that no child is left behind, it seems that

Massachusetts could. As Robert Gaudet noted, the state as a whole does not have an achievement problem. Furthermore, it is among the best situated in terms of its having had an early start at standards-based accountability, having the economic means, and having a broad coalition of committed people and organizations with the resources to meet the educational needs of children less easy to teach. Yet the achievement gap, which correlates more strongly with socioeconomic status than with race itself, persists. It is too early to know whether the extended day and school year initiatives that it has begun will be effective, but it appears certain that such radical innovation will be necessary to raise achievement levels among the most disadvantaged student groups.

## NOTES

1.  Demographic information is taken from the National Center for Education Statistics Web site's NAEP State Profile for Massachusetts at http://nces.ed.gov/nationsreportcard/states/profile.asp

2.  This and other information in this chapter released by the Massachusetts Department of Education, including progress on achievement tests, statements by the commissioner and other Department news was found in the department's press releases archived at http://www.doe.mass.edu/news

3.  Information on the history of the Massachusetts Business Alliance for Education and its role in the development of MERA was found at the Massachusetts Business Alliance for Education's website at http://www.mbae.org/aboutus/history.asp

4.  MCAS and other test results and analysis can be found at the Web site of the Massachusetts Department of Education at http://www.doe.mass.edu

5.  Massachusetts' "Consolidated State Application May 1, 2003 Submission for State Grants under Title IX, Part C, Section 9302 of the Elementary and Secondary Education Act (Public Law 107-110)," can be found at http://www.doe.mass.edu/nclb/stateapp/0503app.pdf. The document includes students' current achievement levels and the state's proposed targets for having all children at proficiency in reading and math by 2013-2014.

6.  State by state comparisons between students' achievement as measured by state tests and as measured by NAEP tests can be sound in *Education Week's Quality Counts 2005 No Small Change: Targeting Money Toward Student Performance*, pp. 84-85.

## REFERENCES

Achieve, Inc. (2004). *Do graduation tests measure up? A closer look at state high school exit exams.* Washington, DC: Author. Retrieved November 12, 2005, from http://www.achieve.org/files/TestGraduation-FinalReport.pdf

Barone, M., & Cohen, R. E. (2005). *The almanac of American politics, 2006*. Washington, DC: National Journal Group.

Berger, N., & McLynch, J. (2005). *Public school funding in Massachusetts: How it works, trends since 1993*. Boston: Massachusetts Budget and Policy Center. Retrieved November 12, 2005, from http://www.massbudget.org/Public_School_Funding_FY03.pdf

Berger, N., & McLynch, J. (2006). *Public school funding in Massachusetts: Where we are, what has changed, and options ahead*. Boston: Massachusetts Budget and Policy Center. Retrieved March 1, 2007 from http://www.massbudget.org/Public_School_Funding-Where_We_Are_What_Has_Changed_-_FINAL.pdf

Boston Foundation. (2004). *Romney endorses findings of Grogan Task Force on Education: Announces immediate action plan to implement turnaround strategies*. (News from the Boston Foundation.) Retrieved December 12, 2005, from http://www.tbf.org/About/about-L2 .asp?id=1714.

Cancell, E. R. (n.d.). *Guaranteeing MCAS failure*. Retrieved November 27, 2005, from http://www.eyeoneducation.tv/about/cancell.html

Cross, R. W., Rebarber, T., & Torres, J. (2004). *Grading the systems: The guide to state standards, tests, and accountability policies*. Washington, DC: Thomas B. Fordham Foundation and Accountability Works. Retrieved November 15, 2005, from http://www.edexcellence.net/doc/GradingtheSystems.pdf

Educational Management Accountability Board. (2000). *First findings: The summative report of the Educational Management Accountability Board on the audits of Massachusetts school districts and the impact of the Education Reform Act*. Boston: Author. Retrieved on November 27, 2005, from http://www.edbenchmarks .org/index/Findings.PDF

Gabrieli, C. (2005, November 16). Get ready for a longer school day. *The Boston Globe*. Retrieved November 27, 2005, from http://boston.com/news/education/k_23/articles/2005/11/16/get_ready_for_a_longer_school_day/

Garcia, J., & Rothman, R. (2002). *Three paths one destination: Standards-based reform in Maryland, Massachusetts and Texas*. Washington, DC: Achieve Inc. Retrieved November 12, 2005, from http://www.achieve.org/files/reportthree-statefinal_2.pdf

Gaudet, R. D. (2002). *Student achievement in Massachusetts: The lessons of nine years of education reform*. Amherst: University of Massachusetts Donahue Institute. Retrieved November 15, 2005, from http://www.edbenchmarks.org/index/StudAchv.pdf

Gaudet, R. D. (2003). *Effective school districts in Massachusetts: A study of student performance on the 2002 MCAS assessments relative to district demography: The fifth annual report*. Amherst: University of Massachusetts Donahue Institute. Retrieved November 27, 2005, from http://www.edbenchmarks.org/index/MCAS_Report_02. pdf

Governor's Task Force on State Intervention in Under-Performing Districts. (2004). *Partners in progress: A framework for raising student achievement in underperforming school districts*. Boston: Author. Retrieved November 27, 2005, from http://www.doemass.org/infoservices/news04/Partners_in_Progress_04_4.pdf

Greenberg, C. L. (2004). *Public school funding in Massachusetts: How does the commonwealth compare to the rest of the nation?* Boston: Massachusetts Budget and Policy

Center. Retrieved November 27, 2005, from http://www.massteacher.org/advocating/news_2004-01-16.cfm.

Hess, F. M. (2002). *I say 'refining,' you say 'retreating': The politics of high-stakes accountability.* Paper presented at the Taking Account of Accountability: Assessing Politics and Policy Conference, Cambridge, MA. (ERIC Document Reproduction Service No. 471865).

Hess, F. M. (2002). Refining or retreating? High-stakes accountability in the states. In P. E. Peterson & M. R. West (Eds.), *No Child Left Behind? The politics and practice of school accountability* (pp. 55-79). Washington, DC: Brookings Institution Press.

Kennedy, E.M. (2005, January 8). *Statement of Senator Edward M. Kennedy signing of education reform legislation Boston Latin School.* Retrieved November 27, 2005 from   http://kennedy.senate.gov/%7Ekennedy/statements/02/01/2002109901.html

Klein, D. (with Braams, B. J., Parker, T, Quirk, W., Schmid, W., & Wilson, S. W.) (2005). *The state of state MATH standards.* Washington, DC: Thomas B. Fordham Foundation. Retrieved November 12, 2005, from http://www.edexcellence.net/doc/ mathstandards05FINAL.pdf

Mass Insight Education. (2005). *Public to policymakers: Full speed ahead on K-12 education reform: Special focus: Teacher and management issues.* Boston: Author. Retrieved December 3, 2005, from http://www.massinsight.org/docs/2005EducationPublicOpinionSurvey.pdf

Massachusetts 2020 Foundation. (n.d.). *Massachusetts 2020 foundation initiatives.* Retrieved November 27, 2005, from http://www.mass2020.org/projects.html

Massachusetts Business Alliance for Education. (n.d.). *History.* Retrieved December 3, 2005, from http://www.mbae.org/aboutus/history.asp

Massachusetts Department of Education. (n.d.). *Massachusetts common core of learning.* Retrieved November 27, 2005, from http://www.doe.mass.edu/edreform/commoncore/

Massachusetts Department of Education. (2005). *Spring 2005 MCAS tests: Summary of state results.* Malden, MA: Author. Retrieved November 27, 2005, from http://www.doe.mass.edu/mcas/2005/results/summary.pdf

Massachusetts Department of Education. (2003). *Consolidated state application May 1, 2003 submission for state grants under Title IX, part C, section 9302 of the Elementary and Secondary Education Act (public law 107-110).* Retrieved November 27, 2005, from http://www.doe.mass.edu/nclb/stateapp/0503app.pdf

Massachusetts Department of Education. (2006). *Progress report on students attaining the competency determination statewide and by school and district: Classes of 2006 and 2007.* Retrieved February 3, 2007, from http://www.doe.mass.edu/mcas/2006/results/ CDreport_0606.doc

Patrick, D. (2005, October 6). *Assuring excellence in public education.* Campaign statement. Retrieved on February 3, 2007, from http://www.devalpatrick.com/resources/pdf/ Moving%20MA%20Forward,%20Education.pdf

Peyser, J. A. (2003). Complying with NCLB is not enough. In *Implementing the No Child Left Behind Act.* Washington, D.C.: Progressive Policy Institute. Retrieved November 27, 2005 from http://www.ppionline.org/ppi_ci.cfm?knlgAreaID =110&subsecID=900023&contentID=251471

Potier, B. (2001, October 18). MCAS put to the test at KSG. *Harvard University Gazette*. Retrieved November 27, 2005, from http://www.news.harvard.edu/gazette/2001/10.18/ 06-mcas.html

*Quality Counts 2005*: No small change: Targeting money toward student performance. (2005, January). [Special issue]. *Education Week*.

*Quality Counts 2007*: From cradle to career: Connecting American education from birth through adulthood. (2007, January). [Special issue]. *Education Week*.

Rennie Center for Education Research & Policy at Mass INC. (2005). *Reaching capacity: A blueprint for the state role in improving low performing schools and districts*. Boston: Author.

Schworm, P. (2004, May 10).Urban charter schools score a win. *The Boston Globe*. Retrieved December 12, 2005 from http://www.boston.com/news/local/massachusetts/articles/ 2004/05/10/urban_charter_schools_score_a_win/

Stotsky, S. (2005). *The State of state ENGLISH standards*. Washington, DC: Thomas B. Fordham Foundation. Retrieved December 3, 2005, from http://www.edexcellence.net/ doc/FullReport[01-03-05].pdf

Stotsky, S. (with Haverty, L.) (2004). Can a state department of education increase teacher quality? Lessons leaned in Massachusetts. In *Brookings Papers on education policy* 2004 (pp. 131-180). Washington, DC: The Brookings Institution.

Wheelock, A. (n.d.). *MCAS pass rates not cause for celebration*. Retrieved November 27, 2005, from http://www.eyeoneducation.tv/about/wheelock.html

# CHAPTER 3

---

# NEW YORK

---

## INTRODUCTION

We introduce the state of New York by reviewing its social, cultural, economic, and political characteristics, after which we turn to the nature of its educational system.

### Socioeconomic and Political Characteristics

For most of the nineteenth and twentieth centuries, New York was America's most populous state, but in 2006 it has 19.2 million residents and stands third behind California and Texas. Yet it is home to America's largest city, New York City, with a population of 8 million. New York has recovered from population losses of the 1970s, but its rate of growth, like that of other rust belt states, has been slow.

The state's population is among the most diverse ethnically in the United States. Today 62% of New Yorkers are Caucasians, 15.1% of Latino origin, 14.8% Black, 5.5% Asian, and the balance of a large number of ethnicities (Barone & Cohen, 2005). New York City is a mosaic of nationalities, and more than a third of its residents were born in other countries. First speakers of languages other than English make up a large minority of the state's population.

---

*Education Reform in the American States*
pp. 55–81

New York has a diverse economic system. Upstate New York has a large agricultural industry. Manufacturing was the backbone of the state's rapid economic development in the late nineteenth and early twentieth centuries, and 16% of New York's residents are still employed in this sector, notwithstanding the hollowing out of the industrial base in the last generation. Most New Yorkers, however, are employed in the services sector—finance, education, government, information, communications, the entertainment industry, and the professions.

Many of America's largest corporations—such as IBM, Kodak, Xerox, and GE—have headquarters in New York's cities, and New York City itself is America's center of arts and letters, the media, and finance. It was the latter distinction that drew terrorists to the World Trade Center on September 11, 2001. Although the city recovered, it hemorrhaged 200,000 jobs.

The median income of New Yorkers is $43,400, but this figure camouflages stark contrasts between rich and poor. Some of the wealthiest Americans live and work in New York City; yet 18% of the population has household incomes lower than $15,000; 15% are classified as poor; and the unemployment rate is 7%. Until New York City went bankrupt in 1975, it had America's largest welfare bureaucracy with quite liberal health and income maintenance benefits for the least advantaged. Even in 2006, state and city governments (which employ 17% of New Yorkers) play large roles in providing social services. New York also has one of the highest rates of union membership in the nation.

Politically, New York is a "blue" state. Registration in the Democratic Party exceeds by 2 million that of the Republican Party. George W. Bush took only 35% of the presidential vote in 2000, but improved his margin to 40% in 2004. In the 110th Congress, both U.S. senators are Democrats, as are 20 of the 29 New York members in the House of Representatives.

State politics have been more balanced between the parties. Traditionally, New York City was a bastion of Democrats and upstate New York of Republicans, and this division continues. In late 2006, New York City has a second-term Republican mayor, Michael Bloomberg, and the state governor, Eliot Spitzer (starting his first term in office) is a Democrat. The state legislature closely reflects New York's partisan divide: the senate is controlled by Republicans (35Rs, 27Ds) and the assembly by Democrats (104Ds, 44Rs).

## The State Educational System

The state's political establishment is strongly involved in public education, including both houses of the legislature (and their education committees), the governor, and the mayor of New York City. Education unions, especially teachers, lobby the legislature in Albany. Business alliances, representatives of the state's ethnic communities, even public policy institutes focus concentrated attention on education issues.

The New York State Education Department (NYSED) is one of the largest state departments, with increasingly centralized control over districts and schools. Members of the Board of Regents are selected by the legislature; they appoint the state commissioner of education. Regents and commissioner work independently of the governor, and commissioners tend to serve long terms in office. The chancellor of New York City schools, an appointee of the mayor, is active and influential in state policymaking.

New York has 2.84 million public school students in 4,624 schools, and 37% of the students attend school in New York City. The private school enrollment at nearly 500,000 is large and comprises over 14% of total student enrollment. The state has a small number of charter schools, just 38 (including 18 in New York City), and they receive generally high marks from parents (Manhattan Institute for Policy Research, 2003). Although the state has a moderately strong charter school law, the large number of private schools is a deterrent to the establishment of charters. About 47% of New York students are ethnic/racial minorities. Some 19.9% are Black, 19.8% Latino, 7.2% Asian/Pacific Islander or American Indian/Alaska Native, and 53.1% Caucasian. Approximately 19% are children in poverty; 14.4% have disabilities; and 6.2% are students with limited English proficiency (LEP). About 38% of students are eligible for free/reduced rate lunches, a primary indicator of low-income status. These students tend to be concentrated in New York City and the state's other large cities.

Serving student educational needs are 227,000 teachers, nearly 44,000 professionals (administrators, counselors, psychologists, nurses), and about 63,000 paraprofessionals (for example, teachers' aides) (National Center for Education Statistics, 2006; New York State Education Department [NYSED], 2004b, 2006c). New York is not a right-to-work state, and educational professionals are organized into strong unions.

## THE NEW YORK ASSESSMENT AND
## ACCOUNTABILITY SYSTEM BEFORE 2002

The state of New York did not develop a comprehensive assessment and accountability system for education until the 1990s. However, New York led the other states in the establishment of a high school exit examination. Then, in the late 1960s, New York decentralized control from its largest district, New York City, to community schools, and experimented

with various forms of site-based management. We review these two processes of education reform before introducing the accountability system.

## The Regents Examination

New York has been administering high school exit examinations,
closely based on the high school curriculum, since 1878. The exams were
taken by students throughout their high school careers, but were effectively a dual-track system: students could graduate from high school
receiving a regents' diploma, indicating passage of the exams, or with a
local high school diploma.

When the Regents Examinations were scrutinized in the early 1980s, as
part of the Regents' Action Plan, there were two sets of examinations. Students satisfied with a local high school diploma needed only complete the
required course units and pass the Regents Competency Tests (RCTs),
which were relatively undemanding. Those seeking a Regents diploma
needed to pass a minimum of eight of the more demanding Regents
Examinations and course units of study (see NYSED, 1995; Natriello &
Pallas, 2001).

The dual structure of the examination system led to students following
different tracks—an easier set of high school classes if they pursued the
local high school diploma, or more challenging courses to prepare them
for the Regents Examination. Even for those students taking the Regents
Examination, it was not a high-stakes test. Bishop and Mane (2001)
report that exam grades counted for less than one-eighth of final grades
in courses. Nor did exam scores figure in college admissions decisions,
which relied mainly on grades and SAT scores. In the 1996-97 school
year, just about 42% of graduating seniors received the Regents diploma,
indicating that students were more likely to follow the easy road to graduation.

In the mid-1990s, the state eliminated the lower track and made the
Regents Examination a bona fide high-stakes test. First, the New York City
Board of Education required students to take three Regents-level math
and three science courses before graduating, beginning with those entering high school in 1994 (Jones, 1994). Chancellor Ramon Cortines
remarked:

> The easy way out is the road to nowhere. If achievement in our schools is to
> improve, we must raise our expectations for students and staff. Our system
> will fail in its obligation to this community unless we equalize educational
> opportunity and raise standards in all of our schools. (Bishop & Mane,
> 2001, p. 67)

Within 2 years, the Board of Regents raised graduation requirements for all public school students in the state. Students would be required to take Regents-level courses and also pass Regents exams for these courses. Beginning with the class of 1996, students progressively would take examinations in English, algebra and geometry, global studies, American history—a total of five required examinations that students would need to pass at the 55% level, but this level would also be raised to 65%. (In fall 2003, the state delayed raising the threshold passing score for the exit exams for 2 years [Loveless, 2005].) Bishop and Mane call this requirement "the first high-stakes, curriculum-based, external exit examination system in United States history" (2001, p. 68).

The toughening of requirements represents change from the traditional Regents Examination in three respects. First, the bottom track was effectively eliminated. Students received a Regents Diploma if they scored 65% on examinations; they received a local diploma if they attained a lower score determined by the local district (but no less than 55%); and they received no diploma if they failed to meet these standards. Second, examinations increasingly were keyed to comprehensive state standards (described below), with connections between grade levels and across subject areas. Third, the system was based on the concept of continual revision, tracking evolving state and national standards and assessment practices (Natriello & Pallas, 2001; NYSED, 2006c). We examine some of the effects of these changes in the following section.

## Decentralization of Education in New York City

The second reform, decentralizing educational control within the state's largest school district, was also the first of its kind in the United States. The New York City decentralization experiment was a product of 1960s social reform in the nation's largest city (many elements were present in other cities as well; see Rogers, 1968; also see Gittel & Hollander, 1968). Reform objectives included improvement in education through equalizing educational services for minority racial and ethnic groups, and by making the system as a whole accountable to its different constituencies.

Leading the charge for reform were blacks who objected to lack of quality in schooling, continued segregation of schools, and lack of effective compensatory programs. Latino and other groups complained about the district bureaucracy, which they thought was insulated and grossly mismanaged (Rogers & Chang, 1973). They pictured it as the epitome of professional control. School wars of the late 1960s in sections of Brooklyn (Ocean Hill-Brownsville) closed the entire city school system for weeks at a time (Ravitch, 1973). Indeed, cracking professional control and bureau-cracy were the ultimate goals of the movement. Rogers and Chung (1973) summarize the goals of the movement as increased accountability of edu-cators to the public, greater public and community involvement in educa-tional decision making, increasing innovation in schooling, greater linkages of schools and communities in hiring and curriculum, more jobs in schools for district residents, creation of more local-level leadership, improved school legitimacy, and ultimately, increased student perfor-mance.

In 1969 the New York Legislature decentralized education in the city, devolving power over hiring and some elements of curriculum in elemen-tary and junior high schools to some 32 elected community school boards (high schools remained under the central board). Early analyses of the decentralization experiment pointed out successes as well as problems in governance, administration, and district-headquarters relations (see Rog-ers & Chung, 1973; also see Gittel, 1973; Ravitch, 1973; and Zimet, 1973). Yet, the experiment ran too short a period to determine its effec-tiveness in raising student performance levels before the financial difficul-ties of New York City leading to its bankruptcy in 1975 brought about significant effective recentralization. Even under conditions of centralized control, the city continued to experiment with forms of shared decision-making. When Joseph Fernandez became chancellor of city schools in 1990, he implemented site-based management in the districts' schools (see Cuban, 2004). In 1997 the state legislature strengthened the power of the chancellor over city schools (Ross, 1998).

## Development of the State Assessment and Accountability System

Before 1995, New York had some elements of an assessment and accountability system. Since 1965, the state had administered a Pupil Evaluation Program (PEP) for elementary and middle-level students. PEP required all students to take criterion-referenced reading and mathemat-ics tests in Grades 3 and 6 and a writing test in Grade 5. As mentioned, for high school students, the state administered the Regents Examination and Regency Competency Tests, a dual-track system. The system as a whole lacked integration, and it was not closely matched with standards to which curricula could be aligned.

This system was transformed in the 1990s under the leadership of then-Commissioner of Education Thomas Sobol. In July 1996, the Board of Regents adopted content standards defining what students should know and be able to do as they progressed through Grades K-12. The standards focused on seven curricular areas: English language arts, mathematics, science and technology, social studies, languages other than English, the arts, health, physical education and family and consumer sciences, and career development (including occupational studies; see NYSED, 2001). The Regents' strategy for raising standards included three elements:

1. Set clear, high expectations/standards for all students and develop an effective means of assessing student progress in meeting the standards;
2. Build the capacity of schools and districts to meet standards; and
3. Use and expand the existing system of public accountability for schools—based on student performance—and provide incentives for improving effectiveness and sanctions for low performance (NYSED, 2001, p. 2).

For the elementary and middle grades, the Regents replaced PEP with a New York State Assessment Program (NYSAP) in English language arts and mathematics and the grade 4 science test. The new tests matched grades tested through the National Educational Assessment Program (NAEP); they were criterion-referenced, based on the state standards, and prepared by McGraw-Hill. For secondary school students, as mentioned, the state toughened the Regents Examination and phased out the RCTs (except for students with disabilities), and required passage of the Regents Examination to receive a high school diploma. (For discussion of New York's high stakes examination system, see DeBray, 2005, and Iatarola, 2005). A second measure of high school performance was the career education proficiency examination.

To measure performance on criterion-referenced tests, NYSED adopted equal-interval scales, each of which was divided into four performance levels. Level 1 encompassed students with the lowest performance, indicating serious academic deficiencies and little or no proficiency in standards for that grade level. Level 2 students showed some knowledge and skill in each of the required standards, but needed extra help to reach all the standards and pass the Regents Examination. Level 3 students met the standards and, with continued steady growth, were thought to be able to pass Regents Examinations. Finally, Level 4 students were at the highest level; they exceeded the standards and were moving toward high performance on the Regents Examinations (NYSED, 2001, 2006c).

Regulations required schools to provide academic intervention services to students scoring at the two lowest levels. Beginning in 1996-97, schools were identified for registration review, if they were determined to be most in need of improvement (farthest from state performance standards). Such schools were called "schools under registration review (or SURR schools)," and were required to make school improvement plans; those on the SURR list for more than 2 years were subject to state intervention. In May 2000, the Regents established accountability standards (for schools) based on NYSAP in English and math, completing graduation requirements in English and math, and dropout rates. Earlier legislation (a 1987 amendment to chapter 655 of the state education law) required NYSED to submit an annual report to the governor and legislature on the educational status of New York schools, and these reports inform this study.

A study commissioned by the educationally conservative Fordham Foundation criticizes the New York standards, calling them "poor" in English-language arts and mathematics. Focusing principally on math, the report says the standards are "vague, poorly written and have noticeable holes in the coverage of core math concepts.... (They) place greater emphasis on thinking, writing, and talking *about* math—so-called "math chat"—than on actual performance" (Cross, Rebarber, & Torres, 2004, p. 38; see also Klein, 2005; and Stotsky, 2005).

However, the Consortium for Policy Research in Education (CPRE) reported favorably on the New York system overall in its review of the 50 states (2000). Darling-Hammond and Falk (1997) describe the New York effort as "a comprehensive system of learning goals and standards, curriculum frameworks, new assessments, and support strategies" (p. 59). *Quality Counts 2005* listed New York as the "top-scoring state":

> New York has all the elements critical to a strong accountability system. New York has clear and specific standards in English, mathematics, science, and social studies/history at the elementary, middle, and high school levels. It also has tests aligned with those standards in each of the subjects in every grade span.... New York uses its test data to hold schools accountable. The state publishes test data on school report cards.... It also provides help to schools rated as low-performing and imposes sanctions on consistently low-performing or failing schools. New York also provides monetary rewards to high-performing or improving schools. (2005, p. 1)

*Quality Counts 2007* ranked New York somewhat lower on a new set of measures. The alignment of its policies "from cradle to career" placed it fourth among the states, while its policies in the area of standards, assessments, and accountability earned it a state ranking of ninth.

In sum, New York has a national reputation for the quality of its accountability system, notwithstanding some critical commentary about its math standards.

## IMPACT OF THE NEW YORK ACCOUNTABILITY SYSTEM

At the time NCLB was moving toward passage in the Congress, New York had administered most of the elements of the new accountability system since the 1998-99 school year. We review information on general levels of proficiency statewide in elementary and middle-school levels, and then turn to differences between New York City students and those in the rest of the state. Before NCLB, New York did not compare ethnic/racial subgroups, but it did compile information on students with disabilities and LEP students. We touch on these differences briefly before looking at trends on the Regents examination.

Table 3.1 displays the proficiency in English-language arts and mathematics of elementary and middle-level students, from 1999 to 2002. Caution must be used in interpreting these data, as they represent cross-sections of students at different points in time. The NYSAP does not facilitate measurement of student gains from year to year. Nevertheless, there appear to be large improvements in some areas. Comparing proficiency percentages in 1999 with those in 2002, one notes a significant improvement of scores in fourth grade English-language arts (from 49 to 62%) and eighth grade mathematics (from 38 to 48%). There is not much change in fourth grade mathematics (from 67% proficient in 1999 to 68% in 2002). Scores in eighth grade English-language arts, however, decline, from 49% in 1999 to 44% in 2002. Overall, it appears that in most areas at the elementary level, the majority of students were meeting state standards.

General education students were over five times as likely as those with disabilities to score at Level 4 on the fourth grade English assessment; the general education students were twice as likely to score at Level 3 or above. Yet performance of students with disabilities increased at all levels after 2001 (NYSED, 2003). The disparity in performance between stu-

### Table 3.1 Proficiency in English and Mathematics, 1999-2002*

| Year | English, 4th | Math, 4th | English, 8th | Math, 8th |
|------|------|------|------|------|
| 1998-1999 | 49% | 67% | 49% | 38% |
| 1999-2000 | 59% | 65% | 45% | 41% |
| 2000-2001 | 60% | 69% | 45% | 39% |
| 2001-2002 | 62% | 68% | 44% | 48% |

*Proficiency percentage is based on students ranking in levels 3 and 4.
*Note:* Adapted by author from NYSED (2003, pp. 35-37).

dents with disabilities and general education students was even greater at the middle level.

Greater differences in performance appear when examining limited English proficient (LEP) students, as one would expect. Only 14% of the LEP students were proficient on the elementary-level English assessment, compared to 63% of non-LEP students. At the middle-level, only about 4% of the LEP students were proficient, as compared to 46% of the non-LEP students (NYSED, 2003, p. 51).

As noted above, before NCLB, New York did not compare ethnic or racial subgroups of the student population, but inferences can be made about the performance of minority students by comparing New York City students with those from the rest of the state. In 2002, fourth grade students in the city had proficiency rates in English and math of 47 and 52%, compared to all other New York students whose proficiency in these subjects stood at 71 and 76% respectively. A similar gap was apparent between English and math scores of eighth grade city students and other students. Some 30% of city children were proficient in both subjects compared to proficiency rates of 52 and 57% for all other New York students (NYSED, 2003, pp. 36-37).

These differences in performance are glaring. In each grade and subject area, students from outside New York City ranked at least 20% higher in proficiency than did city students. New York City students are more likely to have limited English language proficiency. Definitely, they come from families that are poorer on average than those in other New York cities, or in the suburban districts with students from families having high incomes and property wealth. The NYSED report on educational status has this to say about these striking differences:

> These contrasts in performance parallel contrasts in student need and district resources. Seventy-five percent—compared with three percent—were eligible for free lunches. One-third of middle-level mathematics teachers in New York City, compared with four percent in advantaged districts, were not certified in mathematics. Despite New York City's large number of students placed at-risk by poverty and limited proficiency in English, the City's mean expenditure per pupil was 83 percent of that in the most advantaged districts. Consequently, New York City must compete for teachers with more advantaged districts whose median teacher salary exceeds the City's by 30 percent. (2003, p. vi)

Indeed, like a number of other states, New York has two systems of public education—one in New York City (and other large cities) and the second in the rest of the state.

Our final area in examination of the New York accountability system before NCLB is performance of high school students. Test results on the

Regents Examinations show that more students had taken the tests, and a larger number had scored 55 or higher on four of the five core areas (the fifth, where student performance did not consistently improve, was mathematics). NYSED (2003) attributes the downturn in number of students tested in mathematics to the increased amount of time and course work needed to prepare for this revised examination.

Performance of students with disabilities was considerably less good. While nearly three fourths of general education students in the 1996 cohort (those students starting high school in 1996 and graduating in 2000) scored from 65 to 100 on Regents English, only one third of students with disabilities did so (NYSED, 2003). As for students of limited English proficiency, the results were as one might expect: 32% passed at the 65-100 rate in 2002 (compared to 27% in 2001, a significant improvement) compared to 78% of the non-LEP students (a score essentially unchanged from that in the previous year). Mathematics rates were closer, with some 46% of LEP students passing at 65-100% compared to 74% of non-LEP students (NYSED, 2003).

Overall, it would appear that the New York assessment and accountability system made a difference in student outcomes, and this occurred before the implementation of NCLB. Yet the development of national reform legislation caught New York at an awkward moment. It was just in the process of implementing an integrated reform of state education, when it was required to adapt to a new national system, based on a different model. We now turn to this conflict in systems.

## RESPONSE OF NEW YORK TO NCLB REQUIREMENTS

Although the New York accountability system was integrated, it lacked several elements required in the national NCLB legislation. This necessitated modifications and amendments of the state assessment system, determining Adequate Yearly Progress (AYP), providing choice for students in failing schools, and addressing issues of teacher quality.

The Regents Examinations satisfied NCLB requirements for testing high school students, but the state assessments measured students in the fourth and eighth grades only, while NCLB required testing in each grade from third to eighth. Because this represented a near tripling of the size of its assessment program, New York gained permission from the U.S. Department of Education (USDOE) to delay implementation of this requirement until the 2005-06 school year, so that the NYSED and test contractor McGraw-Hill could develop criterion-referenced assessments for Grades 3, 5, 6, and 7.

When the state enacted new assessments in 1996, it decided against dividing students into racial, ethnic, or socioeconomic subgroups and then expecting schools to insure that members of those subgroups achieved the same progress as the student body as a whole. Although education officials were interested in focusing on subgroup performance, they lacked "adequate technical means" to do so (NYSED, 2003, p. 51; see also Keller, 2000). However, this became a requirement under NCLB, and was an additional reason behind New York's request for a delay of implementation.

Following NCLB requirements, the state established Annual Measurable Objectives (AMOs) for English and mathematics at each grade level. The AMOs are neither front- nor rear-loaded; they increase annually, beginning in 2004-05, in equal increments until reaching 100% student proficiency in 2013-14. To minimize the chance that a district or school erroneously will be deemed to have not made AYP, New York gained USDOE approval to use a "confidence interval" to determine whether a group of smaller than minimum size has met its AMO.[1] New York also takes advantage of the "safe harbor" provisions of NCLB for those schools failing to meet "effective AMO" in English and mathematics, but which have improved by specified amounts over the previous year's performance.

New York was one of the first states to gain USDOE approval for the methods it used to comply with the accountability provisions of NCLB. It modified its accountability system to incorporate AYP directly. It rated schools based on separate performance indices in reading and mathematics that give schools credit for the percent of students who have achieved basic or full proficiency on state tests. Those schools that are "high performing" will have to meet or exceed all state standards and achieve adequate progress for each subgroup of students. It has established a similar index at the high school level, based on the percentage of ninth graders who pass the Regents Examinations in math and English by Grade 12. The state had to convince USDOE that only students' first reported scores in Grade 12, including those passing the tests earlier, should be counted for accountability purposes (Olson, 2003).

New York's accountability system required some modification to accommodate NCLB's requirements for schools and districts failing to make AYP for two consecutive years in the same grade and subject. It designated these as Schools Requiring Academic Progress (SRAP, or DRAP for Districts). For Title I schools in this status, it added the additional designation of "School (or District) in Need of Improvement [SINI or DINI]" (NYSED, 2004a, p. 14).

New York had some experience in the choice provisions of NCLB under its own accountability system. For example, New York City students in 331 failing schools (from a total of about 1,100), were eligible to transfer in fall 2002. Although the district informed 280,000 households that they had the right to transfer, only 3,600 students applied; of these, 1,500 were moved to other schools. Levin (2004) comments: "The meager initial response by families, the relatively small number of available spaces, and the distance between failing schools and available places substantially limited the school choice option and its use as a sanction for failing schools" (Levin, 2004, p. 253). New York's experience was echoed in many states.

A final area of response concerns teacher quality. Haycock (2004) found that differences of teacher qualifications in New York were greater than those of the nation as a whole. Statewide, approximately 17% of teachers in high-poverty schools were uncertified, compared to 4% of teachers in low-poverty schools. Teachers in low-performing schools were more likely to have failed the licensure exam at least once, as compared to teachers in high-performing schools. In about 10% of schools, virtually all teachers were experienced; but at the other pole, some 18% of teachers lacked experience. The problem was greatest in New York City, where 10% of the teachers in the median school were inexperienced, and some 23% of the overall teaching force had less than 3 years experience (p. 232; see also Lankford, Wyckoff & Papa, 2000).

Of New York's 217,935 teachers in 2002-03, some 6,573 were "teaching out of certification," or 3% of the total teaching force. Nearly 800 teachers worked under temporary licenses (NYSED, 2004a, p. 2). New York City had long hired under-prepared teachers, filling vacancies with uncertified applicants well after the school year began. However, the NYSED pressured the city to hire qualified teachers and mandated that uncertified teachers would no longer be able to teach in low-performing schools, effective fall 2003. In the 2002-03 school year, the city district sharply increased salaries (to an average of 16% overall and more than 20% higher for starting teachers). Darling-Hammond and Sykes (2004) note that through this action and aggressive recruiting, "90% of new hires were certified, up from 60% the year before. The remaining 10% were in programs that would lead to certification by the end of the school year" (p. 198; also see Hayes & Gendar, 2002).

## INITIAL RESULTS OF NCLB IN NEW YORK (2003-2006)

By late 2006, New York had 3 years of data indicating the performance of its schools under NCLB requirements. The assessment system remained unchanged for these 3 years, as the state received permission to delay implementation of testing in all grades until the 2005-06 school year.

**Table 3.2.   Proficiency in English and Mathematics, 2003-2005**

| Year | English, 4th | Math, 4th | English, 8th | Math, 8th |
|------|------|------|------|------|
| 2003 | 64% | 79% | 45% | 51% |
| 2004 | 63% | 79% | 47% | 58% |
| 2005 | 70% | 85% | 48% | 55% |

*Note:*   Adapted by author from NYSED (2006b, pp. 53-56).

Table 3.2 presents information on student proficiency in English and mathematics for 3 years, 2002-03 to 2004-05:

When we compare these results to the three previous school years (2000, 2001, and 2002), we note general improvement in performance. Scores of fourth grade students in English are better. The mathematics scores are much higher, with levels some 10% better for both fourth and eighth grade students. Only in eighth grade English is there no upward movement. Of course, these are improvement scores on the state's tests, which have proficiency cutoffs easier to attain than those of the NAEP (Dillon, 2005). The NAEP scores for New York in 2003 are 34% in reading at fourth grade and 35% for eighth grade, both increases of 3-4% from the previous testing, but increases that were not statistically significant. In 2005, NAEP scores in reading are 33% for both grade levels, a slight decline (but statistically insignificant).

In 2003, the NAEP math scores were 33% for fourth grade students and 32% for eighth graders, both of which were statistically significant increases (*Quality Counts*, 2005). In the 2005 NAEP, math scores increased 3% for fourth graders but dropped 2% for eighth graders (not statistically significant). Overall, only in the area of mathematics and at the elementary level, does it appear that New York students clearly are registering improvement under NCLB (see also NCES, 2006).

In 2005, New York finally produced statewide information on the performance of ethnic and racial subgroups. Table 3.4 presents these breakdowns for elementary students in English and mathematics on state tests for 2 years (variations across subgroups do not differ greatly from elementary to secondary students).

These subgroup differences are all in the expected direction. White students outperformed both Black and Latino students, by at least 20% points, while Asian students had the highest scores of any ethnic group. Students of minority ethnicity are far more likely to be of limited English proficiency, economically disadvantaged, and from migrant families—and scores of these groups are considerably lower. As we have noted previ-

**Table 3.3.  Student Proficiency by Subgroups, 2004 and 2005**

| Subgroup | 4th Grade English | | 4th Grade Math | |
|---|---|---|---|---|
| | 2003-04 | 04-05 | 03-04 | 04-05 |
| American Indian/Ak. Native | 46% | 58% | 72% | 79% |
| Black | 44% | 54% | 63% | 73% |
| Hispanic | 46% | 57% | 66% | 76% |
| Asian/Pacific Islander | 78% | 83% | 90% | 93% |
| White | 73% | 79% | 89% | 92% |
| Students with disabilities | 22% | 28% | 49% | 55% |
| Female | 66% | 74% | 80% | 85% |
| Male | 59% | 67% | 79% | 84% |
| Limited English proficiency | 21% | 31% | 48% | 59% |
| Economically disadvantaged | 46% | 57% | 68% | 77% |
| Migrant family | 33% | 44% | 62% | 68% |
| Statewide total | 62% | 70% | 79% | 85% |

*Note:* Adapted by author from NYSED (2006b, pp. 15-16).

ously, New York City has a far higher number of such students than other cities and towns in the state.

Large improvements in scores occurred for most minority populations. For example, proficiency scores for black students increased by 10% in both English and math. For LEP students the increase was 10% in English and 11% in math. Given the greater distance of these groups from the norm, the proficiency rate increase appears especially meaningful.

General education students who entered ninth grade in 1999 or 2000 needed to score 55 or higher on the Regents English and mathematics examinations to graduate. Table 3.4 indicates graduation rates for 2002, 2003, and 2004 for all student subgroups.

These data indicate a similar breakdown in subgroups to that presented in Table 3.3. In most of the ethnic/racial groups, little change occurred in graduation rates over the 3 years. Although the graduation percentage of students with disabilities (see discussion below on state compliance), and of students who were economically disadvantaged, increased somewhat in 2003; it fell the following year. The dropout rate for these students, at approximately 20%, remained higher than the statewide average of 12%. Graduation rates of minority students is an election issue, and figured in Michael Bloomberg's mayoral re-election campaign in 2005 (Gootman, 2005), when he had to defend his record against opposition criticism.

**Table 3.4.   Graduation Rates of Cohorts\* in 2002-2004, by Subgroups**

| Student Subgroup | 2002 | 2003 | 2004 |
|---|---|---|---|
| American Indian/AK. Native | 68% | 69% | 66% |
| Black | 57% | 58% | 59% |
| Hispanic | 53% | 53% | 55% |
| Asian/Pacific Islander | 78% | 79% | 78% |
| White | 88% | 86% | 86% |
| Students with disabilities | 55% | 58% | 53% |
| Female | 80% | 80% | 81% |
| Male | 73% | 72% | 77% |
| Limited English proficiency | 49% | 43% | 45% |
| Economically disadvantaged | 54% | 62% | 58% |
| Migrant family | 81% | 67% | 49% |
| Statewide total | 77% | 76% | 77% |

\*The 2002 graduates were from the cohort first entering Grade 9 in 1998; the 2003 graduates entered Grade 9 in 1999, and the 2004 cohort in 2000. Both groups include students who earned a local diploma with or without a Regents endorsement by August 31st of the year.

*Note:* Adapted by author from NYSED (2006b, p. 23).

Under NCLB, New York also measures schools' attainment of AYP by accountability group, and data are available for the 2003-04 and 2004-05 school years. In 2003-04, about 68% of New York's public schools made AYP in all subjects and grade levels. Elementary schools were most likely to make AYP, and 90% did so; least likely to make AYP were secondary schools (53%), with middle schools falling in between (68.5%) (NYSED, 2005, p. 23). A relatively large number of schools failed to meet AYP because of the participation requirement, particularly affecting middle and high schools.

In 2004-05, 82% of public schools made AYP in all subjects and grade levels, an increase of 14%. The rate of attainment for elementary schools, 90%, was identical to that of the previous year. However, performance improved in secondary schools (74.7%) and middle schools (76%) as compared to the previous year (NYSED, 2006c, p. 23).

Most schools not meeting AYP in both years failed for more than one accountability group. The subgroups for which schools were least likely to meet accountability requirements were students with disabilities and LEP students, yet the small numbers in these groups in many schools meant that schools were not required to demonstrate accountability for them

(NYSED, 2005, 2006c). The same performance gaps among racial/ethnic groups noticed on state assessments are found among accountability groups too. Most schools were accountable for white students and economically disadvantaged students. Most elementary schools were accountable for black and Hispanic students. However, in middle and high schools, larger percentages of black and Hispanic groups failed to make AYP in English-language arts and mathematics (NYSED, 2005, 2006c).

New York has one of the oldest educational intervention programs of the American states. Since 1989, it has used the registration review process to strengthen education in schools performing least well as measured by state standards. The process identifies the lowest-performing schools, warns them that their registration might be revoked, and assists in improving educational programs. Schools failing to improve may lose their registrations, in which case NYSED develops a plan to provide educational services for that school's students.

Table 3.5 indicates the number of schools under registration review (SURR schools) from 1990-91 through the 2004-05 school year. Clearly, schools in New York City comprise the vast majority of schools requiring state intervention, for reasons mentioned previously—the large number of minorities and students with educational disabilities, who are economi-

**Table 3.5.  Schools Under Registration Review, 1990-91 to 2004-05**

| Year | New York City | Total Public | NYC % to Total |
|---|---|---|---|
| 1990-91 | 40 schools | 48 schools | 83% |
| 1992-92 | 56 schools | 62 schools | 90% |
| 1993-94 | 55 schools | 61 schools | 90% |
| 1994-95 | 72 schools | 79 schools | 91% |
| 1995-96 | 78 schools | 86 schools | 91% |
| 1996-97 | 92 schools | 99 schools | 93% |
| 1997-98 | 94 schools | 98 schools | 96% |
| 1998-99 | 98 schools | 103 schools | 95% |
| 1999-00 | 94 schools | 102 schools | 92% |
| 2000-01 | 98 schools | 114 schools | 86% |
| 2001-02 | 96 schools | 120 schools | 80% |
| 2002-03 | 58 schools | 81 schools | 72% |
| 2003-04 | 46 schools | 65 schools | 71% |
| 2004-05 | 51 schools | 73 schools | 70% |

*Note:* Adapted by author from NYSED (2006c, p. 39).

cally disadvantaged, and who have limited English proficiency. Since the inception of the registration review process, 267 schools statewide have been identified as requiring intervention. Some 233 of these schools (including 22 during the 2004-05 school year) have been removed from the list; 19 left because they achieved the student performance standards of the state, and the other 5 were closed (NYSED, 2005, 2006c). Some 38 schools have been closed since the inception of the program (NYSED, 2006c; also see Mintrop & Trujillo, 2004). And some schools leave the list temporarily to return a few years later, as occurred to three schools in the 2004-05 school year. A noteworthy development is the smaller number of schools entering the list after the initial implementation of NCLB.

However, NCLB requires a slightly different system of school intervention, which has confused the process of school improvement in New York. During the first years of NCLB implementation, yet based on the state's assessments (because federal rules for annual assessment did not take effect until 2005-06), the number of failing public schools increased by 23%. The NYSED list for public schools outside New York City included 143 schools, an increase of 10 (or 8%) from the previous year. Failing schools in the city increased to an estimated 426, a rise of 95 schools (or 95%) as compared to the previous year. Altogether, the increase of 105 schools raised the New York total to 569 failing public schools, a 23% increase over the previous year (see Foundation for Education Reform & Accountability, 2003a). The number of low-performing schools under NCLB regulations is nearly double that identified following state rules, indicating lack of clarity as to the size of the improvement problem in the state. The main difference lies in subgroup performance, which previously did not figure into state calculations.

## PROSPECTS FOR ATTAINMENT OF NCLB GOALS BY 2014

In many respects, New York was better prepared for NCLB than most states, as it had a well-developed and nationally recognized assessment and accountability system in place, which tested students in essential core areas, incorporated high stakes to focus student performance at the high school level, and provided both positive and negative sanctions for schools. Yet NCLB required that schools meet AYP for a series of subgroups and test students annually in intermediate and middle-levels instead of just twice before high school. New York was allowed to delay its full implementation of NCLB 2 years, which correspondingly increases the AYP targets it must reach each year until 2014.

New York repeatedly negotiates with the U.S. Department of Education (USDOE) on NCLB regulations. In 2005, it gained approval to use a proxy method to calculate AYP for students with disabilities (Ed.gov, 2005). In 2006 federal officials prohibited New York (and Virginia) from using English-language proficiency scores to calculate progress for LEP students. Instead, LEP students who have been in the United States at least one year must take the more difficult language arts test (Zehr, 2006).

As with the other states having large concentrations of ethnic and racial minority populations, economically disadvantaged and limited English language proficient students, the inspirational goal of insuring that each New York student will demonstrate proficiency by 2014 is not likely to be attainable. Yet student gains on tests, and some significant increases in subgroup scores, give NCLB supporters cause to applaud the New York experience.

New York's greatest challenge of educational reform lies in its premier city. In this concluding section we examine three problems associated with the accountability system which are exaggerated in New York City—educational finance, resistance to testing, and support for students in low-performing schools. We also consider a unique challenge to educational accountability in New York because of its school governance structure.

## Resource Equity in Financing New York Education

Although no longer America's richest state, New York does spend more than most states on education. About 44% of school funding comes from state general fund resources, 49% from local governments (largely through property taxation) and the remainder, about 6.5%, from the federal government. In the 2003-04 school year, total expenditures on education were $40 billion (NYSED, 2006c). The average per student spending adjusted for regional cost differentials was $10,002 in 2002. Since then, New York has been the third highest of the nation in per pupil education spending,[2] behind New Jersey and the District of Columbia (Education Counts, 2007; Saulny, 2005a). New York's teacher salaries are also among the highest in the United States.

However, funding of school districts in New York ranks low on the equity scale, because wealthy districts spend significantly more than poor districts. The issue first entered the court system in 1982 when the state's Court of Appeals opined that the New York Constitution guaranteed all children an opportunity for a "sound basic education."[3] In 1993, a group called the Campaign for Fiscal Equity (CFE), with substantial support from teachers' unions, challenged the state's school financing system, arguing that it failed to provide students sufficient opportunity for a sound basic education in New York City. The state's highest court, the Court of Appeals, ultimately accepted CFE's argument, ruling that current funding arrangements were unconstitutional and needed to be altered to insure that funding was "adequate" (American Institutes for Research, 2004, p. 2).

The American Institutes for Research and Management Analysis and Planning, Inc. studied what the incremental cost would be to extend to all New York's public school students an opportunity to acquire knowledge specified by the Regents' Learning Standards. The consultants projected that $6.21 billion beyond current spending (based on the 2001-02 school year) would be required to meet this standard, and that because New York City schools enrolled 37% of the state's students, it should receive an additional $3.62 billion, or an increase of 31% (American Institutes for Research, 2004, p. ii). This was one of several "costing-out" studies presented as part of the Zarb Commission report to Governor George Pataki in March 2004, conducted by Standard & Poor's (which argued that $1.93 billion would be sufficient to address equity concerns).

The governor incorporated the S&P report into his broad proposal for further educational reform, when he called the legislature into a special session in July 2004. He asked the legislature to increase funding for schools by $8 billion in the next 5 years, including $4.7 billion for New York City schools, and to create a dedicated fund for high-need and poorly performing school districts. He also asked the legislature to improve the accountability system to measure whether reforms actually provided the opportunity for a sound basic education (New York, Office of the Governor, 2004a). In Governor Pataki's words, "the Assembly Leadership did not ever intend to reach an agreement by the deadline, and instead chose to simply delay and stall (New York, Office of the Governor, 2004b);" it declined his request for additional funding for schools. Thereupon, the governor submitted his reform plan to the State Supreme Court.

Governor Pataki was term-limited, and the Republican candidate for the governorship in 2006, John Faso, was luke-warm in support of the Pataki plan. The Democratic candidate, Attorney General Eliot Spitzer, made school finance a campaign issue. He pledged to increase funding for city schools as much as $6 billion in stages over 4-5 years (McNeil, 2006a). This, as well as Spitzer's strong agenda for continued school reform in New York (McNeil, 2007), was a large factor in his landslide victory.

In late 2006, the New York Court of Appeals resolved the school finance issue. In a 4-2 decision, the court rejected CFE's cost estimate of $4.7 billion to fix equity problems. It sided with the Standard & Poor's estimate of $1.93 billion, finding that amount would likely be sufficient to remedy constitutional violations.[4] The court was reluctant to tread on legislative and executive budget prerogatives, treating the $1.93 billion as a minimum. However, newly-elected Governor Spitzer said he would ask the legislature for a significant funding increase for New York City schools, saying "We must provide more statewide funding than the constitutional minimum, so that all of New York's schoolchildren have the opportunity to thrive in the 21st century workplace" (McNeil, 2006b, 22).

New York not only is an example of a state with equity issues in school finance and improvement. The state's educational finance as well as its accountability system also question the role of economic resources in school improvement. Conservative citizens' groups have asked whether additional funding will actually improve educational outcomes. For example, the Foundation for Education Reform & Accountability called Governor Pataki's increased funding proposal "an irresponsible and ineffective attempt to throw more money at the same old education problems, ignoring any real solutions that would help improve public education" (Foundation for Education Reform & Accountability, 2003b, p. 1).

This is a familiar criticism of economic conservatives who in the case of this particular interest group as well as others nationwide ask for elimination of regulations for charter schools, extension of the school year (without an increase in educational costs), merit pay for administrators and teachers, elimination of union work rules, and school choice vouchers to expand options for low-income students. In support of their criticism, a recent study indicates that so far as one critical element of education reform is concerned—teachers' qualifications—money in the form of higher salaries is a less important motivator than "the desire to teach easier students" (Lankford et al., 2000, p. 38).

Research conducted in other states (especially in Georgia and Texas) finds a similar pattern: The race of students, their socioeconomic class, and their achievement level together are stronger motivators than high salaries, especially for white female teachers. To counteract the situation of districts with a majority of "difficult-to-teach" students would require paying considerably more—from 20 to 50% higher salaries—than districts with white or Asian students who are academically prepared (Haycock, 2004). Thus money, targeted to significantly higher salaries for teachers in low-performing schools, may be an essential ingredient to successful reform.

## RESISTANCE TO TESTING

The New York case also illustrates the extent to which resistance to testing erodes support of the reform coalition for educational improvement. For example, in March 2001 more than 60% of Scarsdale eighth graders declined to attend school for science tests, prompting NYSED to warn the district that future boycotts would be met with disciplinary action for the district (see Zernike, 2001; and Bert, 2001). The following year, over 100 eighth graders from two Manhattan middle schools boycotted standardized state tests (Chiles, 2002). Although most cases reflect opposition of parents to increased testing requirements, teachers, and particularly union organizations, have been less than sympathetic to the assessment part of New York's accountability system.

What is particular to the New York case is suspicion about the state's ability to manage a sophisticated accountability system, the complexity of which is exacerbated by NCLB requirements. For example, NYSED officials announced in August 2005 that it would take eight months (from administration of tests in January 2006) to grade and distribute English examinations for the 2005-06 academic year, because of the need to meet NCLB requirements of annual testing, for which it lacked sufficient assessment staff, among other reasons. New York City education officials then determined they would administer their own tests in order to have results by June when grade promotion decisions needed to be made (Saulny, 2005b), effectively testing students twice.

## Supplemental Educational Services

We have mentioned the difficulty New York has had in implementing school choice for students of low-performing schools, a problem shared with all states. An alternative for students in these schools is tutoring by outside groups. A recent study indicates that the tutoring service in New York (as in most other U.S. cities) is relatively unused.

Fewer than half of the 215,000 eligible students in New York City applied for free tutoring by mid-2005. Districts are required to use Title I funds to pay for the tutoring, and unless exempted, it must employ groups outside the failing district. This gives districts no incentive to place students in tutoring programs and may explain the low rate of student recruitment. (The USDOE granted NYC a waiver to manage its own program.) Other factors may be the bureaucratic requirements to arrange services, lack of school advertising and recruitment, or even the difficulty of engaging minority communities in this type of program.

New York City's rate of participation in tutoring services is perhaps better than that of other cities (USDOE claims only 12% take advantage of it). As in other areas LEP students and those with disabilities—most in need of services—are least likely to apply for them. The rate of retention in tutoring programs also is low (Saulny, 2006).

## A Variety of Accountability Standards

In this chapter, we have distinguished the educational problems of New York City from other cities and towns of New York state, because the city is distinctive socially, culturally, economically, and politically. It is America's largest city, and center of commerce, finance, communications, and the arts. Since September 11, 2001 it has become a beacon of resistance to global terrorism, while enmeshed in its own disorderly conflicts of ethnic and racial communities, public and private sector organized interests, and tension of local-state and state-federal relationships.

New York City is the primary American city to have attained a degree of control over its educational system, which it partially devolved to community schools in the late 1960s. Control has mostly returned to the city's education bureaucracy and mayor in the early twenty-first century, yet the city remains distinctive. In mid-2005, the city schools chancellor announced plans to develop an independent assessment and accountability system. Instead of relying on the state's measurement of student progress cross-sectionally, the city would measure student gains from year to year (called a "value-added" approach). Additionally, it would measure each school's learning environment, including parental involvement and quality of work demanded of students (Olson, 2005). Indeed, to proponents, the reform elements composed a "model for public accountability and public engagement."[5]

Unlike the other American states, New York's educational reform initiatives and challenges involve three levels of government. As a recent critical study comments: "Schools in NYC currently operate under at least three different accountability systems—federal, State and local—each focused primarily on output rather than input, and none of which are well-aligned with the others" (Citizens Budget Commission, 2004, p. 2) Commenting on the city's accountability system, the writers of the report complain about changes in the decentralization system—for example, the creation of ten instructional regions in the city, headed by regional superintendents, as well as six operational centers—which dilute control. Meanwhile (as in most other states) ultimate responsibility for accountability lies in the hands of publicly-elected school boards, which are not trained for this exercise of responsibility (Citizens Budget Commission, 2004).

Perhaps in response to this criticism, in early 2007 Mayor Bloomberg eliminated the 10 administrative regions he had created to cut into the education bureaucracy. The city now will revert to the postdecentralization system, in which 32 community superintendents oversee schools and report directly to the chancellor. The mayor said this change would give principals more power over hiring and firing staff, controlling educational programs, and managing schools budgets. In return for the empowerment of principals, they will be evaluated more rigorously by community superintendents. Schools will be graded based on student performance, attendance, and parent-teacher-student feedback. High performing schools will be eligible for bonuses; those with lower grades will be subject to intervention (Gewertz, 2007, p. 7).

The resiliency of the American federal system is reflected in the cycles of education reform—initiated from the top-down as well as from the bottom-up—and involving cities as well as states. No better example of this resilience can be found than in the ways in which New York, state and city, have responded to the challenges of No Child Left Behind.

## NOTES

1. A confidence interval recognizes the sampling error associated with an observed score and permits the analyst to determine whether the difference between the observed Performance Index (PI) and the AMO falls within certain bounds or whether the difference falls outside the margin of error. See http://www.emsc.nysed.gov/irts/school-accountabilityi/confidence-intervals.htm, retrieved 11/30/05.

2. The American Legislative Exchange Council's *Report Card* (September 2004, p. 41) cites 2001-02 expenditures per pupil of $11,029 in New York, making it first in the nation for this year.

3. The decision was *Levittown v. Nyquist*, in which the court questioned the constitutional adequacy of the state's educational finance system. The court did not define what a "sound basic education" was, but NYSED convened a task force to define the term. The group defined the term relevant to learning or subject matter, which prompted the department's sponsorship of research and hearings leading to issuance of the Regents' Learning Standards in 1996. See American Institutes for Research, *The New York Adequacy Study: "Adequate" Education Costs in New York State*, February 2004, p. 1.

4. In the 2006 legislative session, New York's lawmakers increased K-12 funding by nearly 8%. They provided New York City almost $2 billion for new school construction, while increasing the city's borrowing authority by $9 billion, an action clearly related to the CFE suit. See *Education Week* (Zehr, 2006, p. 20), Lawmakers increase funding for K-12, school construction.

5. See "New York City Sound Basic Education Plan," retrieved 11/30/05 from: http://www.classsizematters.org/accountbilityplan.html

## REFERENCES

American Institutes for Research. (2004, February). *The New York adequacy study: "Adequate" education cost in New York state*. Washington, DC: Author.
Barone, M., & Cohen, R. E. (2005). *The almanac of American politics*. Washington, DC: The National Journal Group.

Bert, A. (2001, May 9). Scarsdale students boycott state test. *Journal News*, p. 1A.

Bishop, J. H., & Mane, F. (2001). The impacts of minimum competency exam graduation requirements on college attendance and early labor market success of disadvantaged students. In G. Orfield & M. L. Kornhaber (Eds.). *Raising standards or raising barriers? Inequalityi and high-stakes testing in public education* (pp. 51-84). New York: The Century Foundation Press.

Chiles, N. (2002, March 6). 120 8th-graders boycott state test. *Newsday*, p. A14.

Citizens Budget Commission. (2004, November). *Promoting accountability in New York state.* Retrieved January 08, 2006, from www.cbcny.org

Consortium for Policy Research in Education. (2000). *Assessment and accountability in the fifty states: 1999-2000, New York.* Madison, WI: Author.

Cross, R. W., Rebarber, T., & Torres, J. (2004). *Grading the system: The guide to state standards, tests, and accountability policies.* Washington, DC: Thomas B. Fordham Foundation.

Cuban, L. (2004). A solution that lost its problem: Centralized policyimaking and classroom gains. In N. Epstein (Ed.), *Who's in charge here? The tangled web of school governance and policy* (pp. 104-30). Washington, DC: Brookings Institution Press.

Darling-Hammond, L., & Falk, B. (1997). Policy for authentic assessment. In A. L. Goodwin (Ed.), *Assessment for equity and inclusion: Embracing all our children* (pp. 51-76). New York: Routledge.

Darling-Hammond, L., & Sykes, G. (2004). A teacher supply policy for education: How to meet the "highly qualified teacher" challenge. In N. Epstein (Ed.), *Who's in charge here? The tangled web of school governance and policy* (pp. 164-227). Washington, DC: Brookings Institution Press.

DeBray, E. (2005, Octobre/November). A comprehensive high school and a shift in New York state policy: A study of early implementation. *The High School Journal*, 18-45.

*Education Counts.* (2007). New York state information. Retrieved February 10, 2007, from http://www2.edweek.org/

Ed.gov (2005). Decision letter on request to amend New York accountability plan. Washington, DC: U.S. Department of Education. Retrieved February 12, 2007, from http://www.ed.gov/admins/lead/account/letters/acny3.html

Foundation for Education Reform & Accountability. (2003a, September 5). *Number of failing schools grows by 23 percent (*News release). Clifton Park, NY.

Foundation for Education Reform & Accountability (2003b, December 18). *Massive education spending hike proposal called "irresponsible and ineffective"* (News release). Clifton Park, NY.

Gewertz, C. (2007, January 24). N.Y.C. to scrap regions, give principals more authority. *Education Week*, 26(20), 7.

Gittel, M., & Hollander, T. E. (1968). *Six urban school districts.* New York: Praeger.

Gittel, M. (1973). *School boards and school policy: An evaluation of decentralization in New York City.* New York: Praeger.

Gootman, E. (2005, November 30). Few minorities get best high school diploma. *New York Times*, p. 79.

Haycock, K. (2004). The elephant in the living room. In D. Ravitch (Ed.), *Brookings papers on education policy, 2004* (pp. 229-263). Washington, DC: Brookings Institution.

Hayes, E., & Gendar, A. (2002, July 25). Pay hike lures better-qualified teachers. *New York Daily News*, p. 10.

Iatarola, P. (2005, Fall). Learning from experience: New York City's small high schools. *Politics of Education Association, 30*(1), pp. 1-5.

Jones, C. (1994, May 2). New York City to stiffen rules for graduation. *New York Times*, p. A1.

Keller, B. (2000, February 23). New York considers system for rating schools. *Education Week, 19*(24), 18.

Klein, D. (2005). The state of the state math standards

Lankford, H., Wyckoff, J., & Papa, F. (2002). *The labor market for public school teachers: A descriptive analysis of New York state's teacher workforce*. Albany, NY: State University of New York Press.

Levin, H. (2004). Multiple "choice" questions: The road ahead. In N. Epstein (Ed.), *Who's in charge here? The tangled web of school governance and policy* (pp. 228-255). Washington, DC: Brookings Institution Press.

Loveless, T. (2005). Test-based accountability: The promise and the perils. In D. Ravitch (Ed.), *Brookings papers on education policy, 2005* (pp. 7-45). Washington, DC: The Brookings Institution.

Manhattan Institute for Policy Research. (2003). *What parents think of New York's charter schools* (Report no. 37). New York: Author.

McNeil, M. (2006a, November 15). Gubernatorial results may signal policy shift. *Education Week, 26*(12), 23.

McNeil, M. (2006b, November 29). Aid award cut in suit over N.Y.C. *Education Week, 26*(13), 22.

McNeil, M. (2007). "Reform agenda" in New York. *Education Week, 26*(22), 1, 18.

Mintrop, H., & Trujillo, T. (2004, December). *Corrective action in low-performing schools*. Los Angeles: National Center for Research on Evaluation, Standards, and Student Testing, UCLA.

National Center for Education Statistics. (2006). *State profiles: New York*. Retrieved February 15, 2007, from http://nces.ed.gov/ntionalsreportcard/states/profile.asp

Natriello, G., & Pallas, A. M. (2001). The development and impact of high-stakes testing. In G. Orfield & M. L. Kornhaber (Ed.), *Raising standards or raising barriers? Inequality and high-stakes testing in public education* (pp.19-38). New York: The Century Foundation Press.

New York, Office of the Governor. (2004a, July 20). Governor Pataki calls legislature into special session. Albany, NY: Press release.

New York, Office of the Governor (2004b, July 30). Governor vows not to give up (Press release). Albany, NY.

New York State Education Department. (1995). *The strategy for raising standards*. Albany, NY: Author.

New York State Education Department. *New York: The state of learning: A report to the governor and the legislature on the educational status of the state's schools*. Albany, NY: Author.

New York State Education Department. (2003, July). *New York: The state of learning: statewide profile of the educational system.* Albany, NY: Author.

New York State Education Department. (2004a, June). *The state of learning: statewide profile of the educational system.* Albany, NY: Author.

New York State Education Department (2004b, July 20). *New York state public report card, comprehensive information report.* Albany, NY: Author.

New York State Education Department (2005, July). *The state of learning: Statewide profile of the educational system.* Albany, NY: Author.

New York State Education Department (2006a, May). *New York state total public report card comprehensive report.* Albany, NY: Author.

New York State Education Department (2006b, May). *Overview of performance in English language arts, mathematics, and science and analysis of student subgroup performance for public schools in New York state.* Albany, NY: Author.

New York State Education Department (2006c, October). *New York, the state of learning: Statewide profile of the educational system.* Albany, NY: Author.

Olson, L. (2003, January 22). Approval of states' ESEA plans suggests flexibility. *Education Week, 22*(19), 14, 18.

Olson, L. (2005, June 15). N.Y.C. schools to measure gains, not just raw test scores. *Education Week, 24*(40), 10.

*Quality Counts.* (2005, January 6). Report card, New York. *Education Week, 24*(17), 126.

Ravitch, D. (1973). *The great school wars.* New York: Basic Books.

Rogers, D. (1968). *110 Livingston Street: Politics and bureaucracy in the New York City schools.* New York: Random House.

Rogers, D., & Chung, N. H. (1973). *110 Livingston Street revisited: Decentralization in action.* New York: New York University Press.

Ross, T. (1998). Grassroots action in East Brooklyn: A community organization takes up school reform. In *Changing urban education* (pp. 18-38). Lawrence, KS: University Press of Kansas.

Saulny, S. (2005a, January 6). New York is third in country in per-pupil school spending. *New York Times,* p. 81.

Saulny, S. (2005b, August 12). Delayed test results trouble New York. *New York Times,* p. 81.

Saulny, S. (2006, February 12). Tutor program offered by law is going unused. *New York Times,* p. 81. Retrieved February 12, 2007, from http://www.nytimes.com/2006/02/12/education/12tutor.html?ei=5088&en=b29baae78f12b753&ex=1297400400&partner=rssny

Stotsky, S. (2005). *The state of the state English standards.* Washington, DC: Fordham Foundation.

Zehr, M. A. (2006, December 20). *Education Week, 26*(16), pp. 18, 21.

Zernike, K. (2001, May 4). Scarsdale mothers succeed in first boycott of 8th grade test. *New York Times,* p. B5.

Zimet, M. (1973). *Decentralization and school effectiveness.* New York: Teachers College Press.

# CHAPTER 4

# VIRGINIA

## INTRODUCTION

Virginians revel in their heritage. They contributed more to the founding era than any other state. Thomas Jefferson wrote the Declaration of Independence, George Washington served as commander in chief during the American Revolution and as America's first president, and in the interim, the Virginia delegation contributed more to the Miracle at Philadelphia than any other state delegation. James Madison is known as the Father of the Constitution and George Washington was the presiding officer at the Convention. Virginia has been the home of eight U.S. presidents; but also, it was the seat of the Confederate government (Richmond) and the home of Confederate heroes General Robert E. Lee and Stonewall Jackson.

Today the multiple strands of Virginia's heritage that reflect the greatest and the most discredited principles in American history, provide the backdrop for a diverse culture and economy that includes the industrial Tidewater Region; the affluent, highly educated and powerful bedroom communities of Washington, DC; the bucolic Piedmont region; the Blue Ridge in the East; and the rural and economically challenged southside and southwest region.

*Education Reform in the American States*
pp. 83–114
Copyright © 2008 by Information Age Publishing
All rights of reproduction in any form reserved.

## State Socioeconomic and Political Characteristics

The largest state at the founding, Virginia ranks 12th among the American states with an estimated population of 7.5 million early in the twenty-first century. The population is 70% White, just over 19% Black, nearly 5% Hispanic, and nearly 4% Asian (Barone & Cohen, 2005). Agriculture remains important in the commonwealth that began as a predominantly tobacco producing colony. Virginia now has numerous large manufacturing industries, such as transportation equipment, electronics, chemicals, textiles and wood products. Early in the twenty-first century the service sector provides about one third of jobs in Virginia, most notably computer and data processing services, and of course government services. Virginia is also a major producer of coal.

The traditionalist sentiments that reflected Virginia's socially stratified and racially segregated past, and which were represented in conservative Democratic party ideology, began to give way to modern partisan divisions in the 1980s. Moderate Democrats Charles Robb, Gerald Baliles and Douglas Wilder were elected governors in the 1980s (Virginia is the only state that allows only one 4-year term in the governor's office) by distancing themselves from a labor-liberal agenda and promising to use government to improve education and the economy. Republican George Allen was elected governor in 1993 by campaigning for lower taxes, traditional cultural values, longer prison terms, and education reform focused on the basics (Barone & Cohen, 2005). Governor Allen's education reform initiative with accountability measures had faced Democratic opposition in the General Assembly, but Republican membership had increased in the past two decades. Republicans were less responsive to the two most powerful groups likely to oppose the high-stakes testing associated with the new academic standards, the Virginia Education Association and the National Association for the Advancement of Colored People, because they were generally viewed as hostile to the Republicans (Hess, 2002). In 1997, Republican Jim Gilmore became governor, and Republicans gained majorities in both chambers of the General Assembly; thus for the first time, Republicans controlled the executive and legislative branches in Virginia.

Governor Mark Warner (D), elected in 2001, was a staunch supporter of education reform, holding schools and students accountable, while offering multiple support programs to improve achievement. In 2005, education and other child welfare issues were at the top of voters' priorities. Democrat Timothy Kaine, lieutenant governor under Governor Warner, called for universal prekindergarten programs, which he called the Start Strong Initiative, and Republican Jerry Kilgore promoted merit pay for teachers. Kaine won the election, but apparently his victory was based more on the anti-Republican tide related to President Bush's low ratings, rather than voters choosing Kaine's education policy over Kilgore's (Samuels, 2005). Governor Kaine's education policies included instituting a new requirement that all classroom teachers be evaluated regularly, working to expand pre-kindergarten classes, and raising teacher salaries (Official Site of the Governor of Virginia, n.d.).

In 2007, both of Virginia's U.S. Senators were Republican and 11 of its 14 U.S. Representatives were Republican. In the General Assembly Republicans dominated the Senate with 23 of 40 seats. Of the 100 seats in the House of Delegates, Republicans held 57, Democrats held 40, and Independents held 3. Democrats had gained a total of 3 seats in the 2006 elections.

## The State Educational System

Virginia's educational system is directed by the State Board of Education (BOE), a nine-member governor-appointed board, which in 2007 is chaired by Dr. Mark E. Emblidge. The Superintendent of Schools is Dr. Billy K. Cannaday. He is responsible for implementing BOE policies, which are based on state law. As appointed public servants, these administrators are relatively insulated from political pressure, but not completely, as Virginia's history with education reform reveals. Public opposition to the more punitive aspects of Virginia's Standards of Learning (SOL) system apparently influenced Governor Gilmore to replace Governor Allen's conservative appointees who strongly backed the high-stakes elements of Virginia's reforms with moderates. The new BOE moderated some of its predecessors' education reform policies to mollify aggrieved parties, though they remained committed to the principles of the reform.

Virginia's being a right-to-work state, along with the fact that Republicans have control of both chambers of the General Assembly, suggests that the teachers union is not as influential in opposing the high-stakes aspects of the SOL system as teachers have been in opposing high- stakes reforms in some states.

In 2004-2005, Virginia enrolled 1,204,739 students in 2,084 schools and 135 school divisions. The student population was 60.6% White, 27.1% Black, 7.1% Hispanic, 4.9% Asian/Pacific Islander and .3% American Indian/Alaskan Native. About 31% of students were eligible for free or reduced lunch. About 14.5% of students were on Individualized Education Plans (IEP's) and 5.6% of students were English learners (Limited English Proficiency, LEP) (National Center for Education Statistics, 2005b). Among Virginia's school children were 18,693 who were home-schooled in 2006-2007.

State law allows local school boards to charter schools, but in 2006, only five operated in the state. Charters are held to the same laws, regulations and policies as other public schools, though some flexibility may be negotiated with local school boards. Under the law, enrollment is open to students within the district and other at-risk students. Charter schools that aim to serve at-risk children have a better chance of having their applications approved (Center for Education Reform, n.d.).

Virginia spent $8,729 per pupil in 2004-2005, which placed it 22nd in the nation in per-pupil spending on education (National Education Assocication, 2006). Virginia's General Assembly adopted a budget for the years 2004-2006 that increased public school funding by $1.5 billion. Among other items, the Assembly approved funding of one preparation period per school day for all middle and high school teachers. Another important change was the funding of 17 (up from 10) instructional positions per one thousand ESL students (Virginia Board of Education, 2004), whose numbers were increasing disproportionately.

## VIRGINIA'S ACCOUNTABILITY SYSTEM PRIOR TO THE NCLB ACT

### The Standards of Learning and Standards of Accreditation

Virginia has been a leader among the states in standards-based reform, launching its Standards of Learning (SOLs) for students and Standards of Accreditation (SOAs) for schools and school divisions in the 1990s. The commonwealth made several attempts, beginning in the 1970s, to raise academic standards, adopting minimum competency testing, raising teacher standards and per-pupil expenditures, and adopting a Literacy Passport Test (LPT) in the 1980s, but ultimately public outcry at the numbers of students who were retained resulted in weakening tests and sanctions to the point that they were rendered meaningless. A *common core of learning* that broadened the curriculum and emphasized outcomes replaced the earlier standards-based approach in 1990, but by 1993 it, too, had been abandoned. Conservatives had charged that it attempted to decrease the rigor of the curriculum while infusing it with value-laden premises (Hess, 2002).

In his 1993 gubernatorial campaign, Republican George Allen critiqued the *common core* program and called for higher standards and accountability. It was not difficult to generate public concern over the quality of public education in Virginia when nearly one third of Grade 6 students were failing the LPT, Virginia students' reading scores on the National Assessment of Educational Progress (NAEP) had declined against national averages, and SAT scores had been declining for several years (Hess, 2002).

In May 1994, newly elected Governor Allen appointed a Governor's Commission on Champion Schools and more conservative members to the Board of Education, and he charged them with developing rigorous statewide academic standards. In response to the governor's directive, the BOE called upon teams of teachers, parents and community members from four leading school districts in the state to develop *Standards of Learning* in English, math, science and history/social studies. After some revision the BOE enacted the Standards of Learning in June of 1995. The SOLs sparked considerable controversy, particularly among educators and administrators who feared that they would be punished for low student test scores. However, Allen's conservative appointees to the BOE steadfastly supported the Standards of Learning, the high stakes testing of students and the sanctions for teachers and administrators in low performing schools. Governor Allen's successor, Republican Governor Jim Gilmore, replaced Allen's conservative appointees[1] with moderates on education policy (Wurtzel, 2002), which may partially explain the BOE's later willingness to soften the impact of the SOLs through reducing the requirements for the standard diploma, allowing students to take substitute tests, such as Advanced Placement (AP) tests, and giving Limited English Proficiency students a 1-year reprieve on taking SOLs.

The public battle over education standards in Virginia reflected the political challenges that all states have faced in balancing the interests of a public, including parent, tax payer and business community perspectives, that calls for high standards and accountability in public education with those of stakeholders, including administrators, teachers and students and their parents, who are most likely to be negatively affected by the sanctions built into such systems. The public generally supports the notion of improved quality in public education and the notion of accountability in the abstract, but opposition mounts when high-stakes accountability programs are implemented. While the benefits are broadly dispersed, the costs are concentrated, and those whom the sanctions target have incentives to organize.

Virginia's accountability system included four main components: (1) the creation of demanding Standards of Learning for Grades K-12; (2) criterion-referenced tests that were aligned with the SOLs, (3) school accreditation and student graduation linked to student performance on the tests; and (4) reporting on school performance to parents in annual School Performance Report Cards, which included information on school safety, student performance and numerous other factors. The tests were administered to students in Grades 3, 5, 8 and in high school (to earn a diploma). There are 27 SOL tests for various subjects, all of which are multiple choice, except English, which includes a writing component (Hess, 2002).

The Board of Education approved a number of diplomas to differentiate among more and less rigorous programs of study.

- *The Advanced Diploma* reflects the most rigorous course of study, requiring the most standard credits (courses taken) and nine verified credits (SOLs passed).
- *The Standard Diploma* requires (since 2002) that students pass three English, two math and one lab science (no history or social studies) and earn six verified credits.
- The *Modified Standard Diploma*, created in 2000, is for students with disabilities who desire a rigorous alternative to the Standard Diploma. Students with disabilities must demonstrate English and mathematics achievement on Grade 8 SOL tests.
- The *Special Diploma* is for students with disabilities who complete the requirements included in their individualized education programs (IEPs).
- A *General Achievement Diploma* can be earned by passing the GED exam, completing an education and training program established by the BOE, and satisfying other BOE requirements.
- *Certificates of Completion* are awarded by local school boards to students who complete the course of study required by local school boards, but not State BOE requirements (Virginia Code 22.1-253.13:4. Standard 4 [of Standards of Quality]).

Virginia spent approximately $18 million in developing its assessments, contracting with Harcourt Brace Educational Measurements to develop test questions based on Virginia's SOLs, and refining the tests through a lengthy review and field testing process. Identifying specific content for the SOLs engendered much controversy, particularly in social studies, but Virginia's history SOLs eventually won national acclaim for their rigor and clarity (Hess, 2002). Only Virginia received the highest ranking in all four academic areas of its standards from the American Federation of Teachers, and more than 20 states have used Virginia's standards as models for their own (Thayer, 2000).

The first tests based on standards were administered in 1998, and the graduation requirements were scheduled to take effect for the first time in 2004. Establishing the pass and proficient scores for the tests proved challenging. Setting cut scores too high would invite such opposition that the SOLs might be scuttled, whereas setting them too low would render them meaningless. The Board of Education set *passing* scores for the tests ranging from 52% in high school biology to 73% for Grade 5 English. The Board set the *proficient* scores for the tests at 90% or higher for most tests. When the vast majority of students failed the first tests, pressure mounted for accommodations (Hess, 2002). Both accommodations and assistance followed.

In 1999 the Board decided that Virginia's Limited English Proficiency students could opt out of one year of SOL testing and that they could use a bilingual dictionary when taking the tests. Moreover, the scores of LEP students would not be included in their schools' composite scores for two years. In 2000 the BOE also allowed students to substitute such tests as the Advanced Placement, International Baccalaureate or SAT II tests for the related SOL tests (Hess, 2002). This accommodation quelled complaints from students, parents and teachers in rigorous academic programs that preparing for the much less rigorous SOLs was a waste of time.

In 2003 Governor Mark Warner began *Project Graduation*, a program to identify and aid students at risk of not graduating with the class of 2004. Academies offering intensive study in reading, writing and algebra helped prepare students for passing the SOLs. In spring 2004, Project Graduation Online Tutorial began preparing students who failed the SOL reading test to retake it. Of the students who used the service, 93% subsequently passed the test. Project Graduation also offered regional "continuation academies" to nongraduating students who sought to upgrade their Certificates of Completion to Standard Diplomas (Warner, 2004).

In 1997, the State BOE adopted a performance-based accreditation system (Standards of Accreditation) for schools. School accreditation depends on 70% of the schools' students' passing SOL tests in the four core academic areas. For Grades 3 and 5 the BOE requires that 75% of students pass the English tests, but that only 50% pass the science and history/social studies tests (Thayer, 2000). Beginning with the 2000-2001 school year, schools Accredited with Warning were subject to on-site academic reviews by outside teams of professional educators. Schools were required to develop and implement school improvement plans that outlined the actions the schools would take to address identified weaknesses. The BOE also had the authority to carry out district level reviews, if evidence suggested that problems with accreditation were districtwide (Virginia Board of Education, 2004). No consequences were specified, except that schools not accredited by 2005-2006 would have to adopt 3-year School Improvement Plans, and state law required the Superintendent of Public Instruction to assist schools in the development of such plans and monitor their effectiveness.

Thus, Virginia had implemented a strong accountability system well before the No Child Left Behind Act was enacted in 2002. After early failed attempts at reforming public education and strengthening the curriculum in the 1970s and 1980s, declining student performance and mobilization of a supporting coalition provided the impetus for a rigorous standards-based reform movement in the mid-1990s. Virginia established its Standards of Learning, which outlined curricula, assessments and expectations for students, and it established the Standards of Accreditation for schools. The process was contentious and the public apprehensive, but reformers stood their ground, and Virginia's standards and accountability system served as a model for many other states. Nevertheless, Virginia's SOL and SOA system would continue to evolve, as defects were noted, as test scores reflected unfavorably on public education itself, as deadlines for sanctions loomed, and as the reforms were not producing anticipated achievement gains.

## Public Opposition to Standards-Based Education With High-Stakes Accountability

As occurred elsewhere, Virginia's SOL system drew opposition from various sectors, and it grew more strident, even as test scores were improving, likely because the dates when students and schools would be sanctioned were approaching, and because serious shortcomings and manipulation of the system to improve numbers were detected. Tom Loveless writes,

> Formidable political factors are arrayed against accountability. Progressive education supplies an ideology hostile to test-based accountability. Politically powerful teachers unions represent actors with interests divergent from the aims of accountability systems. Governance in education is both open and porous, providing multiple venues for challenging implementation. (Loveless, 2005, p. 25)

Of the 1,031 registered Virginia voters surveyed in August 2000 by the *Washington Post*, 51% said that the SOL testing program was "not working," whereas 34% said that it was "working." Asked what should be done, 43% said the SOLs should be substantially changed and 21% said they should be abandoned. Only 24% felt the program should remain "as is." Polls of students revealed overwhelming dissatisfaction with the SOLs. Meanwhile, the state poured millions of dollars into efforts to increase educators' comfort with and support for the SOLs, including providing web-based materials for teachers, funds for staff development in low-performing schools and an SOL Academy for teachers at James Madison University (Hess, 2002).

Opponents of school-level accountability argued that factors outside the control of the schools explained most of the variation in student achievement levels, and that the performance requirements did not reflect these disproportionate challenges. Inner city and southeast Virginia schools with high minority and high poverty populations had to achieve the same 70% passage rates that much more affluent and already high-achieving Fairfax County schools did. This required extraordinary gains by the former schools and little additional effort in the latter (Wurtzel, 2002). Ironically, Fairfax had its own problems with a significant achievement gap, as noted below.

A group calling itself Parents Across Virginia United to Reform SOLs (PAVURSOL) formed to improve the SOLs and SOA system. The internet-based group, which claimed 6,000 members in 2005, sought "to ensure that the standards and assessments used with our children are educationally defensible." The group asserted on its Web site that "our current 'one-size-fits-all' SOL system" did not meet the needs of all students and was harmful to students, schools and communities. The group critiqued the state's over reliance on test scores and pass rates and called for multiple assessments of students and schools. PAVURSOL also raised concern that the SOL and SOA systems discriminated against low-income, minority or disabled children, and it called for alternate paths to earning standard diplomas (PAVURSOL, n.d.).

Information on PAVURSOL's Web site called into question the state's claims of improved achievement since the introduction of the SOLs. For instance, an editorial by Mickey VanDerwerker, member of the Bedford County School Board and founder of PAVURSOL, noted that Virginia's Grade 4 and 8 students had not improved their reading and writing scores on the NAEP between 1992 and 2003, while the national average had increased during that time period. Furthermore, claimed VanDerwerker, Virginia's exclusion rate on the NAEP had increased to one of the highest in the nation (VanDerwerker, 2004).

In fact, Virginia's exclusion rates for the NAEP reading tests were among the highest in the nation. With 10% of Grade 4 students with disabilities and 3% of Grade 4 LEP students excluded, Virginia had an overall Grade 4 exclusion rate of 12%. Six percent of Grade 8 students with disabilities and 1% of Grade 8 LEP students were excluded, for an overall Grade 8 exclusion rate of 7%. The national average exclusion rate on the reading tests was 4%. Thus, Virginia's exclusion rates for reading clearly were high. The American Institutes for Research found little relation between exclusion rates and overall state scores, but scores did tend to rise in states that raised their exclusion rates (Viadero, 2005). Exclusion rates for Virginia students on the math NAEP were 5% (National Center for Education Statistics, 2005a).

Another article posted on PAVURSOL's Web site claimed that the state had used various methods to distort and inflate student pass rates and increase the number of schools accredited since the implementation of the SOA program. For instance, they claimed that the "bonus point" given for students who passed SOLs on retakes after the school year ended inflated pass rates. State regulation allowed schools to include in the number of student who passed SOLs those students who retook and passed the test, but the retakes were not added to the number of students taking the test. PAVURSOL argued that this practice significantly inflated the percentage of students who passed the test (PAVURSOL Web site, "Apples," n.d.). However, given that the state and the public were interested in the number (or percentage) of students who passed the tests (even if on the second or third attempt), rather than what percentage of *tests taken* received a passing score, then the state's method of measuring was rational.

Teacher opposition to the SOLs appeared to soften over time. In the early years of implementation, newer teachers were rather accepting of the SOLs, having more recently completed their teacher training programs, which familiarized them with preparing lesson plans in accordance with standards. Veteran teachers, on the other hand, felt that the SOLs compromised their autonomy and professionalism. With time, support grew among veteran teachers, the most resistant perhaps having left teaching and others having come to recognize benefits of the program (Hess, 2002).

In Virginia opposition to high-stakes accountability emanated from similar sectors to those opposing education reform in other states: stakeholders who would be sanctioned by the policies, such as students who failed to pass tests and their parents; students (along with their parents) who felt the standards were much too low and that studying for the tests diverted them from time spent in more valuable educational pursuits; the Virginia Education Association, which like its parent group, the National Education Association, claimed that high-stakes testing resulted in teaching to the test and a narrowing of the curriculum; and school administrators who objected to the onerous and expensive implementation requirements. The Department of Education (DOE) responded to these concerns by allowing for alternative assessments and providing professional development for teachers and remediation for students. However, Virginia's DOE held fairly firmly to its reform agenda.

By 2001, growing public acceptance of SOL's could be seen in the incorporation of SOL-related material, such as coin recognition, map reading and learning about prominent historical figures, in preschool curricula, largely in response to parental requests. In the 2001 gubernatorial campaign, both candidates supported SOLs (Hess, 2002), reflecting both institutionalization and broadening public acceptance of the policy.

## Evaluations of Virginia's Standards

Several organizations have evaluated the states' standards and/or accountability systems. These evaluations place different values on various criteria. Thus, Virginia has received a variety of grades on its education accountability system. Nevertheless, an overview of the results of these evaluations is instructive. Virginia generally receives fairly high assessments on the articulation of standards and the alignment between its standards and assessments, but it falls short of the highest marks for various reasons, including low expectations for performance on the assessments, lack of defined content in English, and reliance on calculators and neglect of deductive reasoning in math.

The Fordham Foundation, in collaboration with AccountabilityWorks, produced in 2004 what it deemed "the most comprehensive and rigorous appraisal ever undertaken of the entire standards-based (education reform) movement across a large number of states" (Cross, Rebarber, & Torres, 2004, p. iii). Virginia received an overall ranking of "fair" on its standards, which the Fordham Foundation said were best "by far" in elementary school mathematics. The SOL tests were deemed fairly solidly aligned with Virginia's standards, in some cases impressively so. However Virginia received demerits on the rigor of its tests, because Fordham's analysts felt the cut scores were about 20 points too low (Cross et al., 2004, pp. 33-34).

The Fordham Foundation also sponsored thoroughgoing evaluations of English and Math standards in 2005. Virginia's English standards ranked eighth in the nation and placed the state on the 2005 Honor Roll for English Standards, with a grade of 3.23 (B). Virginia received praise for the specificity and clarity of its English standards, though the reviewer lamented the lack of a specific reading list and the lack of emphasis on vocabulary in Grades 9-12 (Stotsky, 2005).

Fordham's State of the States' MATH Standards assessed Virginia's math standards at .38 above the national average (12th in the nation) with a score of 1.97, a "C." The evaluators were most critical of the extensive reliance on (required use of) calculators from kindergarten forward, excessive use of manipulatives, even in high school algebra; and in high school geometry, spending too much time on "time-consuming diversions," rather than building a solid foundation in deductive reasoning (Klein, 2005, pp. 111-113). Similar critiques were found in the evaluations of all the states.

The Southern Regional Education Board (SREB) produced an assessment of the southern states' accountability systems in 2005. In Virginia, the SREB researchers found that lower-performing student groups had improved in general, and achievement gaps had narrowed, but substantial gaps remained, and high school graduation rates had not improved. SREB awarded Virginia an overall grade of "B" on its accountability system, based on its adoption of strong content standards that were clear, specific and grounded in content, the alignment of assessments to its standards, and its provision of report cards for all schools by 2004.

Virginia fared relatively well in *Education Week's Quality Counts 2005* assessment of the states' education systems. The state received a B in Standards and Accountability; a B in efforts to improve teacher quality; a C– in School Climate, which includes such factors as safety, parental involvement and facilities; and a C– in Resources Equity, which assesses the equitability of funding of schools in the state. *Education Week's Quality Counts 2007, From Cradle to Career: Connecting American Education from Birth Through Adulthood,* ranked Virginia fourth in the nation on its Standards, Assessment & Accountability index. The education journal ranked Virginia first in terms of its children's Chance for Success index. *Education Week* used a number of criteria for determining the states' rankings, including family income, student achievement levels, parental employment and whether parents spoke English. Thus, Virginia was a leader in developing content standards and aligning them with assessments, and its accountability system was ranked among the best in the nation.

## STUDENT ACHIEVEMENT PROGRESS UNDER VIRGINIA'S ACCOUNTABILITY SYSTEM

Under Virginia's SOL program, students made steady gains in achievement, as measured on the SOLs. In 2002, 86% of high school students passed the English/reading test, up 14 points since 1998. In English/writing, the pass rate increased by 15 points to 86% in 2002. Gains in mathematics were much more dramatic. In 1998 only 40% of students had passed the algebra I test; in 2002, 79% passed it. On the algebra II test, the pass rate jumped 47 points to 78% between 1998 and 2002. The geometry pass rate rose from 52% to 77% between 1998 and 2002. Since adoption of the SOLs, Virginia students' scores had improved on the verbal and math portions of SAT I by 3 and 7 points respectively. Table 4.1 below shows the progress made by Virginia high school students on the SOLs between 1998 and 2002.

On the National Assessment of Educational Progress (NAEP), which allows cross-state comparisons of achievement levels, Virginia's Grade 4 average *reading* score rose from 217 in 1998 to 223 in 2003, which was 7 points above the national average. However, there was no significant change in the gap between Virginia's Black and White Grade 4 students (26 points in 1992 and 25 in 2003). Nor had the gap between economi-

**Table 4.1.  Percentages of Virginia High School Students
Receiving Passing SOL Scores 1998-2002**

| Years | English/Reading | English/Writing | Algebra I | Algebra II | Geometry |
|-------|-----------------|-----------------|-----------|------------|----------|
| 1998 | 72 % | 71 % | 40 % | 31 % | 52 % |
| 2002 | 86 % | 86 % | 79 % | 78 % | 77 % |

*Source:*  Virginia Board of Education (2005).

cally disadvantaged and nondisadvantaged students changed; it was 27 points between 1998 and 2003. On the Grade 8 reading test, there were no significant changes between 1998 (average 266) and 2003 (average 268). The gap between White and Black students did not change significantly; it was 24 in 1998 and 25 in 2003. Nor did the gap between economically disadvantaged students narrow significantly; it was 25 points in 1998 and 23 in 2003.[2]

In contrast to the negligible changes in NAEP reading scores under Virginia's accountability program, the state's NAEP *math* scores rose significantly between 1992 and 2003. The average score of Virginia's Grade 4 students on the NAEP rose from 221 in 1992 to 239 in 2003, which was 5 points above the national average. The gap between White and Black Grade 4 Virginia students narrowed in math, from 29 points in 1992 to 23 points in 2003. Similarly, achievement among Grade 8 students rose in math from an average of 264 in 1990 to 282 in 2003, which was 6 points above the national average. However, the gap between Blacks and Whites did not change significantly from 29 points in 1990 to 28 in 2003. Table 4.2 below shows Virginia's average scores on the NAEP in both reading and math from 1990 to 2003.

Thus Virginia had mixed results in reading under its accountability system, as measured by the NAEP. In math, on the other hand, significant gains were made under Virginia's SOL system, on both the state tests and the NAEP. Yet, progress on narrowing the gap between Whites and non Whites was negligible.

As for the Standards of Accreditation (SOAs) for schools, the first school report cards, issued in January 1999, shocked the public with the results that more than 97% of Virginia's schools failed to meet the new state standards. The following year, 6.5% of schools met the mark with 70% or more of their students passing the SOLs. Black student performance rose relative to that of Whites, but the gap was still wide: 75% of Black students failed at least one SOL, while 41% of White students failed at least one test. By 2000, 22% of Virginia schools met the 70% threshold and another 38% met provisional benchmarks. Black students continued to make gains (Hess, 2002).

**Table 4.2.   Virginia's Scores on the NAEP 1990-2003**

|  | 4th Grade | | | | 8th Grade | | | |
|  | Math | | Reading | | Math | | Reading | |
| Year | VA Avg. | Nat. Avg. | VA Avg. | Nat. Avg. | VA Avg. | Nat. Avg. | VA Avg. | Nat. Avg. |
|---|---|---|---|---|---|---|---|---|
| 1990 | | | | | 264 | 262 | | |
| 1992 | 221 | 219 | 221 | 215 | 268 | 267 | | |
| 1994 | | | 213 | 212 | | | | |
| 1996 | 223 | 222 | | | 270 | 271 | | |
| 1998 | | | 217 | 213 | | | 266 | 261 |
| 2000 | 230 | 224 | | | 275 | 272 | | |
| 2002 | | | 225 | 217 | | | 269 | 263 |
| 2003 | 239 | 234 | 223 | 216 | 282 | 276 | 268 | 261 |

*Source:*   National Center for Education Statistics (2005b).

In 2002 Governor Warner initiated the Partnership for Achieving Successful Schools (PASS) program to assist at-risk schools. It identified one hundred academically warned schools which would receive special services from visiting academic review teams to help them in raising performance on their SOLs. Thirty-four of the schools were identified as PASS priority schools and would receive additional intervention and monitoring to assess the progress made by students, teachers and administrators (Virginia Board of Education, 2002). As will be seen below, the various interventions and assistance offered produced significant results. The state continued to make small but steady gains in passage rates on elementary school SOLs, and significant gains on Grade 10 SOLs, all of which translated into large gains in the percentage of schools accredited.

By 2002, those who had supported the system could point to various indications of success: generally good reviews of the accountability system itself as evidenced by its use as a model in numerous states, significant increases in the SOL scores of students, and progress in the number of schools that were accredited by 2002. Virginians could also take pride in the numerous efforts the state had undertaken to provide students with the assistance needed to succeed, such as professional development for teachers and Project Graduation, which is discussed below. Yet, the modest gains, where there were any, in achievement on the NAEP and the persistence of the achievement gap provided clear evidence that meeting the requirements of NCLB would be no easy task.

## VIRGINIA'S RESPONSE TO NCLB

Virginia's response to the No Child Left Behind Act perhaps can be best described as ambivalent. On the one hand, Virginians were proud to be seen as a leader in the field of educational accountability. Virginia's scores on the National Assessment of Educational Progress (NAEP) were among the highest in the nation. However, NCLB requirements exposed large achievement gaps between minority and White students and required that they be eliminated, which called for much greater resourcefulness and innovation than Virginians had asked of themselves. As public awareness of the implications of NCLB grew, opposition from the state legislature, from the BOE, from parents and from teacher organizations grew more strident. The General Assembly called for a cost-benefit analysis of Virginia's participation in Title I programs. At the same time that the BOE issued sanguine statements about the progress of Virginia's students under NCLB, the board asked for waivers from several of NCLB's regulations. On closer analysis, these seemingly contradictory responses are not so puzzling, however. Virginia deserves credit for having taken the lead in standards-based reform, and for standing firm on accountability when it would have been easier to back down in the face of criticism. Now the federal government was requiring that the state redouble, perhaps quadruple, its efforts to teach even those children for whom achieving proficiency will require dramatically disproportional effort on the part of school systems. It is not surprising that Virginia, like other states, is asking the federal government for reasonableness, flexibility, and credit for progress made. Nevertheless, it is clear that the commonwealth must be more creative and assertive to hasten achievement gains.

Because Virginia had already institutionalized its state standards and accountability system before the NCLB requirements took effect, and because it had already made significant progress in student achievement, it was able to set a relatively ambitious timeline for meeting the NCLB target of all students' reaching proficiency by 2013-2014. Virginia's starting point for reading/language arts was 60.7% of students at proficiency in reading in 2001-2002 (Virginia Department of Education, 2003). In comparison, California's starting point was 15% in 2001-2002, which required the state to make extraordinary gains between then and 2013-2014 when 100% of students would have to be proficient to remain in compliance with NCLB (Tracey, Sunderman, & Orfield, 2005). Virginia's start point for math proficiency was nearly as high as that for reading/language arts, at 58.4 in 2001-2002 (Virginia Department of Education, 2003). Table 4.3 shows Virginia's targets for proficiency in math and English under NCLB.

Table 4.3.  Virginia's Targets for 100 Percent
Proficiency in Math and English by 2013-2014

| Years | Math | Reading/Language Arts |
|---|---|---|
| 2001-02 | 58.4% | 60.7% |
| 2002-04 | 59% | 61% |
| 2004-07 | 70% | 70% |
| 2007-10 | 80% | 80% |
| 2010-13 | 90% | 90% |
| 2013-14 | 100% | 100% |

Source: Virginia Consolidated State Application Accountability Workbook, May 1, 2003, accessed at http://www.pen.k12.va.us/VDOE/nclb?VAConSolApplWorkbook5-1-03.pdf

Virginia clearly was dedicated to improving the quality of its education system through its Standards of Learning and to meeting the requirements of NCLB. The Board of Education's *Six-Year Plan: 2003-2008* identified six priorities, among which it affirmed its commitment to challenging academic standards for all students, enhancing the training, recruitment, and retention of highly qualified teachers and administrators, improving reading among students, especially those in elementary school, and providing leadership in implementing NCLB (Virginia Board of Education, 2002).

The 2003-2008 Plan noted dissatisfaction with the lack of improvement in reading achievement in Virginia, especially given the resources the state has directed at reading. The fact that Virginia's non-English speaking population was growing disproportionately exacerbated the challenge of improving student achievement in reading. Virginia's LEP student population had increased approximately 300% from the early 1990s to the early twenty-first century and was expected to continue to rise (Virginia Board of Education, 2002).

The Board of Education's *2004 Annual Report on the Condition and Needs of Public Schools in Virginia* identified as some of the major challenges facing Virginia's public school in the coming years the following, all of which related directly or indirectly to NCLB:

- fully funding the state share of the Standards of Quality;
- closing the achievement gap;
- ensuring meaningful, on-going professional development for teachers and administrators;
- coping with the huge growth in the population of students who did not speak English;

- assisting chronically low-performing schools and students;
- ensuring that all children learned to read at grade level;
- implementing and meeting the requirements of the No Child Left Behind Act of 2001;
- developing, implementing and using a student-level data base;
- helping the "hard-to-staff" schools; and
- advocating for higher teacher salaries and helping schools recruit and retain highly qualified teachers (Virginia Board of Education, 2004).

To improve reading, the commonwealth had a comprehensive program in place that trained teachers to diagnose individual students' reading readiness and capacities. The state used the NCLB-approved Reading First, along with Phonological Awareness Literacy Screening (PALS), a program developed at the University of Virginia, to screen for early intervention in reading. PALS provided teachers with specific diagnostic information on each child that allowed teachers to match instruction methods and materials to the needs of the child. Virginia had begun using PALS in 1997, well before NCLB was enacted, in Grades K-1. The program was expanded to Grades 2 and 3 in 2000, and was used in 98% of school districts in Virginia in 2005. "Virginia has been in the vanguard in terms of assessment.... We probably are the state with the best research design behind Reading First," commented Dr. Mary Abouzeid of the Curry School of Education at the University of Virginia, director of Reading First in Virginia and developer of PALS (personal communication, 2005).

TEMPO, a statewide outreach program housed in the McGuffey Reading Center of the Curry School, offered 65 graduate courses in reading training, which contributed to developing a network of well-trained reading instructors throughout the state. A central tenet of the training was *assessment*, which Abouzeid emphasized was essential to effective instruction.

Abouzeid noted that nationwide, about 25% of children were not ready to read upon entering school. Preschool children living in poverty spent very little time, compared with their middle class counterparts, in preliteracy activities, such as listening to books read by parents or playing rhyming games. Given the extraordinary differences in literacy readiness between disadvantaged and middle class kindergarten children, it was clear that much more aggressive intervention was needed to bring disadvantaged children up to the achievement level of their advantaged peers.

One of the greatest challenges to states in meeting the AYP requirements of NCLB was providing technical assistance and other guidance to administrators and teachers in schools that were failing. To meet this need, Governor Warner created a program to train a group of principals in turning around troubled schools. The program would train 10 principals each year for two years in business and educational strategies that had been effective in revitalizing low-performing organizations. Each specialist would be assigned to a school for three years (Education Commission of the States, 2004).

Another especially onerous requirement of NCLB was that by 2005-2006 *all* students would be taught by highly qualified teachers. Recruiting and retaining highly qualified teachers in all of Virginia's schools would not be easy, with a decreasing teacher supply and an increasing student population. In 2002 Virginia was already experiencing acute teacher shortages in special education, science and most severely in mathematics (Virginia Board of Education, 2002). Furthermore, the 2004 Annual Report notes that Virginia had 230 "hard-to-staff" schools; these tended to be high-poverty inner-city schools or schools in economically depressed rural areas that offered relatively low salaries (Virginia Board of Education, 2004).

In 2004, as an incentive program, the Virginia Board of Education and surrounding states formed a consortium to create a Meritorious New Teacher Candidate designation to recognize "exceptionally well-prepared and high performing new teachers" from approved teacher education programs. The Board supported numerous other efforts to build a stronger and more numerous teaching corps through the Teacher Quality Enhancement project. In 2003-2004, highly qualified teachers taught 94.5% of classes; however, the percentage of highly qualified teachers was 96.5 in low-poverty schools and 92.2 in high-poverty schools (Virginia Board of Education, 2004).

In October 2005, in response to complaints from states that having 100% of their students taught by "highly qualified" teachers by 2005-2006 was both unreasonable and impossible, given teacher shortages, Secretary of Education Margaret Spellings notified state education officials that they could apply for a 1-year extension on this requirement. If states could show a good faith effort in accomplishing the goal of all students' being taught by highly qualified teachers, they could have until 2006-2007 to accomplish that directive (Keller, 2005). This extension was a relief, but the challenge of having all teachers be "highly qualified" even by 2006-2007 remained daunting, at best. Indeed, the BOE's 2006 Annual Report showed that 5% of classroom teachers in the state still were not highly qualified (though many states had higher percentages yet of teachers who were not highly qualified).

Concerns about the costs of implementing NCLB, especially given the onerous accounting and reporting requirements, were mounting within the states. In January 2004, Virginia's House of Delegates passed a resolution by a vote of 98-1 that demanded that Congress exempt states like Virginia that had accountability programs in place from the requirements of NCLB. The resolution declared that the federal law "represents the most sweeping intrusions into state and local control of education in the history of the United States" and claimed that its implementation would cost the state millions of dollars that it did not have. Several states had expressed complaints about NCLB, but Scott Young, an education policy specialist with the National Conference of State Legislatures said that Virginia's resolution was the "strongest-worded Republican-sponsored initiative to pass." Eugene W. Hickok, Acting Deputy Secretary of the US Department of Education responded that Virginia's resolution "essentially says that if states feel like they have been doing a good job, we should give them the money and leave them alone. What state wouldn't say that?" (Becker & Helderman, 2004, p. A01.)

In January 2005, the Virginia Board of Education made several requests to the U.S. Department of Education (USDOE) for flexibility in the implementation of NCLB. These included the following that were approved:

1.  that students with disabilities and LEP students earning diplomas within the time specified on their Individual Education Plans (IEPs) be considered on-time graduates;
2.  that students passing expedited retakes of high school SOL tests be regarded as proficient in calculating AYP ratings;
3.  that Virginia be allowed to establish a minimum "n" for schools, divisions and the state of 50 or 1%, with a cap at 200 students for measuring AYP;
4.  that only school divisions failing to make AYP in the same subject *across all grade spans* for two consecutive years be regarded as in need of improvement (Jackson, 2005).

USDOE's agreement to Virginia's using the "grade-span" method for failing to make AYP, the fourth request approved above, would reduce significantly the number of districts deemed not to have made AYP under NCLB. Districts were otherwise considered out of compliance if in *any one grade level* schools and districts failed to meet the state's proficiency targets. By 2006, the USDOE had allowed at least 35 states to use the grade span method, as opposed to the original method stipulated in NCLB, known as the AYP method (Center on Education Policy, 2007).

Several other of Virginia's requests were denied. In a written statement, Board of Education President Thomas M. Jackson, Jr. expressed frustration with the USDOE's lack of cooperation with Virginia. He noted

USDOE's 5-month delay in responding to Virginia's requests for amendments to its accountability plan, most of which had already been granted to other states. "This continued disrespect toward a state that has faithfully implemented the No Child Left Behind Act of 2001 (NCLB) is bewildering." Jackson stressed the reasonableness of the state's requests, which were based on experience and progress. "By ignoring this progress and rejecting most of Virginia's proposed amendments, the United States Department of Education continues on a course that undercuts support for NCLB in the commonwealth and encourages confrontation" (Jackson, 2005, p. 2).

By 2006, Virginia had also received permission from the USDOE for the following:

1. averaging participation rates over three years if the current year fell under the 95% required to make AYP;
2. averaging the percentage of students scoring at the proficient level ("uniform averaging") over 2 or 3 years if students fell below the AYP targets;
3. converting the non proficient test scores of students with disabilities who took *regular tests* to proficient scores (for a total of not more than 2% of the total student population) (Center on Education Policy, 2007).

However, in the meantime, frustration had been growing. In February 2005, Virginia's Legislative Assembly had ordered a cost analysis of Virginia's participation in the NCLB Act, to be completed by October 2005, so that the commonwealth could consider withdrawing from the program. Virginia received about $350 million per year from the federal government through Title I, and the receipt of these funds would be jeopardized by noncompliance with NCLB. Delegate James H. Dillard II (R-Fairfax) predicted that the cost to the state of implementation of NCLB would outweigh the aid received from the national government (Helderman, 2005).

In response to the legislative directive, Virginia's DOE joined a consortium of state departments of education sponsored by the Council of Chief State School Officers (CCSSO) to coordinate the effort of analyzing the costs of implementing NCLB. CCSSO contracted with Augenblick, Palaich and Associates (APA) to develop a framework to determine the requirements and costs to states and localities. CCSSO, together with APA, produced two cost analyses, which were presented to and adopted by the Virginia BOE. The analysis of costs *to the state* versus federal revenues received showed that for fiscal years 2005-2008, the state would retain a modest surplus after implementing NCLB's mandates, ranging from

$234,400 the first year to $1,974,212 the second year, with surpluses in the third and fourth years of approximately $650,000. The analysts were careful to note that this was a conservative estimate that did not take into account the costs that could be incurred in actually bringing all students to proficiency by 2013-2014 (Virginia Department of Education, 2005).

The second report, which analyzed the costs *to school divisions* (districts) of implementing NCLB, showed that the revenues provided by the national government did not meet the costs incurred by school divisions. Costs incurred by school divisions ranged from $238 to $267 million per year for fiscal years 2005-2008, which amounted to per pupil costs of $204 to $209 per year, $53 of which was unfunded. The report noted that the $53 cost to the state was less than 1% of the total per pupil expenditures by the state of $8,552 in 2003-2004 (Pailich, Aaugenblick, Silverstein, & Brown, 2005). Thus, there was a modest surplus at the state level and a deficit at the local levels which exceeded the state surplus, but did not approach the $350 million that the state received in Title I funds from the Washington.

In the spring of 2005, Virginia Senator (former Governor) George Allen, along with Virginia Congressman Bob Goodlatte, introduced legislation in Congress to amend NCLB to exempt from NCLB's AYP formulas states that had accountability systems in place, while at the same time expanding the academic content areas covered by NCLB to include US history, civics and writing. In an article in the *Washington Post*, Allen charged that NCLB, while "noble in its intent to educate every child," in practice led to micromanagement of the states' education practices "to an extent well beyond that of any previous federal effort in our nation's history." Like Board President Jackson, Allen said that NCLB failed to recognize the progress in student achievement that Virginia and other states had made with their own accountability systems instituted well before NCLB was enacted. Allen warned that NCLB's micromanagement could undercut the high accountability standards that were already in place in states (Allen, 2005), but there was no evidence that this was occurring. H.R. 1821, the Flexibility for Champion Schools Act, was never passed (GovTrack.us, 2007).

Ross Wiener, a policy director for The Education Trust, which strongly supports accountability in education and reducing the achievement gap, responded in an article in the *Washington Post* that Allen's proposal would allow states to ignore the achievement gap, the reduction of which was a central aim of NCLB, by hiding lower scores of minority students within average scores. For instance, Wiener noted that in northern Virginia's Fairfax County, one of the most affluent and highly regarded school districts in the nation, 91% of White students demonstrated proficiency in English, whereas only 66% of Black students did so in the 2003-2004 school year. This proficiency rate for Black students in Fairfax was lower than the proficiency rate for Blacks in less affluent regions of the state. Wiener said the bill paid "lip service" to closing the achievement gap, but required no goals or quantifiable benchmarks for doing so (Wiener, 2005).

Thus Virginia's response to NCLB was ambivalent. Having been a leader in setting standards and adopting assessments, the state was not averse to the notion of accountability in education. And the state had much to be proud of in its education system. Its students ranked well above the national average on many measures. However, NCLB required more of the state and its education system than it had been doing, most notably with regard to closing the achievement gap between White students and various other subgroups. Virginians bristled at the federal directives within NCLB and the additional costs involved in complying with them, and they issued some of the most scathing denunciations of the act itself and the USDOE. Nevertheless, the state DOE and BOE continued to endeavor to meet the federal requirements and to express pride in the state's students for their progress.

## Achievement in Virginia Under NCLB 2003-2005

By the most noticeable measure, having achieved AYP in 2004-2005 and 2005-2006, Virginia appeared to be advancing in the years following the enactment of NCLB. And certainly, Virginia students were doing well on the NAEP, with few states surpassing Virginia's scores. However a closer look at achievement data shows that Virginia's academic gains have slowed in recent years and suggests that the goals of eliminating the achievement gap and having all students at proficiency by 2013-2014 appear far out of reach.

Virginia achieved AYP for the first time as a state in 2004-2005, by meeting or exceeding objectives for participation and by increasing achievement. Eighty percent of the state's public schools made AYP, up from 74% the previous year, even though the bar was higher in 2005. In 2005-2006, the state again made AYP, with 73% of its schools making AYP. In both 2004-2005 and 2005-2006, 80% of Virginia's Title I schools made AYP. In 2005-2006, 47 Title I schools made AYP for the second year and thereby exited school improvement status, bringing the number of sanctioned Title I schools down from 111 to 64 (VA DOE 2006 Annual Report, 2006). As mentioned above, Virginia's initial AYP objectives were some of the highest in the nation, owing to the progress its students had made since the introduction of the SOLs in the mid 1990s. Table 4.4 shows Vir-

**Table 4.4.   Virginia's NCLB AYP Targets
and Performance for years 2003-2006**

| Years | AYP Target Reading/ELA | AYP Target Math | State Made AYP? | % Schools Made AYP | % Title I Schools Made AYP | # School Divisions Made AYP |
|---|---|---|---|---|---|---|
| 2003-2004 | 61 % | 59% | No | 74% | | |
| 2004-2005 | 65 % | 63% | Yes | 80% | 80% | 68% |
| 2005-2006 | 69 % | 67% | Yes | 73% | 80% | 72% (55%) |

ginia's AYP targets and the percentages of its schools and divisions making AYP from 2003-2006.

Black and Hispanic students improved their test scores and narrowed the gaps slightly between their performances and those of White students in 2004-2005 on the state tests in both reading and math (Virginia Board of Education, 2005). In reading, Black and Hispanic students narrowed the gap a point or two further in 2005-2006. In math, new, more challenging tests were adopted in 2005-2006, and student scores dropped across the board. It was difficult to make comparisons, but it appeared that the gap had widened slightly between Whites and minorities, as White students' math scores dropped an average of 8 points, whereas both Black and Hispanic students' math scores dropped an average of 11 points (Virginia Board of Education, 2006 Annual Report, 2006).

Progress in terms of accreditation of schools under Virginia's SOA system continued after NCLB was enacted, as well. By November 2003, 78% of Virginia schools were fully accredited, up from 23% in 2000. By 2004, 84% of schools were accredited, and by 2005, 92% were accredited. In 2005-2006, the percentage of accredited schools remained at 92% (Virginia Board of Education, 2006).

Responding to public pressure, the BOE broadened the accreditation criteria to include in-puts such as course offerings, facilities and staffing patterns. As of 2004, Virginia Code specified the following for accreditation criteria: student outcome measures; requirements for instruction, including integration of educational technology; administrative and instructional staffing; course and credit requirements for graduation; community relations; and "the philosophy, goals, and objectives of public education in Virginia," though the State Board was not limited to those criteria in developing standards for accreditation (Virginia Code, 2004, ss.22.1-253.13:3).

The number of accredited schools rose even as accreditation requirements in reading, science and history increased for elementary schools. Pass rates in reading of 75% of students in Grades 3 and 5, 70% (up from

50%) in Grade 5 science and history, and 50% pass rates in Grade 3 science and history were required for accreditation by 2003-2004. The category of provisional accreditation was no longer available, and schools were either fully accredited or accredited with warning, except for alternative schools, which were allowed alternative accreditation plans (Virginia Department of Education, 2004).

High school SOL scores and graduation rates continued to climb, as well. The class of 2004 was the first to be held to Virginia's high stakes accountability system, which required students to earn verified credits by passing high school SOL tests to graduate. Contrary to the dire predictions that the more stringent requirements would leave large numbers of students without high school diplomas, 94% of Virginia seniors received advanced, standard, modified standard or special diplomas. Using the formula established by Congress in NCLB, 73.5% of the ninth grade class of 2000-2001 earned a diploma in 2004, which is the "on-time graduation rate" (Commonwealth Educational Policy Institute, 2005) down slightly from the average of the previous 5 years, 74.7% (Warner, 2004), and down nearly 3% from the on-time graduation rate for the class of 2002-2003. Another 3% completed high school by receiving GEDs, ISAEPs (individual student alternative education plans) or certificates of completion (Commonwealth Educational Policy Institute, 2005).

Grade retention and dropping out accounted for most of the 25% of students who were enrolled in Grade 9 with the graduating class of 2004 but did not graduate. Failure to earn standard credits—those earned from courses passed— was a greater deterrent to graduation than was failure to pass SOL tests, an interesting finding. More than three times as many students failed to graduate because they had earned an insufficient number of standard credits. Of those who did not earn the Standard Diploma, the majority needed only one verified credit, and one fourth needed two verified credits. School divisions reported that 57% of Grade 12 students who did not graduate were continuing in high school, suggesting that many of them would graduate, though they would not be counted as on-time graduates (Commonwealth Educational Policy Institute, 2005).

Project Graduation initiatives, including Spring and Summer Regional Academies and online tutorials, as well as Term Graduation testing (administration of retakes of SOLs in the summer after senior year), WorkKeys, an alternative writing assessment, and ePat, which allowed students to practice assessments in various subjects, attracted thousands of students, earning them verified credits and significantly raising graduation rates (Commonwealth Educational Policy Institute, 2005).

Of students who earned diplomas, 54.6% earned Advanced Diplomas, 43.3% earned Standard diplomas, 2% received Modified Standard and 3.6% received Special Diplomas (Commonwealth Educational Policy Institute, 2005). The class of 2004 was the first in which a majority of the seniors who earned diplomas had earned Advanced Diplomas (Warner, 2004).

On the other hand, the number and percentage of students earning the Modified Standard Diploma had increased substantially since its inception in 2000-2001, from .1% (37 students) in 2001 to 2% (1,437 students) in 2004. The percentage of students receiving Special Diplomas had almost doubled since 2001, from 2% to 3.6%. The number of completers who received GEDs or certificates of completion remained steady with less than 1% receiving certificates of completion and 1.3% receiving GEDs (Commonwealth Educational Policy Institute, 2005).

The graduation figures reflected a significant gap in achievement among White, Black and Hispanic students, as well as between males and females. Graduation rates were highest in northern Virginia at 80% and lowest in southeast and southside (south central) Virginia at about 66%. All of these disparities were consistent with other research that showed that socioeconomic status, race/ethnicity and gender were the strongest predictors of graduation (Commonwealth Educational Policy Institute, 2005). Table 4.5 below shows Virginia's 2004 graduation rates disaggregated by race and gender.

The 2005 and 2006 graduation rates were nearly the same as those of 2004, while the percentage of Advanced Diplomas earned rose from 47.6% in 2004 to 49.4% in 2005 to 50.7% in 2006 (VA BOE, 2006 Annual Report, 2006).

The number of Virginia students taking Advanced Placement (AP) courses also showed improvement since the implementation of NCLB, another indication that students were seeking more challenging options in high school. By 2006, 20.7% of Virginia's public high school seniors earned a grade of 3 or higher on at least one AP exam, up from 15.9% in 2000. The national average in 2006 was 14.8%. The gap between White

**Table 4.5.  Graduation Rates for Virginia's 2004 Students Disaggregated by Race**

| Group | Total Rate | Advanced Diplomas | Standard Diplomas | Modified Diplomas | Special Diplomas |
|-------|-----------|-------------------|-------------------|-------------------|------------------|
| Black | 61.3% | 29.8% | 60.1% | 3.3% | 6.8% |
| Hispanic | 66.5% | 35.6% | 59.6% | 2.5% | 2.4% |
| White | 77% | 53.5% | 42.3% | 1.6% | 2.8% |
| Total | | 44.8% | 44.1% | 1.9% | 3.4% |

*Sources:*   Commonwealth Educational Policy Institute (2005) and Warner (2005).

and other students who were taking more challenging courses was narrowing, as well. The number of AP exams taken by Black students had increased 85.7% between 2001 and 2006, and the number of Hispanic students who had taken at least one AP exam had more than doubled during the same time period (Virginia Department of Education, 2007).

Virginia students fared well in comparison to students nationwide in 2004-2005, but their lead over their peers nationwide had been gained prior to NCLB. On the National Assessment of Education Progress (NAEP) 2005 reading and math exams for Grades 4 and 8, Virginia students out performed students nationally, as a whole, and in all ethnic subgroups. However, the achievement gap in reading between White and Black students had not changed from 26 and 24 points for Grades 4 and 8 respectively. The gap between economically disadvantaged and non disadvantaged students had not changed significantly, either. The math gaps between White and Black Virginia students widened by one point for Grade 4 and two points for Grade 8, both of which increases were insignificant, but certainly did not show progress since 2003. Table 4.6 below shows the Virginia's NAEP scores from 1990 through 2005.

Proficiency clearly had a different meaning on the NAEP than on Virginia's SOLs, considering that at least 65% of all students and all subgroups scored proficient in reading in Virginia, thereby allowing the state to make AYP in 2005 (and in 2006), whereas only 37 and 35% of Grades 4

**Table 4.6.   NAEP Reading and Math Scores for Virginia and the U.S. 1990-2005**

| | 4th Grade | | | | 8th Grade | | | |
|---|---|---|---|---|---|---|---|---|
| | Math | | Reading | | Math | | Reading | |
| Year | VA Avg. | Nat. Avg. | VA Avg. | Nat. Avg. | VA Avg. | Nat. Avg. | VA Avg. | Nat. Avg. |
| 1990 | | | | | 264 | 262 | | |
| 1992 | 221 | 219 | 221 | 215 | 268 | 267 | | |
| 1994 | | | 213 | 212 | | | | |
| 1996 | 223 | 222 | | | 270 | 271 | | |
| 1998 | | | 217 | 213 | | | 266 | 261 |
| 2000 | 230 | 224 | | | 275 | 272 | | |
| 2002 | | | 225 | 217 | | | 269 | 263 |
| 2003 | 239 | 234 | 223 | 216 | 282 | 276 | 268 | 261 |
| 2005 | 240 | 237 | 226 | 217 | 284 | 278 | 268 | 260 |

*Note:*   http://nces.ed.gov/nationsreportcard/states/profile.asp

and 8 students respectively were deemed proficient on the NAEP. Similarly in math, at least 61% of all students and all subgroups were deemed proficient on Virginia's SOLs, whereas 39 and 33% of Grades 4 and 8 students were deemed proficient on the NAEP, respectively.

Students' comparative performances on the NAEP provide state and national policymakers with important information on the relative achievement levels of students in the various states, information that cannot be gleaned from the state progress reports required by NCLB and based on AYP. As explained in the Introduction, under NCLB, states set their own goals for improvement in student achievement, and they design their own tests to measure the progress they make. Not surprisingly, the states' accountability systems, their assessments, and their timetables for compliance with NCLB vary dramatically. In the vast majority of states far greater percentages of students are considered proficient by state standards for the purposes of NCLB than are proficient on the NAEP. The most extreme example is Mississippi; 87% of the state's Grade 4 students were proficient on the state reading test, whereas only 10% were proficient on the NAEP reading test.

Diane Ravitch, a member of the governing board of NAEP from 1997 to 2004, argues that these discrepancies show that "the states have embraced low standards and grade inflation." Political considerations drive educational and elected leaders to produce positive results; thus they maintain standards that correspond with the public's comfort level, instead of demanding excellence from schools, teachers and students, she observes. "Americans must recognize that we need national standards, national tests and a national curriculum," Ravitch declares, if we are to raise student achievement to internationally competitive levels (2005).

Certainly, allowing states to develop their own standards and accountability systems and definitions of proficiency under NCLB was a political concession. Without that provision, the bill would not have received majority support in Congress. Even with the wide flexibility allowed under the law, states, including Virginia, have harshly criticized NCLB's intrusive effects on education policy, which has historically lain within the purviews of the states. So despite its shortcomings, NCLB has succeeded in forcing states to set standards, albeit many seem pitifully low. And despite these disparate definitions of proficiency, states are being called upon to make unprecedented efforts to comply with NCLB and raise student achievement in the next few years, efforts that would not have taken place without congressional pressure. Thus, even if what states deem *proficient* is closer to NAEP's *basic* achievement level, it would be a remarkable accomplishment if by 2013-2014 all American students were achieving at that level.

## CONCLUSION AND PROSPECTS FOR
## STATE ATTAINMENT OF NCLB OBJECTIVES BY 2014

Frederick Hess notes that the central challenge to success for standards-based accountability systems is maintaining the integrity of the program in the face of political opposition, especially from stakeholders who are the targets of sanctions. These interests tend to be much more organized and vocal than those who benefit (arguably everyone) in the long term from higher expectations of schools, teachers and students. Critics rarely explicitly oppose the notion of accountability; they almost always target the "punitive" specifics of programs that deny students diplomas or sanction schools or teachers for low student performance. Thus they endorse the notion of transformative accountability, but "only if it is stripped of its transformative character" (2004, pp. 56-58). Hess observes, "Resisting the protests of the aggrieved is the central political challenge confronting advocates of high-stakes reform. In the face of heated opposition, proponents often agree to a series of compromises on program design and implementation, eventually undercutting the coercive promise implied by high-stakes testing" (2004, p. 60).

Virginia's experience with standards and accountability provides strong evidence that such policies can improve achievement significantly. The state's Standards of Learning and Standards of Accreditation have raised student achievement on state tests in both reading and math, and Virginia students have made significant gains in math on the NAEP. The task before Virginia of raising all students to proficiency in both reading and math by 2013-2014 is much less onerous, given its high starting point, than that before many other states. However, many more resources and greater innovation will be needed to raise the reading scores of all students and to close the achievement gaps between White and middle-class students and their disadvantaged counterparts.

Given the energy directed at reading improvement and the resources available in Virginia, reading achievement is likely to rise, though not quickly enough to meet NCLB objectives. The fact that Virginia students' reading achievement, as measured by the NAEP, is several points above the national average renders the state's potential for meeting its NCLB objectives better than most, especially in terms of students' truly being proficient at reading.

The achievement gap is a much more intractable characteristic of public education throughout America and is a consequence of numerous factors associated with income disparities and other family assets or deficits. Virginia's SOL and SOA systems were not designed to address the achievement gap specifically, and this is a challenge that, based on the rhetoric of policymakers, it appears that the state has not fully embraced.

Even with concerted will and effort on the part of those responsible for Virginia's public education system, it is highly doubtful that the state will attain its NCLB proficiency targets in all groups by 2014.

## NOTES

1. Wurtzel described two of three Allen appointees as "hard-core right wing, religious right" (2002, pp. 106-107).
2. Virginia's test scores on the NAEP can be found at the Web site for the National Center for Education Statistics at http://nces.ed.gov/ nationsreportcard/states/profile.asp

## REFERENCES

Allen, G. (2005, May 22). Undermining school progress. *Washington Post*, p.B7.

*Apples to processed and refined applesauce: How Virginia plays the accreditation numbers games*. (n.d.). Retrieved August 8, 2005, from http://solreform.com/ hardapples.htm

Barone, M., & Cohen, R. E. (2005). *The almanac of American politics, 2006*. Washington, DC: National Journal Group.

Becker, J., & Helderman, R. S. (2004, January 24). Va. seeks to leave Bush law behind: Republicans fight school mandates. *Washington Post*, p. A01.

Center for Education Reform. *Virginia, charter law*. Retrieved December 18, 2005, from http://www.edreform.com/index.cfm?fuseAction=cLaw&stateID=3

Center on Education Policy. (2007, January). *No Child Left Behind at Five: A Review of Changes to State Accountability Plans*. Washington, DC: Author. Retrieved February 26, 2007, from http://www.cep-dc.org/nclb/stateaccountability/ StateAccountabilityPlanChanges.pdf

Commonwealth Educational Policy Institute. (2005). Final report: The Virginia class of 2004: Graduation rates, trends, and remedial initiatives. Richmond: Virginia Commonwealth University, School of Education. Retrieved February 19, 2007, from http://141.104.22.210/VDOE/ FinalGradeReportwithIntrodLetter.pdf

Cross, R.W., Rebarber, T., & Torres, J. ( 2004). *Grading the systems: The guide to state standards, tests, and accountability policies*. Washington, DC: The Thomas B. Fordham Foundation and AccountabilityWorks.

Education Commission of the States. (2004). *ECS report to the nation: State implementation of the No Child Left Behind Act*. Denver: Author.

*From cradle to career: Connecting American education from birth through adulthood*. [Virginia]. (2007). *Quality Counts 2007*. [Special state-focused supplement to the special issue]. *Education Week*. Retrieved February 19, 2007 from http:// www.edweek.org/rc

H.R. 1821—109th Congress. (2005). *Flexibility for champion schools act*. Retrieved March 1, 2007, from http://www.govtrack.us/congress/bill.xpd?bill= h109-1821

Helderman, R. S. (2005, February 25). Cost analysis of 'No Child' law backed. *Washington Post*, p. B01. Retrieved July 25, 2005, from http://www .washingtonpost.com/wp-dyn/articles/A51520-2005 Feb25

Hess, F. M. (2002). Reform, resistance . . . retreat? The predictable politics of accountability in Virginia. *Brookings Papers on Education Policy 2002* (pp. 69-122). Washington, DC: Brookings Institution.

Hess, F. M. (2004). Refining or retreating? High-stakes accountability in the states. In P. E. Peterson & M. R. West (Eds.) *No Child Left Behind? The politics and practice of school accountability* (pp. 55-79). Washington, DC: Brookings Institution Press.

Jackson, T. M. (2005, June 14). *Statement of board of education president Thomas M. Jackson, Jr. regarding USED response to Virginia's request for NCLB flexibility.* Retrieved July 16, 2005, from http://www.pen.k12.va.us.VDOE/NewHome/pressreleases/2005/jujun14b.html

Keller, B. (2005, November 2). States given extra year on teachers. *Education Week.* Retrieved November 5, 2005 from http://www.edwek.org/ew/articles/2005/11/02/10reprieve.h25.html

Klein, D. (with Braams, B.J., Parker, T, Quirk, W., Schmid, W. & Wilson, S. W.). (2005). *The state of state MATH standards.* Washington, DC: Thomas B. Fordham Foundation.

Loveless, T. (2005). Test-based accountability: The promise and the perils. *Brookings Papers on Education Policy 2005.1* (pp. 7-45). Washington, DC: Brookings Institution Press.

National Center for Educational Statistics. (2005a). *NAEP reading mathematics 2005-Mathematics state exclusion rates.* Retrieved November 6, 2005, from http://nces.ed.gov/nationsreportcard/nrc/reading-math2005/s0094

National Center for Education Statistics. (2005b). *NCES state profiles 2005, Virginia.* Retrieved February 3, 2007, from http://nces.ed.gov/nationsreportcard/states/profile.asp

National Education Assocication. (2006). Education statistics: Rankings & estimates 2006. Retrieved February 26, 2007, from http://www.nea.org/edstats/RankFull06b.htm

Official Site of the Governor of Virginia. (n.d.). Governor Tim Kaine. Retrieved February 21, 2007, from http://wwwgovernor.virginia.gov/AboutTheGovernor/biography.cfm

Palaich, R., Aaugenblick, J, Silverstein, J., & Brown, A. R. (2005). *The cost of fulfilling the requirements of the No Child Left Behind Act for school divisions in Virginia.* Denver: Augenblick, Palaich and Associates.

Parents Across Virginia United to Reform SOLs. (n.d.). Retrieved August 8, 2005 from http://www.solreform.com/

Ravitch, D. (2005, November 7). Every state left behind. *New York Times.* Retrieved November 11, 2005, from http://www.nytimes.com/2005/11/07/opinion/07/ravitch

Samuels, C. A. (2005, October 19). Virginia gubernatorial hopefuls differ on school policy: Statewide preschool, teacher merit pay lead competing plans. *Education Week.* Retrieved December 14, 2005, from http://www.edweek.org/ew/articles/2005/10/19/ 08politics.h25.html?rale=KQE5d7nM%2

Southern Regional Education Board. (2005). *Focusing on student performance through accountability.* Challenge to Lead Series. Atlanta: Author.

Stotsky, S. (2005). *The state of the state ENGLISH standards.* Washington DC: The Fordham Foundation.

Summary of Grades by State. (2005). *Quality Counts 2005 no small change: Targeting money toward student performance.* [Special issue]. *Education Week.* Retrieved October 20, 2005, from http://www.edweek.org/ew?/qc/2005/tables/17archieve-t1.html

Thayer, Y. (2000). Virginia's standards make all students stars. *Educational Leadership, 57*(5), 70-72.

Tracey, C. A., Sunderman, G. L., & Orfield, G. (2005). *Changing NCLB district accountability standards: Implications for racial equity.* Cambridge: Harvard University's The Civil Rights Project.

VanDerwerker, M. (2004, November 7). SOL progress hasn't meant greater overall student achievement. *Fredricksburg Free Lance Star.* Retrieved August 8, 2005, from http://www.solreorm.com/

Viadero, D. (2005, November 2). States vary on students excluded from NAEP tests. *Education Week.* Retrieved November 6, 2005, from http://www.edweek.org/ew/ articles/2005/11/02/10naepexclude.h25.html

Virginia Board of Education. (2002). *Board of education six-year plan: 2003-2008.* Richmond: Author. Retrieved July 30, 2005, from http://www.pen.k12.va.us/VDOE/VA_Board/ home.shtml

Virginia Board of Education. (2004). *2004 Annual report on the condition and needs of public schools in Virginia.* Richmond: Author. Retrieved July 30, 2005, from http://leg2.state.va.us/dls/h&sdocs.nsf/By+Year/RD1372004/ $file/RD137.pdf

Virginia Board of Education. (2005, January). Raising Student Achievement. Retrieved July 28, 2005 from http://www.pen.k12.va.us/VDOE/VA_Board/ home.shtml

Virginia Board of Education. (2006). *2006 Annual report on the condition and needs of public schools in Virginia.* Richmond: Author. Retrieved 19 February 2007 from http://www.pen.k12.va.us/VDOE/VA_Board/annualreport2006.pdf

Virginia Code ss.22.1-253.13:3. Standard 3 (of standards of quality). Accreditation, other standards of evaluation. A-B.

Virginia Code 22.1-253.13:4. Standard 4 (of standards of quality). Student achievement and graduation requirements.

Virginia Department of Education. (2003). *Virginia consolidated state application accountability workbook submitted May 1, 2003.* Washington: US Department of Education. Retrieved July 25, 2005, from http://www.pen.k12.va.us/VDOE

Virginia Department of Education. (2003, November 10). *Seventy-eight percent of Virginia schools now fully accredited: More than 90 percent of high school juniors pass required reading and writing tests in 2002-2003.* Richmond: Author. Retrieved July 11, 2005, from http://www.pen.k12.va.us/VDOE/NewHome/pressreleases/2003/no

Virginia Department of Education. (2004). *Eight out of ten schools now fully accredited: More elementary schools achieve full accreditation while meeting high standards for reading.* Richmond: Author. Retrieved July 16, 2005, at http://www.pen.k12.va.us/VDOE/ NewHome/pressreleases/2004/oct

Virginia Department of Education. (2005, September). *Report to the governor and general assembly on the costs of the federal No Child Left Behind Act to the Virginia Department of Education.* Richmond: Author.

Virginia Department of Education. (2007, February 6). Virginia advanced placement performance even stronger in 2006. Richmond: Author. Retrieved February 26, 2007, from http://www.pen.k12.va.us/VDOE/NewHome/pressreleases/2007/feb6.html

Warner, M. R. (2004). *Governor Warner announces final graduation rate for class of 2004 and results of Project Graduation—2004 graduation requirement is first consequences milestone since SOLs adopted in 1995.* Richmond: Official Website of the Governor of Virginia. Retrieved July 16, 2005, from http://www.governor.virginia.gov/Press_Policy/ Releases/2004/Oct0

Warner, M. R. (2005). *Governor Warner announces graduation rates for class of 2005—nearly half of graduates earn advanced studies diplomas; 2,639 benefit from governor's Project Graduation initiative.* Richmond: Official Website of the Governor of Virginia. Accessed at October 17, 2005, from http://www.governor.virginia.gov/ Press_Policy/Releases/2005/Oct0

Wiener, R. (2005, June 6). In Virginia, reopening the gap. *Washington Post,* p. A19. Retrieved July 28, 2005, from http://www.washingtonpost.com/wp-dyn/content/article/2005/06/0

Wurtzel, A. (2002). Comment by Alan Wurtzel. *Brookings Papers on Education Policy 2002* (pp. 104-110). Washington, DC: Brookings Institution Press.

CHAPTER 5

# NORTH CAROLINA

## INTRODUCTION

### State Socioeconomic and Political Characteristics

North Carolina is one of America's fastest growing states; its population grew by 45% between 1980 and 2004. The U.S. Census (n.d.) estimated North Carolina's population at 8,856,500 in 2006. In 2004, 70.2% of the population was White, 21.4% was Black, 4.7% was Hispanic, 1.4% was Asian, and 1.2% was Native American. The Hispanic population was growing rapidly, having increased nearly 500%, from 77,000 to 379,000, in the past decade (Barone & Cohen, 2005).

Half of the growth since 1990 centered in the Charlotte and Raleigh-Durham areas. In 2005, 60% of the state's population was urban, but the rich rural traditions of the state endured. North Carolina's economy has diversified as it has lost low-skill jobs in tobacco, textiles, and furniture to foreign producers and gained higher skilled service and technology jobs. Governor Mike Easley (D) expanded the state's incentives to businesses to locate and enhance their operations in the state to counteract the loss of blue-collar jobs, with success. The Research Triangle Park, between Raleigh, Durham, and Chapel Hill, with North Carolina State, Duke, and the University of North Carolina Chapel Hill, is one of the world's largest pharmaceutical and high-technology research centers. The Piedmont Research Triad in Winston-Salem plays a similar role in biotechnology.

*Education Reform in the American States*
pp. 115–145
Copyright © 2008 by Information Age Publishing
All rights of reproduction in any form reserved.

The state hosts several banking centers as well. Though tobacco declined since the federal government's price supports ended in 2004, many residents are still engaged in agriculture, and the state is second in the nation in hog production. North Carolina experienced an economic boom during the 1990s followed by the worst recession since the Great Depression early in the twenty-first century, forcing government to make substantial public sector cutbacks (Barone & Cohen, 2005).

The state has a strong Democratic tradition, but in recent years, as in the rest of the South, Republicans have made gains. In 2006, the state's voter registration data showed that 45% of the registered voters were Democrats, 35% were Republicans, and 20% were unaffiliated (North Carolina State Board of Elections, n.d.). Split-ticket voting is common. In 2004, 56% of North Carolina voters chose President Bush, and 56% reelected Democratic Governor Mike Easley. The state has two Republican senators and elected seven Democrats and six Republicans to the U.S. House of Representatives in 2006. The General Assembly was dominated by Democrats, 31 to 19 in the Senate and 68 to 52 in the House after the 2006 elections.

The state's residents tend to divide on cultural, rather than economic lines and fall into either progressive or traditional values groups. Both recently have contributed to the state's economic growth and education reform. In 2004 exit polls, 40% of voters self-identified as conservative, 43% as moderate and 17% as liberal (Guillory, 2005).

## The State Educational System

The state plays a strong role in education in North Carolina, providing 70% of the school districts' budgets, whereas the national average is 51% from state funding. The governors since the 1990s, Jim Hunt (D) from 1992 to 2000 and Mike Easley from 2000 have been staunch advocates of education reform, increasing funding to education in the 1990s and 2004-05 and maintaining funding during the recession of 2001-2003, though education funding as a proportion of the state's budget has declined, as is discussed below.

North Carolina has an unusual governance system for its public schools, with leadership divided between the elected Superintendent of Public Instruction and the appointed State Board of Education (SBE); the SBE generates policy based on state law, and the superintendent implements both. Relations between the superintendent and the SBE were strained during the 1990s to the point that the General Assembly eventually gave the SBE operational control of the Department of Public Instruction (DPI). With the election of State Superintendent Mike Ward in

1996, relations improved, but the potential for conflict remains as long as the state retains the dual system of governance.[1] Superintendent June Atkinson (D), elected in 2004, exemplifies the strong ties between business and public education in the state, as well as the strength of leadership in public education. Dr. Atkinson began her teaching career in a high school business education program in Roanoke where she worked with business people to find employment opportunities for students. She earned a PhD in educational leadership and policy from North Carolina State University in 1996 and has made presentations to business and educational groups on education policy throughout the nation (North Carolina Public Schools, n.d.b).

North Carolina is a right-to-work state and teachers are not permitted to bargain collectively, so teachers unions are less a force than in some states. The North Carolina Association of Educators (NCAE) membership included 55.5% of North Carolina teachers in 2003-2004. Ladd and Zelli note that the most fully-developed educational accountability systems tend to operate in states in which the state contributes a large percentage of school funding and in which teachers' unions are relatively weak (2001). Both of these conditions exist in North Carolina.

In 2004-2005, North Carolina public schools served 1,360,209 students. Fifty-nine percent of students were White, 31% were Black, and 6% were Hispanic. Asian and American Indian/Alaska Native students comprised very small percentages of North Carolina's students. Between 1994 and 2004, the Hispanic population grew by 612%. The school-age population was more diverse than the general population, as is typically the case. Just under 14% of students were on Individualized Education Programs (IEPs), 4.9% were English learners (LEP) and 45.1% were eligible for free or reduced price lunch (National Center for Education Statistics, n.d.), a measure of poverty.

Of the state's 2,268 public schools, 97 were charter schools in 2006-2007. The state allowed up to 100 charter schools, to provide students and parents with a wider variety of learning opportunities through innovative instructional methods and expanded learning experiences. The schools were publicly funded, with federal, state and local dollars following the student. School administrators were released from some state regulations to allow for flexibility, but students were required to take state-mandated assessments. The State BOE issued charters and could withdraw them for such reasons as fiscal malfeasance and failure to meet student performance requirements, or at the request of two thirds of the faculty and staff of the school (North Carolina Public Schools, n.d.a).

North Carolina ranked well below the national mean in per pupil spending between 1998-99 and 2003-04. However, per pupil expenditures rose significantly between 1970 and 2005. Education reform benefited from the booming economy in North Carolina in the 1990s. The state was able to increase school funding while cutting taxes, which relieved policymakers of the difficult fiscal choices many states have to make in reforming their education systems (Grissmer & Flanagan, 1998). However, education expenditures as a percentage of the total state budget have fallen significantly since the 1970s. In 1970 the state spent 52% of its budget on K-12 education, and by 2006-2007, education's percentage of the budget had fallen to 38.1%.

School financing is influenced by *Leandro v. State of North Carolina* (1997), a suit brought by five school boards and 20 residents in low income school districts who charged that the state was not fulfilling its constitutional obligations with regard to providing funding for public education. Judge Howard Manning, Jr. determined that every North Carolina child had a constitutional right to a sound basic education, including the right to competent teachers and principals. The court put the onus on the state to ensure adequate funding to all districts. However, the judge said that school districts could commit additional funds to their schools. In 2004, Judge Manning extended *Leandro* rights to all the state's children from infancy, which obligated the state to provide prekindergarten services.

North Carolina's accountability system, the ABCs of Public Education, rests on the principles of **A**ccountability, **B**asic skills with high educational standards and local **C**ontrol. The program was launched in 1996 with strong bipartisan support in the legislature, as well as enthusiastic support from the business community and the public. The ABCs built on a series of reforms in the 1980s and early 1990s that contributed to the highest gains in the nation in National Assessment of Educational Progress (NAEP) scores in the 1990s.

Reforms continued following the implementation of the ABCs. In 1999, Governor Jim Hunt, in his State of the State address, challenged North Carolina to become "First in Education" by 2010. His successor, Mike Easley, remained committed to that goal (Reid, 2002). In the first years of the twenty-first century, in the midst of a deep recession, the state continued to prioritize education, implementing initiative after initiative aimed at raising achievement, while reducing achievement gaps, improving teacher quality, enhancing recruitment and retention of teachers, and reducing the dropout rate.

A study of North Carolina and Texas (Grissmer & Flanagan, 1998), the states with the highest gains in academic achievement during the early and mid 1990s, found that critical aspects of North Carolina's (and Texas') approach to education reform were:

• clear statewide grade-by-grade teaching objectives,

- state-wide assessments linked to the learning standards,
- an accountability system with both positive and negative incentives,
- a computerized feedback system providing test scores at the student, classroom, school and district levels which were used for diagnostic purposes,
- expectations that all students would meet the standards,
- increasing flexibility of local school systems,
- maintaining the reforms over several years without significant changes, and
- shifting of resources to schools with more disadvantaged children (pp. 19-20).

Especially important to the early successes of North Carolina's program and its endurance have been the establishment of an infrastructure for continuing support of improvement in education, including research institutes and centers, business-school partnerships, and the development of "cottage industries" to assist in school improvement through training and technology, along with reliance on outside experts to help guide reform. Perhaps most important, say the study's authors, have been the relationships forged among taxpayers, educators, policymakers and business leaders.

The Education First Task Force in 2002 credited, more than any specific initiative, the state's decision to focus relentlessly on improved student performance with having produced the state's remarkable achievement gains during the 1990s. The Task Force report, *Let's Finish the Job*, notes that state economic leaders had recognized since the 1990s that substantive reform and improvement of the state's education system was needed if it were to survive and thrive. Low-skill manufacturing jobs were decreasing, and the jobs of the future would go to states "that have a large pool of educated workers who are capable of learning and relearning through a lifetime of work. North Carolina must focus on becoming a 'knowledge state' where citizens are prepared to think for a living in a more demanding, complex economy" (p. 11).

## NORTH CAROLINA'S ACCOUNTABILITY AND ASSESSMENT SYSTEM PRIOR TO 2002

In response to *A Nation at Risk*, low SAT scores and concerns about the state's economic prospects, North Carolina began education reforms in the 1980s. In 1984 the business community established the Commission on Education for Economic Growth, which produced an agenda for reform that included pay increases and career development for teachers, funding for school facilities and new construction, and increased funding for a "Basic Education Program" (NC Department of Public Instruction, n.d.b). In 1985, in response to consensus among business people, elected officials and educators that North Carolina needed a "standing blue ribbon commission on education and the economy" to provide consistent support for improving schools, the Public School Forum was created. Its 60-member board of directors included approximately equal numbers of business leaders, elected officials and educators (Public School Forum, n.d.a, p. 1).

The forum produced "Thinking for Living: A Blueprint for Educational Growth" in 1988. The Blueprint called for alignment of standards, curriculum and assessments; accountability at the building level, with school report cards providing student performance information, and with teachers' advancement and pay based on student scores; greater local control in administration, along with enhanced training for principals; and increased preschool programs (Grissmer & Flanagan, 2001). These recommendations were adopted by the state in the North Carolina School Improvement and Accountability Act of 1989, which called for *district accountability*, partly based on student exams taken annually in Grades 3 through 12 (Buxton, 2003). The act called on schools and school systems to develop improvement plans, including setting measurable goals and milestones. Local administrators could receive waivers from state laws and SBE policies, if they could show how such flexibility would improve student achievement. In 1992 the General Assembly amended the School Improvement and Accountability Act to require increased participation by parents and teachers in developing school improvement plans, and the state placed more emphasis on *school* level decision making. In the meantime, in 1991 the General Assembly had provided for supplemental funding for small and needy school systems totaling $60 million annually, also at the recommendation of the Public School Forum (North Carolina Department of Public Instruction, n.d.a).

In the early 1990s, State Superintendent Bob Etheridge targeted early childhood education with Chapter I funds and sought state funding, as well, for early childhood programs for disadvantaged children. He also sought to lower dropout rates and raise SAT scores and to raise professionalism among teachers and principals, among other efforts to improve public education. Dropout rates declined, and between 1989 and 1993, the state's SAT scores rose by 23 points. Various efforts, including greater emphasis on rigorous coursework, raised expectations, and increased access to the PSAT contributed to the gains. For instance, in 1991, North Carolina required high school students to complete Algebra I successfully, to graduate; it was the first state to do so (North Carolina Department of

Public Instruction, n.d.a). Dr. Jay Robinson, the first president of the Public School Forum and SBE chairman from 1994-1997, was a driving force in the reform movement, championing the ABCs program, particularly its positive incentives, and the Teaching Fellows program (Buxton, 2003).

Political leaders were crucial to the success of the reform initiatives, as well. Governor Jim Hunt (1992-2000) sponsored several initiatives that built on the reform agenda, including efforts to improve instruction and to align teacher education with state standards, and Smart Start. Initiated in 1993, Smart-Start established local nonprofits, through which state funding is directed at early childhood programs. Communities determine where the greatest needs lie—in day care, preschool programs, health needs, social services or even recreation for preschool children (Grissmer & Flanagan, 1998). By 2002 the program had expanded to each of the state's 100 counties and served as a national model for early childhood development programs (Education First Task Force, 2002).

Furthermore, a "massive public relations campaign" accompanied the development of the ABCs program. In school board and chamber of commerce meetings, in editorial boardrooms and town meetings, in legislative committees and in schools across the state, stakeholders learned of the goals of accountability and how the program would operate (Buxton, 2003). Ladd and Zelli credit the high support for the ABCs program among school principals in part to the "strong educational leadership at the state level and to the state's efforts to communicate with local school officials" (2001, p. 16).

Other initiatives of the Public School Forum were the establishment of NC Partners, a statewide umbrella organization that networked local chambers of commerce, nonprofit organizations, businesses and school officials who recognized the benefits of partnering to improve public education, with the NC Institute for Educational Policymakers. The institute, the first of its kind in the nation, was created in 1997 as a collaborative effort among the forum, the Burroughs Wellcome Fund, which is located in the Research Triangle and supports scientific and educational activities, and Bell-South Foundation. It provided educational policymakers facts and information necessary for good decision making on education-related issues. It focused on members of the General Assembly and SBE, as well as on members of the media who reported on education issues. The institute held regional briefings on important education topics, held regional symposiums, and issued quarterly newsletters. It also sponsored orientation sessions for newly appointed members of the SBE and held briefing sessions on education issues for all interested candidates for the General Assembly.

## The ABCs of Public Education

With the *ABCs of Public Education*, the state in 1996 implemented school accountability and called for annual end-of-grade (EOG) criterion-referenced tests in Grades 3-8 in 10 subject areas including English, math and science. Students in Grade 8 take computer skills tests, as well. Alternate Assessment Portfolios or Academic Inventories are used for qualified students with disabilities. The ABCs program measured not only performance of students at the various grade levels, but achievement growth in individual students from year to year (Buxton, 2003). The goal was a year's worth of growth during a year of school. In this measure, North Carolina's accountability system addressed a weakness that many have identified in NCLB: the latter measured and compared performances of cohorts of students, rather than measuring academic growth in individual students. NCLB's requirements thus did not acknowledge progress in individual students, nor did NCLB sufficiently recognize progress in schools that started far behind. During the 1997-98 school year, North Carolina applied school accountability measures to high school, implementation at the secondary level having been delayed, owing to the greater complexity of the academic structure of high schools.

In 2000-2001, the Standards, or Gateways, were applied to Grade 5, which meant that their promotion depended upon performance on EOG tests. The following year the Gateways were applied to Grades 3 and 8. In high school students take eight end-of-course (EOC) tests: Algebra I, Algebra II, biology, chemistry, English I, geometry, physical science, and physics. Each school has an individualized growth standard, based on previous performance and statewide average growth (North Carolina Public Schools, North Carolina State Board of Education, and North Carolina Department of Public Instruction, n.d.).

North Carolina schools could receive various levels of recognition or sanctions based on the scores of their students on state tests.

- Schools with 90 to 100% of students performing at Achievement Level III (of four) or higher and which made expected or high growth were named *Schools of Excellence*.
- Schools with 80 to 89% of students performing at Achievement Level III or higher and which made expected or high growth were designated *Schools of Distinction*.
- Schools with 60 to 79% of students performing at Achievement Level III or higher and which made expected or high growth were designated *Schools of Progress*.

- Schools with the above percentages performing at Level III or higher and which did not make expected or high growth received *No Recognition*.

- Schools with 50 to 59% of students performing at Achievement Level III or higher were called *Priority Schools*, regardless of growth, as were those with less than 50% of students at Achievement Level III who made expected or high growth.

- Schools with less than 50% of students performing at Level II or higher who made less than expected growth were designated *Low-Performing* (North Carolina Public Schools et al., n.d.).

For the low-performing schools deemed most in need, for instance those in which performance appeared to be declining, the SBE assigned state assistance teams comprised of current and retired educators, people in higher education, and school administrators who were specially trained to review the policies and operations of low performing schools and to develop recommendations for improvement (NC Public Schools et al., n.d.). The assistance teams observed teachers in the classroom, conducted demonstration lessons, assisted in aligning the curriculum to the standards and led instructional team meetings, as well as working with building principals on schoolwide issues (Holdzkom, 2001). The teams or the principals of the schools could recommend that certified personnel be required to take SBE-designated general knowledge tests, if they questioned the employees' general knowledge. Local superintendents or the SBE could recommend the dismissal of principals of low-performing schools (North Carolina Public Schools et al., n.d.).

In all schools that attained high growth (10% more than expected growth), regardless of level of achievement, certified staff received up to $1500 each as incentive awards; teaching assistants received up to $500. In all schools that attained expected growth, but less than high growth, certified staff received up to $750, while teaching aides received up to $375 (North Carolina Public Schools et al., n.d.).

To enhance the potential of the ABCs program, the state made extraordinary efforts to improve the professionalism of its teaching corps and to attract high quality teachers. A 1996 report titled *A Profession in Jeopardy*, which was produced by the Public School Forum, called on the state to increase substantially its efforts toward teacher preparation and support. The following year, the General Assembly passed the Excellent Schools Act, which responded to many of the forum's recommendations. The act was a comprehensive plan for improving student achievement, reducing teacher attrition and rewarding teachers' knowledge and skills. It raised teacher salaries, increased standards for teacher preparation, encouraged their continuing education, and enhanced support for beginning teachers, including providing each with a compensated mentor teacher and providing extra paid school days for the new and mentor teacher prior to the school year (Education First Task Force, 2002).

North Carolina's efforts to improve teacher quality were among the most energetic in the nation. *Education Week's Quality Counts '99* awarded North Carolina an "A" for its efforts in this area. It had developed standards and assessments for beginning teachers and had implemented incentives for practicing teachers to improve their skills. In 1999 North Carolina had more teachers certified by the National Board for Professional Teaching Standards than any other state. The state rewarded teachers who achieved national certification with 12% salary raises. The state led the nation in investments in school-based performance incentives and had backed away from sanctions, such as requiring teachers in low-performing schools to take competency tests.

Recognizing the critical importance of the formative years in children's education, the state made substantial investments in early childhood education, as well. As mentioned above, Governor Jim Hunt had initiated Smart Start in 1993. In 2001 the General Assembly approved, at newly elected Governor Easley's urging, the creation of "More at Four," a program aimed at increasing at-risk preschool children's readiness for school, along with significant class-size reductions in Grades K-3 (Education First Task Force, 2002). That year most of the state's kindergarten class sizes were reduced, and in the 36 highest poverty and lowest performing elementary schools, K-3 classes were reduced to 15 students. Governor Easley had prioritized these education expenditures, even as he had proposed deep cuts elsewhere in the budget owing to economic recession.

Pursuing the vision that Governor Hunt had articulated, Governor Easley in 2001 created a task force of educators, business people, community activists, elected leaders and other concerned citizens from throughout North Carolina, and he charged the Education First Task Force, as the group was called, with "developing a road map to make North Carolina the national leader in education by 2010." He directed the group to strive to create an education system that was "superior and competitive." The task force divided itself into three committees which focused on (1) examining what was working in what came to be called "Hallmarks of Excellence" schools, those which had been substantially increasing student achievement, (2) finances and resources, and (3) teaching issues, drop-out rates and high school structures (Education First Task Force, 2002, pp. 2-3).

In its report, *Let's Finish the Job*, the task force emphasized four proposals:

- earned flexibility for high performing schools and districts,
- increased support to low-performing and high poverty districts,
- increased innovation in high schools, and
- modification of the ABCs to include targeting the achievement gap.

The Education First Task Force found that leadership was "an indispensable factor" in the "Hallmarks of Excellence" schools. Principals in these schools "set the tone." Sometimes leadership emanated from groups of committed teachers or from district leadership, the task force reported, but "(w)hatever the source of leadership it (was) an essential part of the school improvement equation" (p. 10).

The task force recommended that the state redouble its efforts to ensure that all children could read at grade level by Grade 3. To that end and to enhance the quality of the teaching corps in general, it urged the state to direct increased energy and resources toward recruiting and retaining highly qualified teachers. It noted that the teacher shortage was critical in North Carolina, and the schools and communities most in need of highly qualified teachers were least able to attract them. The task force made several recommendations to strengthen the teaching force, including incentives to draw highly qualified teachers to hard-to-staff schools and monetary incentives to recruit teachers into math, science and special education positions.

The task force endorsed Governor Easley's request in his proposed budget for 2002-2003 that the state increase the number of awards in the Teaching Fellowship Program by 100 per year and that the state continue its efforts to attract male and minority candidates. The task force noted that the fellowship program had already produced over 2,000 teachers who were working in the state, and that both the North Carolina Teacher of the Year and the national Walt Disney Teacher of the Year had been graduates of the program.

Thus, North Carolina continued its reform efforts well after the implementation of the ABCs. Progress seemed to inspire more dedication from private and public sector interests to the goal that North Carolina should be a national leader in education.

Yet, education reform in North Carolina was not without its detractors. For instance, the independent North Carolina think tank, the John Locke Foundation, which espoused conservative principles, such as reducing taxes, reducing welfare programs, reducing regulation of business, and ending government corruption and wasteful spending, as well as providing a sound, basic education to all children (John Locke Foundation, n.d.a), argued that the state's achievement expectations were too low and that since the 1990s, the state had adopted numerous costly reforms with-

out conducting cost-benefit analyses of the policies. The foundation recommended that the state jettison its ABCs assessments and rely on more
rigorous assessments with higher expectations. It also recommended
rewarding individual teachers based on the value they added to students'
performances. Finally, the foundation recommended deregulation and
decentralization of public school systems, while maintaining accountability for results, specifically abolishing tenure and inflexible certification
rules, giving districts more flexibility in allocation of resources and lifting
the state cap of 100 on charters to allow for the establishment of more
innovative schools (John Locke Foundation, n.d.b).

The merits of these criticisms notwithstanding, early in the twenty-first
century, North Carolina had in place a standards-based accountability system that was viewed as a model. The state had been a leader in the reform
movement, and it remained strongly committed to raising the academic
achievement of all North Carolina children. The state had supplemented
its ABCs program with early childhood programs and had worked aggressively to remediate low performance. Education advocates appeared to be
poised to do what was necessary to make North Carolina first in the
nation in education.

## Progress Under the ABCs of Public Education

North Carolina made significant progress in achievement during the
1990s; in fact its growth was the highest in the nation as measured on the
National Assessment of Educational Achievement (NAEP). Students progressed on the state achievement tests, as well. The state received praise
for the clarity of its standards and their alignment with assessments, for its
emphasis on raising teacher quality, for the comprehensiveness of its
reforms, and for the widespread support from various sectors of the state
and community which backed the reforms, all of which contributed to the
success of the reforms in raising achievement. Indeed, there was a rare
degree of unity behind North Carolina's ABCs.

Beginning in 1992-1993, students made gains on state tests. In 1992-
93, 52.9% of students scored at or above Achievement Level III, or *proficient*, in both reading and math. From there proficiency rose each year
through 2001-2002, when 74.7% of students were at Level III or higher in
both reading and math. In 2000-2001, 60% of schools made Expected
Growth or High Growth, and that percentage rose to 75% in 2001-2002
(Fabrizio, 2005).

Comprehensive assistance was provided to low performing schools,
with impressive results. Fifteen low performing schools from throughout
the state were assigned assistance teams in August 1997, and by July 1998,

14 of the 15 schools had made their expected growth, and 13 had achieved exemplary status (later called "high growth") by attaining 10% above "expected growth." The 15th school was designated "adequate" on its performance. The percentage of students at or above grade level rose from 43% in 1996-97 to 53% in 1997-98. In each of the 15 schools, assistance teams of 3 to 5 educators had worked throughout the school year assisting the staff in aligning instruction with state standards, modeling effective teaching practices, mentoring teachers and helping locate additional resources for the schools. Local school systems provided assistance such as equipment and materials, volunteers, funding, staff, building improvements and staff training (North Carolina Public Schools, 1998).

Lou Fabrizio, director of the Division of Accountability Services, North Carolina Department of Public Instruction (DPI), explained that the assistance teams found good teachers in the low-performing schools, but they had not been teaching to the standards. So the process identified a critical gap in the system, that while solid standards had been developed, the information was not well disseminated to teachers. The DPI acted on this information to ensure that students were being taught to the standards (personal communication, December 6, 2005). In 2001, North Carolina implemented the High Priority Schools Act, which concentrated state resources on the highest-poverty and lowest-performing elementary schools and on continually low-performing middle and high schools (Fabrizio, 2005).

The SBE announced that it would offer support to more low-performing schools through a new program called NC HELPS, North Carolina Helping Education in Low-Performing Schools, a joint project among the governor's office, the university system, community colleges, and the SBE and DPI. NC HELPS would provide financial resources and professional development for teachers and administrators "to build and sustain their capacity for long-term change." A wide variety of services would be directed at curriculum alignment, teaching practices and data analysis (North Carolina Public Schools, 1998, p. 2). Funds would come from existing federal grants and from fundraising efforts, and schools could qualify for as much as $100,000 to design and institute reforms (Manzo, 1999). In 1996-1997, 7.5% of K-8 schools were low performing by state standards. In 2001-2002, only .8% of K-12 schools were low performing. It was believed that North Carolina was the first state in which such intervention had shown significant progress (North Carolina Department of Public Instruction, 2003).

North Carolina Grade 4 *reading* scores on the NAEP rose from 212 in 1992 to 222 in 2002, while the White-Black gap grew from 26 to 29 points, though the latter increase was not statistically significant. The Grade 8 reading score rose from 262 in 1998 to 265 in 2002, and the

**Table 5.1.   North Carolina Fourth and Eighth Grade Scores
on the NAEP 1990-2003**

| | 4th Grade | | | | 8th Grade | | | |
|---|---|---|---|---|---|---|---|---|
| | Math | | Reading | | Math | | Reading | |
| Year | NC Avg. | Nat. Avg. | NC Avg. | Nat. Avg. | NC Avg. | Nat. Avg. | NC Avg. | Nat. Avg. |
| 1990 | | | | | 250 | 262 | | |
| 1992 | 213 | 219 | 212 | 215 | 258 | 267 | | |
| 1994 | | | 214 | 212 | | | | |
| 1996 | 224 | 222 | | | 268 | 271 | | |
| 1998 | | | 213 | 213 | | | 262 | 261 |
| 2000 | 230 | 224 | | | 276 | 272 | | |
| 2002 | | | 222 | 217 | | | 265 | 263 |
| 2003 | 242 | 234 | 221 | 216 | 281 | 276 | 262 | 261 |

*Source:*   National Center for Education Statistics (n.d.): http://nces.ed.gov/nationsreport-card/states/profile.asp

White-Black gap of 25 points in 1998 did not change significantly. Data were not sufficient to permit a reliable estimate of the White-Hispanic gap. On the NAEP *math* test, gains were quite dramatic. The North Carolina Grade 4 score rose from 213 in 1992 to 242 in 2003. The White-Black gap for Grade 4 math narrowed slightly during the interim from 30 to 26 points. The Grade 8 math score rose from 250 in 1992 to 281 in 2003. The White-Black gap widened during the time span from 30 to 34 points, but this widening of the gap was not statistically significant.

North Carolina's SAT scores improved significantly from the early 1990s through 2002, as well, and the gap between the average U.S. score and North Carolina's average score narrowed substantially. In 1990, North Carolina's average SAT score of 948 was 53 points below the U.S. average of 1001. By 2002, the gap had narrowed to 22 points with North Carolina's average score at 998 and the U.S. average at 1020.

While North Carolina had made strong growth in the 1990s, educators throughout the state expressed ambivalence about the ABCs, given that the program held them accountable for students' performances. In 2001, the North Carolina Association of Educators (NCAE) conducted focus groups with educators throughout the state to gather their concerns and recommendations. The resulting report expressed general support for the notion of accountability, while noting numerous unintended consequences of the ABCs program that required attention "if we are to fully embrace the state's system of accountability." The report listed numerous positive outcomes of the ABCs program, including: recognition of the need to close the achievement gap, increased attention to underserved schools, measurement of growth in students, and improvement of North Carolina's status in education. The report also related concerns raised in the focus groups, such as the need for professional development to understand and use assessment information, the need for increased public education on the various performance categories for schools, frustration with the overemphasis on drilling and test preparation, and the need for greater family and community accountability. The NCAE's recommendations included increased communication and information; professional development; more individualized feedback on student performance on tests and refinement of tests for severely cognitively challenged students; greater stakeholder accountability, especially for families and communities; delaying of testing for ESL students; and finally, respect for the contributions of educators and greater responsiveness to their concerns about the accountability system (NCAE, 2002). The document was noteworthy for its overall support of education standards and accountability, for its concern for students, and for the reasonableness of the recommendations.

Lou Fabrizio opined that the relationship between the NCAE and the SBE is open and respectful. SBE members tend to be K-12 teachers or people in higher education. NCAE lets the SBE know of its concerns and the Board is receptive. Several years ago the state surveyed teachers on working conditions, and the governor worked closely with NCAE on the surveys, with what Fabrizio felt were positive results (personal communication, December 6, 2005). Thus, it appears that a relatively collaborative relationship between teachers and education governance exists in North Carolina, in contrast to the much more adversarial relationship that is found between teachers and education governance in some states, especially non right-to-work states, such as Massachusetts.

While progress under the ABCs program was impressive, the program did not disaggregate student scores by race, as NCLB would later require, so it was possible for schools to make or exceed their growth goals while leaving minority students far behind. And in fact, nearly half of minority students were not achieving proficiency on the tests. On the 2001 SAT tests, the Black-White gap for North Carolina was 206 points, 5 points wider than the national gap. Moreover, minority students in North Carolina were underrepresented in honors and Advanced Placement courses. And more than twice the percentage of White than percentage of Black students who took AP exams in 2000 received a score of 3 or higher (Reid, 2002). These gaps were not unique to North Carolina, of course, but they were nevertheless troubling.

The North Carolina Justice Center, a nonprofit antipoverty organization, reported on the Achievement Gap in North Carolina in 2000, 2001 and 2002, finding a "disturbingly wide and persistent gap in achievement" between White and minority students in 2000 and finding the gap virtually unchanged in 2002. The Justice Center reported that, despite *Leandro*, "a significant number of children of color—Black, Hispanic and Native American students—(were) not receiving a sound basic education" (Reid, 2002, p. 1), as evidenced by wide achievement gaps. The General Assembly in 2001 mandated that closing the achievement gap be incorporated into the ABCs by 2002-2003.

The ABCs, like the accountability systems of the other states, have been evaluated by several education-focused organizations and foundations. The Fordham Foundation published a thoroughgoing analysis of the states' accountability systems in 2004, and it deemed the overall quality of North Carolina's standards *fair* (3), with considerable variability, for example, outstanding middle school math standards, but poor middle school reading standards. Fordham found North Carolina's accountability policies to be *solid* (4) before the enactment of the NCLB, and expected them to rise to *outstanding* (5) if the state implemented NCLB requirements (Cross, Rebarbar, & Torres, 2004).

In a separate 2005 evaluation, "The State of State ENGLISH Standards," Fordham gave North Carolina a B on its English standards; the major fault noted was the lack of a list of recommended literature for high school (Stotsky, 2005). Fordham's 2005 "The State of State MATH Standards" gave North Carolina a C, identifying "pervasive shortcomings such as an overemphasis on patterns, data analysis, and probability, and an inappropriate use of technology." The evaluators noted the overuse of calculators and the lack of progressive skill development (Klein, 2005, pp. 89-90).

In 2005 *Education Week* awarded North Carolina generally high scores on its standards and accountability system, ranking the state 26th with an $83 = B$ as an overall grade for standards and accountability. Thus ratings of North Carolina's standards and accountability system were generally good, though evaluators found fault with various aspects of the program, such as the lack of a reading list in English, and over reliance on calculators in math.

Helen Ladd and Arnaldo Zelli of the Terry Sanford Institute of Public Policy at Duke University conducted an assessment of North Carolina's ABCs program, focusing on its ability to modify the behavior of school principals in ways consonant with the goals of the program. They interviewed a random sample of seventy-four principals in 1997 and again in 1999, and they found that the ABCs program was a "powerful tool" in changing principals' behaviors in ways that furthered the objectives of the

ABCs (2001, p. 9). The overwhelming majority had focused attention on low-performing students since the program's inception. They had redirected resources to teaching reading, writing and math and had encouraged work on test taking skills.

However, an unintended consequence of the ABCs program that Ladd and Zelli detected was that it appeared to lessen the ability of low-performing schools to attract strong teachers and principals, which would increase the disparities among students' and schools' performances. Principals in the lower performing schools felt that they had limited ability to remove poor teachers, because they could not attract highly qualified replacements. High performing schools, where teachers might win bonuses and would not risk being labeled incompetent and removed, were clearly more attractive to teachers. For the same reasons, the incentives and sanctions associated with the ABCs would make it difficult to attract strong principals to low performing schools. Schools and districts throughout the nation faced this challenge of attracting and retaining highly qualified teachers in schools with high percentages of high risk students.

## NORTH CAROLINA AND NCLB

### North Carolina's Response to NCLB

North Carolina stands out not only for its early adoption of standards-based reform, but for its positive response to NCLB. The State Board of Education (SBE) and the Department of Public Instruction (DPI) stressed the compatible goals of the state's ABCs of Public Education and the No Child Left Behind Act. "North Carolina is working to blend our state standards with the new federal standards" proclaimed a public information brochure sponsored by the Public Schools of North Carolina, the SBE and DPI titled "ABCs of Public Education Connects With No Child Left Behind" (n.d., p. 1). The SBE proposed incorporating NCLB into the ABCs incentive bonuses for 2002-2003, awarding $600 to each certified staff member in schools earning the ABC designation of Expected Growth, an additional $600 to each certified staff member in schools designated High Growth, and $600 to each certified employee in schools making AYP under NCLB. Thus, certified staff could receive $1,800 each. As mentioned above, North Carolina's General Assembly had mandated in 2001 that beginning in 2002-2003, closing the achievement gap would be a component of growth in student performance in all schools. In addition to what NCLB required of the state, North Carolina continued to measure the progress of individual students through its ABCs model.

Meanwhile, the Public School Forum asked the SBE and the DPI to join the forum in identifying the strategies that would enable the state to meet the challenges of NCLB. The Public School Forum Study Group 10, consisting of over 70 educators, business and community leaders and elected officials collaborated for six months in developing their recommendations for integrating NCLB's requirements with the state's ABCs program and achieving the goals of each. The study group divided its task into three central issues: (1) identifying elements critical to transitioning to NCLB, (2) meeting the NCLB requirement for testing in science (NCLB required that states add science to the subjects to be tested by 2005-2006), and (3) educating the public about the requirements and implications of NCLB.

The study group acknowledged that meeting AYP requirements within all subgroups would be an extraordinary challenge for North Carolina, as would meeting the NCLB requirement that all children be taught by highly qualified teachers. At the time 17% of students were taught by teachers without a major or minor in their subjects. Schools with high turnover rates, which were often low-performing schools, were forced to accept underqualified teachers. Many more schools were expected to be identified as needing improvement under NCLB than under the ABCs, so the state would have to expand greatly its support for low-performing schools. The study group suggested that the "overriding challenge" might not be meeting the performance goals of NCLB, but maintaining public confidence in the public school system as NCLB testing requirements exposed weaknesses in the public education system that the ABCs had not addressed, especially the lower performance of subgroups, such as Blacks, Hispanics and economically disadvantaged students. Therefore the study group recommended that state and local school systems launch a "massive re-education job to make sure that policymakers, parents and the public at large understand the differences between accountability as defined by the ABCs and by NCLB" (pp. 5-6).

Owing to recent downsizing of the DPI, it had eliminated its role in professional development, and other entities, such as the UNC Center for School Leadership Development, schools of education and school-business partnerships had taken over educational professional development. The study group urged that the state assess its capacity to support low-performing schools and better align and coordinate the resources and programs that existed. Furthermore, the study group recommended that the state revise its funding formula to provide much greater resources to the schools that had the most at-risk students, especially students who might fall into more than one at-risk category.

Regarding Task One—identifying the elements critical to transitioning to NCLB, the Group recommended ensuring that Congress fulfill its financial obligations to the state as the state reorganized and refocused its resources to achieve greater efficiency and to target the greatest needs, and as it adopted aggressive strategies to ensure that all children were taught by highly qualified teachers. As for Task Two, meeting NCLB's science mandates, the study group noted that 1994 NAEP scores showed that North Carolina students were poorly prepared in science, and it suggested that the state's focus on reading and math was partially to blame for this. The study group urged that the state prioritize science education in order to ensure the state's economic well-being. The study group recommended that the SBE enter into a formal agreement with the Burroughs Wellcome Center for Mathematics, Science and Technology and create a "blue ribbon advisory board" to make North Carolina a leader in science education by drawing on the best practices from throughout the nation. The group recommended greater coordination with DPI staff, the Math & Science Network at UNC Center for School Leadership and Development, and other institutions of higher education to develop the curriculum and assessment, as well as to provide professional development for science teachers.

By the time that the study group's report was produced, Task Three the massive public education campaign regarding the implications of NCLB, had already begun. Members of the General Assembly had been briefed, five regional seminars for education reporters and public school information officers were scheduled, and Public School Forum and DPI staff were presenting information programs on request to gatherings of educators, business leaders and community organizations. This energetic and proactive approach exemplified the actions and attitudes of North Carolina education advocates since the 1990s.

As mentioned above, one of the greatest challenges for North Carolina in meeting the requirements of the NCLB was to have a highly qualified teacher in every classroom by 2006. Each year the state had to fill 10,000 to 11,000 teaching positions, yet the state's teacher education programs produced only 3,500 qualified candidates each year, of whom only about 2,500 entered North Carolina classrooms. Only 35% of the state's paraprofessionals met NCLB requirements in 2003. The state subsequently began including paraprofessionals in staff development with positive results, both in terms of building morale and in enhancing their credentials (North Carolina Association of School Administrators, 2004). Through the North Carolina Partnership for Excellence, the business community provided professional development for teachers, often using private sector models, such as its High Performance Model, which focused on "customer" needs (North Carolina Partnership for Excellence, n.d.).

Because of the progress that North Carolina students had made on their ABCs tests in the past decade, the state was able to set high initial proficiency targets for NCLB. The targets for Grades 3-8 in math and reading/language arts were 74.6 and 68.9% at proficiency, respectively, in

**Table 5.2.   NC Targets for Having All Students at Proficiency in English and Math by 2013-2014**

|  | Grades 3-8 (%) | | Grade 10 (%) | | | |
|  |  |  | Reading/ELA* | | Math* | |
| Year | Reading | Math | Original | Revised | Original | Revised |
|---|---|---|---|---|---|---|
| 2004-07 | 76.7 | 81 | (64.4) | 35.4 | (66.2) | 70.8 |
| 2007-10 | 84.4 | 87.3 | (76) | 56.9 | (77.4) | 80.5 |
| 2010-13 | 92.2 | 93.7 | (88) | 78.4 | (88.7) | 90.2 |
| 2013-14 | 100 | 100 | (100) | 100 | (100) | 100 |

*Grade 10 proficiency goals were revised in 2005 to reflect the new method of measuring AYP for high school.
Notes: North Carolina Consolidated State Application May, 2003 Submission and "Adequate Yearly Progress in North Carolina" accessed at http://www.dpi.state.nc.us/nclb/abcayp/overview/aup?&print+true

2002-2003. For Grade 10 the proficiency targets were 54.9 and 52% for math and reading/language arts, respectively, in 2002-2003. The average baseline proficiency rates for all students were higher than these starting points, but some subgroups, especially Black, LEP and disabled high school students were performing at levels significantly below these initial targets (North Carolina Department of Public Instruction, 2003a). These relatively high initial targets would mean that North Carolina had a much less daunting task to meet NCLB's requirement of all students in all subgroups attaining proficiency by 2013-2014 than would California, for instance, with its beginning targets of 15% at proficient. Yet, even for North Carolina and other states with high baselines of proficiency, meeting the NCLB targets for 2013-2014 would require Herculean efforts.

In 2003, the General Assembly required the SBE to identify the schools that had made AYP, study the instructional, administrative and fiscal practices at those schools, and develop models to assist struggling schools based on those practices. The law called for enlisting the help of the schools of education in the state university system and the University of North Carolina Center for School Leadership Development in this endeavor (Education Commission of the States, 2004).

In keeping with other concerted efforts within North Carolina to maximize the potential of NCLB, the North Carolina Association of School Administrators in 2004 made numerous recommendations for amendments to NCLB and for increased funding for its implementation. The document enthusiastically endorsed the objectives of NCLB and pledged the dedication of its members to the causes of closing the achievement gap and helping all children to achieve proficiency. It asked for revisions to NCLB's requirements in order to render the act more workable and successful. Among its requests were that Congress or USDOE modify the AYP formula to recognize progress and to distinguish schools that had missed AYP by only one or two targets from schools that were failing in numerous categories; that Congress make allowances for the special challenges of students with disabilities and LEP students, and not penalize them and their schools unreasonably; and that USDOE allow North Carolina to measure progress based on individual student growth, in accordance with its ABCs model. The association also asked for more flexibility in meeting the highly qualified teacher in every classroom requirements, especially with regard to special education teachers, who taught children in all subjects. Finally, the group noted that for the past three fiscal years Congress had not allocated the full amounts budgeted for NCLB implementation, which left states unfairly burdened with the costs associated with the congressional mandates. The group reiterated its commitment to complying with NCLB and to fulfilling its objectives, averring "While No Child Left Behind presents us with many challenges, we find those challenges worthy of our best efforts as education leaders" (2004, p. 11). Thus this group of education leaders, like so many others in North Carolina, demonstrated its commitment to the ABCs' and NCLB's goals.

## North Carolina's Progress Under NCLB

As was the case with the vast majority of the states, North Carolina's definition of "proficiency" that was used for AYP calculations for NCLB was substantially different from what was deemed proficient on the National Assessment of Educational Progress (NAEP). In 2001-2002, for instance, 72% of North Carolina students scored at or above Level III on Grade 4 reading tests, which was North Carolina's definition of proficient. On the NAEP, 25% of Grade 4 students scored at or above proficient, and 60% scored at or above basic. Such discrepancies called the legitimacy of the ABCs into question and explained the John Locke Foundation's call for jettisoning the ABCs' assessments and adopting more rigorous ones with higher cut scores.

Similarly, growth was measured differently under the ABCs and the NCLB, which resulted in discrepancies between schools that made acceptable progress (expected or higher than expected progress) under the ABCs and those that made acceptable progress (AYP) under NCLB. In 2003-2004, North Carolina's SBE approved the category of *Honor School of Excellence* to acknowledge *Schools of Excellence* (the top ranking for schools under the ABCs) that made AYP. The DPI and SBE were making concerted efforts to educate the public about the differences in national and state accountability systems and to assure them that North Carolina's children were making academic progress.

North Carolina students continued to make gains in achievement following implementation of NCLB, through progress was slow. On state tests, students showed improvements among all groups and narrowed the achievement gaps as well in both reading/English Language Arts and math (The Education Trust, 2004). Despite this improvement, because of increasing expectations of growth, fewer schools were measuring up according to the ABCs model and in terms of making AYP under NCLB.

In 2003-2004, under the ABCs, 75% of schools made high or expected growth, whereas in 2004-2005, 69% made expected or higher growth (Fabrizio, 2005). Fabrizio explained that each year growth expectations were recalculated, and it was increasingly difficult to keep up the same pace of improvement (personal communication, December 6, 2005). All states faced the same challenge. By 2005-2006, the percentage of schools making expected or higher growth was down to 54.3 (North Carolina Department of Public Instruction, 2007). This drop was a function not only of the difficulty in keeping up the pace of improvement, but of the state's having raised the passing score on the math tests.

In October 2006, in response to concern regarding the gap between proficiency in math on the ABCs and on the NAEP, the state raised the passing bar on the math tests. The new cut scores were applied to the tests for the 2005-2006 school year and resulted in fewer students passing the test, though the raised standards made it difficult to compare student performances in 2004-2005 to 2005-2006. As to the ever more daunting task of meeting the higher standards, SBE Chair Howard Lee declared, "The standards being set today are designed to help prepare North Carolina youngsters for the challenges of the twenty-first century. We know our students need a higher level of preparation to be ready for the challenges ahead" (Public School Forum, 2006b, p. 1).

North Carolina set its proficiency goal for measuring AYP under NCLB for 2003-2004 at 68.9% for reading and 74.6% in math in Grades 3-8, and at 52.0% in reading and 54.9% in math in Grade 10. That year 70.5% of schools made AYP. The following year, performance targets rose to 76.7% in reading and 81% in math in Grades 3-8, and they changed to 35.4% in reading and 70.8% in math in Grade 10. (As shown in Table 5.2, AYP targets had been recalculated based on new tests and cut scores for high school students.) With the higher targets in 2004-2005, the percentage of schools that made AYP dropped to 56.3% (Fabrizio, 2005).

Yet in many cases, schools that had not met their proficiency targets were very close to reaching them. For instance, of the 10,878 school targets in the state (each subgroup in each school had a target in each sub-

**Table 5.3. Percentages of North Carolina Schools
Meeting State and NCLB Growth Standards**

| Years | Expected or Higher Growth—ABCs | AYP-NCLB |
|---|---|---|
| 2003-2004 | 75% | 70.5% |
| 2004-2005 | 69% | 56.3% |
| 2005-2006 | 54.3% | 45.2% |

ject), 95.5% were achieved. The subgroups with the highest percentages of achieved targets were multiracial (100%), White (99.7%) and Asian (99.2%), while students with disabilities (76.8%), LEP students (81.7%) and Black students (87.7%) had met the lowest percentages of their targets. Of Title I schools, 63% made AYP in 2004-2005 (Fabrizio, 2005).

In 2005-2006 only 45% of North Carolina's schools made AYP (North Carolina Department of Public Instruction, 2007). Table 5.3 shows the percentage of schools making expected or higher growth under the ABCs and the percentage of schools making AYP under NCLB. The table illustrates the increasing difficulty in keeping up the expected rate of academic growth and in reaching the 2013-2014 targets for NCLB.

The significant progress that North Carolina students made on the *NAEP* during the 1990s slowed in the early years of the twenty-first century, and in some cases was partially lost after implementation of NCLB. The math score for North Carolina Grade 4 students rose from 213 in 1992 to 242 in 2003, and then dropped to 241 in 2005, though this drop was not statistically significant. The Grade 8 average score rose from 250 in 1990 to 281 in 2003 and to 282 in 2005.

The average Grade 4 reading score rose from 212 in 1992 to 221 in 2003, but then declined slightly to 217 in 2005. The average Grade 8 reading score was 262 in both 1998 and 2003, but declined slightly to 258 in 2005. The achievement gap between Black and White students narrowed slightly in Grade 4 math from 30 points in 1992 to 25 points in 2005, but only by 2 points between 1990 and 2005 in Grade 8 math. The Black-White gap did not change significantly in Grade 4 reading, but it increased by 3 points in Grade 8 grade reading between 1998 and 2005. Thus, results of 2005's NAEP showed stagnation.

Finally, North Carolina's SAT scores continued to climb and gain on the national average, although the state's average dipped two points in 2006. The state's average score rose from 998 in 2002, which was 22 points below the national average, to 1010 in 2005, which was 18 points below the national average of 1028. It dropped two points to 1008 in 2006, but owing to a larger drop in the national average, North Carolina

**Table 5.4.   North Carolina and U.S. SAT Scores 1990-2006**

| Year | North Carolina | U.S. Average | Gap |
|------|---------------|--------------|-----|
| 1990 | 948 | 1,001 | 53 |
| 1991 | 952 | 999 | 47 |
| 1992 | 961 | 1,001 | 40 |
| 1993 | 964 | 1,003 | 39 |
| 1994 | 964 | 1,003 | 39 |
| 1995 | 970 | 1,010 | 40 |
| 1996 | 976 | 1,013 | 37 |
| 1997 | 978 | 1,016 | 38 |
| 1998 | 982 | 1,017 | 35 |
| 1999 | 986 | 1,016 | 30 |
| 2000 | 988 | 1,019 | 31 |
| 2001 | 992 | 1,020 | 28 |
| 2002 | 998 | 1,020 | 22 |
| 2003 | 1,001 | 1,026 | 25 |
| 2004 | 1,006 | 1,026 | 20 |
| 2005 | 1,010 | 1,028 | 18 |
| 2006 | 1,008 | 1,021 | 13 |

*Source*:   Public School Forum (2006a, n.d.b).

narrowed the gap between its and the national average to 13 points in 2006. Table 5.4 shows North Carolina's remarkable improvement in SAT scores and the narrowing of the gap between the North Carolina and national average scores.

The fact that growth in the early twenty-first century did not match the pace of the remarkable growth in the 1990s suggested that the improvements and innovations to the school system, such as developing standards, aligning them with assessments, making sure that teachers were actually applying the content standards, and targeting more resources at low-performing schools had produced the bulk of the results they would produce and that even greater resources and more innovation would be needed to address the needs of the most at-risk children.

## CONCLUSION AND PROSPECTS FOR ATTAINMENT OF NCLB BY 2014

North Carolina's approach to standards-based reform has been proactive, holistic, collaborative, and energetic. The state led the reform movement as one of the first to adopt curriculum standards that were aligned with assessments and to hold districts, schools and students accountable for achievement. Leadership from various sectors in the state rallied behind education reform as an obligation to the state's youth and as a necessity for the state's economic future. When schools were first identified as low-performing, the state responded quickly by providing additional resources and expert support teams that showed remarkable success in turning schools around. Performance improved across the board. In fact, North Carolina led the nation in improvement in NAEP math and reading scores in the 1990s. When the booming economy of the 1990s ended and the first years of the twenty-first century saw increasing deficits for the state, education advocates and other political leaders ensured that education would not suffer. Advocate groups like the Public School Forum urged that this was the time to redouble the state's efforts in education, because the workforce of the future required a much stronger knowledge and skill base than that of the past.

The Education First Task Force also urged forging ahead with even more determination to bring the state to its goal of being First in Education in 2010. In the past decade, North Carolina students had risen from among the lowest performing in the nation to just above average. "Barely above average, however, is not where North Carolina young people belong," declared the Education First Task Force in its report *Let's Finish the Job*. "It's time for the state to finish the job that it started in the eighties" (2002, p. 6). The report listed the challenges the state still faced: the achievement gap, unacceptably high dropout rates, too many under-qualified or out-of-field teachers, too many graduates who were unprepared for the work force and too many students needing remediation upon entering postsecondary education institutions. When the state was confronted with the more demanding requirements of NCLB, rather than balking at the impossibility of the demands, or lashing out at the unprecedented intrusion by the national government in public education, or complaining about the additional costs, the state met the challenge, and public and private sector interests came together to determine how the state could martial its resources to meet the extraordinary challenges posed by NCLB.

In December 2006, the Public School Forum's Study Group XII produced another report, *Creating Internationally Competitive Schools*, which called on the state to rethink fundamentally its notion of competitiveness. No longer could the state afford to compare itself to other states. In the current climate of off-shoring and outsourcing, American workers would have to compete globally, and it was up to state education systems to prepare them to do so. Study Group XII supplied recommendations in response to three questions: (1) What should be done to bring the state's math and science education up to internationally competitive standards? (2) How could the state become a national leader in developing a curriculum that would prepare students for global competition? (3) How could North Carolina best provide the professional development for its teaching corps to achieve these goals? The study group's recommendations included raising standards beyond proficient in math and science, and focusing not just on bringing up the lowest-performing students, but on challenging the strongest students; lengthening the school year (America, it noted has the shortest school year in the industrialized world); more aggressive recruiting of math and science teachers, including differentiated pay; revising the curriculum to provide a more global focus, for instance through expanded language options and promoting exchanges, and through more emphasis on technology; and various measures to strengthen teaching quality (Public School Forum's Study Group XII, 2006). This was yet another example of how the state and its political and educational leadership, rather than shrinking from the overwhelming demands of NCLB, were preparing to meet those requirements and more.

North Carolina was also taking steps to acknowledge and address its high dropout rates. While the state had been reporting its dropout rate at approximately 5% per year, national studies had ranked North Carolina among the 10 states with the highest dropout rates, at nearly 40%. The Public School Forum conducted its own research into the matter and reported in February 2007 that it had found the 40% figure to be correct. The SBI announced that it would be adopting a formula similar to that used by the forum.[3]

Grissmer and Flanagan identified several key components of North Carolina's accountability system that explained its early success, including sound and integrated standards and assessments and good computerized feedback that allowed the tests to be used for diagnostic purposes; positive and negative incentives for improvement; shifting of resources to lowest performing schools, along with expectations that all children would achieve; increased flexibility at the local level; and perseverance over an extended period of time. The widespread continued commitment that Grissmer and Flanagan deemed essential was still very visible in 2007. For instance, Governor Easley, who had run on his education record and had been reelected in 2004, announced in late October 2005 his plan to raise teacher salaries to the national average. This would help reduce the teacher shortage in North Carolina.

A 2004 study of first-generation accountability systems (Mintrop & Trujillo) found that the effectiveness of such systems depended on, among other factors, their including a comprehensive bundle of strategies, emphasis on relationship building and a strong commitment by the state. All of these factors were present in North Carolina. The state continued to exhibit the leadership, energy, resourcefulness, innovation and determination that had spawned the reform movement in the 1980s and 1990s. For example, Wake County, which included the Research Triangle, had been operating an innovative program to integrate students by family income levels so as to reduce concentrations of at-risk children in any one school. Furthermore, several of North Carolina's universities were collaborating with the business sector and education leaders to improve the quality of public education in the state. The synergy produced from the partners' collective vision of their state as a national leader in education, from the capacities and resources that each had to offer, and from the confidence generated by the progress of the 1990s more than compensated for the slowing of progress in the early twenty-first century. With this leadership, vision and resources, North Carolina appeared to be well situated to realize its goal of being a national leader in education. Whether it would be First in Education in 2010 in terms of NAEP scores was questionable, given its high percentage of children in poverty and its critical teacher shortage, but if it stayed the course, North Carolina surely would be viewed as a national model in terms of education leadership, education reform and progress.

Reaching the NCLB goal of having all children proficient in reading and math by 2012-2014 was more elusive. North Carolina's greatest challenges to meeting the goals were its increasing percentages of Hispanic and Black students, who tended to perform less well on tests, and the critical shortage of highly qualified teachers, especially in schools and districts with higher percentages of high-risk students. The latter challenge exacerbated the former, as it was these minority and oftentimes disadvantaged children whose need for highly qualified teachers was especially great. Fabrizio suggested that educators would have to be much more innovative to meet the needs of these at-risk or low-performing students.

The resources, capacities and commitment that would serve the state in progressing toward its goals of being First in Education in 2010 and of being internationally competitive would advance the state toward NCLB's targets. However, the former two goals were relative and conceivably achievable, especially given North Carolina's determination, whereas the latter goal was absolute and much less foreseeable, not only for North Carolina, but for any state, if the Act's requirements were not modified substantially.

## NOTES

1.  This and other information on school finance, student demographics, and teacher union membership in this section, as well as information on the

history and efforts of the Public School Forum in this and later sections was found, unless otherwise noted, at the Web site of The Public School Forum at http://www.ncforum.org

2.  Information on the recommendations of Study Group 10 was found in a document titled "Meeting the education challenge of 2003: Building the capacity and the will to meet the challenges of the federal government's No Child Left Behind Act, 2003, retrieved November 13, 2005 from www.ncforum.org/about/milestones.html.

3.  North Carolina has gathered drop out data since 1999-2000, when the rate was reported as 6.43%. It declined to 4.78 in 2002-2003 and then began to climb again. Thus is is not clear whether the ABCs of Public Education have had an effect on drop out rates. The 2006 Drop Out Report can be seen at http://www.ncpublicschools.org/docs/ schoolimprovement/effective/ dropout/2005-06/annualreport.pdf

## REFERENCES

Barone, M., & Cohen, R. E. (2005). *The almanac of Amercian politics*. Washington, DC: The National Journal Group.

Buxton, J.B. (2003, April). *Eight lessons from orth Carolina*. Paper presented at the Implementing the No Child Left Behind Act Conference in Washington, DC sponsored by the Progressive Policy Institute, National Center on Education and Economy, and Thomas B. Fordham Foundation.

Cross, R., Rebarber, T., & Torres, J. (2004). *Grading the systems: The guide to state standards, tests, and accountability policies*. Washington DC: The Fordham Foundation.

Education Commission of the States. (2004, July). *ECS report to the nation: State implementation of the No Child Left Behind Act: Respecting diversity among states*. Denver, CO: Author.

Education First Task Force. (2002). *Let's finish the job: Building a system of superior schools*. Raleigh: Author. Retrieved from http://ncforum.org/doclib/publications/collateral/ Finish_the_%20Job.pdf

The Education Trust. (2004). *Measured progress: Achievement rises and gaps narrow, but too slowly*. Washington, DC: Author.  Retrieved August 15, 2005, from http://www2.edtrust.org/NR/rdonleyres/F1C402F7-AB53-49ED-A9DC-27A41AA6E7E5/0MeasuredProgressSumma99F.pdf

Fabrizio, L. (2005). *North Carolina's testing and accountability program: A progress report*. Retrieved August 14, 2005, retrieved November 13, 2005 from http://www.lexile.com/conference2005/ presentations/Fabrizio.pdf

Grissmer, D., & Flanagan, A. (1998) *Exploring rapid achievement gains in North Carolina and Texas*. Washington, DC: National Education Goals Panel. Retrieved August 20, 2005 from http://govinfo.library.unt.edu/negp/reports/grissmer.pdf

Guillory, F. (2005). Straight-party and split-ticket voting. Chapel Hill: South Now, Center for the Study of the American South, University of North Carolina at

Chapel Hill. Retrieved November 13, 2005, from http://www.southnow.org/pubs/datanet.php

Holdzkom, D. (2001). Low-performing schools: So you've identified them—Now what? Charleston, WV: AEL policy briefs. (Appalachia Educational Laboratory, now called Edvantia). Retrieved July 25, 2005 from http://www.edvantia.org/ publications/pdf/PB0202.pdf

John Locke Foundation. (n.d.a). About the John Locke foundation. Retrieved November 13, 2005 from http://www.johnlocke.org/about/

John Locke Foundation. (n.d.b). Education: School standards & testing. Retrieved November 13, 2005 from http://www.johnlocke.org/agenda2004/standardstesting.html

Klein, D. (with Braams, B.J., Parker, T, Quirk, W., Schmid, W. & Wilson, S. W.). (2005). *The state of state MATH standards.* Washington, DC: Thomas B. Fordham Foundation. Retrieved November 12, 2005, from http://www.edexcellence.net/doc/ mathstandards05FINAL.pdf

Ladd, H. F., & Zelli, A. (2001). *School-based accountability in North Carolina: The responses of school principals.* Durham, NC: Terry Sanford Institute of Public Policy, Duke University.

Leandro v. State of North Carolina. (1997) 346NC336.

Manzo, K. K. (1999). North Carolina: Seeing a payoff. *Education Week Quality Counts '99,* p. 3. Retrieved November 12, 2005, from http://counts.edweek.org/sreports/qc99/ states/policy/nc-up.htm

Mintrop, H., & Trujillo, T. (2004). *Corrective action in low-performing schools: Lessons for NCLB implementation from state and district strategies in first-generation accountability systems* (CSE Report 641). Los Angeles: National Center for Research on Evaluation, Standards, and Student Testing (CRESST), University of California Los Angeles.

National Center for Education Statistics. (n.d.). *NAEP state profile, NC, 2006-2007.* Retrieved February 3, 2007, from http://nces.ed.gov/nationsreportcard/states/profile.asp

North Carolina Association of Educators. (2002). *NCAE recommendations for improving the ABCs.* Retrieved November 12, 2005 from http://www.ncae.org

North Carolina Association of School Administrators. (2004). *North Carolina Association of School Administrators' recommendations regarding the 'No Child Left Behind' Act.* Retrieved November 12, 2005, from http://www.aasa.org/ files/Word/PublicPolicy/North%20Carolina%20Association%20of%20School%20Administrators.doc

North Carolina Department of Public Instruction. (2003). *North Carolina and No Child Left Behind* (Briefing, p. 4). Raleigh: Author. Retrieved November 12, 2005, from http://www.ncforum.org/doclib/presentations/collateral/Presentations/nclb.pdf

North Carolina Department of Public Instruction. (2007). *The ABCs of public education: 2005-2006 growth and performance of North Carolina Public Schools, executive summary.* Raleigh: Author. Retrieved February 15, 2007, from http://www.ncpublicschools.org/ docs/accountability/reporting/abc/2005-06/exec-summ.pdf

North Carolina Department of Public Instruction. (n.d.a). *History of education in North Carolina.* Retrieved November 14, 2005, from www.ncpublicschools.org/ student/ history_of_ed.pdf

North Carolina Department of Public Instruction. (n.d.b). *North Carolina education initiatives.* Retrieved November 12, 2005, from http://teach4nc.org/schools/ initiatives.html

North Carolina Partnership for Excellence (n.d.) *NCPE business planning highlights.* Retrieved November 15, 2005, from http://www.ncpe-online.org/about/ index.htm

North Carolina Public Schools. (1998, July 7). *North Carolina's low-performing schools make progress* (News release). Retrieved July 30, 2005, at http:// www.ncpublicschools.org

North Carolina Public Schools. (n.d.a). *Office of Charter Schools.* Retrieved November 13, from http://www.ncpublicschools.org/charterschools/

North Carolina Public Schools. (n.d.b). *Organization: Superintendent.* Retrieved November 18, 2005, from http://www.ncpublicschools.org/organization/super- intendent

North Carolina Public Schools, North Carolina State Board of Education and North Carolina Department of Public Instruction. (n.d.). *ABCs of Public Edu- cation connects with No Child Left Behind.* Raleigh: Authors. Retrieved August 18, 2005, from www.abss.k12.nc.us/system/policies/nclb/abc-nclb.pdf

North Carolina State Board of Elections. (n.d.). 2006 Voter registration statistics. Retrieved February 10, 2007, from http://www.sboe.state.nc.us/

Public School Forum. (2006a, September 8). *The public school forum's Friday report.* Retrieved February 16, 2007, from http://www.ncforum.org

Public School Forum. (2006b, October 13). *The public school forum's Friday report.* Retrieved February 16, 2007, from http://www.ncforum.org

Public School Forum. (2007, February 16). *The public school forum's Friday report.* Retrieved February 16, 2007, from http://www.ncforum.org

Public School Forum. (n.d.a). *Our organization.* Retrieved November 17, 2005, from http://www.ncforum.org

Public School Forum. (n.d.b). *SAT gap narrows: Comparison of US & NC SAT scores.* Retrieved November 13, 2005, from http://www.ncforum.org

Public School Forum Study Group 10 (with North Carolina State Board of Educa- tion and Department of Public Instruction). (2003). *Meeting the education chal- lenge of 2003: Building the capacity and the will to meet the challenges of the federal government's No Child Left Behind Act.* Raleigh: Authors. Retrieved November 12, 2006, from http://www.ncforum.org/about/milestones.html

Public School Forum Study Group XII. (2006). *Creating internationally competitive schools.* Raleigh: Author. Retrieved February 15, 2007 from http://www .ncforum.org/doclib/ news/collateral/PSF%20Study%20Group.pdf

*Quality Counts* '99 North Carolina report card. [Special issue]. (1999). *Education Week,* 18(17), 165. Retrieved November 12, 2005, from http://counts.edweek .org/sreports/ qc99/states/ grades/nc-rc.htm

Reid, S. (2002). *The achievement gap 2002: An update.* Raleigh:  North Carolina Education & Law Project. (ERIC Document Reproduction Service No. ED471159)

Standards and accountability. *Quality Counts 2005*: No small change: Targeting money toward student performance. (2005, January). [Special issue]. *Education Week*. 86-91.

Stotsky, S. (2005). *The state of state ENGLISH standards*. Washington, DC: The Fordham Foundation.

U. S. Census. (n.d.) *Annual estimates of the population for the United States, regions, and states and for Puerto Rico: April 1, 2000 to July 1, 2006*. Retrieved February 10, 2007, from http://www.census.gov/popest/states/tables/NST-EST2006-01 .xls

# CHAPTER 6

---

# FLORIDA

---

## INTRODUCTION

For decades, those in the north have seen Florida as a sunny, pleasant, and just about perfect place to retire, especially since the state has no state income tax and no inheritance taxes. Maybe that accounts for Florida's being known as "the sunshine state" and for its being the fourth largest state in population size. In the first section of this chapter, the social, economic, and political environment for education reform in Florida will be discussed.

## Historical, Sociceonomic, and Political Characteristics

Many believe that the availability of air conditioning in Florida, which grew from 20% in 1950 to 95% in 2000, has been a crucial factor in the remarkable population growth in the state. Because of its temperate weather, Florida has the largest population of retired people in the United States, 19% of the state population in 2004. These physically active and healthy "baby boomers" will face retirement in growing numbers and are predicted to live many years beyond retirement (Barone & Cohen, 2005).

During the 1980s and 1990s, a healthy economy attracted many southerners and foreigners who flooded the state. Political refugees from Cuba

---

*Education Reform in the American States*
pp. 147–170

147

and Haiti were drawn to the state due to Florida's booming economy, the freedom of the United States, and the relative political stability. Many made their homes in Florida adding to its dramatic growth. Prior to this, Florida had the slowest population growth in the south. The state has also benefited financially from increases in foreign investment, especially investments coming from Latin America. This influx of money, the strong economy, and the large number of retirees have contributed to making Florida what is considered a "rich" state due to several major components such as a military presence, tourism, and agriculture (Barone & Cohen, 2005).

Florida voted overwhelmingly for George H. W. Bush in 1988 and again in 1992 due to a combination of support from southerners, comfortable retirees, business minded individuals, and Cubans in Miami and Dade Counties. But in 2000, the state had grown so rapidly and was so deeply divided that it became an important state to win for both of the major political parties. Only after the intervention of the U.S. Supreme Court did Florida enter the Republican column and thus determined the outcome of the presidency.

Historically Democratic, the state today is considered competitive politically, as was seen during the 2000 presidential election. The new diverse Florida has been influenced by military southerners, business minded Republicans, and anti-Castro Cubans, all of whom mostly support the Republican Party. In recent years, these groups, joined by right-leaning poor Whites, have voted Republican and have outnumbered the Democrats. In statewide elections, Republicans Governor Jeb Bush won by 2.9 million votes in 2000, and by 3.9 million in 2004.

Groups like the immigrants from Haiti, the Caribbean and Latin America, and African Americans from the South are joined by liberal retirees from the north to constitute the Democratic block. Many consider the state politically volatile since most of its residents are from somewhere else (although two thirds are from the United States) and most made their fortunes somewhere else.

According to the estimated 2004 U.S. Census, Florida has a population of 17,397,161, with a growth of 23.5% between 1990 and 2000. The state has a diverse population that includes 62.1% White (not Hispanic or Latino), 15.7% African American, 19.5% Hispanic or Latino, 2.1% Asian, and .5% Other (U.S. Census Bureau, 2005). A total of 23.1% of Florida residents speak a language other than English, and 16.7% are foreign born. A total of 79.9% are high school graduates, and 22.3% have a bachelor's degree or higher. The homeownership rate is 70.1%, and the median household income in 1999 was $38,819, with 12.5% of the state's population below the poverty line (U.S. Census Bureau, 2005).

## The State Educational System

Florida is a right to work state. The Florida Education Association (FEA), affiliated with National Education Association, American Federation of Teachers, and American Federation of Labor and Congress of Industrial Organizations, was first created in 1886. Today, it has more than 250,000 members and is the largest professional organization in the state.

There are 37 school districts in the state, 3,529 schools, and 260 charter schools. Per pupil expenditure in Florida is $,6540, giving the state a rank of 47th nationwide according to *Quality Counts 2005*. There are 144,955 teachers in the state. In 2005, there were 2,587,628 students in Florida's schools, with 37.7% of them in Title I schools. Almost half, 46%, are eligible for free or reduced lunch. The K-12 student population is diverse (*Quality Counts*, 2005). In 2007, the National Center for Education Statistics (NCES) reported that the ethnic/racial composition of Florida schools was 50.5% White; 24.1% Black; 23% Latino; 2.1% Asian/Pacific Islander, and 3% American Indian/Alaska Native.

In 2006, the state spent $16.4 billion on pre-K–12 education, and earned an overall equity grade of B from *Quality Counts* for allocation of funds for education. The state used the Florida Education Finance Program, a foundation formula that includes a cost-of-living adjustment, to establish a base per-pupil allocation (*Quality Counts*, 2006).

Private schools in Florida operate as businesses and are not licensed, approved, accredited or regulated by the Education Department. Students in private schools, 15% of the entire public school population, are not required to participate in the state's testing program (Florida Department of Education, 2007a). The current number of private schools is estimated at 3,095, which serve a total of 430,880 students (LaPolt & St. John, 2002; National Association for the Advancement of Colored People, NAACP, 2002). Florida is known for its school choice and voucher plans nationwide.

Governor Jeb Bush, who is fluent in Spanish in a state that is 16.8% Latino (the state's largest minority group) and is the president's brother, had worked hard on educational accountability long before NCLB and is known as a strong supporter of vouchers (Broder, 2005). Under his administration, Florida recently approved a plan to spend $400 million on a universal preschool program for 4-year-olds, which will be further discussed (*Quality Counts*, 2005).

In the 2006, Florida gubernatorial election Governor Jeb Bush was term-limited and could not run again for the office. Republican Charlie Crist won the election for governor receiving 52.2% of the vote. Crist had been attorney general, had served in the Florida Senate, and had been the state education commissioner (Answers.com, 2007; *Florida Bar News*, 2003).

## FLORIDA'S EDUCATIONAL SYSTEM BEFORE 2002

Florida established an innovative educational system long before NCLB. State accountability legislation was established as early as 1971, and educational accountability has been promoted by a combination of business, political and education interest groups. The 1971 Florida Educational Accountability Act served as the basis for the state's assessment program and created statewide academic objectives for Grades 2 and 4. Committees of content specialists and teachers were charged with identifying and listing each objective (first in reading, then in 1976, math). These were then submitted to the State Board of Education for approval. In 1976, the act was expanded to include a criterion-based, high school graduation exam students were required to pass; however, several lawsuits delayed implementation (see *FCAT Handbook—A Resource for Educators*, 2005).

There have been several legal challenges to the state assessment system. The first came in 1979 from the NAACP in Dade County who challenged the Department of Education's right to limit public access to the Functional Literacy Test. This basic literacy test, which was required for graduation, had been mandated in 1978-79, by Florida's Educational Accountability Act of 1976. On its first administration, a high percentage of 11th graders passed the different portions of the test; 92% passed the communication skills portion of the test, and 64% passed the mathematics portion of the test. This test was renamed the State Student Assessment Test, the SSAT, Part 1I (Tesolowski, 1980). The case was dropped the year it was filed.

From 1999 to 2000, opposition also arose from parents and teachers after an expanded voucher system became part of Florida's A+ Plan for Education in 1999 (Heritage Foundation, 2005). A case still not resolved was filed by the ACLU challenging state funding of vouchers to send students to private schools (*Quality Counts*, 2005). In 2006, after various challenges, reversals, and appeals, the Florida Supreme Court ruled that the state's Opportunity Scholarship Program was unconstitutional (Heritage Foundation, 2007).

Out of these concerted efforts came Florida's celebrated A+ Plan. The 1999 plan was a comprehensive accountability plan that provided grades from A to F to each school in the state based on student performance, sanctions for poor performing schools, and private school vouchers for eligible students. Florida became the first state in the nation to assign grades to schools based on student performance (National Conference of State Legislatures, 2005).

Minimum performance standards were revised and in October 1994, the first administration of the High School Competency Test (HSCT) was conducted, and passing both the communications and math sections of the HSCT became a requirement for graduation. Students who did not pass the HSCT were given additional opportunities to pass. The State Board of Education established passing scores.

School reform in the 1990s enjoyed wide support from the general public, some teachers, a GOP controlled legislature, and the popular governor, Jeb Bush. School reform also had strong support from the business sector including a business coalition consisting of the state chamber of commerce, Associated Industries in Florida, the National Federation of Independent Business, Citizens for a Sound Economy, and the Florida Farm Bureau (see The Heartland Institute, 1999).

In 1996, the Florida legislature and State Board approved the Florida Sunshine Standards in seven content areas (language arts, math, science, social studies, health and physical education, foreign languages, and the arts) for students in Grades pre-K to 2, 3 to 5, 6 to 8, and 9 to 12. The state contracted CTB/McGraw-Hill to design the Florida Comprehensive Assessment Test (FCAT) and the High School Competency Test (HSCT), which were field-tested and planned for students in Grades 4, 5, 8, and 10.

In conducting research on Florida's educational system, Figlio and Getzler (2002) used the term "gaming" to describe how the Florida Comprehensive Assessment test in 1996, led schools to reclassify students, as disabled for example, in order to exclude low performing students' scores from schools' aggregate test scores. As to be expected, this tendency was found most often in schools with large student populations that were low income.

In 1999, Florida's A+ Plan was approved and expanded the state's assessment system to include calculation of students' academic growth over time, additional grade levels, and norm-referenced components. The plan also required high school students to pass FCAT tests, which replaced the HSCT, in reading and math for graduation beginning in 2002.

Florida had three important components in place to support the A+ Plan. These included the Sunshine State Standards, the criterion-referenced FCAT, and a grading system and performance levels for schools, which had been approved in 1998. Florida's A+ Plan built on these to include accountability, choice, more resources, rewards for improvement, and mandated changes when students were not improving. The plan was considered innovative and aggressive, but was generally well received. Some school educators were unhappy with the plan's focus on test results (Prawdzik, n.d.).

However, one survey found that the majority of Florida teachers responding, while opposing vouchers plans, conceded that vouchers or the threat of vouchers were driving improvement. In the survey of 750 teachers, only 17% reported that the state plan played "no role" in the improvements (Heritage Foundation, 2007, p. 23).

In 2000, the third administration of FCAT was conducted in February and March for students in Grades 3-10. A total of 1,440,000 students took the test, and results were used in Grades 4, 5, 8, and 10 in assigning school grades. In February/March 2001, the fourth administration of the FCAT was conducted and included assessments in writing, reading, and math for students in Grades 3-10. Although students received test results, the districts received these late due to technical problems, and they proved unusable (History of Statewide Assessment Program, 2005).

In 2001, the first operational tests for the FCAT in reading, writing and math for students in Grades 3 through 10 were given, which were also used to calculate school grades. In August 2001, the State Board approved FCAT passing scores, required for graduation, for high school students to be effective in 2003. Although NCLB was enacted in 2001, no major changes were necessary in the state's assessment system due to the state plan already developed, although a developmental scale score was introduced in 2002.

Sanctions for schools were based on a school grading system, and students could transfer out of any school that received a grade of F for 2 years to either a high performing school or a private school using a state funded Opportunity Scholarship. However, due to legal challenges to the state's A+ Plan from the ACLU, the NAACP, People for the American Way, American Federation of Teachers, and others, school sanctions were suspended during the 1999-2000 school year.

In March 2000, a state judge struck down the school choice provision of the plan and ruled that the Scholarship Program violated a state mandate that "the state provide a free education through a system of public schools" (Heritage Foundation, 2007, p. 3). After several reversals, the Florida Supreme Court in 2006, ruled that the state's Opportunity Scholarship Program was unconstitutional since it violated the state's Blaine Amendment, which prohibits state funding from going to sectarian schools. Then Governor Bush said that the state would "explore all legal options" to allow the program to continue (Heritage Foundation, 2007, p. 8).

In 2001, the governor signed an expanded publicly funded voucher bill, which established the McKay Scholarship program, and in 2001, 4,000 students participated; this number increased to 8,082 in 2002 (Crist, 2001). In 2002, then Education Commissioner Charlie Crist, who was elected governor in 2006, and Governor Jeb Bush released the 2001-

2002 school grades from A to F that for the first time contained students' annual learning gains.

In 2001, the Teacher Quality Act made revised existing policy. One change required school boards to give bonuses to classroom teachers. The Florida International Baccalaureate Program allowed high school students to earn college credits and signaled a need for a more rigorous curriculum. Teachers in the international baccalaureate program received a $50 bonus for each student who scored a 4 or higher on the international baccalaureate exam and an additional $500 when the teacher taught in a school designated with a grade of D or F and had at least one student scoring 4 or higher (Clowes, 2000).

In 2002, the NAACP, other civil rights groups, and a coalition of public school activists organized in support of Amendment 9, which would by 2010 institute class size limits of 18 students per teacher from kindergarten to Grade 3; 22 students per teacher through Grade 8; and 25 students per teacher at the high school level. Governor Bush, appointed State Board members, and other Republican leaders in the state vigorously opposed the legislation, which state accountants estimated would cost an additional $368 million for 2002 for new teachers and $1.8 billion for new classrooms. Nevertheless, in November 2002, Florida voters approved the amendment indicating strong support for public education by the general population (Barone & Cohen, 2005).

As in other states, questions about the accuracy of the state tests surfaced. In a Florida study involving 41,803 incidents, Figlio (2003) sought to investigate whether schools employed harsher discipline punishments for low-performing students during the "testing window" to keep them away from school. The researcher found evidence that schools used selective discipline, harsher punishments for low-performers/lighter punishments for high performers, in response to the pressures of testing, but only for students in grades being tested in a given school. Figlio concluded that "results indicate that schools may be using student discipline as a tool to manipulate aggregate test scores" (p. 15).

In spite of these "glitches," which were certainly not unique to Florida, researchers from the Center of Civic Innovation at the Manhattan Institute found that the Florida plan was working. Based on 2003 FCAT results, researchers of the study concluded that low performing schools were improving perhaps due to real or perceived voucher competition, which will be discussed more fully ("A+ for Florida Vouchers," 2005).

## IMPACT OF NCLB ON THE FLORIDA STATE ASSESSMENT SYSTEM

As in other states, the Florida State Board of Education was designated as responsible for enforcement of the NCLB legislation. Under the legislation, a school meets the NCLB standard only if students in all identified subgroups make yearly academic progress. Thus, it was necessary to disaggregate student test scores by group, including all ethnic/racial groups, students with disabilities, students learning English, and economically disadvantaged students. If students in any one subgroup do not meet the standard, the whole school is affected and will be designated as not meeting the Adequate Yearly Progress (AYP) requirement.

This NCLB requirement is a clear difference from the state plan whereby improvement is rewarded and affects a school's overall grade, an important distinction. The state plan provides for both rewards and sanctions based on performance results. By state mandate, districts must offer a school choice program, which provides Opportunity Scholarships to students attending a low-performing school. For rewards, the state provides greater autonomy and financial rewards to schools for sustained or significantly improved student performance (National Center for Education Statistics, 2005).

## Student Performance on the FCAT and NAEP Tests

*Quality Counts 2005* data for Florida, showing the percent of students scoring at or above proficient levels in the NAEP from 2004 through 2006, are presented in Table 6.1 alongside with FCAT scores in reading and math for students in Grades 4 and 8.

As in most states, results on the state tests for student performance are shown to be significantly higher than those in the national NAEP tests, which are often referred to as "the Nation's Report Card."

For example, in 2005, 30% of students in Grade 4 were proficient in reading under NAEP, but in reading scores on the FCAT, 71% of students in Grade 4 were proficient. In 2005, 26% of students in Grade 8 math tested proficient on the NAEP, but 59% tested proficient on the FCAT. Commenting on the differences, Frances Marine, from the Florida Department of Education, said, "It's difficult to compare; the cutoffs don't match.... What's fair is to look at the trends. Students are improving in both assessments" (NCLB Public School Choice, 2005).

Despite the discrepancies in test results, improvement has been made in raising student proficiency rates in Florida. As shown on Table 6.1, there was slight improvement in scores in reading and math on the state tests from 2004 to 2006, with one exception (scores, at the Proficient or Advanced levels for reading in Grade 4 went from 70% in 2004, to 71% in 2005, and to 66% in 2006). In 2003, Florida ranked eighth in the nation for reading in Grade 4 (NCLB Public School Choice, 2005).

**Table 6.1. FCAT and NAEP Test Results, 2004-2006**

*FCAT, Level Three (Proficient) and Advanced, in %*

|  | Grade 4 | | | Grade 8 | | |
|---|---|---|---|---|---|---|
|  | *2004* | *2005* | *2006* | *2004* | *2005* | *2006* |
| Reading | 70 | 71 | 66 | 45 | 44 | 46 |
| Math | 64 | 64 | 67 | 56 | 59 | 60 |

*NAEP, 2005, at the Proficient and Advanced Levels, in %*

|  | Grade 4 | Grade 8 |
|---|---|---|
| Reading | 30 | 25 |
| Math | 37 | 26 |

*Note.* FCAT scores accessed from the Florida Department of Education Web site (http://firn.edu/doe/sas/fcat/fcinfopg.htm). NAEP scores accessed from the NCES Web site (http://nces.ed.gov/nationsreportcard/states/profile.asp). No accommodations were permitted for the NAEP reading tests.

*Quality Counts 2005* also provided summary data on Florida's high school students. The percentage of students in Florida taking upper level math courses was only 38%, and only 26% were taking upper level science courses. Graduation rates are low for all students, but particularly so for African American and Latino students. Perhaps this is the reason that *Quality Counts* predicted that Florida's students' chances for college in 2002, were a dismal 31%. As discouraging as these statistics are for minority student populations, some improvement has been made since implementation of the State's A+ Plan.

NCLB requires that all students reach 100% proficiency by 2014. McCombs and Carroll concluded there is "a gulf between the national goal and the state realities (that) poses a challenge in all states" (Florida School Recognition, 2005b). Nevertheless, in Florida as in other states, NCLB focused attention on the improvement of all schools and on the performance of all students and brought an increase in Title I funding.

## SANCTIONS FOR TROUBLED SCHOOLS/REWARDS FOR SCHOOLS WITH HIGH STUDENT PERFORMANCE

Under NCLB, schools that receive Title I funds are at risk of being sanctioned. In Florida, 1,400 schools of about 3,700 receive Title I money. The new law came with an increase in Title I money, from $172 to $214 per student, meant to help students from low-income homes (FCAT Handbook, 2005). Florida established additional criteria to meet the state's accountability plan: improve student performance in writing by 1%, and improve the graduation rate by 1%. With approval of a "Safe Harbor" provision, a school can still make AYP but the percentage of non-proficient students must be decreased by 10% from the previous year in the area evaluated (Winn, 2005-2006). As noted above, only Florida schools that receive Title I funds (37%) are at risk of being sanctioned; however, all schools in the state are affected by the legislation since results are made public.

The Florida Department of Education is required to provide timely student performance results to all Local Education Authorities (LEAs), and this information is made public both by press releases and on the state education Web site. For NCLB, the Department developed a system of escalating level of sanctions that apply only for low performing Title I schools and that remain in place until the school makes AYP for two consecutive years. It outlined different levels of sanctions for schools identified as a 'School in Need of Improvement' (SINI) that include: "Under Improvement," "Corrective Action," and "Restructuring."

Although low performing Title I schools are subject to the mandated interventions and sanctions, all schools, that are low performing or meet other state requirements can be identified and designated as needing assistance (State of Florida Consolidated State Accountability Workbook, 2003). Under the plan, administrators in a low performing school must offer parents the option to transfer their children to another school including a charter school not identified as low performing with priority given to students from low income homes (NCLB Public School Choice, 2005).

In the "Under Improvement" phase, 3 months after being identified as a SINI, the school must develop an improvement plan, to be reviewed by the district that includes incorporation of a research-based curriculum, that directly addresses student achievement, and that informs parents of the school's designation and offers "public school choice." The LEA with the SINI school can use an amount equal to 20% of Title I funds to pay for a variety of options, such as magnet schools, charter schools, virtual schools, and private tutoring. Under the state's Voluntary Choice Program, an LEA can offer funding of $50,000, to a high performing district to mentor and work with a SINI school.

After 3 years of the SINI rating, the Florida Department of Education requires that the school, now in "Corrective Action," continues to follow all requirements of the "Under Improvement" designation including choice options for all priority students (identified as low performing students from low income homes) until the school makes AYP for two consecutive years. The SINI must provide transportation or supplemental educational services with funding taken from the LEA's Title I allocation.

As in other states, legislation also provides sanctions for repeatedly failing schools that include closure, reconstitution, charter status, or contracting out.

From 1999 to 2004, the State Board utilized the School Recognition Program under Florida's A+ School Accountability Plan to provide monetary awards to schools with higher or improved student achievement. In 2005, the Florida Legislature provided $263 million to the program, and the Department of Education identified 1,502 schools as qualified for this award (Florida Department of Education, 2005e).

The Standards Setting Committee, composed of educators, Education Department staff, the Education Commissioner, and the State Board, determined cut scores. Based on scale scores, students are assigned one of five levels, from Level 1, the lowest, to Level 5, the highest. For NCLB, proficiency was set at Level 3 to 5 (FCAT Handbook—A Resource for Educators, 2005).

In January 2005, historic legislation was signed by Governor Bush to fund a universal prekindergarten voucher system for 4-year-olds worth $2,500. Clearly, legislators in the state believe that expanding the options for students is the way to solve the problem of under performing schools (Heritage Foundation, 2005).

## Teacher Quality and NCLB—New Requirements for Teachers and Paraprofessionals

NCLB legislation concerning "highly qualified" requirements for teachers and paraprofessionals was interpreted by the Florida Department of Education to mean that highly qualified teachers and paraprofessionals in Title I schools had to meet outlined requirements by the 2002-2003 year. In a memorandum to all district superintendents, directors of Title I Programs, and other personnel, Betty Coxe, deputy commissioner of educational programs, outlined NCLB requirements for highly qualified teachers stating that the requirements would be in effect for teachers in core areas paid by Title I funds beginning the first day in the 2002 school year (Coxe, 2002). Administrators began making teaching assignments based on the new requirements.

In 2001, 16% of teaching vacancies were filled by teachers not certified in the appropriate content areas: state officials exhibited an early concern with teacher quality and many teacher programs had been established to deal with the issue (see Horne & Coxe, 2003 report to the House of Representatives Education Appropriations Committee). Florida's teachers are evaluated partially on student performance on state tests; Florida schools are required to notify parents when their children are taught by an uncertified or unqualified teacher. Florida was one of only three states to require this notification prior to NCLB (*Quality Counts*, 2005).

To meet the need for qualified teachers, the state developed several programs to assist in the recruitment and retention of high quality teachers. These include:

1.  Excellent Teacher Program—Governor Bush and the Legislature allocated $47 million to the program. Under this program, teachers completing National Boards receive a bonus of $3820 to be awarded every year, up to 10 years. In addition, they receive a one-time $500 bonus. Candidates meeting these qualifications who choose to become teacher mentors receive an additional bonus equal to 10% of an average teacher's pay with built-in increases for each additional year.

2.  State Improvement Grants—These grants are funded by the US DOE, instituted prior to NCLB, and provide funding to support pre-service programs.

3.  The Great Florida Teach-In—This is a recruitment conference that attracts candidates within and outside the state.

4.  The Dale Hickam Excellent Teaching Program—This program, established prior to NCLB, provides scholarships and bonuses to teachers completing the National Board of Certification (Florida Department of Education, 2005d).

In 1997, Florida had six teachers certified by the National Board of Professional Teaching Standards. By 2003, 1,448 had been awarded this certification.

After NCLB, new state legislation required that new teachers must be certified in the content area for each teaching assignment and earn a passing score on the Florida Subject Area Exam. Paraprofessionals in instructional roles are now required to show that they have the ability to deliver instruction by completing two years of college, obtaining an associate's degree, or by passing a state or local assessment. The new law specified that a paraprofessional could provide direct instruction only under the supervision of a highly qualified teacher. Districts were allowed to use Title I funds to assist teachers and paraprofessionals in becoming highly qualified.

The Florida Department of Education has developed about 50 subject area exams for core content courses. Core areas include English, reading, language arts, math, science, foreign languages, civics, government, economics, arts, history, and geography. Extensive licensure requirements are in place for new teachers. For example, teacher candidates must demonstrate general knowledge in reading, English/language arts, and math; they also must pass a professional education exam, in addition to exams in the specialized content area/s chosen. The exams are aligned to the state curriculum and were developed by teachers, district personnel, and content university faculty.

In 2003, the Florida State Education Department reported that 89% of teachers in core content areas were highly qualified, with 87.2% in high poverty schools and 91% in low poverty schools considered highly qualified in core content areas. In the core content areas at the elementary level, 93.9% of teachers are considered highly qualified, and 85.4% of teachers in core content areas at the secondary level are considered highly qualified.

*Quality Counts 2005* gave Florida a grade of C on "Efforts to Improve Teacher Quality" stating that the state does not evaluate teachers through performance assessments for advanced licenses, does not require or pay for a mentoring system for new teachers, and does not include teacher qualifications on their state report card. In *Quality Counts 2006*, the state's "grade" of C did not improve and the report stated that

> Florida does not do well in teacher quality, falling below the national average (C+). The state loses points … because it does not require all prospective high school or middle school teachers to have a major, minor, or equivalent coursework in the subjects they will teach in order to receive a beginning teaching license. (*Quality Counts*, 2006, p. 2).

## IMPLEMENTATION ISSUES: STATE RESPONSE TO NCLB REQUIREMENTS

Although Florida had begun working on an accountability system decades prior to the new legislation, NCLB brought forth a significant response. With a sense of urgency officials at the Florida Department of Education looked for ways to understand and implement the new legislation. In March 2002, a Superintendents' Conference with State Department of Education officials met to try and make sense of the 1200 page NCLB document. Several regional meetings were held to outline NCLB requirements to superintendents, Title I Directors, District Certification Contacts, and Directors of Personnel (Coxe, 2002).

On April 30, 2003, Jim Horne, Florida Commissioner of Education, wrote a memo to the State Legislature, the State Board of Education, and K-12 superintendents that U.S. Secretary of Education Paige had completed review of the state's NCLB proposal and had approved it. Florida became the 13th state to receive approval. There were 10 principles to

Florida's NCLB proposal, which included applying a single statewide assessment system for schools, holding schools and districts accountable for the performance of students in specified subgroups, and defining AYP. Horne added that Florida would receive an additional $960 million in federal funds to implement NCLB (U.S. Department of Education, 2003).

Two years later, however, in April 1, 2005, the Florida Education Commissioner requested approval from the U.S. DOE to revise the state plan by lowering proficiency targets in reading and math, increasing a subgroup's size so that their performance would not impact a school's AYP rating, and replacing the Safe Harbor measure with individual student improvement.

While the majority of schools earned A's and B's under the state system, as many as 60% would fail under NCLB adding that federal and state systems will continue to be "at odds" (Matius, 2005, p. 1). According to David Mosrie, chief executive officer of the Florida Association of District School Superintendents, up to 370,000, students would be eligible to receive tutoring, which would cost districts millions of dollars.

Matius reported that some districts were making plans to offer tutoring and that some administrators (like Principal Jeff Eakins of Hillsborough County) did not see this as a burden. Superintendent Clayton Wilcox of Pinellas stated, "We just have to keep doing the right thing regardless of what label they put on a school" (Matius, 2005, p. 2).

The state had already approved a plan for a "Provisional AYP" designation that recognized achievement in some of the state's best schools. The plan would affect 825 schools with grades A or B under the Florida system that would not make the federal requirements due to scores of poor and minority students. However, negotiations between the state and the U.S. DOE apparently fell through amidst wide criticism that wealthy/suburban schools were not being held fully accountable for the low performance of poor and/or minority students who were numerical minorities within these schools (Peteilli, 2005).

When the plan was submitted to the U.S. DOE for approval and drew national attention, Secretary of Education Margaret Spellings wisely rejected the plan, which would have seriously undermined the heart of the NCLB legislation. Although Secretary Spellings appeared willing to consider a value added approach, where some states (including Florida) give credit to schools making progress meeting performance levels for poor and minority students, she was not willing to approve Florida's broad plan that would essentially dilute the main priority of the legislation (Fordham Foundation, 2005).

In a phone interview to the Florida Department of Education, one official stated that although the Provisional AYP designation as approved by the state was used for A and B schools, it was not used for the purposes of the required reporting for NCLB (Florida Department of Education, personal communication, February 28, 2007).

## Fiscal Challenges of NCLB

Florida uses a foundation based school finance policy. *Quality Counts* gave Florida an overall grade of B in the area of equity in funding. The state spends $1.8 billion on categorical education programs, and in 2002, spent an average of $6,492 per student. The state ranks 30th for teacher pay and 47th for per pupil expenditure (*Quality Counts*, 2005; Neal & Poole, 2004). The State Board has increasingly moved to connect funding to student performance.

When the U.S. Department of Education approved the Florida Accountability Plan in 2003, it received more than $2.4 billion in federal education funding including $960 million to implement NCLB. The amount of federal funding to the state is 10.5% of its total education budget (Heritage Foundation, 2005).

The main fiscal challenge for Florida is meeting the ever-expanding cost of funding public education in the state, a problem for every state. Jeb Bush's innovative and admirable pre-K voucher plan will cost $11.8 to implement (Workforce Innovations, 2005). Amendment 9, the teacher union backed and Bush opposed legislation approved by Florida voters in November 2002, was estimated to cost over $1.8 billion for new teachers and new classrooms (LaPolt & St. John, 2005).

## Charter Schools in Florida

Charter school laws were established in 1996, but legislation supporting charter schools has continued to be strengthened due to support from the business sector, the general public, the legislature, and the governor. The Heritage Foundation (2005) rates Florida's charter school laws as strong. Florida charter schools are a popular but small percent of the total student enrollment in the state and serve 46% White, 29% African American, and 22% Latino students. In 2005, there were 82,000 students enrolled in charter schools in the state. Florida had 5 charter schools in 1996, which increased in 2002, to 222.

There are three types of charter schools in the state: Start ups, which serve at-risk, disadvantaged or special needs students; conversion schools, which serve as experimental schools, and community partnerships, which may have workplace, cities or university collaboration. Teachers who work in charter schools must be certified (Florida Department of Education, 2003).

## Voucher Experiments in Florida

Signed into law in 1999, Florida's A+ Plan allows state funded scholarships for students attending low performing public schools to attend another public, private or religious school. A series of lawsuits immediately followed until 2000, when the first public choice plan was approved (Heritage Foundation, 2005).

Providing school choice to parents of students in failing schools has been at the heart of Florida's accountability plan even before NCLB. The state has two voucher laws, FS 1002.38 that allows students to attend a school with students who perform well, and FS 1002.39 that allows parents of SPED students to use vouchers to attend a private or parochial school. The business sector, the legislature, the general public, the superintendent of Catholic Schools for the Diocese of Pensacola-Tallahassee, and the governor have largely supported these efforts.

An early evaluation of Florida's A+ Accountability and School Choice Program found that schools with failing grades that had students using tuition vouchers showed more than 50% stronger gains than students in other schools. Greene (2001) concluded that student performance improves when schools have students using vouchers.

Levin (2002) outlined a framework for evaluating school vouchers. In his view, no voucher system can meet four desirable goals of freedom of choice, efficiency, equity, and social cohesion, and he obviously believes that the plan needs further modification to better meet the needs of working families with children.

In analyzing the new pre-K voluntary program (VPK), which was signed by Governor Bush in 2005, Kennedy-Salchow (2005) stated, "The Florida VPK program appears to favor the principles of freedom of choice and efficiency at the expense of equity and social cohesion" (p. 23). In her analysis, she used the term "equity" to discuss the fairness of the program for children with disabilities since there is no incentive built into the plan for a pre-K program to accept a child with disabilities. Kennedy-Salchow predicted that families with disabled children might not be able to find a pre-K program that will enroll the children

For those who support vouchers in education, in Florida and elsewhere, families need more choices, and creating competition for public schools will increase their effectiveness. Other legislation to expand Florida's voucher system is pending.

Many have interpreted NCLB legislation as creating explicit incentives for private-sector involvement in public education (*TC Record*, 2005). Perhaps that is why in March 14, 2005, Jim Warford, Florida Department of Education's K-12 chancellor, sent out a memo to "interested parties" based on a request by the State Board for information on options for continuing failing schools where more than 75% of students were not reading at grade level. Warford stated that the Florida Department of Education was beginning an informal process of identifying "viable parties" (contracted services) and outlined performance expectations in this memo (Florida Department of Education, 2005c, March 14). Due to the wide support of vouchers in Florida, their continued growth is anticipated.

## Opposition to Current Educational Reform

As stated previously, after the state's *A+* Plan was signed into law in 1999, various state and national groups challenged the law over the use of state funds for school vouchers. Groups that challenged these laws have included People for the American Way, teachers unions, the ACLU, and others. Although some researchers question the results of the states' accountability plan in general, Greene, Winters, and Forster (2003) studied several school programs across the country using high and low stakes tests and found that Florida's program provided an accurate measure of student performance and schools' impact on that performance. They determined that Florida had the most aggressive high stakes public school testing in the United States.

However, voucher opponents in the state filed various lawsuits challenging the *Opportunity Scholarship* program basing their argument on the state constitution's Blaine Amendment that prohibits the use of state monies to aid religious institutions. Although the state has prevailed in many of the cases filed, as noted above, in 2006, the Florida Supreme Court ruled that the state's *Opportunity Scholarship* program was unconstitutional (Heritage Foundation, 2007; Romano, 2006).

Additional opposition to the accountability movement in Florida and elsewhere has come from educational researchers and academics. For example, Levin and Belfield (2002) believe that student performance is based both on the family and the school, with the family being the most critical component considering the established link between socioeconomic status and student performance. They assert that a contractual agreement between families and schools (they use the term "society") would effectively improve student performance.

## INITIAL RESULTS OF NCLB

*Quality Counts* (2006) analyzed state policies and performance across five areas: student achievement, standards and accountability, efforts to improve teacher quality, school climate, and resources to arrive at a grade of A through F for each state. Under this system, Florida earned an overall grade of A for its standards and accountability plan in 2005 and 2006. Other "grades" include a C for "Efforts to Improve Teacher Quality"; a C for "School Climate," and a B- for "Resources Equity" ("Florida State Highlights," 2006). In their summary of grades, *Education Week* writers state,

> Florida scores above the national average on two of four graded categories.... The state scores very well on measures related to standards and accountability, ranking near the top of the nation" (Florida's State Highlights, 2006).

In this section, student FCAT performance will be reviewed. Under FCAT, five student achievement levels were defined with Level 3 set as the criterion for meeting state standards:

| | |
|---|---|
| Level 1 | Below proficient |
| Level 2 | Basic |
| Level 3 & 4 | Proficient |
| Level 5 | Advanced |

Table 6.2 shows FCAT statewide results for students testing at Level 3 or above in Grades 4 and 8 in reading and mathematics.

Post-NCLB scores show some improvement in both reading and math in Grade 4, but not for students in Grade 8, where grades actually went down in 2004, and again in 2005. Reading scores went down between 2005 and 2006 for students in Grade 4. Math scores improved for students in Grade 4 between 2003 and 2004, remained unchanged between 2004 and 2005, but improved slightly for students in both groups in 2006 (FCAT, 2005, 2006).

On the FCAT tests, students in all the subgroups are making slow progress in reading and mathematics. This can be seen clearly in Table 6.3. For example, in the area of reading, 28% of African American students in grades 3 to 10, performed at a Level 3 (Proficient) or above in 2002; this percentage increased to 39% in 2006. In reading, 38% of Latino students performed at a Level 3 or above in 2002; this percentage increased to 50% in 2006. In the same content area, 60% of white students performed at a Level 3 or above in 2002; this percentage increased to

**Table 6.2.   FCAT Scores in Reading and Math, 2003-2006, in %**

*Grade 4, Percent at Level 3 (Proficient) or Above*

|  | *Reading* | *Math* |
|---|---|---|
| 2003 | 60% | 54% |
| 2004 | 70% | 64% |
| 2005 | 71% | 64% |
| 2006 | 66% | 67% |

*Grade 8, Percent at Level 3 (Proficient) or Above*

|  | | |
|---|---|---|
| 2003 | 49% | 56% |
| 2004 | 45% | 56% |
| 2005 | 44% | 59% |
| 2006 | 46% | 60% |

*Note*:   Results can be accessed from the Florida Department of Education http://firn.edu/doe/sas/fcat/fcinfopg.htm

**Table 6.3.   FCAT Sunshine State Standards Tests, Reading and Mathematics Scores, by Group**

*At Level 3 (Proficient) and Above, Grades 3-10, by %*

| *Reading* | *2002* | *2004* | *2006* |
|---|---|---|---|
| African American | 28 | 32 | 39 |
| Latino/Hispanic | 38 | 42 | 50 |
| White | 60 | 63 | 67 |
| LEP | 12 | 14 | 25 |
| *Math* | | | |
| African American | 27 | 34 | 41 |
| Latino/Hispanic | 42 | 49 | 56 |
| White | 64 | 68 | 72 |
| LEP | 22 | 25 | 33 |

*Note*:   Adapted from data found at the Florida Department of Education, http://firn.edu/doe/sas/fcat/fcinfopg.htm

67% in 2006. In 2002, 12% of LEP students performed at Level 3 or above in reading; in 2006, this percentage increased to 25%. The same pattern was seen in student performance in the area of mathematics (*FCAT*, 2006).

Florida has its own grading system based partially on the number of schools making AYP. In 2005, 90% or more of "A" schools (a total of 1,174) made AYP, and 80% or more of "B" schools (a total of 536) made AYP. However, 50% of Florida schools with a grade of "F" under the state system (a total of 69 schools) also made AYP (see Florida Department of Education, 2005d). However, in 2006, schools making AYP fell from 36% the year before to 28%, with 39% receiving Provisional AYP status. Nevertheless, the number of schools not making AYP fell from 37% in 2005, to 33% in 2006 (Florida Department of Education, 2007b).

There has been little change in the public perception of support for education and for the Florida assessment system, which has been strong for decades. The number of lawsuits from opponents of vouchers has decreased due to the 5 to 2 ruling by the Florida Supreme Court in 2006. In that ruling, the court stated, "The diversion of money not only reduces public funds for a public education but also uses public funds to provide an alternative education in private schools that are not subject to the "uniformity" requirements for public schools" (Romano, 2006, p. A05). Nevertheless, those who support vouchers have signaled a commitment to continue to pursue options including amending the state constitution.

## CONCLUSION

The state has a well-developed and highly regarded assessment system in place. Florida has a large and diverse student population. The median income in the state is $37,512, with 12% of its citizens in poverty (LeFevre, 2005). Florida is a right-to-work state with no strong teachers' union. Policy makers and others in the state appear to believe that an expanded voucher system is the way to solve the problem of low performing schools. Yet, a Rand report found that in 11 states, fewer than half the students met the state proficiency standards, and in all states less than 50% met NAEP proficiency standards (Sloan & Carroll, 2003). Sloan and Carroll assert that states are not even close to meeting the national goal of 100% proficiency.

In Florida, the state legislature and leadership historically provided by the governor's office, supported by a strong coalition of business interests, education groups, and the general public, have shown a strong commitment to education and have not shied away from innovation. The solid investment in education in this state, which preceded NCLB, is admirable. Nationwide, it is clear that the new legislation has sparked wide interest, controversy, discussion, and resistance. But in Florida, there has been much less controversy and resistance than in others, perhaps because educational reform began early in this state.

Despite these tremendous efforts, increases in student performance for students from poor homes, minority students, and other student populations remain small although they are moving up. At this point, it is difficult to predict whether it is realistic to expect that all students in Florida will achieve 100% proficiency by 2014.

## REFERENCES

*A+* for Florida vouchers. (2003, August 24). *The Washington Times*. Retrieved December 15, 2005 from http://www.washingtontimes.com/functions/print .php?StoryID=20030823-112745-4625r

Answers.com. (2007). *Florida's gubernatorial election 2006*. Retrieved February 13, 2007, from http://www.answers.com/topic/florida-gubernatorial-election-2006

Barone, M., & Cohen, R. (2005). *The almanac of American politics 2006*. Washington, DC: National Journal Group.

Broder, J. (2005, November 25). States'coffers swelling again after struggles. *The New York Times*. Retrieved November 28, 2005, from http:// select.nytimes.com/ gst/abstract.html?res= FA0616FC3C550C768EDDA80994DD404482

Clowes, G. (2000, September 1). Florida educators still criticize A+ Plan. *The Heartland Institute*. Retrieved December 13, 2005, from http://www.heartland .org

Coxe, B. (2002, October 4). Memorandum from Coxe, Deputy Commissioner, to state superintendents and other administrators. Retrieved December 12, 2006, from http://www.fldoe.org

Crist, C. (2001, July 1). Teacher Quality Act. *Legislative Review*. Florida Department of Education. Retrieved August 20, 2005, from http://www.fldoe.org/gr/ pdf/review2001.pdf

*FCAT*. (2005). Florida Department of Education. Retrieved November 2, 2005, from http://fcat.fldoe.org

*FCAT*. (2006). Florida Department of Education. Retrieved February 13, 2007, from http://firn.edu/doe/sas/fcat/fcinfopg.htm

*FCAT Handbook—A Resource for Educators*. (2005). Florida Department of Education. Retrieved August 20, 2005, from http://www.firn.edu/doe/sas/fcat/ handbk/background.pdf

FCAT. (2006). Reading and math scores. Florida Department of Education. Retrieved February 28, 2007, from http://firn.edu/doe/sas/fcat/fcinfopg.htm

Figlio, D. (2005). *Testing, crime, and punishment*. Cambridge, MA: National Bureau of Economic Research.

Figlio, D., & Getzler, L. (2002, November). *Accountability, ability and disability: Gaming the system* (Working Paper No. 9307). Cambridge, MA: National Bureau of Economic Research.

*Florida Bar News*. (2003, July). AG Crist: lawyers have the skills to make justice happen. Retrieved February 13, 2007, from http://findarticles.com/p/articles/ mi_go1672/ is_200307/ai_n9019926

Florida Department of Education. (2003, February 20). *Florida Charter Schools*. Florida Department of Education. Retrieved December 22, 2006, from http:// www.fldoe.org

Florida Department of Education. (2005a). *Florida School Grades.* Retrieved December 13, 2006, from http://schoolgrades.fldoe.org/0405/summaries.cfm

Florida Department of Education. (2005b). *Florida's School Recognition.* Retrieved December 12, 2006, from http://www.fldoe.org/faq/faq.asp?Dept=177&ID= 621&Cat=71#621

Florida Department of Education. (2005c, March 14). Memorandum from Jim Warford, Florida Department of Education's K-12 Chancellor. Retrieved December 14, 2006, from at http://www.fldoe.org

Florida Department of Education. (2005d). *Professional information.* Retrieved August 22, 2005, from http://www.fldoe.org/educator/

Florida Department of Education. (2007a). *Florida school choice.* Retrieved June 4, 2007, from http://www.floridaschoolchoice.org/Information/Private_Schools/ annual_reports.asp

Florida Department of Education. (2007b). *No Child Left Behind adequate yearly process.* Retrieved June 4, 2007, from http://schoolgrades.fldoe.org/pdf/0506/ schlGrds_13.pdf

Florida state highlights. (2006). *Education Week.* Retrieved February 13, 2007, from http://www.edweek.org/ew/articles/2006/01/05/17shr.fl.h25.html

Fordham Foundation. (2005, August 25). Secretary Spellings aging well. *The Education Gadfly: A Weekly Bulletin of News and Analysis.* Thomas B. Fordham Foundation, 5(29). Retrieved August 26, 2005, from http://www.edexcellence.net/ foundation/gadfly/issue.cfm?edition=&id=204#2437

Greene, J. (2001, February). An evaluation of the Florida A-Plus Accountability and School Choice Program. *Civic Report,* pp.1-15. Retrieved December 6, 2006, from https://mail2.uaf.edu/webmail/src/read_body.php?mailbox= INBOX&passed_id=6

Green, J., Winters, M., & Forster, G. (2003, February). Testing high stakes tests: Can we believe the results of accountability tests? *Civic Report, No. 33.* New York: Manhattan Institute for Policy Research.

The Heartland Institute. (1999, June 1). How Florida achieved school choice. Retrieved from http://www.heartland.org/Article.cfm?artId=11252

Heritage Foundation. (2005). *Research: Education, Florida.* Retrieved November 11, 2005, from http://www.heritage.org/research/education/schoolchoice/Florida .cfm

Heritage Foundation. (2007). *Research: Education, Florida.* Retrieved February 19, 2007, from http://www.heritage.org/research/Education/SchoolChoice/Florida .cfm?renderforprint=1

History of Statewide Assessment Program. (2005). Florida Department of Education. Retrieved November 7, 2005, from http://www.firn.edu/doe/sas/hsap/ hsap9000.htm#2000

Horne, J., & Coxe, B. (2003, February 5). *Teacher recruitment and retention follow-up report.* Florida Department of Education. Report to the House of Representatives Education Appropriations Committee. Retrieved February 20, 2007, from http://www.fldoe.org/gr/pdf/presentations/02-05 03_Coxe_House_Ed_ Approp_Teacher_Recruitment.pdf

Kennedy-Salchow, S. (2005, May). *An analysis of Florida's voluntary pre-K program.* New York: Teachers College.

LaPolt, A., & St. John, P. (2005, October 3). Bush would seek to kill class-size amendment. *Florida Capitol News*. Retrieved December 12, 2005, from http://www.floridacapitalnews.com/campaign/stories/1003classsize.htm

LeFevre, A. (2004). *Report card on American education: A state-by-state analysis, 1981-2003*. Washington, DC: American Legislative Exchange Council.

Levin, H. (2002). *A comprehensive framework for evaluating educational vouchers*. Occasional Paper #5. National Center for the Study of Privatization in Education. Retrieved December 1, 2005, from http://www.ncspe.org

Levin H., & C. Belfield, C. (2002). *Families as contractual partners in education*. Occasional Paper. New York: Columbia.

Matius, R. (2005, August 18). Feds say all Florida schools must pass. *St. Petersburg Times*. Retrieved December 20, 2005, from http://www.sptimes.com/2005/08/18/ news_pf/State/Feds_say_all_Florida_.shtml

National Association for the Advancement of Colored People. (2002). *Florida class-size reduction amendment victorious*. Retrieved December 15, 2005, from http://www.naacp.org/news/2002/2002-11-06.html

National Conference of State Legislatures. (2005). *Reporting, accrediting, rewarding, and sanctioning school performance*. Retrieved December 15, 2005, from http://www.ncsl.org/programs/educ/areporting.htm

Neal, T., & Poole, J. (2004, June 15). A test in Florida. *Washington Post*. Retrieved June 4, 2007, from http://www.washingtonpost.com/wp-srv/politics/articles/battleground_florida.htm

National Center for Education Statistics. (2005). *State profiles*. Retrieved November 17, 2005, from http://nces.ed.gov/nationsreportcard/states/profile.asp

National Center for Education Statistics. (2006). *State profiles*. Retrieved February 10, 2007, from http://nces.ed.gov/nationsreportcard/states/profile.asp

*NCLB Public School Choice*. (2005). Florida Department of Education. Retrieved November 1, 2005, from http://www.floridaschoolchoice.org/

*NCLB Report*. (2003). Florida Department of Education. Retrieved December 5, 2006, from http://doewebprd.doe.state.fl.us//eds/nclbspar/index.cfm

*People for the American Way*. (n.d.). Holmes v. Bush and other voucher cases. Retrieved December 16, 2005, from http://www.pfaw.org/pfaw/general/default.aspx?oid=2944&print=yes

Petrilli, M. (2005, July 11). School reform moves to the suburbs. *New York Times*, p. 17.

Prawdzik, C. (n.d.). Florida teachers concede vouchers spurred improvement. *Alexis de Tocqueville Institute*. Retrieved December 13, 2005, from http://www.adti.net/education/ florida_survey_prawdzik08032000.html

*Quality Counts*. (2005). *Education Week*. Retrieved November 23, 2005, from http://www.edweek.org/ew/qc/2005/state_data.html?state=fL&opt=data

*Quality Counts*. (2006). Florida report card. *Education Week*. Retrieved February 13, 2007, from http://www.edweek.org/ew/articles/2006/01/05/17shr.fl.h25 .html

Romano, L. (2006, January 6). Fla. Voucher system struck down: Court's ruling could affect programs in other states. *Washingtonpost.com*, p. A05. Retrieved February 27, 2007, from http://www.washingtonpost.com/wpdyn/content/article/2006/01/05/ AR2006010501983_pf.html

Sloan, J., & Carroll, S. (2005, Spring). Ultimate test: Who is accountable for education If everyone fails? *Rand Review*. Retrieved December 10, 2006, from http://www.rand.org/publications/randreview/issues/spring2005/ulttest.html

*State of Florida Consolidated State Accountability Workbook*. (2003). Florida Department of Education. Retrieved December 1, 2005, from http://www.fldoe.org/news/NCLB/NCLB-

*TC Record*. (2005, December 15). The new educational privatization: Educational contracting and high stakes accountability. Columbia Teachers College. Retrieved December 16, 2005, from http://www.tcrecord.org/

Tesolowski, D. (1980, July). The Functional Literacy Test: Florida's approach to competency testing. *Viewpoints in Teaching and Learning*, *56*(3), 67-94.

U.S. Census Bureau. (2005). *State & county quick facts, Florida*. Retrieved August 15, 2005, from http://quickfacts.census.gov/qfd/states/12000.html

U.S. Department of Education. (2003). Approved state accountability plans. Can be accessed, from http://www.ed.gov/admins/lead/account/stateplans03/index.html

Winn, J. (2005-2006). *2006 Guide to calculating adequate yearly progress (AYP): Technical assistance paper*. Florida Department of Education. Retrieved February 9, 2007, from http://schoolgrades.fldoe.org/pdf/2006AYPTAP.pdf

Workforce Innovations. (2005). My Florida.com. Retrieved December 10, 2005, from http://www.upkflorida.org/index.cfm?Section=GovLeg&Page=GovSignsLaw

CHAPTER 7

# TEXAS

## INTRODUCTION

There are many songs and stories in the popular media and in traditional lore about Texas and its people, and the state enjoys a unique and colorful history. Songs like *The Yellow Rose of Texas* have a historical context, as do the *corridos*, Mexican ballads, which were especially important to the Spanish speaking population during the 1800s and early 1900s.[1] In contemporary times, Texans are often admired for their open honesty, down-to-earth common sense, resourcefulness, and heroic character. Shedding an outdated and mostly inaccurate stereotype, being a Texan became almost "cool" in the 1980s. Only two U.S. Presidents were born in Texas, Eisenhower and Lyndon Johnson, yet both ex-President George H.W. Bush and President George W. Bush consider themselves Texans. Because Texans like to be, almost insist on being, "Number 1," it should surprise no one that Texas has been a leader in helping craft the newest educational reform for the entire nation. It should be emphasized that Texas is less a before and after study of NCLB implementation than other states, simply because Texas had a well-developed accountability model long before this legislation.

In this first section, the state's social, economic, and political environment for education reform will be reviewed.

*Education Reform in the American States*
pp. 171–198
Copyright © 2008 by Information Age Publishing

## HISTORY, SOCIOECONOMIC, AND POLITICAL CHARACTERISTICS

Texas has had the second largest population since the early 1990s, and was the largest state territory until Alaska gained statehood in 1959. Southerners founded the state, although historically it also has the significant cultural and economic influence of the Latino population, African Americans (especially in east Texas and in the urban areas), and a small but important American Indian population.

After the Civil War, most Texans were very poor until 1901, when oil was discovered and the state became for a while the world's leading producer of oil. Some Texans became very wealthy, very quickly. Perhaps it is this up-and-down history that has made Texans admire success coupled with hard work, while being disdainful of failure. Texans love winners, and the winners they like the most are those who formerly were underdogs. Understanding the history of Texas helps us gain an understanding of its citizens.

Texans have earned an enviable reputation for their work on educational accountability, especially considering the large minority public school population (currently over 60%) in the state, but this was not always the case. The educational history of the state includes shameful chapters for its segregated schools and its treatment of poor and minority public school children. As late as the early 1960s, Texas children showing up to school without knowledge of English were routinely placed in special education classes. At the secondary levels, minority students regardless of how talented were placed on a vocational track. Such policies were common educational practices across the United States, especially in states with large minority populations.

The high school dropout rate of Latino students prior to the 1980s was over 50%, and as late as the 1970s, Mexican American females had a high school dropout rate of over 70% (Reyes, 1991). Much damage occurred as ineffective school practices followed the cultural deficit theories popular among educators nationwide at the time that essentially blamed the academic failure of minority children on their home culture. Such theories may have served as the basis for what some scholars consider the long term negative effect of some of the social policies developed in the 1960s under President Johnson.[2] The Texas Office of the State Demographer estimated the total state population for 2003 as 20,851,820, with 50.6% White, 34.2% Latino (primarily Mexican American), 11.5% African American, and 3.7% other (Texas Education Agency, 2004b). A sizeable number of Texans, 25.9%, speak Spanish, and many especially in south Texas are bilingual in English and Spanish. Most Texans (82.5%) live in the urban areas of Houston, San Antonio, Dallas, Austin, and Fort Worth. The public school K-12 student population has been over 50% minority for about a decade. In 2004, the public school student population was 38% White, 44% Latino, 14% African American, and 3% Asian/Pacific Islander (Murdock, 2005).

Depending on the state's labor needs at any given time, Texans (including Mexican Americans) have had a love-hate relationship toward Mexico, primarily because of the constant influx of Mexican immigrants along its porous borders, which continues today. However, in dramatic departure from business as usual, the adoption of the North American Free Trade Agreement (NAFTA) in 1993, (legally) opened up the Texas-Mexico border, a move supported by both political parties. There had always been an officially unacknowledged mutually beneficial economic relationship between Texas and Mexico considering the number of undocumented workers in the state and their contributions in the service and labor market, but NAFTA greatly expanded trade between the United States and Mexico.

In the 1980s, Texas further diversified its economy and became a high-tech Mecca that included the medical technology and the biotech industries. Texas became an economic powerhouse propped by a strong university system (The University of Texas and Texas A & M), an excellent highway system, and a historically strong military presence (Texas Educactional Agency, 2004a). Fusarelli (2002) credits Anne Richards, the 45th Texas governor, a Democrat, as helping diversify the state towards technology and the entertainment industry and by encouraging investment. Richards, a civil rights advocate, gained national attention when she gave a rousing keynote address at the 1988 Democratic National Convention.

Texas was considered a Democratic state until the 1970s, but as the state economy diversified, politicians, and the business sector turned towards the Republican Party, which was considered more "business friendly." Low taxes and the lack of a state income tax became attractive to big business, especially in large urban areas like Dallas-Fort Worth and Houston. Austin became the heart of the high tech industry.

Because of NAFTA and the dramatic growth in the Latino population, Texans took economic advantage of their proximity to Mexico and were able to weather the economic challenges of the 1980s and 1990s. Around this time, the government of Mexico also began aggressively courting Texas leaders and signaled efforts to build a relationship with the country's long neglected expatriates at a time when the economic, educational, and political clout of the Latino population was growing.

In the 1990s, South Texas, once one of the most impoverished areas in the nation, enjoyed some of the nation's most dramatic economic growth, largely fueled by the investment and buying power of Mexican citizens. The majority (70%) of U.S. exports to Mexico flow from Texas, although not all originate there. The last three governors, Anne Richards, George W. Bush, and Rick Perry have supported the Texas-Mexico relationship.

In fact, Perry prepared for the governorship by taking Spanish lessons perhaps as a tribute to George W. Bush who enjoys speaking Spanish to a Latino audience (Fusarelli, 2002). It could have been also due to the ever-growing Latino population in the state, the new status of Latinos as the largest U.S. minority group in the country, or maybe a combination of these factors. During the 2006 gubernatorial race, among a typically colorful group of candidates, Perry was re-elected governor receiving 39% of the vote (Washingtonpost.com, 2007).

One of the most interesting regions in Texas is the unique area along the Texas-Mexico border. South Texas has been an attractive agricultural region of the state for decades due to its sunny weather, warm beaches for tourism, and its proximity to Mexico. It retains a simpatico multicultural flair and most citizens, both the Latinos and Gringos, are bilingual in English and Spanish. Visitors from the northern states, the so-called "Winter Texans," spend the winter living in south Texas enjoying the region and the friendliness of the local citizens. In fact, friendliness is a recognized characteristic of Texans in general.[3] For the last couple of decades, the region has benefited economically from the buying power of the growing Mexican middle class (who like to shop in the area, invest in real estate, and use U.S. banks).

Schools in these areas of the state, where students of Mexican origin are the majority, have historically shown the lowest performance on state tests and the highest dropout rates. According to state statistics, Latino students account for 60.8% of the high school dropouts in the state. Results are influenced by variables such as the high poverty rates of families, generation differences (the number of generations in the U.S.), educational level of parents, and the high number of Limited English Proficiency (LEP) students.

Texas continues to have a stubborn disparity between rich and poor and a high crime rate. Historically, the state has discouraged labor unions, struggles to equalize school funding, and has the unpleasant distinction of having the highest number of executions in the country. Once a solid Democratic enclave, today, Texas is no doubt a "red state."

In 2000, Bush carried the state 59 to 28%, and in 2004, 61 to 38%, with Democrats barely winning the Latino vote in south Texas, where historically citizens voted the Democratic ticket and are considered more politically liberal than the general population. Republicans hold the majority of legislature seats and all Supreme Court seats. Barone and Cohen (2005) see two threats to the Republican hold on the state: the growing Latino population, which generally votes for Democratic candidates, and any failure in state policy due to Republican dominance.

## Fiscal Challenges to School Funding

The Texas school finance system includes a foundation formula, a tax base formula, and caps on the amount wealthier districts are taxed. The system is controversial because districts with a higher property value tax base contribute revenues to poor districts. Because of the increasing cost of public education, from $4.6 billion in 1985, to $16.4 billion in 2002, wealthier districts are reaching their tax limit, and many believe the system requires a major overhaul. Several lawsuits have challenged the state's overreliance on local property taxes to fund public education (Alexander, Gronberg, Jansen, Keller, Taylor, & Triesman, 2002; Imazeki & Reschovsky, 2003).

One of the most compelling cases was *Rodriguez v. San Antonio School District* in 1973, when the Mexican American Legal Defense Education Fund (MALDEF) represented the plaintiff who charged that the formula violated the equal protection clause of the U.S. Constitution and raised other equity issues such as the disparity between the property wealth per pupil in the poorest and the richest districts. The court ruled that the system did not discriminate against poor children. Since this ruling, school finance challenges argue that the system violates the state constitution.

It is not very surprising that these cases continue. There have been wide rich-poor disparities in Texas for centuries; today, there is a growing and increasingly politicized minority population. As minorities make gains in education and the workplace, many also organize for political clout and clamor for social justice and equity. As has been the case with other minorities in the United States, minorities organized early in the twentieth century. The United Latin American Citizens (LULAC) formed in 1929 to address political disfranchisement and racial discrimination. In 1948, a group of 700 Mexican American veterans, led by Dr. Hector Garcia, formed the GI Forum after the Naval Air Station in Corpus Christi refused to accept ailing WWII veterans who were Latino (PBS, 2007). These groups and others, like the Hispanic Association of College and Universities (HACU), included the education of Latino children as a major focus of their advocacy.

On behalf of poor Mexican American families and their children from the west side of San Antonio, Al Kaufman, of the Mexican American Legal Defense Fund (MALDEF), challenged the system again in *Edgewood Independent School District et al. v Kirby et al.* (1984) on the variation in per pupil expenditures and the state's overreliance on the state property tax, which the plaintiffs argued led to a violation of the equal protection clause under the Texas Constitution.

In 1987, the court ruled in favor of the plaintiffs on the basis that the system was unconstitutional taking note that the property wealth of

$48,854 per student in the Edgewood School District was significantly lower than the $570,109 per student in the Alamo Heights School District, both in San Antonio. This decision was reversed on appeal, but the Texas Supreme Court ruled that the state had not addressed differences in wealth among districts, affirming the lower court ruling 2 years later (Texas Politics, 2005).

In response, the legislature passed a school reform measure to increase state funding of poor schools. The new legislation was immediately challenged by MALDEF as "intolerably illegal" (Texas Politics, 2005). The state district judge ruled in favor of the plaintiffs, and the legislature was ordered to devise a new system to fund schools. The state appealed the decision again, but in 1989, a unanimous decision by the Texas Supreme Court ruled in favor of the plaintiffs and ordered the state to create an equitable funding system.

In June 1990, with assistance from a court appointed master, the legislature approved a $528 million bill to increase funding to schools. Litigation continued but ultimately led to the creation of Senate Bill 7 in 1993. Several other lawsuits were filed until January 1995, when the Texas Supreme Court ruled that Senate Bill 7 had finally provided a finance system that was constitutional (*Edgewood Independent School District v. Meno*, 1995).

Senate Bill 7 outlined a plan for a basic framework with a complex system of formulas, adjustments and weights that equalized funding of Texas schools. When a school exceeds a set revenue limit, it can give away funds by several means including merging/consolidating with a poor district, sending money to the state, educating students in other districts, or moving taxable property to another district. Senate Bill 7 also provided Texas with the basis for its educational accountability plan (Texas Educational Agency, 2005a).

Imazeki and Reschovosky (2003) convincingly argue that the present funding system will not be sustainable in the long term to meet NCLB requirements. They predict that NCLB will force the state to find new funding sources other than a state income tax, which most think that Texans will never accept.

Hanushek (2003), a senior fellow at Stanford's Hoover Institution and a leading expert on educational policy specializing in school finance, concluded that although the Texas accountability system has been extremely successful in raising achievement, the system, like many in the United States, is vulnerable due to the state's inability to tie school reform effectively to school funding. Hanuskek argues that (1) the courts have played a large role in outlining finance policy, (2) court decisions have tended to centralize power at the state level, and (3) student performance and education finance have largely not been considered together when they should be inseparable.

On September 15, 2005, District Judge John Dietz ruled that the state's cap on property tax rates prevents the state from raising enough funding for public schools to ensure that all students reach state proficiency levels. Although many considered the decision a victory for schools, the state immediately appealed the decision to the Texas Supreme Court where it remains (Hoff, 2004).

## Texas Educational System

Texas used the lack of a public school system as one reason to sever ties to Mexico in 1836. The Texas Constitution charged the Legislature with the task of establishing "an efficient system to fund public schools," interpreted to mean that the largest share of education costs would be paid by property taxes. A state sales tax adopted in 1961 has generated a great deal of additional funding for the state and for schools. For decades, various efforts have been made to create a new system of funding, owing to rising property taxes and the cost of funding public education, which grew from $4.6 billion in 1985 to $16.4 billion in 2002 (Texas Public Policy Foundation, 2005).

With more than 4 million students, the Texas public school system is the second largest in the nation. Although the state has a history of segregated schools and a troubled school finance system, a modern educational reform effort began in earnest in 1984, with House Bill 72, a landmark bill developed by the Perot Commission. Wealthy businessman Ross Perot, who was a presidential candidate twice on the Reform Party ticket, led the organization, which was supported by Governor Mark White, the Texas Business Council and the Texas Business Education Coalition. HB72 was the most significant educational legislation in Texas history. Opposition came quickly from public school teachers (who under HB72 were required to pass a basic skills test in order to retain their jobs) and special interests groups like MALDEF.

The legislation called for the testing of all K-12 public school teachers, a pay raise for teachers, and additional funding for property-poor districts. The bill contained the so-called "no-pass, no play" rule still hated by most Texas coaches.[4] In addition, House Bill 72 included several other important provisions:

- appointment of a 15-member State Education Board by the governor (reduced from a 27-member elected board);
- limits on class size in the early grades;

- increased graduation requirements (a high school exit exam);
- student testing in Grades 1, 3, 5, 7, 9, and 11;
- entrance and exit exams for preservice teachers; and
- a career ladder system (Fusarelli, 2002, p. 147).

Shortly after HB72 was adopted, Democratic Governor White increased taxes to compensate for lower oil prices, angered public school teachers over having to pass a basic skills test, and subsequently lost his bid for re-election. Although Texas is a right-to-work state and teachers cannot collectively bargain, which makes them a less powerful force than in other states, they can vote. While it is widely believed that White lost his re-election bid because of anger over teacher testing, others think more issues were involved. In 1989, White in retrospect stated, "I think that (teacher testing) was a mistake. We could have achieved the same goal with less emotionally damaging techniques" (McNeeley, 1989).

Newly elected Republican Governor Bill Clements continued implementation of HB72, as did his successor Ann Richards, a liberal Democrat elected in 1990. In 1993, Governor Richards got into political hot water by supporting the so-called "Robin Hood" plan of school finance, which would have redistributed funds from property-rich school districts to poor ones. The plan was defeated by a 2 to 1 margin, and gained the attention of George W. Bush who became the next Republican challenger.

In his campaign, Bush focused on crime, education, and lower taxes, popular themes with Texas voters. Both Richards and Bush promoted greater educational accountability by increasing student testing, staff development for teachers, and school choice, although Bush was friendlier to the idea of school vouchers than was Richards. In 1994, ushering in the Republic dominance in the state, Bush defeated Richards by 300,000 votes.

Under Bush, the educational accountability system was strengthened as the new governor built relationships with the state's leading educational leaders, some of whom had national reputations. In 1995, Bush signed Senate Bill 1, which authorized charter schools and allowed home-rule districts, and in 1997, House Bill 318, which improved on charter school legislation by raising the number of charter schools and allowing an unlimited number of charter schools serving at-risk students.

In 1999, a strong state economy allowed Bush to champion large tax cuts while providing funding for all day kindergarten for all children, a reading program, and pay raises for teachers and other state employees. In 2000, Governor Perry and many in the Texas Legislature voiced strong support for charter schools and vouchers and for increasing student options.

For purposes of K-12 public education, the state is divided into 20 geo-graphic areas each served by an educational regional service center. Each center provides planning, consultation, professional development (in some centers, even teacher licensure programs), and technical assistance to districts (Texas Educational Agency, 2005c). There are 1,040 districts and 7,646 schools in the state. Of all students, 57.7% are in Title I schools, and 46.2% of all students in the state are eligible for free/reduced lunch.

Texas ranks 38th among the states in per student spending. The national average is $7,734 and, when adjusted for regional cost differences, Texas spends $7,183. It ranks 9th for average class size with an average of 18.5 students per class. The average beginning teacher makes $31,874.7 (*Education Week*, 2005).

Texas has a diverse K-12 student population that is over 60% minority, and 55.6% of students were identified as "economically disadvantaged" as seen on Table 7.1.

Because of the ethnic/racial diversity in the student population, a long recognized concern by educators is the lack of diversity among Texas teachers. It is projected that by 2025, two out of every three children in Texas will be members of minority groups. However, the majority (73%) of all teachers in Texas are White, while 23% are minorities with 14% reporting a Latino ethnicity, which is considered the fastest growing teacher group. African American teachers make up 1.3% of all teachers. Some state researchers think that the disparity in academic achievement between White and minority children can be mitigated with strong recruitment of a diverse teacher force, especially in districts with high

**Table 7.1.  Texas Student Enrollment, 2005-2006**

| *Ethnicity/Race* | *In %* |
|---|---|
| African American | 14.7% |
| Latino | 45.3% |
| Native American | 0.3% |
| Asian/Pacific Islander | 3.1% |
| White | 36.5% |
| Economically disadvantaged | 55.6% |
| At risk | 48.7% |
| Total Student count | 4,505,572 |

*Source:*  From data available on the Texas Educational Agency Web site: http://www.tea.state.tx.us/perfreport/aeis/2006/state.pdf

minority school enrollments (Texas Educational Agency, 2006). However, it is only within the last 35 years that Texas colleges and universities have begun seeing a significant presence of minority college students.

As mentioned above, Texas has a large number of private schools. In 2003-2004, the total number of K-12 private schools was 1,282, with a significantly large student enrollment of 220,206 and 20,673 teachers (Broughman & Swain). Per pupil expenditures were $7,136, with 9.9% of this revenue coming from the federal government.

Jimmy Aimes, executive director, Texas Private School Accreditation Commission, explained that private schools in the state are unregulated, which limits the amount of information available on these schools. About 820 private schools have voluntarily joined the state association and received accreditation, but Aimes stated that there are probably an additional 3000 or more private schools in the state (personal communication, August 10, 2005).

## TEXAS ASSESSMENT AND
## ACCOUNTABILITY SYSTEM BEFORE 2002

House Bill 72 was the first state law to raise high school graduation requirements. The Texas assessment system established under HB72 featured these elements: a standards-based curriculum; student testing including a high school graduation exam; a reporting system that specified test results by ethnic/racial group and economic status; and accountability for students, teachers, schools, and districts. The state department responsible for oversight of the plan has been the Texas Education Agency (TEA). Many believe that the Texas model influenced the creation of the No Child Left Behind legislation in 2001. For example, Watt, Powell, Mendiola, and Cossio (2006) made references to the "similarities between NCLB and the Texas accountability model" (p. 58; see also Achieve, Inc., 2002.) Education has been a priority for each of the last five Texas governors (Texas Educational Agency, 2002).

From 1980 to 1989, Texas assessed students for minimum skills in reading, writing, and math with the Texas Assessment of Basic Skills tests, which were norm-referenced. In 1990, the standards-based Texas Assessment of Academic Skills (TAAS) was developed as part of House Bill 72, and in 1999, educational reform legislation called for development of the Texas Assessment of Knowledge and Skills (TAKS) and End-of-Course requirements for high school students (Texas Educational Agency, 2005c).

From 1993, students in Grades 3 to 8 and 10 (exit level) were tested in reading and math, and students in Grades 4, 8, and 10 (exit level) were tested in writing. An effort was made to schedule tests so that results could reach schools and districts before fall. In 1994, the Spanish TAAS was developed for students in Grades 3-6, to serve the large number of students in Spanish bilingual programs.

TAKS was scheduled to be phased in from 2002 through 2005. However, for the 2002-2003 academic year, all students Grades 3 to 8, and 10 were required to take the TAAS tests. It wasn't until 2005 that the TAKS was fully phased in for students in Grades 3-10 (Texas Educational Agency, 2005b).

By law, students had to show satisfactory performance on the TAKS and the End-of-Course tests as graduation requirements since 2001. All students unless exempt, under certain conditions, based on special education (SPED) or limited English proficiency (LEP) status are required to take end-of-course tests for algebra I, biology, English II, and history, even if the student has passed the TAAS test in a specific content area. LEP students are also required to take the end-of-course tests, although recently arrived immigrants may postpone the timing of the tests. The state education agency issued a press release in 2005 that 91% of seniors had passed the TAKS (Texas Educational Agency, 2005b).

By legislation, the Texas Essential Knowledge and Skills (TEKS), the state curriculum in social studies, with standards for history, geography, economics, government, citizenship, culture, technology, and social science skills, established what all K-12 students in Texas should know and be able to do in the social sciences. The legislature further mandated that the Assessment of Knowledge and Skills (TAKS) be redesigned to be aligned with the TEKS standards and be given to students in more grade levels beginning in 2002-2003.

First developed in 1984 as part of HB72, the Academic Excellence Indicator System (AEIS), the state reporting system at TEA, has responded to changing legislation. AEIS collects a wide range of information on each Texas school and district. It provides a database to track student performance, attendance rates, college admission results, dropout rates, and other performance indicators.

By state mandate, AEIS has reporting responsibilities that include the School Report Card since in 1987. The School Report Card serves as the basis for rating schools and providing other information related to K-12 schools to parents and to the general public, with information made available on the TEA Web site. A school's rating is based on performance on the TAAS, dropout rates, and attendance rates. Based on 1995 provisions, there are four ratings for districts and individual schools: Exemplary (for either a school or a district), Recognized (for either a school or a district), Accredited (for a school), and Accredited-Warned (for a school).

Texas provides for both sanctions and remedies for poor student performance. Once identified, districts and schools receiving low accountability ratings receive site visits from a peer review team from the Education Agency and are required to develop and implement an improvement plan. If the district or school continues to receive poor ratings over two or more consecutive years, the level of intervention increases. Schools and district ratings from 1994 through 2002 included: Exemplary, Recognized, Academically Acceptable, Academically Unacceptable, and Academically Unacceptable: Special Accreditation Investigation (SAI) (Texas Educational Agency, 2005f).

The Texas system includes monetary rewards for high performance or improvement under the Successful Schools Award System. In 1999, the Texas legislature appropriated $5 million for these school awards to be based on the 2000 ratings. Decisions on how this money is used are made at the district or school level.

In 1995, the Texas legislature designed the Public Education Grant Program (PEG), a program that would allow parents with children who attended low-performing schools to transfer their children to another public school, even if that school was outside district boundaries, but had higher performance results.

Teacher shortages and attrition are recognized as significant problems, and teacher quality was an early concern as seen in 1984, when new legislation mandated testing in basic skills for all Texas public school teachers. From 1984 to 1993, by statute, the Texas Teacher Career Ladder provided salary stipends of $1,000 to $6,000 for teachers meeting certain requirements based on tenure and evaluation results.

The Career Ladder program proved controversial among Texas teachers and has been difficult to administer. In many schools, competition for the stipends created an unfriendly school environment, as teachers were afraid to share ideas with each other. Administrators, especially if not well trained, appeared to favor some teachers regardless of classroom effectiveness, and skewed teacher evaluation results. Because of mounting complaints, many schools gave all tenured teachers some sort of stipend funded by state and local revenues.

Other programs developed to address teacher quality included: the Texas Beginning Educator Support System (which reached only 10% of new teachers); professional development by the Regional Service Centers; student loan forgiveness and Cancellation Opportunities (for students in subject-matter shortage areas and designated low-income schools); and Improving Teacher Quality State Grants (available to State Agencies, local educational agencies (LEAs), and state agencies for higher education).

Taken together the comprehensive Texas Assessment system before 2002 moved the state towards closer alignment of standards to the state tests, attempted to address the issue of teacher quality, but created anxiety among the educational establishment, parents, and students by demanding accountability from all of them. As the results in the next section indicate, the system worked and moved Texas out of the education "dark ages."

## TAKS and NAEP Scores

The National Assessment of Educational Progress (NAEP), often called "the Nation's Report Card," provides a basis for comparing student performance across the United States. In 2001, the *Austin American Statesman* reported that African American and Latino Grade 4 students in Texas ranked number one in the nation in math, and White Grade 4 students tied for first place with students in Connecticut ("Minority Fourth Grade Scores," 2001). Student performance in other areas was reported strong, although 14 other states had significantly higher proficiency levels in Grade 8 math than did Texas.

The spring 2000 TAAS results for students meeting the standards in Grades 3 to 8 and 10 are shown on Table 7.2.

In 2003, the Texas Education Agency (TEA) announced in two press releases that the 2002 NAEP reading scores for students in the major ethnic/racial groups and for students who qualified for free/reduced lunch in Texas were higher than those in other states. Texas scores in the NAEP writing exam were not significantly higher than the average national scores (Texas Educational Agency, 2003, 2005b).

Based on this information, the Texas assessment system, established long before the NCLB legislation, appeared to be an effective system that produced early impressive results. The state's modern reform efforts date back to Perot's reforms in 1984, which served as the basis for the develop-

**Table 7.2.   TAAS Results, 2002, Grades 3-8, and 10**

|  | *Student Group, by Percent Passing* | | | |
|---|---|---|---|---|
|  | *All* | *African American* | *Latino* | *Economically Disadvantaged* |
| Reading | 91.3% | 86.7% | 86.9% | 86% |
| Math | 92.7% | 86.5% | 90.1% | 88.9% |
| Writing | 88.7% | 84.5% | 83.7% | 82.7% |

*Source:*   From data found in the "Texas Assessment of Academic Skills (TAAS) Table," Texas Educational Agency (http://www.tea.state.tx.us/perfreport/account/2002/state/html)

ment of educational standards in the state. Reforms established by the Perot Commission efforts mandated (1) specific requirements for high school graduation, (2) annual testing of students at every level, and (3) reporting by the state on the results of student performance by ethnic and socio-economic levels. These also have served as central components of NCLB legislation.

## INITIAL NCLB IMPACT ON STATE SYSTEM

When the U.S. Congress passed the No Child Left Behind (NCLB) in 2001, it mandated sweeping changes for schools and districts based on the concept of accountability. NCLB, Public Law 107-110, was enacted on January 8, 2002, although most provisions of the statute went into effect on July 1, 2002. Because Texas had an effective accountability plan prior to NCLB, the basic structures and the leadership were already in place to meet the new federal legislation, although certain refinements were made to comply with the new requirements. For example, a new Texas Educational Agency (TEA) unit was created, the Division of NCLB Program Coordination.

As early as 2001, TEA had been posting accountability tables on its website showing data such as the dropout rates for minority and economically-disadvantaged students, student performance scores on the Texas Assessment of Academic Skills (TAAS), school attendance data by various student groups, and college admission rates for different student groups. The agency had also designed an accreditation system that provided for monitoring and alternative interventions of schools based on student test performance.

Elements in the Texas accountability plan submitted for NCLB approval as posted on the U.S. Department of Education are based on a variety of principles including the following:

- accountability for schools,
- accountability for students,
- accountability for AYP of schools and districts,
- accountability for students in subgroups,
- accountability for graduation rates and other additional indicators, and
- accountability for a system for calculating rate of statewide participation for all students and small schools (Texas Educational Agency, 2004c).

On June 6, 2003, U.S. Education Secretary Rod Paige (a Texan and former Houston School District superintendent) approved the basic elements of Texas' accountability plan. Representing Paige, Laurie Rich, along with Texas Commissioner of Education Felipe Alanis and U.S. Representative John Carter, made the announcement from the State Capitol in Austin. Texas became the 33rd state to gain approval of its NCLB plan. Texas received $9 billion in funding, including $8 billion to implement its plan (Texas Educational Agency, 2005e).

Under NCLB, schools, districts, and the state must meet Adequate Yearly Progress (AYP) based on certain indicators that include student performance in reading/language arts and math, and either high school graduation rates or attendance rates (for elementary and middle schools). Information about schools, districts, or the state on any failure to make AYP is made public, although publicizing school ratings was a feature of the Texas assessment plan prior to NCLB. New sanctions were developed for Title I schools and districts when a unit did not make AYP, and all instructional staff working with Title I had to be "highly qualified."

## Initial Response to Teacher Quality Concerns and NCLB

Teacher quality has been a concern for state policy makers since House Bill 72, in 1984. Prior to NCLB, there were several programs with various success rates that addressed teacher quality, the most notable of which was the master teacher program created in 1999. However, the state had no systematic statewide strategy to manage the issue of teacher quality in the lowest-performing schools, something the new legislation sought to address. The NCLB definition of "highly qualified" was not in complete alignment with state certification regulations, something TEA quickly sought to remedy. Regional Service Centers prepared to provide support for professional development.

TEA was informed that the use of various permits, temporary credentials, or waivers issued by the State Board Educator Certification office were not in compliance with NCLB, with certain exceptions. In charter schools, teachers had not previously been required to be certified unless they were special education (SPED) or bilingual teachers, but under the new legislation, all teachers were required to be "highly qualified," including teachers in charter schools. To be considered highly qualified under NCLB, a teacher must hold a college degree in a content area if she or he teaches in a core subject area, and he or she must demonstrate competency in the state mandated ExCET/TexES content exams.

NCLB also outlined changes in the requirements for Texas paraprofessionals under Title I. Before NCLB, the state had required all paraprofessionals to hold high school diplomas. After January 8, 2002, newly hired paraprofessionals working under Title I also had to have completed 2 years of college or be able to demonstrate that they had the ability to teach. Paraprofessionals had until January 8, 2006 to meet these requirements, and local educational agencies (LEAs) can use Title I funds to assist them in meeting the new qualifications. The new qualifications applied only to paraprofessionals working in schools receiving Title I, Part A funding (Texas Educational Agency, 2005d).

Thus, Texas was well positioned to respond to the NCLB, given that it had a well-established accountability system prior to NCLB's implementation. In fact the federal act incorporated several components of the Texas system. Nevertheless, it was a year before Texas' accountability system received approval from the US Department of Education (U.S. DOE). Below we present the major challenges that Texas experienced in responding to NCLB's requirements, including charter schools and vouchers, and opposition to student testing.

## IMPLEMENTATION ISSUES

In April 2004, Texas State Commissioner of Education Shirley Neeley requested a timeline extension and exception to the 1% cap on use of alternative assessments for students with disabilities for purposes of AYP. The commissioner cited the need for more time to modify existing standards and to amend state statutes. The request included a proposal for inclusion of test scores for LEP students tested on alternative assessments, which followed a similar request for flexibility on this issue earlier that year. Dr. Neeley stressed the importance of having proposed changes to state education law reviewed and approved by the legislature. In a decision letter dated July 27, 2004, to Shirley Neeley, Raymond Simon of the U.S. DOE fully approved Texas' amended plan.

A second appeal on September 8, 2005, requested waivers and other flexibility owing to the influx of students into the state following Hurricane Katrina. About 250,000, evacuees, one quarter of whom were children, poured into the state due to the hurricane. Dr. Neeley also asked for additional funding (Neeley, 2005).

In September 2005, U.S. Secretary of Education Margaret Spellings responded to Dr. Neeley's requests. Spellings' detailed response included a proposal to provide up to $1.9 billion to school districts and charter schools enrolling at least 10 displaced students, and granted waivers and modifications for the following: (1) postponement and flexibility of Office of Special Education Program requirements, and (2) flexibility in NCLB timelines, reporting and monitoring.

However, Spellings stated that waivers were not needed for meeting highly qualified teachers/paraprofessionals requirements and for meeting the IDEA timelines, as provisions already existed to address this special circumstance. As Secretary Spellings stated, "The Department has determined that Texas has sufficient flexibility under its Ed-Flex agreement to waive these sections." In the letter, Spellings requested additional information on Neeley's requests on the use of NCLB funds, possible extension of participation in research projects, student assignment under NCLB, and information on state amendments relating to AYP, which Spellings called "the linchpin of No Child Left Behind accountability system." Showing the federal commitment to the new legislation, Secretary Spellings ended her letter by expressing reluctance to modify any required timelines related to NCLB (Texas Educational Agency, 2005e).

## Choice for Students in Texas

Under the new Texas Plan, agency interventions became more clearly defined than the system in place prior to NCLB, and they included various stages of intervention for both the individual schools and their LEAs. The new system included LEA requirements to provide information, including options to parents once a school is identified for improvement by TEA. Under the state plan, sanctions for low-performing schools are given the first year the school is identified.

Various interventions/sanctions are instituted for low-performing schools or districts as determined by the State Commissioner. For schools, interventions/sanctions range from issuing a notice of deficiency to school closure for continued low performance. Under the state plan, which was in place prior to NCLB, students are provided with a transfer option from a low-performing school identified under the Public Education Grant. Under the grant, a school is identified as low-performing when less than 50% of students pass the TAAS tests in any one of the following content areas in a 3-year period: reading, writing, or math.

Under NCLB's requirements for school choice, students and parents are provided with another transfer option. Districts are required to offer students in Title I schools identified as needing improvement with the option to transfer to a school not identified as needing improvement. Table 7.3 shows district and school ratings for 2002 through 2005; ratings for 2003 were not available.

The ratings indicate a drop in the number of districts and schools rated "Exemplary" or "Recognized" and an increase in the number of districts rated "Academically Unacceptable" after NCLB. In 2002, 98.5% of districts were "Academically Acceptable" or above, but in 2005, this num-

**Table 7.3.   Texas District and School Ratings**

|  | 2002 | 2004 | 2005 |
|---|---|---|---|
| Districts* |  |  |  |
| Exemplary | 14.3% | .9% | .9% |
| Recognized | 40.9% | 14% | 14% |
| Academically acceptable | 43.3% | 80.5% | 80.5% |
| Academically unacceptable | 1.3% | 4.2% | 4.2% |
| Academically unacceptable | .2% |  |  |
| :SAI (Special Accreditation Investigation) [Not used after 2002] | | | |
|  |  |  |  |
| Exemplary | 27% | 3.8% | 6.6% |
| Recognized | 33.7% | 24.1% | 32.5% |
| Academically acceptable | 29.1% | 60% | 45.8% |
| Low performing** | 2.3% |  |  |
| Academically unacceptable |  | 3.3% | 1.2% |
| Not Rated |  | 8.6% | 4.9% |

*Note:*   Other categories not included. For example, under District rankings, there is a category called "Not Rated: Data Integrity Issues." Ratings for 2004-2005 include charter schools. Data can be located in the "Accountability Rating System for Texas Schools and Districts," TEA Web site, http://www.tea.state.tx.us/perfreport/account/

ber dropped to 95.4%. In 2002, 89.8% of schools were "Academically Acceptable" or above, and in 2005, this number dropped to 84.9%. However, between 2002 and 2005, the majority of districts and schools earned a rating of "Academically Acceptable" or higher under both the old assessment system and the one after NCLB.

## Texas Charter Schools and Vouchers

Major educational reform (Senate Bill I) in 1995, passed by the 74th Legislature and signed into law by Governor George W. Bush modified the Texas Education Code giving the State Board the authority to grant open enrollment charter schools. House Bill 318, which received strong public support, significantly strengthened charter school legislation (Heritage Foundation (2005).

The number of charter schools grew from 17 in 1996 to 185 in 2003. Texas charter schools are accredited, supervised and funded by the state, and must comply with some of the provisions of the state education code.

Many offer alternative methods of instruction. The Heritage Foundation rated Texas' charter school law as strong, and the state had 284 schools in operation in 2005, with 80,000 students enrolled.

Several studies have found that Texas charter schools serve larger proportions of low-income, African American and at-risk students than public schools statewide. According to a study conducted by the Texas Policy Foundation on charter schools, researchers Gronberg and Jansen (2005) concluded that elementary and middle school students in charter schools showed greater improvement on standardized tests over time than did students in regular schools, based on 2003 and 2004 student assessments.

At the high school levels, Gronberg and Jansen (2005) concluded that students in charter schools made greater gains in reading than students in regular schools, but students in regular public schools showed more improvement in math. The researchers concluded that:

- students who exited charter schools were doing better than if they had remained in traditional public schools;
- charter schools serve as a viable alternative to public schools and encourage educators in public schools to do better; and
- charter schools offer an important, informative, and encouraging institutional design.

However, another study of Texas charter schools found substantial variation in school quality among charter schools and no significant difference in school quality after the initial start-up period. Researchers also concluded that parents were more sensitive to the education quality in charter schools than in regular schools. In other words, parents were more likely to exit what they considered to be a low quality charter school and were more likely to let their children stay in a high quality charter school, a significant finding (Hanusheck, Kain, & Rivkin, 2002).

A study commissioned by the U.S. Department of Education found that charter schools were less likely to meet state performance standards. In Texas, researchers found that while 98% of students in public schools met performance standards, 66% of students in charter schools met the standards. In addition, the researchers found that charter schools tend to be in urban areas and serve higher percentages of minority students than do regular public schools. Commenting on the findings, Paul Peterson stated, "When you target a needy population, you will have more difficulty reaching state standards" (Dillon & Shemo, 2004, p. 2). However, even when researchers controlled for race and poverty in Texas, students still underperformed their public school counter-parts. Other studies have both supported and refuted these findings (Dillon & Shemo).

Because of these conflicting findings, it is difficult to judge the efficacy of Texas charter schools. The Hanushek et al. (2002) study found that parents are more likely to exit badly run charter schools, which shows that parents are "paying attention" and are willing to take their children out of a bad school. This, in turn, suggests that parents of students enrolled in charter schools are at least somewhat satisfied with the school's performance. The fact that charter schools increased in numbers so dramatically between 1996 and 2003 and served 80,000 students in 2005 affirms that they are filling an important role in offering choice in public education in Texas.

Since the late 1990s, several bills have been introduced to create a statewide school voucher system in Texas, but so far none has received approval of both the House and Senate. Nevertheless, evidence suggests that expanded school choice appears to be strongly supported by Governor Rick Perry, many legislators, and the general public.

## Opposition to Student Testing

Initial opposition to school reform came from teachers and from special interest groups representing minority legal rights in the state. In 1995, the NAACP filed a complaint with the U.S. Department of Education Office of Civil Rights (OCR) on the basis that the student tests discriminated against minority students. However, OCR found no evidence of discrimination.

In 2000, MALDEF filed a lawsuit, *GI Forum v. Texas Education Agency*, alleging that the TAAS high school exit exam (which measures basic proficiency in reading, writing, and math) discriminated against minority students, citing a history of discrimination in Texas schools. Federal judge Edward Prado, from San Antonio, ruled for the state. In his ruling, Prado asserted, "Ultimately, resolution of this case turns not on the validity of the parties' views on education but on the state's right to pursue educational policies that it legitimately believes are in the best interest of Texas students" (READ Institute, n.d.). MALDEF did not to appeal the ruling.

In a subsequent news release announcing the ruling, Texas Commissioner of Education Jim Nelson said,

> We've had an exit-level test requirement in law since 1984, when the Legislature passed House Bill 72, and it's here to stay.... Let's all work together to make sure our children have access to the best possible education.... Our world is only going to get more complex and challenging, and our children need to be well prepared to thrive in that world and meet those challenges (Texas Education Agency, 2000).

Opposition to state testing in Texas has also come from university academics including Angela Valenzuela from the University of Texas at Austin, who has written extensively on the topic. Dr. Valenzuela believes standardized testing is especially harmful to language minority students (Valenzuela & McNeil, 2000; Valenzuela, 2000; also, see Grant, 2004). Of the TAAS tests, Valenzuela and McNeil stated,

> For children, successful performance on the TAAS in no way insures either a quality education or a promising future. An education aimed at TAAS scores does unequivocally reduce children's chances of a real education. The pressure to raise scores is greatest in our poorest, historically least well-funded schools (p. 20).

Also opposed to the current use of standardized testing in schools are organizations such as FairTest that have established national websites and have started a grass-roots movement in 36 states, including Texas, against the misuse of standardized testing in K-12 schools.

## Results on Student Performance Statewide After NCLB

It is difficult fully to assess the impact of NCLB on student performance in Texas because the state already had many of the elements of the legislation in place prior to the federal mandate. A preliminary examination reflects the tougher standards of the TAKS tests discussed earlier that resulted in lower scores in their initial implementation in response to NCLB. We begin this section by reviewing test results by student group on the Texas Assessment of Academic Skills (TAAS), the tests offered in 2002 to every student in Grades 3 through 8 and 10, and results from the Texas Assessment of Knowledge and Skills (TAKS) in reading and math for 2003-2005 for students in the same grades. The TAKS scores listed for "Reading" include assessment in English language arts. Table 7.4 summarizes results from the NAEP tests from 2002-2005.

Generally, results indicate that in both reading and math, all students performed less well on the more rigorous TAKS tests. In 2003, 72% of all students met the TAKS standards in reading; this percentage rose to 83 in 2005. In math, 57% of all students met the TAKS standards in 2003; by 2005, this percentage rose to 72. The 2006 scores for students were not fully available on the state website at the time of this writing.

In August 11, 2005, a TEA press release reported that 87% of all Texas districts had made AYP. To make AYP, a district had to have higher scores or show improvement from previous years. Using 2005 criteria, 149 districts did not make AYP, which included 147 districts and 678 schools with Title I programs. Nevertheless, the overall findings on student perfor-

**Table 7.4.    Texas Student Assessments, Statewide, Percent Passing or Met Standard (Grades 3-8, and 10)**

| Reading | 2002 | 2003 | 2004 | 2005 |
|---|---|---|---|---|
| All students | 91.3% | 72% | 80% | 83% |
| African American | 86.7% | 61% | 79% | 76% |
| Latino | 86.9% | 63% | 79% | 77% |
| White | 96.3% | 83% | 93% | 91% |
| Economically disadvantaged | 86% | Not listed | 78% | 76% |

| Math | 2002 | 2003 | 2004 | 2005 |
|---|---|---|---|---|
| All students | 92.7% | 57% | 76% | 72% |
| African Am. | 86.5% | 41% | 62% | 57% |
| Latino | 90.1% | 47% | 68% | 64% |
| White | 96.5% | 71% | 86% | 84% |
| Economically disadvantaged | 88.9% | Not listed | 67% | 62% |

*Note:*   Data used can be found in the Texas Education Agency Web site, accessed at http://www.tea.state.tx.us and http://www.tea.state.tx.us/perfreport/aeis/2006/state.html

mance based on state standards appear impressive, until one reviews results on the NAEP.

In contrast to this rosy picture on incremental improvement on student performance, the *Quality Counts 2005* Report Card shows the following results for students at the proficient level and above levels based on 2003 NAEP results: 33% proficient or above in Grade 4 math; 25% proficient or above in Grade 8 math; 27% proficient or above in Grade 4 reading; and 26% proficient or above in Grade 8 reading (*Quality Counts*, 2005).

Table 7.5 illustrates the national averages in math and reading for the period under review.

NAEP results generally show improvement for students in reading and math during the 2 years of testing, which many consider too short a time span to attribute improvements in student performance to NCLB, especially because the state already had a comprehensive assessment system in place. A comparison of the state and NAEP tests shows that the state's definition of proficiency compares more closely with the basic level, rather than the proficient level on the NAEP. Proficiency definitions for purposes of AYP for most states are far less rigorous than the proficiency level on the NAEP. Numerous critiques of these discrepancies and the variability of state standards have been made (see Dillon, 2005).

The *Quality Counts 2005* Report rates Texas' accountability plan with a grade of C+ noting that the plan is well known but their analysis suggests

**Table 7.5.   NAEP Results, 2003-2005, at the Basic Level and Above**

|  | Grade 4 | | Grade 8 | |
|---|---|---|---|---|
|  | *Math* | *Reading* | *Math* | *Reading* |
| 2003 | 82% | 60% | 69% | 71% |
| 2005 | 87% | 64% | 72% | 69% |
| National | 79% | 65% | 68% | 65% |
| Proficient Level and Above | | | | |
| 2003 | 33% | 27% | 25% | 26% |
| 2005 | 40% | 29% | 31% | 26% |
| National | 35% | 30% | 32% | 29% |

*Note.* Data used can be found in the "State Profiles, Texas," NCES, Available from http://nces.ed.gov/nationsreportcard/states/profile.asp

that it could be improved. The report cites the state's failure to mandate a complete set of course requirements for teachers that are content specific; the lack of financial incentives for high performing/improving schools; and the state's unequal school funding and per-pupil funding below the national average. Equal funding of schools has been a problem for the state that continues to be reflected in this analysis. Texas did have the Texas Successful Schools Award System from 1999 through 2001, but discontinued the program owing to a lack of funding. It is curious that content specific course requirements for teachers have not been outlined under the current plan given the state's early concern with teacher quality.

For 2007, the Editorial Projects in Education Research Center, that designed the *Quality Counts* assessments, developed a "transitional document" based on a state's own assessment, including improvements over time. *Quality Counts 2007* ranked Texas 48th among the states on its Chance-for-Success Index; 11th on the alignment of its education system with the state's economy and work opportunities; 16th in achievement indicators and 9th on its standards, assessments and accountability system.

Under the grading system developed by the Fordham Foundation in 2004, Texas received a grade of "Fair" for its standards, which are called "clear, specific, and measurable, and almost entirely focused on essential skills" (Cross, Rebarber, Torres, & Finn, 2004, p. 32). On its accountability policies prior to NCLB, the state received a rating of 4 out of 4 points with the Fordham Foundation researchers stating that the system was well designed and predicting that when Texas' NCLB plan was fully implemented, the expectation was that it also would be an effective system.

NAEP and state test results and the history with educational reform in this state support this prediction.

Nationwide, NCLB gets mixed reviews because of the small gains seen in the NAEP data, despite the enormous and expensive efforts on the part of the states. Nevertheless, Secretary of Education Spellings recently stated, "I'm very pleased that we're making steady progress, which is driven by increased progress by Hispanic and African American students, which is the whole point of No Child Left Behind" (Olson & Manzo, 2005). Many Texans agree with this assessment.

## CONCLUSION AND PROSPECTS FOR MEETING NCLB GOALS

Texas shows strong gains in education considering the state's large minority student population, and the fact that close to 40% of students are eligible for free lunch (often used as an indicator of poverty). Texas' progress in education was prompted by a strong early push from the business community and was further refined by the results of the state's litigious history. It has also benefited from strong leadership at the state level, particularly from the governor's office. All of these factors have contributed to impressive gains in education the last 20 years. Educators and policymakers in the state have crafted an admirable accountability system since the 1980s in attempting to meet the education needs of all students. There are other states that served as the model for the NCLB legislation, but many believe that Texas' accountability plan has been the most influential.

Under the state's system, the 2005 report on accreditation and sanctions for school districts and charter schools indicated that 19 were rated exemplary, 378 were recognized, and 712 were unacceptable. Of 1,227 school districts and charter schools, 24 were deemed academically unacceptable, 85 were not rated (all alternative charter schools), and 9 were not rated (charter schools) (Texas Education Agency, 2005a).

Coupled with results from the state and NAEP tests, these are all hopeful indicators. Researchers Fuller and Johnson (2001) believe that Texas has made significant gains especially with minority children and children from low-income homes. It wasn't that long ago that the educational system was failing and failing miserably in educating the state's most vulnerable citizens.

Will Texas meet those 2014 NCLB goals? The evidence indicates that educators in Texas, who provided the rest of the nation with an effective educational reform model, have worked hard to upgrade their public school system and evidence suggests that they are making every effort to meet these goals. We predict that Texas will come as close as humanly possible in meeting the lofty goals set by NCLB and that Texans will continue to persevere in their historic and admirable efforts to improve public education.

## NOTES

1. Corridos (ballads) often provided news and stories based on historical events related to the Latino population in Texas often with an interpretation not available in the newspapers and textbooks of the 1800s and 1900s. For information on corridos in Texas, there is not a better source than the incomparable Americo Paredes, folklorist, journalist, English and anthropology professor, and mentor extraordinaire from the University of Texas at Austin. His first book told the 1901 story of a Mexican American hero/ Texas outlaw Gregorio Cortez. See *With a Pistol in His Hand*, 1958, University of Texas Press: Austin. For his work, Paredes himself became a much beloved hero to the Mexican American population in Texas.

2. Manuel Ramirez, a psychology professor from the University of Texas at Austin, was the first academic to challenge the cultural deficit theories. See Ramirez, Taylor, and Peterson (1971), and Ramirez's other work. Another well-known scholar on social policies, poverty and minorities in the United States has been William Julius Wilson (1987).

3. One small but telling example: Most state education Web sites will give the state name followed by the words "Education Department." The Texas Web site reads "Welcome to the Texas Education Agency."

4. Under the "No Pass, No Play" provision, a student had to be passing his courses in order to be eligible to participate in sports. Football is pretty serious business in Texas.

## REFERENCES

Achieve, Inc. (2002). *Aiming higher: Meeting the challenges of educational reform in Texas*. Retrieved June 4, 2007, from http://www.tea.state.tx.us/curriculum/aimhitexas.pdf#xml=http://www.tea.state.tx.us/cgi/te

Alexander, C., Gronberg, T., Jansen, D., Keller, H., Taylor, L., & Treisman, P. (2002). *A study of uncontrollable variations in the cost of Texas public education* (Technical Supplement). Austin, TX: Dana Center.

Baron, M., & Cohen, R. (2005). *The almanac of American politics, 2006*. Washington, DC: National Journal Group.

Broughman, S., & Swaim, N. (2006, March). *Characteristics of private schools in the United States: Results from the 2003-2004 private school universe survey* (NCES 2006-319). Washington, DC: U.S. Department of Education, NCES.

Cross, R., Rebarber, T., Torres, J., & Finn, C. (2004). *Grading the systems: The guide to state standards, tests, and accountability policies*. Retrieved December 20, 2005, from http://www.edexcellence.net/ foundation/topic/topic.cfm?topic=Testing percent20 percent26 percent 20Accountability.

Dillon, S. (2005, November 26). Students ace state tests, but earn D's from U.S. *The New York Times*, p. A1.

Dillon, S., & Schemo, D. (2004, November 23). Charter schools fall short in public school matchup. *The New York Times*, p. 2.

*Education Week*. Texas state information. (2005). Retrieved November 18, 2005, from http://www.edweek.org/rc/states/texas

Fuller, E., & Johnson, J. (2001). Can state accountability systems drive improvements for children of color and children from low-income homes? *Education and Urban Society, 33*(3), 260-283.

Fusarelli, L. (2002). The political economy of gubernatorial elections: Implications for educational policy, *Educational Policy, 16*(1), 139-159.

Grant, C. (2004). Oppression, privilege, and high-stakes testing. *Multicultural Perspectives, 6*(1), 3-11.

Gronberg, T., & Jensen, D. (2005). *Texas charter schools: An assessment*. Austin: Texas: Policy Foundation.

Hanushek, E. (2003, October 22). *Thinking about school finance in Texas: Testimony to the subcommittee on cost adjustments of the select House Committee on Public School finance*. Austin: Texas Public Policy Foundation.

Hanushek, E., Kain, J., & Rivkin, S. (2002). *The impact of charter schools on academic achievement*. Unpublished paper, Stanford University.

Heritage Foundation. (2005). Research education, Texas. *School Choice*, pp. 1-9. Retrieved November 1, 2005, at http://heritage.org/Research/Education/SchoolChoice/Texas.cfm.

Hoff, D. (2004, September 22). Texas judge rules funds not enough: State school aid formula found unconstitutional. *Education Week*, p. 1.

Imazeki, J., & Reschovsky, A. (2003). *School finance reform in Texas: A never ending story?*Madison, WI: University of Wisconsin-Madison.

Minority fourth grade scores lead nation: Minority eighth graders scores up but need help. (2001, August 3). *Austin American Statesman*. Retrieved June 4, 2007, from Texas Math Initiative Web site, http://tea.state.tx.us/math/TexNAEPSco.htm

McNeeley, D. (1989, June 15). White ponders another run for governor. *Austin American Statesman*, A13.

Murdock, S. (2005). *Population change in Texas: Implications for human and socioeconomic resources in the 21st century*. San Antonio: The University of Texas San Antonio.

Neeley, S. J. (2005). Letter to Raymond Simon, Deputy Secretary U. S. Department of Education. Retrieved 2 March 2007 from http://www.tea.state.tx.us/taa/comm090905a1.pdf

Olson, L., & Manzo, K. (2005, October 20). Despite NCLB's emphasis on reading and math, national test scores show little change. *Edweek.org*. Retrieved, November 1, 2005, at http://www.edweek.org.

PBS. (2007). *The border/1948 American G. I. Forum*. Retrieved February 2, 2007, from http://www.pbs.org/kpbs/theborder/history/index.html

*Quality Counts*. (2005). Report card: Texas. *Education Week*. Retrieved November 1, 2005, at http://www.edweek.org/rc/states/texas.html?print=1

*Quality Counts.* (2007). From cradle to career: Connecting American education from birth through adulthood. *Quality Counts 2007*, 1-7. Retrieved January 29, 2007, from www.edweek.org/rc

Ramirez, M., Taylor, C., & Peterson, B. (1971). Mexican-American cultural membership and adjustment to school. *Developmental Psychology, 4*(20), 141-148.

READ Institute. (n.d.). Passing THE TEST: A summary of GI Forum v. Texas Education Agency. The READ Institute, 1-7, Retrieved December 20, 2005, from http://www.ceousa.org/READ/clegg.html.

Reyes, M. (1991). *Female Hispanic college students: Upper-division and graduate students at four major public institutions in Texas.* Unpublished dissertation, The University of Texas at Austin.

Texas Educational Agency. (2000). *TAAS case ends as MALDEF fails to file appeal on judge's ruling.* Press Release, February 7, 2000. Retrieved August 15, 2005, at http://www.tea.state.tx.us/press/pro000207c.html

Texas Educational Agency. (2002). Aiming higher, Meeting the challenges of education reform in Texas. *Achieve Benchmarking Initiative.* Posted on the state education website. Retrieved November 2005, at http://www.tea.state.tx.us/

Texas Educational Agency. (2003). *Major Texas ethnic groups outscore similar groups across the country on NAEP reading exam* (Press release). Retrieved December 2, 2006, from http://www.tea.state.tx.us/press/naepwrit02.html.

Texas Educational Agency. (2004a). *Pocket edition, 2004-05, Texas public school statistics* (Texas Education Agency Division of Performance Reporting). Retrieved June 4, 2007, from http://www.tea.state.tx.us/perfreport/pocked/2005/pocked0405.pdf

Texas Educational Agency. (2004b). *Student enrollment, statewide totals.* Retrieved at http://www.tea.state.tx.us

Texas Educational Agency. (2004c, July 27). *Texas consolidated state application accountability workbook.* (Available on the U.S. Department of Education Web site.) Retrieved June 4, 2007, from http://www.tea.state.tx.us/research/ed_links.html

Texas Educational Agency. (2005a). *Accountability system: State summary.* Texas Education Agency. Retrieved December 14, 2005, at http://www.tea.state.tx.us/perfreport/account/index.html

Texas Educational Agency. (2005b). 91 percent of seniors pass TAKS: state performance up overall. May 20, 2005, Press release. Retrieved December 2006, at http://www.tea.state.tx.us/

Texas Educational Agency. (2005c). *The history of public education in Texas.* TEA: Austin. Retrieved December 19, 2005, at http://www.tea.state.tx.us/tea/history-overview.html

Texas Educational Agency. (2005d). Paraprofessional requirements under Title I, Part A. Retrieved December 19, 2005, from http://www.tea.state.tx.us/

Texas Educational Agency. (2005e). *Secretary Paige approves Texas' state accountability plan under No Child Left Behind* (Press release). Retrieved November 30, 2005, from the TEA website http://www.tea.state.tx.us/

Texas Educational Agency. (2005f, July 15). *Report on the accreditation, interventions, and sanctions of school districts and charter schools.* Austin, TX: Author.

Texas Educational Agency. (2006). *Texas teacher diversity and recruitment.* Retrieved November 28, 2005, at http://www.tea.state.tx.us/cgi/texis/webinator/search/?db=&db=db&query=teachers percent2C+number percent2C+ethnicity&search.x=0&search.y=0&search=Search

Texas Public Policy Foundation. (2005). *Four myths of public school finance.* Retrieved November 9, 2005, at http://www.texaspolicy.com/publications.php

Texas Politics. (2005). *The Texas Constitution, equality and public education, Edgewood ISD v. Kirby.* Austin: The University of Texas at Austin. Retrieved December 20, 2005, from http://texaspolitics.laits.utexas.edu/html/cons/features/0404_01/edgewood.html.

Valenzuela, A. (2000). The significance of the TAAS Test for Mexican immigrant and Mexican American adolescents: A case study. *Hispanic Journal of Behavioral Sciences, 22*(4), 524-539.

Valenzuela, A., & McNeil, L. (2000). *The harmful impact of the TAAS system of testing in Texas: Beneath the accountability rhetoric.* (ERIC Document Reproduction Service No. ED 443872)

Washingtonpost.com. (2007). Election 2006, Texas elections. Retrieved February 15, 2007, at http://www.washingtonpost.com/wp-

Watt, K., Powell, C., Mendiola, I., & Cossio, G. (2006). Schoolwide impact and AVID: How have selected Texas high schools addressed the new accountability measures? *Journal of Education for Students Placed at Risk, 11*(1), 57-73.

Wilson, W. J. (1987). *The truly disadvantaged.* Chicago: University of Chicago Press.

# CHAPTER 8

# MICHIGAN

## INTRODUCTION

We introduce the state of Michigan by reviewing its social, cultural, economic, and political characteristics, after which we turn to the nature of its educational system.

## Socioeconomic and Political Characteristics

In 2006, the estimated population of Michigan exceeded 10 million. The state population grew 6.9% between 1990 and 2000, and it is ranked eighth in the nation by size of population. The ethnic/racial makeup of the state is 78.6% Caucasian, 14.1% Black, 3.3% Latino, and 1.8% Asian. Racial minorities are concentrated in Michigan's cities, and its largest, Detroit, has a majority-minority population. Michigan has grown more slowly than the rest of the United States due to natural population decreases, lower immigration rates, and loss of residents to other states. Detroit, once the home of 2 million residents, has lost more than half its population in recent decades.

Most of the state's population (75%) lives in the urban parts of the state. Some 83% of state residents hold a high school diploma, while 22% are college graduates. The median household income is $44,667, with 10.5% of state residents living in poverty (Barone & Cohen, 2005, p. 845).

*Education Reform in the American States*
pp. 199–222

These statistics place Michigan well above the median of the 50 American states in income and education, reflected in the somewhat higher than average performance of the state's students on national tests. However, the numbers do not reflect the significant economic restructuring that continues to transform the Michigan economy.

Once the headquarters of the global automobile business, troubles in this industry from the 1970s to the present have reduced by more than half the number of high paid manufacturing jobs. Manufacturing still commands nearly 30% of the state's workforce, but growth in jobs has occurred in light, not heavy, industry such as auto parts, consumer goods, and technological products.[1] Service production employs a majority of the state's residents, including education (such as one of the nation's premier public universities, the University of Michigan at Ann Arbor), retail sales, finance, medical arts and other professions, and entertainment. Michigan also has a small agricultural sector.

Michigan's distribution of political forces followed the rise and fall of the auto industry. From the 1930s to the 1970s, Michigan was a solidly Democratic state, and during this time period it became one of the nation's strongest union states, represented by the power of the United Auto Workers (UAW), Teamsters, and by the state's primary teachers' union, the Michigan Education Association (MEA). The decline of jobs in manufacturing drained union power and diluted Democratic partisan identification. In the 1980s and 1990s, Republican candidates once again were competitive in elections at all levels, and in 1990, Republican John Engler won the governorship, holding it for 12 years. Engler cut taxes more than 30 times as governor; he attempted to develop a more diversified (and faster growing) economy, while protecting public education. Toward the end of his tenure as governor, Engler worked with a Republican-majority state legislature. He was the strongest advocate in Michigan for school vouchers, and an adamant enemy of MEA throughout his terms in office (see Boyd, Plank, & Sykes, 2000).

In the early twenty-first century, Michigan is called a "red" state politically, but in fact it sits close to the edge of the partisan divide and has been a battleground in presidential elections. In 2000, Al Gore collected 51% of Michigan's votes, and John Kerry held this margin in the 2004 presidential election. George W. Bush took 46 and 48% of the popular vote in the two elections, respectively. In the 110th Congress, Michigan is represented by two Democratic senators and a house delegation divided between Republicans (9) and Democrats (6). The state legislature mirrors state partisanship more closely. The Democrats control the House (58 Ds and 52 Rs) while the Republicans control the Senate (21 Rs, 17 Ds).

Jennifer Granholm won the governorship in 2002 with 51% of the vote, and she was reelected by a larger margin in 2006. Granholm won office with strong union backing, especially that of the teachers' unions. She is an opponent of school vouchers and less than lukewarm about charter schools. She has strongly supported public school funding. Michigan's educational system often seems caught up in a tug-of-war between competing political and economic forces.

## The State Educational System

The state has 4,042 public schools, 1,785,160 students, 89,595 teachers, and a pupil/teacher ratio of 19.9. A total of 27.6% of students in Michigan schools are minority and 13.3% are identified as students with disabilities (National Center for Educational Statistics, NCES, 2005). The ethnic/racial composition of the school population in 2002-2003 is 72.4% Caucasian, 20.3% Black, 3.8% Latino, 2.0% Asian/Pacific Islander, and 1.5% American Indian/Alaska Native.

The 1,012 private schools in the state have a total student enrollment of 179,579, a small percentage of the state's student K-12 enrollment. A total of 11,771 teachers work in Michigan's private schools. The state has a strong charter school law, which was enacted in 1993. In 2005, there were 196 charter schools in the state serving 60,236 students (Heritage Foundation, 2004). Under state law, the superintendent of public instruction, who is appointed by the State Board of Education, supervises all private, denominational, and parochial schools with children under 16.

Michigan's school system traditionally has been decentralized. As Cohen notes, although it has become more centrally directed, it has done so in "a more piecemeal fashion than California, Kentucky, or Vermont, with few signs of the guiding vision of reform that could be found in those three states" (Cohen, 1996, p. 104). Also, as indicated above, the state's educational system is relatively less well buffered from penetration by economic and political forces than systems in other states.

## EDUCATION REFORM IN MICHIGAN BEFORE 2002

The pattern in development of standards, assessments, and accountability was one of fits and starts before NCLB. We describe the pattern briefly, and then consider expressions of choice—both the charter school and voucher movements.

## Development of the State Accountability System

Michigan has a loosely coupled system of assessments, standards, and accountability. Elements in the system include content standards, assessments, teacher quality regulation, and rewards for students and schools based on performance. The basis for educational accountability was established nearly 40 years ago in the Michigan Educational Assessment Plan (MEAP), enacted as Public Act 307 (in 1969). That year MEAP tests were administered for the first time. MEAP tests are based on the performance standards in the Michigan Essential Goals and Objectives for Mathematics Education, Reading Education, Science Education, and Writing Education approved by the state board from 1988 to 1991 (Michigan Department of Education, MDE, 2002a), as well as the Model Core Curriculum Outcomes and the Content Standards approved by the state education board in 1994 (MDE, 2002a). In 1995 the state board approved further revised content standards, and the MEAP tests were based on the content standards approved by the board. The state contracted with Measurement Incorporated to score the MEAP tests although written tests were scored in Michigan (MDE, 2004a). Cohen (1996) describes state reform efforts of the 1990s in these terms:

> In certain respects it (reform legislation) expanded state influence in curriculum and sought to clarify lines of responsibility over matters of curriculum and instruction. But ... (the legislation) also reflected a deep tension between efforts to simplify instructional governance by establishing stronger state-level leadership over curriculum and instructional matters and efforts to preserve local control on these matters. (p. 109; also see Thompson, Spillane, & Cohen, 1994)

In 1996, the Michigan Department of Education (MDE) crafted Curriculum Frameworks in the core academic subjects, which replaced the Goals and Objectives as well as the Model Core Curriculum. *Achieve*, a bipartisan standards advocacy group created by governors and business leaders after the 1996 National Education Summit, conducted a benchmarking evaluation of the Michigan plan in 1998. It noted:

> The state assessments form the foundation for an accountability system focused on public reporting of individual schools' achievement results, identifying and warning schools in trouble; providing extra financial resources to chronically under-performing schools; and applying financial penalties and taking over or closing schools that continue to fail. (*Achieve*, 1998, p. 1)

In 2001, test development and planning committees (composed of Michigan educators) drafted significant changes in the content and scoring of the MEAP tests. They decided on proficiency levels and cut scores were set for students in Grades 4, 5, 7, and 8 (in reading and science), 5 and 8 (in writing and social studies), and for students in high school. By the time of testing in 2002, the assessments were aligned to content standards.

For high school graduation, the state assessment plan includes four categories for student performance in math, science, writing, reading, and social studies: Level 1 Endorsed, exceeds standards; Level 2 Endorsed, meet standards; Level 3, Endorsed, at basic level; and Level 4, Not endorsed. There is no exit exam for high school students in Michigan; however high school students passing the high school tests in math, science, writing, reading, and social studies do receive endorsements on their high school diploma.

Since 1998, the state has provided rewards for student performance in high school. Students passing MEAP tests in math, reading, science, and writing can receive $2,500 Michigan Merit Awards. These awards have been funded by the state's 1998 settlement with tobacco companies; they are available to all public school, charter school, nonpublic school, and home schooled students. In 2000, the state granted 43,068 awards, and by 2004, 52,727 awards were given to Michigan students to be used for a postsecondary education in an approved institution (MDE, 2004b).

MDE has one of the oldest school recognition programs in the nation. Established in 1982, the Blue Ribbon Exemplary School Program recognizes outstanding public and private schools, based on academic achievement, accreditation, school organization and culture, student focus and support, curriculum, quality teaching, and family/community partnerships. Since NCLB new requirements have been added: the recognized school must have made AYP and have a school grade of A or B under the Education YES! Program (the current assessment system), and not have a Native American based school mascot, nickname or logo. More than 350 schools have been recognized under this program.

The state's accountability system also had elements pertaining to teacher quality. Since 1967, the state has offered teacher licensure under various experimental programs for individuals holding a bachelor's or higher degree. However, the state board must first approve the program, and the provision has three years of certification and professional development requirements (MDE, 1997a). Since 1991, under the Michigan Test for Teacher Certification law, new teachers are required to pass a basic skills test. Requirements for new teachers to pass content area tests and elementary education tests were added in 1992. Current completers of this program also must meet all NCLB "highly qualified" teacher requirements. In 1995, the legislature established the Teacher Induction and Mentor Program. This required all new teachers to be mentored by a master teacher identified by a district or school committee for 3 years and in addition called for 15 days of intensive professional development. The state also has invested in professional development for teachers that matches standards-based reform (see Dutro et al., 2003).

## The Charter School Movement

Michigan established charter school laws in 1993, and now has 216 charter schools serving 82,000 students, almost 5% of the total enrollment in school districts (Heritage Foundation, 2004). On the *Education Freedom of Choice Index*, the state ranks ninth in the nation for its permissive laws. In 2002, the Commission of Charter Schools recommended creation of a statewide accountability system that would increase state authority over charter schools and the number of university sponsored charter schools. However, legislation to achieve this objective (HB 4800) was defeated by a close vote (Heritage Foundation, 2004). A 2002 survey by the Institute of Public Policy and Social Research at Michigan State showed wide support of state supported charter schools; several other studies have found charter schools to be both effective and cost efficient. Yet charter schools are politically controversial, with Republican governors supporting them and Democrats less warm in support (Heritage Foundation, 2005; see also Clowes, 2003). A number of critics believe that charter schools do not provide equitable access, and that they are the initial step toward a voucher-style system (see Lubienski, 2001; Miron & Nelson, 2002)

A 2002 study by the Mackinac Center found that children attending charter schools scored below those in public schools but were making more significant academic gains on the MEAP tests. In another study, which reviewed charter schools in Michigan, researcher Caroline Hoxby found that charter schools did not present a competition problem in Michigan. She believes that what little rivalry there is, is more substantial in elementary grades, because per pupil foundation funds received cover the cost of education at this level. Achievement was boosted in public schools faced with some competition. She concluded that achievement in public schools subjected to competition from charter school was statistically significant, but not large. Hoxby reasoned that this was because some Michigan schools (like those in Detroit) will take about two decades to catch up to the achievement levels of more affluent schools (Hoxby, 2004). Finally, Loveless (2002) found that student achievement was lower in charter schools.

Research studies on the effectiveness of charter schools are inconclusive. Yet charter schools enjoy the support of Michigan's Catholic bishops, and while controversial, also receive wide public support. Research established that competition of charter schools encouraged public schools to be more effective. In addition, charter schools were cost effective, and there was growth in student achievement in the charter schools when compared with student achievement in schools of the students' home districts (Heritage Foundation, 2005; see also Hill & Lake, 2002).

## The School Vouchers Controversy

In 1996, Public Act 180 established inter-district school choice that permitted students to transfer to a school in other participating districts within a county. The Postsecondary Enrollment Options Act of 1996, which continues today, permitted high school students to enroll in college course work while in high school (MDE, 1997b). These are relatively non-controversial means of expanding choice for parents. But in Michigan, the issue that has galvanized the most support and the most opposition has been the use of public funds for school vouchers that would allow parents to place their children in private (including religious) schools.

In 1991, Senate Bill 31, which would have given vouchers to urban students who came from low-income homes, was introduced and defeated in committee. In 1996, Amway founder and state board member Richard DeVos led school choice advocates (including many business leaders) in establishing a provouchers organization called *Kids First!* The group focused on the fact that in about 30 out of the 798 state school districts, the majority of students failed to graduate from high school. To remedy this, they sought to amend the state constitution to create a system of school vouchers for parents (worth half of public per-pupil expenditure) so that their children could attend "a school of their choice." Protestant and Catholic religious leaders voiced strong support for the proposal (Heritage Foundation, 2004, p. 8).

In 2000, *Kids First!* asked voters to approve Proposal 1, a constitutional amendment to provide: (1) that public school spending would never fall below a certain level, (2) that teachers in public and non-public schools would be tested in content areas, and (3) that students who lived in low-performing districts would receive Opportunity Scholarships worth half the public school expenditures (about $3,300 per student), so that they could attend a school of choice. A 2000 *Detroit News* survey reported that 53% of respondents favored the proposal and 23% opposed it (Heritage Foundation, 2004).

Opposition to Proposal 1 grew quickly. Teachers' unions and a coalition of 30 groups founded an antivoucher organization called *All Kids First!* (Clowes, 2001). The Michigan Association of School Boards (MASB) opposed the legislation because the amendment would also eliminate the prohibition against providing public funds to private and religious schools. MASB estimated that in Detroit alone, schools would lose $50 million (Michigan Association of School Boards, 2000).

In the November 2000 general election, Proposal 1 was soundly defeated by a more than 2 to 1 ratio, but the voucher idea did not die. Voucher proponents formed Choices for Children and the Great Lakes Education Project, private foundations to provide scholarships to children from low-income homes to attend a school of choice (private, religious, other). These organizations established the Education Freedom Fund, a private scholarship organization; using a lottery system, it awarded $1,000 scholarships to K-8 children who qualified for free/reduced lunch. The number of children who have won awards grew from 3 in 1991 to almost 4,000 in 2001. In addition, supporters of vouchers formed two other organizations, the Educational Choice Project and the Children's Fund of Detroit (Heritage Foundation, 2005).

## Evaluation of the Michigan System

*Quality Counts* (2005b) gave Michigan's standards and accountability plan a B+, much higher than the ratings for many other states. Yet the Fordham Foundation rated states' accountability systems and found Michigan's assessment system weak. It graded Michigan standards as poor; test content as fair; test trustworthiness and openness as poor; and accountability policies as fair (Fordham Foundation, 2003; also see Cross, Rebarber, Torres, & Finn, 2002).

In its assessment, Fordham concluded that the Michigan standards were poorly written, and middle and high school math tests were particularly weak. It criticized the reading test at middle school as poorly aligned with state standards. However, it gave the system developed prior to NCLB an overall grade of "fair" while concluding that the state's solid efforts were "undermined by the lack of serious educator consequences and the lack of interventions for low performing students in early grades" (Fordham Foundation, 2003, p. 22) The report opined that changes in leadership at the state level are positive.

## IMPACT OF THE
## MICHIGAN ACCOUNTABILITY SYSTEM BEFORE NCLB

Before the enactment of NCLB in 2002, the Michigan accountability program was not well integrated. Yet it had many of the assessment and accountability features in NCLB, and had developed these without much infusion of ideas from the federal government or other states. In this section, we consider the impact that the Michigan system had on student outcomes. We are limited in our ability to compare changes across years because of changes in content and performance standards and, in 2001, changes in the definition of proficiency.

Table 8.1 presents information on the performance of students in elementary and middle schools, in school years 1999 and 2002.

**Table 8.1. Performance in Math and English, 1999 and 2002**

| Subject | 1999 (Satisfactory*) | | 2002 (Proficient**) | |
|---|---|---|---|---|
| | *4th Grade* | *7th Grade* | *4th Grade* | *8th Grade* |
| Reading | 59.4% | 53.0% | 56.0% | 53.8% |
| Mathematics | 71.7% | 63.2% | 64.5% | 53.8% |

*Satisfactory means that the student scored 520 or above on the mathematics test; to achieve a satisfactory score on the reading test, the student had to meet a specified standard on both the story and the informational reading selection.
**Proficient means that the student scored at Level 1 (exceeded Michigan standards) or Level 2 (met Michigan standards)
Source: Michigan Educational Assessment Program, Statewide results, winter, 1999 (released June 1999), and 2002 Elementary and Middle School MEAP Score (released September, 2002). Retrieved March 1, 2007, from http://www.michigan.gov/mde/0,1607,7-140-22709_31168_40135-50110--,00.html

Even though it is not possible to compare scores in the 2 years selected, the ratings on state tests are much higher than the scores for 2000 on the National Assessment of Educational Progress (NAEP). For example, in fourth grade math, the state scored 28% on the NAEP, while scores on state tests are twice as high. In fourth grade reading (on the 2002 NAEP), Michigan's students scored at the 28% level; again, scores on state tests were twice as high as this number. In both 1998 and 2000, for grade levels tested, Michigan students scored no more than three to seven points higher than the national average (NCES, 2005).

## RESPONSE OF MICHIGAN TO NCLB REQUIREMENTS

NCLB did represent a change of system for Michigan educators. The new federal legislation tested students in every year from 3 to 8 and one year in high school, whereas the Michigan system tested just some of these years. NCLB had more comprehensive requirements regarding teacher quality and reporting on student and school progress to parents. Also, NCLB had provisions on accountability for schools and school districts (and especially sanctions) not used in Michigan. The state responded to NCLB by developing a new accreditation system, by re-emphasizing teacher quality, and by focusing on low-performing schools and strengthening high school programs.

### School Accreditation

In 2002, the State Board established the Accreditation Advisory Committee to make recommendations for baseline scores for the MEAP school performance and student indicators consistent with the new mandate (MDE, 2002b). The board also created a new monitoring structure called Education YES! Under Education YES! every school in the state would be given a grade of A, B, C, or D-Alert, or "Unaccredited." An unaccredited school is subject to a number of sanctions. The composite grade for each school is based on evaluation of: MEAP achievement status, MEAP achievement growth, indicators of engagement, indicators of instructional quality, and indicators of learning opportunities (MDE, 2002b). Superintendent Tom Watkins said of the new system, "This truly is an accreditation system for the new 21st century that helps Michigan align with new federal mandates" (MDE, 2002b, p. 2). The new system gained the support of the AFL-CIO affiliated Michigan Federation of Teachers & School Related Personnel, which called it "a yardstick for excellent schools" (Michigan Federation of Teachers & School Related Personnel, 2002, p. 1).

Michigan became the 30th state to obtain U.S. DOE approval for its accountability plan under the NCLB legislation in June 2003.[2] Education Secretary Rod Paige authorized federal education funding in the amount of $1.5 billion for the state, including $669 million to implement NCLB (USDOE, 2003).

## Focus on Low-Performing Schools

Not only did NCLB legislation bring major changes to Michigan's assessment system, but it also shifted the focus to identifying low-performing Title I schools and districts; and it offered other education options to students —such as transfer to other schools. The state established priority for transfer requests to be given to low-achieving students from low-income families.

The state chose the starting points for meeting annual AYP objectives in student proficiency. To reach AYP, the Michigan state board approved the baseline as the 20th percentile for MEAP scores in reading and math, as shown in Table 8.2 (Banakik, 2003).

Under NCLB, when a Title I school does not make AYP for two consecutive years, it must follow these steps:

- Develop a 2-year improvement plan.
- Submit the plan to the district for peer review and district approval.
- Implement the improvement plan by the beginning of the school year following the year the school was identified.

**Table 8.2.   Michigan's AYP Objectives for 2002-2003**

|  | *Math* | *Reading* |
|---|---|---|
| Elementary | 47% | 38% |
| Middle School | 31% | 31% |
| High School | 33% | 42% |

*Source:*   Michigan Accountability Workbook, February 12, 2003, Michigan State Department of Education. Retrieved December 29, 2006, from http://www.michigan.gov/documents/NCLB_Michigan_Accountability_Workbook_Revised_63716_7.pdf

- Spend at least 10% of Title I allocation each year for the next 2 years on professional development that addresses the achievement problems.

The district must also offer students who are enrolled the option to transfer to other schools within the district not identified for improvement, and provide or pay for transportation for students who choose the transfer option within certain cost limits. At each step, parents for students in these schools are required to be kept informed. The state incorporated NCLB requirements into state law. A school that has been unaccredited for three consecutive years was subject to one or more of the following:

- The state can appoint an administrator at the expense of the affected district;
- Parent/s of a child in the school may send the child to any accredited school with an appropriate grade level within the district;
- The school, with the approval of the state, can align itself with an existing research based improvement plan or model or establish an affiliation with a college or university;
- The school can be closed down.

## Teacher Quality and NCLB

Education YES!, the new accountability plan approved in 2002, also included language on teacher quality, based on recommendations of a task force composed of educational leaders, civic and business leaders, teachers, teacher union representatives, and other groups. The group prepared a report called "Ensuring Excellent Educators" that outlined five goals covering teacher education, attracting and retaining high quality teachers, reorienting teacher professional development, the importance of collaborative partnerships, and elevating the profession. In April 2002, the state board approved "Polices on Ensuring Excellent Educators" based on the committee's recommendations (MDE, 2005a).

The following year, the state board released a document "The Michigan Definition For Identifying Highly Qualified Teachers" as part of its response to NCLB. The board outlined existing requirements for teacher licensure and proposed new guidelines for content area portfolios to assist experienced teachers (not required to take the state tests) to demonstrate their competency and "highly qualified" status to meet the "highly qualified" definition.

The new guidelines apply to teachers with at least a bachelor's degree, a valid state teaching license, assigned to a classroom in the content area certified, as well as other considerations, such as holding National Board Certification or an advanced degree. Competency is to be determined by a review team at the local or school level, which examines: years of successful teaching based on evaluations, college level coursework in the content area, content specific professional development and service in the content area (Watkins, 2003).

Teacher quality is a large education issue in every state, because of NCLB requirements. Michigan has fewer problems than most states, and one reason may be that the state pays teachers well (an average salary in 2002-03 of $54,000). Less than 4% of Michigan's teachers are uncertified or teaching on emergency waivers. However, teachers in urban schools (and especially in low-income areas) are less likely to be highly qualified in their main teaching assignment than their counterparts in suburban and rural areas. As in other states, minority youth are less likely to have access to highly qualified teachers than their White peers (Harris & Ray, 2003).

## Focus on High Schools

On February 2005, Governor Jennifer Granholm, in her State of the State Address, proposed a new scholarship program that would provide $4,000 in tuition for students to use on postsecondary education. Students could use the funds to help pay for an associate's degree, a 4-year degree, or technical training ("Granholm Plan," 2005).

The new Merit Scholarships will be funded by state resources, including $129 million from the tobacco settlement, and Pell grants. Beginning in 2007, the scholarships will reward students completing an associate's degree or earning junior status at an institution of higher education in Michigan. The state education department believes that this funding will encourage more students to seek a postsecondary education since even students who failed the MEAP could still receive an award if they complete two years of post secondary education (MDE, 2005b).

Creating a positive incentive for students to take high school seriously was one road toward improvement. The second was raising standards. In fall 2005, under the leadership of Mike Flanagan, Michigan Superintendent of Public Instruction, the Department of Education, in collaboration with researchers across the United States, conducted a study on how best to improve student performance at the high school level. In November 2005, the Michigan State Board began reviewing a set of more rigorous high school graduation standards proposed by Superintendent Flanagan. On December 13, 2005, the state board approved the proposals to improve the rigor of the state high schools. The superintendent announced:

> We can't wait any longer.... The mindset has to be urgent to get this done. The perfect storm is heading toward Michigan—the pressures of the global economy that our current system is not set for, and that the old auto industry will come back and everything will be fine the way things were. Well, those days are over and we need to change the culture of education in Michigan. (MDE, 2005c)

This change shoved Michigan forward, from having few statewide requirements for high school graduation to having some of the most demanding standards in the country (Jacobson, 2006).

## INITIAL RESULTS OF NCLB IN MICHIGAN, 2003-06

To assess NCLB's initial impact on student performance, we review student performance data on both national and state tests. First, we present ratings given by NAEP, called "the Nation's Report Card," at the proficient and above levels for Grades 4 and 8 (including national averages for 2005).

These data indicate first that the percentage of students in Grade 4, in math and reading, at the proficient or above level was not significantly different in 2005, than in 2003. The average scores for students in Grade 8, in math and reading in 2005, were not significantly different than the average scores in 2003 or the national average. Reading scores for eighth graders declined from 33 to 28%; math scores increased but not significantly.

Subgroup analysis indicates that African American and Latino students in all grades tested and in all content areas tested had significantly lower scores than did White students. Also, Michigan students eligible for free/reduced lunch in all grades and in all content areas had average scores that were significantly lower than Michigan students not eligible for free/reduced lunch.

**Table 8.3.   NAEP Student Achievement Results in
Reading and Math, for 2003 and 2005**

|  | 2003 Reading | 2005 Reading | 2003 Math | 2005 Math |
|---|---|---|---|---|
|  | Proficient & Above | Proficient & Above Level | Proficient & Above | Proficient & Above Level |
| Grade 4 | 32% | 31% | 35% | 37% |
| National |  | 30% |  | 35% |
| Grade 8 | 33% | 28% | 28% | 30% |
| National |  | 29% |  | 29% |

Source:   Michigan, The Nation's Report Card, 2005, National Council for Educational
Statistics. Retrieved February 15, 2007 from http://nces.ed.gov/nationsreportcard/states/
profile.asp

**Table 8.4.   MEAP Student Performance Results, 2003-2006—
Students Achieving Proficiency**

|  | Grade 4 | | Grade 8 | |
|---|---|---|---|---|
| Years | Math | Reading | Math | Reading |
| 2003 | 65% | 75% | 53% |  |
| 2004 | 73% | 79% | 52% |  |
| 2005 | 73% | 82% | 63% |  |
| 2006 | 85% | 85% | 73% | 77% |

Source:   Statewide MEAP Results, Michigan Department of Education. Retrieved February
27, 2007 from: http://www.michigan.gov/mde/0,1607,7-140-22709_31168_31175---
,00.html

Clearly, the NAEP data show no improvement in scores between 2003
and 2005. Average scores in reading for students in Grade 4 for 2005
were not significantly different than in 2003 or 1992 for that matter.
Scores for eighth grade students declined slightly in reading, and rose
somewhat in math. Next, we turn our attention to student performance
results on the state tests.

Table 8.4 presents data for those students demonstrating proficiency
(Levels 1 and 2) on the MEAP assessment, from 2003 to 2006.

It is clear that the results posted for students on the MEAP tests are significantly higher than on the NAEP tests, a common pattern observed in
other states. When studying the MAEP results in Table 8.4, the following
conclusions can be drawn:

- Scores in math for students in Grade 4 improved between 2003 and 2006, by 20 percentage points, even though scores were flat in 2004 and 2005;
- Scores in reading for students in Grade 4 show an improvement of 7% between 2003 and 2005, and 10% from 2003 to 2006;
- Scores in math for students in Grade 8, show little improvement between 2003 and 2004, but a 20% gain between 2003 and 2006;

Overall, the gains on the state tests appear to be significant; and the increases in scores caused education officials to boast about progress of students and schools. However, student gains on MEAP were not matched by gains on the NAEP.

MEAP tests for high school students in Michigan do not show markedly different results. Based on posted MEAP data, student performance at the high school level appears mixed with little significant improvement except for increases in reading between 2003 and 2006. There was little incremental improvement across the content areas tested, with one exception, and a disturbing downward trend in math scores since 2002. In 2006, state Superintendent of Public Instruction Mike Flanagan pointed to low MEAP scores as fresh evidence of the need for more rigor in the high school curriculum. MEAP scores for the high school graduating class of 2006 showed decreases in all but one of the five assessments (MDE, 2006b).

Press releases by the Michigan State Department of Education made these selected statements on the 2005 MEAP scores:

- There has been improvement in reading scores;
- Decline in writing scores is due to a more difficult test for 2005, which is an important qualification;
- Greatest increase in improvement was for reading in Grade 7;
- Scores at the high school level dipped in writing, math, science and social studies compared to previous years, but there was improvement in reading, from 76.2% meeting or exceeding reading standards in 2004 to 77.9% meeting or exceeding reading standards in 2005;
- More students continue to participate in state testing (MDE, 2006a).

NCLB intends to close achievement gaps among ethnic/racial, socioeconomic, and other subgroups. Table 8.5 presents comparison data from 2003 and 2006, assessing differences among Michigan's major subgroupings.

These selected observations can be made on the available test data for students in special populations who met or exceeded state standards as shown in Table 8.5:

- Asian/Pacific Islanders outperformed other student groups in all content areas and in all grades;
- In Grade 4, 2006 pass scores in reading and writing increased sometimes significantly from scores in 2003 across all groups, which might be due to changes in the test;
- In Grade 4, 2006 results in math were higher than in 2003 across all groups, which also might be due to changes in the test;
- In Grade 4, African American students had lower passing scores in math and in reading and writing than did students in all other groups (except for Grade 4 LEP students in reading/writing).

Data from these 2 years indicate mixed results with regard to the narrowing of achievement gaps between minorities and Caucasian students. Noting particularly scores of African-American students, we find a reduction in the gap with White students only in reading/writing, from 2003 to 2006, and this appears to be a significant reduction. In math, however, for both Grades 4 and 8, there is no significant reduction. The use of the same test over several more years will enable reviewers to make more definitive statements about the achievement gap.

A final topic is failing schools, those not meeting AYP targets. In spring 2005, 88% of schools and 95% of districts made AYP, an increase from 2004, when 77.9% of schools and 79.8% of districts made AYP, higher than in many states. The state assessment system measured student achievement and other performance indicators, such as curriculum, teacher quality, professional development, school facilities and family involvement (MDE, 2005d).

## PROSPECTS FOR ATTAINMENT OF NCLB GOALS BY 2014

Two areas are worth special consideration as Michigan continues its implementation of NCLB mandates—education finance and resistance to reform. We discuss each is turn.

### Fiscal Challenges

Current expenditures for education in Michigan are $15 billion. The state school finance system uses a foundation formula and the level of funding is set by the legislature. Michigan has a state lottery that supports education and funding for education also comes from a variety of sources,

**Table 8.5. MEAP Results for Selected Student Without Disabilities—Meeting or Exceeding Standards, 2003 and 2006**

| | Grade 4 | | | | Grade 8 | | |
| | 2003 | | 2006 | | 2003 | 2006 | |
| | Math | Reading & Writing | Math | Reading & Writing | Math | Math | Eng./Language Art |
|---|---|---|---|---|---|---|---|
| American Indian/AK Native | 70% | 42% | 72% | 76% | 64% | 67% | 73% |
| Asian/Pacific Islander | 86% | 58% | 93% | 89% | 80% | 86% | 86% |
| African American | 55% | 30% | 67% | 65% | 37% | 45% | 54% |
| Latino | 60% | 51% | 66% | 70% | 50% | 58% | 63% |
| White, non-Hispanic | 79% | 70% | 90% | 87% | 72% | 81% | 82% |
| Economically disadvantaged | 62% | 34% | 75% | 70% | 47% | 57% | 62% |
| LEP | 62% | 33% | 91% | 60% | 44% | 48% | 43% |

*Note:* Statewide MEAP Results, Michigan Department of Education 2005, and State Demographic Report, Fall 2006. Available at http://www .michigan.gov/mde/0,1607,7-140-22709_31168_31175--,00.html

for example, sales tax, the tobacco tax, education property tax, and liquor tax (*Quality Counts*, 2005a).

*Quality Counts* researchers gave Michigan a grade of C- in the area of "Resources: Equity," left the area of "Resources: Spending" ungraded, and gave Michigan a state rank of 14 in the amount spent per student. Per pupil expenditure was $8,521 for 2001. According to its review, Michigan does not provide money for school construction or renovation. However, spending for education has increased and 91% of students in the state are in districts that spend at least the national average. In the area of equity, "a moderate amount of inequity in the availability of state and local funding is based on local property wealth" (MDE, 2005d; see also Center on Educational Policy, 2005). When Engler served as governor, he succeeded in reducing property taxes. The state then paid more of the bill for K-12 education; in the process it reduced inequity in the education allotment (see Courant & Loeb, 1997).

## Resistance to Reform

As in other states without right-to-work laws, teachers' unions have resisted several of the changes mandated under NCLB. Also, in Michigan, the media have focused on drop outs, and they have feasted on political conflict during the early stages of putting NCLB requirements into effect.

Represented by the National Education Association (NEA), the largest teachers' union in the country, Michigan was one of three states (including Texas and Vermont) that challenged the federal government on the grounds that the NCLB mandates would have to be funded by the states and local districts. In 2005, a federal judge in Michigan dismissed this lawsuit, a major setback for critics of the law, which included some Michigan Department of Education officials and other state officials (Peterson, 2005).

In 2005, a series of articles relating to the cost of educational failure began appearing in the press. *Detroit News 2005* reported on the cost of Michigan's high school drop out rate especially among minority student populations (African Americans and Latinos). Reporters MacDonald and Heath pointed out that the state reports showed 85% of students graduating, while the figure was closer to 77%. They discussed problems with schools' inaccurate reporting of high school graduation rates. In their calculations, for example, the graduation rate in Detroit is only 48% (MacDonald & Heath, 2005). However, a 2003 report in *Education Week* pegged Detroit's graduation rate at 21.7% for the 2002-03 school year, the lowest of the nation's 50 largest school districts (Maxwell, 2006).

In a follow-up story, MacDonald reported that high school dropouts cost the business sector in Detroit losses due to absenteeism, high turnover, and having to provide remedial education. According to MacDonald, the problem was so acute that philanthropist and businessman Bob Thompson, who stated that he had problems with both high school dropouts and high school graduates, planned to build a charter school to teach basic skills (MacDonald, 2005). In December 2005, Thompson began collaboration with the Skillman Foundation to build a charter school in Detroit (Thompson, 2005).

A troublesome barrier to addressing the challenges was the highly politicized environment among Michigan education leaders. In 2005, a rift opened between the governor, the Michigan Education Association, and the superintendent of instruction, which led to the resignation of the superintendent.

The governor and Tom Watkins, superintendent of public instruction, had sparred over Watkins' leadership. The incident that brought things to a head was a difference of opinion on whether Watkins, an appointed official, had lawfully funded the Bay Mills Community College charter school. At one point, Governor Granholm stated, "(Watkins) needs to resign for the good of the state board, for the good of public education" ("State Superintendent," 2005, p. 1)

Previous comments by Watkins to the press were sometimes inflammatory, such as when, in defense of charter schools, he said, "Let's take a look at traditional schools. Some of them will complain about losing 300 (students) to a charter, but you won't hear a peep out of them when 3,000 (dropouts) go to the streets" ("State Superintendent," 2005, p. 2). Although Watkins had strong community support, the state board was divided on his tenure and tabled an extension to his contract prior to his resignation. In spring 2005, Jeremy Hughes, Michigan's chief academic officer, was appointed acting superintendent ("State Superintendent," 2005, p. 4).

## CONCLUSION

Michigan had experimented with many aspects of assessment and accountability well before NCLB was enacted. Of the Michigan Report Card, *Quality Counts* (2005a) states, "It [the state] imposes sanctions, such as closing schools or withholding state aid, on schools consistently rated as low-performing, including non-Title I schools" (pp. 1-2). In 2005, 88.1% of Michigan schools made AYP, an increase from 77.9% in 2004. More schools in 2005 earned grades of A and B under the state's Education YES! Report Card system. Yet, the mediocre performance of Michigan students on the state tests at the high school level has been cause for concern and appears to have brought about an effective response. It is too early to make a fair assessment on the impact of NCLB on the state assessment system and on student performance. Results on student performance on the state tests, especially for high school students in some subgroups, are discouraging. NAEP results for students in Grades 4 and 8 appear to not be significantly different than national averages. On the other hand, math and reading scores on state tests show signs of improvement for elementary and middle grades.

There are also reasons for optimism concerning Michigan's public schools. Our discussion about charter schools, choice, and vouchers indicates that the public school environment gradually is becoming more competitive. Many private citizens in the state care about education judging from the number who became actively involved in school reform. A 2005 Center on Education Policy report found that 85% of Michigan schools in restructuring, 113 schools out of 133, had improved student test scores in 2004-2005, well enough to make AYP. For most this was the first time making AYP (p. 4).

The private sector is stepping up, a historic pattern in this state. In a bold move, the Kalamazoo School District recently celebrated creation of the Kalamazoo Promise, funded by anonymous donors who will provide graduates with funding of up to 100% for tuition and fees for 4 years at a public university or community college in Michigan. The plan requires that students attend Kalamazoo schools from kindergarten through 12th grade. Students attending Kalamazoo schools from Grade 9 to Grade 12 will have 65% of tuition and fees paid. The district has a 25% poverty rate (Michigan Education Association, MEA, 2005). District superintendent Brown stated that the plan, "brings hope, opportunity and revival, and it says that every child is important and will have every chance to succeed" (MEA, 2005, p. 3).

Would that business firms and millionaires could adopt all of Michigan's low-performing schools. Until that time, Michigan's schools seem likely to follow the fits-and-starts pattern expressed in previous education reform eras.

## NOTES

1.  The sections on Michigan's economy and polity are based on Barone and Cohen (2005).
2.  The Michigan state accountability plan mandated by NCLB legislation was approved June 9, 2003. However, certain conditions for that approval were outlined in a July 1, 2003 letter from the U.S. DOE to the State Department of Education. The state had requested that it be allowed to compare

the current 2003 test results with an average of the last two or three years' results, including results from the current year, and use the most favorable results to make AYP determinations for Michigan schools. U.S. DOE officials replied that while the Michigan Superintendent of Public Instruction could use a uniform average of student test results as proposed in the plan, information had to be provided on the possible impact and implications. Once provided, federal officials said that they would fully approve Michigan's accountability plan.

3.  A subsequent communication requested additional information. Michigan Department of Education officials were asked three questions: (1) How many schools made AYP under this system? (2) Exactly how many years of test results were used to determine AYP? And, (3) if subgroups within a school are judged using a different number of years of data, how many schools were evaluated in this way? (US DOE, 2005) In a January 6, 2005 letter, U.S. DOE officials, making reference to the Department's flexibility for states' implementation of NCLB, fully approved Michigan's plan including requested changes as being aligned with federal regulation.

## REFERENCES

Achieve. (1998). *Academic standards and assessments benchmarking evaluation for Michigan schools.* Cambridge, MA: Author.

Banakik, B. (2003). *NCLB: The legal requirements school boards need to know, part 1.* Michigan Association of School Boards, presentation. Retrieved December 20, 2005, from http://www.masb.org/page.cfm/823/

Barone, M., & Cohen, R. E. (2005). *The almanac of American politics.* Washington, DC: The National Journal Group.

Boyd, W. L., Plank, D. N., & Sykes, G. (2000). *Teachers unions in hard times.* Washington, DC: The Brookings Institution.

Center on Educational Policy. (2005, November). *Hope but no miracle cures: Michigan's early restructuring lessons.* Washington, DC: Author.

Clowes, G. (2001, September 1). Voucher wars: Dispatches from the Michigan front. *The Heartland Institute,* p. 1.

Clowes, G. (2003). *The Friedman report: School choice roundup.* Retrieved September 3, 2004, from http://www.heartland.org

Cohen, D. K. (1996). Standards-based school reform: Policy, practice, and performance. In H. F. Ladd (Ed.), *Holding schools accountable* (pp. 99-127). Washington, DC: The Brookings Institution.

Courant, P. N., & Loeb, S. (1997, Winter). Centralization of school finance in Michigan. *Journal of Policy Analysis and Management, 16,* 114-36.

Cross, R. W., Rebarber, T., Torres, J., & Finn, C. E., Jr. (2002). *Grading the systems: The guide to state standards, tests, and accountability policies.* Washington, DC: Thomas B. Fordham Foundation.

Dutro, E., Fisk, M. C., Koch, R., Roop, L. J., & Wixson, K. (2002). *When state policies meet local district contexts: Standards-based professional development as a means to individual agency and collective ownership.* Ann Arbor, MI: University of Michigan, CIERA Report.

Fordham Foundation. (2003). *State of the states' standards*. Washington, DC: Author

Granholm plan would cover two years of college costs. (2005, February 16). *Education Week, 24*(23), 30.

Harris, D., & Ray, L. (2003). *No school left behind? The distribution of teacher quality in Michigan's public schools*. East Lansing: Michigan State University, Education Policy Center, Policy Report.

Heritage Foundation. (2004, April). *Policy research & analysis: Michigan*. Retrieved August 31, 2005, from http://www.heritage.org/Research/Education/Schools/michigan.cfm

Heritage Foundation. (2005). *Research, education. Michigan*. Retrieved August 31, 2005 from: http://www.heritage.org/ResearchEducation/Schools/michigan.cfm

Hill, P. T., & Lake, R. J. (2000). *Charter schools and accountability in public education*. Washington, DC: The Brookings Institution.

Hoxby, C. (2004). *Achievement in charter schools and regular public schools in the United States: Understanding the difference*. PEPG Working Paper.

Jacobson, L. (2006). Michigan poised to implement tough new graduation rules. *Education Week, 25*(31), 26.

Loveless, T. (2002). *How well are American students learning?* Washington, DC: The Brookings Institution.

Lubienski, C. (2001). *Institutionalist and instrumentalist perspectives on "public" education: Strategies and implications of the school choice movement in Michigan*. New York: Columbia University, National Center for the Study of Privatization in Education.

MacDonald, C. (2005, May 29). Businesses are forced to teach the basics. *The Detroit News*, 1.

MacDonald, C., & Heath, B. (2005, May 29). *The Detroit News special report*. Retrieved July 31, 2005, from http://detnews.com/2005/specialreport/0505/30/A01-196693.htm

Maxwell, L. (2006, July 12). Detroit schools struggle to stem student loss. *Education Week, 25*(42), 1, 20.

Michigan Association of School Boards. (2000). *Frequently asked questions*. Retrieved November 2, 2005, from http://www.masb.org/page.cfm/322/

Michigan Department of Education. (1997a). *Michigan teaching certification code*. Retrieved July 17, 2005, from http://www.state.mi.us/orr/emi/admincode.asp?AdminCode=Single&Admin_Num=39001101&Dpt+ED&RngHigh=

Michigan Department of Education. (1997b). *Postsecondary Enrollment Option act 160 of 1996*. Retrieved October 21, 2005 from: http://www.michigan.gov/documents/5H-ReducedSchPupils_41448_7.pdf

Michigan Department of Education. (2002a). *Design and validity of the MEAP test*. Lansing, MI: Author.

Michigan Department of Education. (2002b). *State board approves Education YES! Accreditation system* (News release). Lansing, MI: Author.

Michigan Department of Education. (2004a). *MEAP questions and answers class of 2004*. Retrieved October 8, 2004 from: http://www.michigan.gov/documents/QASpring2004_105966_7.doc

Michigan Department of Education. (2004b). *Snapshot of high school class of 2004.* Retrieved September 12, 2005, from http://www.michigan.gov/documents/snapshot-class-of-2004_106141_7.pdf

Michigan Department of Education. (2005a). *Michigan standards for ensuring excellent educators.* Retrieved January 6, 2006 from: http://www.michigan.gov/mde/0,1607,7-140-6530_5683_5703---,00.html

Michigan Department of Education. (2005b). *Frequently asked questions about the new merit scholarships.* Retrieved December 22, 2005 from: http://www.michigan.gov/documents/faq_126309_7.htm

Michigan Department of Education. (2005c). *State board reviews Flanagan's recommendations for state high school graduation requirements* (News release). Lansing, MI: Author.

Michigan Department of Education. (2005d). *Michigan's school report card.* Retrieved January 13, 2006 from: http://ayp.mde.state.mi.us/ayp/

Michigan Department of Education. (2006a). *Improved reading scores highlight 2005 MEAP results* (News release). Lansing, MI: Author.

Michigan Department of Education. (2006b). *Flanagan says HS MEAP scores show need for tougher requirements* (Press release). Retrieved February 27, 2007, from http://www.michigan.gov/printerFriendly/0,1687,7-140-11709_31168_40135-147256--,oo.html

Michigan Education Association. (2005, November 22). *Challenge ahead to fulfill Kalamazoo promise,* 1-4.

Michigan Federation of Teachers & School Related Personnel. (2002). *MFTSRP position statement: Education YES! A yardstick for excellent schools.* Retrieved November 2, 2005, from http:www.mftsrp.org/edyesposition.html

Miron, G., & Nelson, C. (2002). *What's public about charter schools? Lessons learned about choice and accountability.* Thousand Oaks, CA: Sage.

National Center for Educational Statistics. (2005). *State education data profiles: Michigan.* Retrieved August 31, 2005 from: http://nces.ed.gov/programs/stateprofiles/sresult.asp?mode=short&s1=26

Peterson, K. (2005). *Schools lose round in NCLB challenge.* Retrieved December 1, 2005, from http:/www.stateline.org/live/ViewPage.actionsiteNodeId=137&languageId=1&contentId=70843

*Quality Counts.* (2005a). Finance snapshots, Michigan. *Education Week.* Retrieved December 8, 2005, from http://www.edweek.org/ew/articles/2005/01/06/17statesums-mih24

*Quality Counts.* (2005b, January 6). Report card: Michigan. Retrieved December 20, 2005, from http://www.edweek.org/ew/articles/2005/01/06/17sos-mi.h24.html?s

State superintendent Watkins resigns. (2005, April 11). *Michigan Education Report,* 1-4.

Thompson, B. (2005, December 18). Charter supporter hosts new DPS board in private retreat. *The Michigan Citizen,* p. A1.

Thompson, C., Spillane, J. P., & Cohen, D. K. (1994). *The state policy system affecting science and mathematics education in Michigan.* East Lansing: Michigan State University, College of Education.

U.S. Department of Education. (2003). *Secretary Paige approves Michigan state accountability plan under No Child Left Behind.* Retrieved December 10, 2005, from http://www.ed.gov/print/news/pressreleases/2003/06/06092003a.html

U.S. Department of Education. (2005, January 6). Letter to Thomas Watkins, Michigan Superintendent of Public Instruction. Retrieved July 20, 2005 from: http://www.ed.gov/searchResults.jhtml

Watkins, T. (2003). *The Michigan definition for identifying highly qualified teachers.* Retrieved November 23, 2005, from http://www.michigan.gov/mde

# CHAPTER 9

---

# CALIFORNIA

---

## INTRODUCTION

We introduce first the social, economic, and political environment for education reform in California, and then turn to a discussion of education policy makers and student characteristics.

### State Socioeconomic and Political Characteristics

California is America's largest state in terms of population (with an estimated 2006 population in excess of 36 million) and the most diverse ethnically and racially. The state's economy is the nation's largest, and it is also the most diverse. California has a large and important high tech industry; large service sectors in finance, communications, education, retail/wholesale sales, government, and entertainment; traditional manufacturing plants and innovative light industries; and an highly productive agricultural sector. The state's economic product is greater than that of all but five of the world's nation-states, yet the state has a large low-income population. Because socioeconomic status (SES) is the most reliable predictor of student academic success, California's income gap needs to be kept in mind: the state has more high-income people and more in poverty (14.2% in 2005) than any other state in the nation (Barone & Cohen, 2005). As Korey (2004) notes: "On the one hand, the state is faced with meeting the needs of a large population dependent on government ser-

*Education Reform in the American States*
pp. 223–254

223

vices. On the other hand, in meeting these needs, the state is able to draw upon the wealth of a large number of affluent residents"(p. CA-5).

California is the second "majority-minority" state (after Hawaii), meaning that most of its people are now minorities. Non-Latino Caucasians are the plurality of the population, at approximately 47%, but the Latino population is large and growing at a rapid rate, comprising approximately 33% of the population. In 2006, African Americans make up about 6.5% of the state's population; Asian Americans 11%; and other minorities including American Indians comprise the remainder. Significantly, some 16% of the population are not U.S. citizens, and the immigrant proportion of the state population has grown in recent years. Indeed, California has replaced New York as America's immigrant capital.

California is a "blue" state in national politics, voting for Democrats for the presidency at an increasing rate since the 1960s. In the 2000 presidential election, 53% of voters opted for Democratic candidate Al Gore; in 2004, 54% voted for Democratic candidate John Kerry. Its U.S. Senate delegation in the 110th Congress is Democratic and has been for 14 years, as are the majority (34) of the 53 House seats. The California state legislature also has been in Democratic hands most of the time since the 1960s, and since 1996 Democrats have approached a two thirds majority in both the Assembly and the Senate. Through a series of redistricting plans, California legislators have made seats held by incumbents increasingly "safe," meaning that major changes in the legislature's political composition do not seem likely in the near-term (Korey, 2004). However, the governorship is competitive between the two major parties. California was the springboard for Ronald Reagan's political career, and he served as governor from 1967 to 1974. In 2003, Democratic governor Gray Davis (first elected in 1998) was recalled by the voters and replaced with Republican Arnold Schwarzenegger, who was re-elected in 2006. Notwithstanding competitiveness for the governorship, the nominal complexion of the state's political establishment is Democratic and liberal-centrist. This partisan and ideological slant is reflected in high rates of taxation on personal income, a high minimum wage (and the highest workmen's compensation premiums of the nation), the absence of right-to-work legislation in the state and, as a result, the strength of education unions. The strength of unions was revealed in the defeat of Governor Schwarzenegger's attempt, in November 2005, to increase from 2 to 5 years teachers' service requirement for tenure (Korey, 2006).

## The State Educational System

The state's educational policymaking system has a large number of actors, and they have competed for primacy in setting state educational policy. The governor, as the major elected official statewide, has considerable influence on education policy. For example, in 1996 Republican Governor Pete Wilson threatened to veto the entire state budget unless Democrats agreed with his plan to test academic performance of all students in 2nd through 11th grades (Sokolow, 1997). Then, in 1999, Democratic Governor Gray Davis proposed a high school exit examination, which students would need to pass in order to graduate (Bateman & Lascher, 2000). As we note below, Governor Davis was also a strong proponent of the new accountability system, and in 1999 proposed to "fund newly enacted legislation to hold schools accountable for their performance and to reward high achieving and improving schools" (California Office of the Governor, 1999).

Both houses of the state legislature, and particularly their education committees, direct attention to the state's K-12 education budget, and the California legislature has enhanced powers because of the influence of the Legislative Analyst's Office. This office analyzes the governor's budget and suggests legislative responses to it (Korey, 2005). When the Democratic legislature has faced a Republican governor, such as during Governor Pete Wilson's two terms (1990-98) and Governor Arnold Schwarzenegger's first and second terms (2003 to present), it has sought to increase education funding above the governor's proposal. Even under unified Democratic control, as during the Gray Davis administration, the legislature sparred with the governor on education issues.

Too, Democrats in the legislature have been receptive to lobbying by teachers' unions, school boards, the state school board association, and school administrators; they have been particularly defensive of teacher tenure and collective bargaining rights of school employees. The intergovernmental education lobby, and particularly the California Teachers Association (CTA), has been active independent of legislators and governor, whenever it perceives its interests to be threatened. For example, CTA officials objected strenuously to new budget funding for bonuses to high-performing teachers as part of the state's accountability system, because of the divisiveness this would create in the teacher workforce (Hess, 2003).

California's state Board of Education is somewhat weaker than those in the other American states. It is appointed by the governor. However, the California Department of Education is headed by the superintendent of public instruction, and this is a statewide office, elected by the voters. Under situations of both divided and unified partisan control, there are opportunities for tension between the state board and the education department, because the head of the latter is effectively independent from the governor.

The state's business elite has been strongly involved in education politics and school reform. Emery (2002) notes the early involvement of the California Business Roundtable (CBR) in education issues. Established in 1976 in San Francisco, this group of CEOs decided to lobby state legislators, CDE administrators, and the governor:

> The California Business Roundtable issued a 295-page blueprint for reform in 1988, entitled *Restructuring California Education: A Design for Public Education in the Twenty-first Century*.... This report, which would be the basis for educational reform for the next fifteen years, incorporated the concerns over dropouts and test score disparities into a new theory of education reform. (p. 122)

Emery points out the CBR's emphasis on Total Quality Management, its focus on accountability based on performance, choice, and high-stakes testing, and the congruence of its agenda with that of the national Business Roundtable, and most elements of its *Nine Essential Components of a Successful Education System* to school reform (p. 148). In California, the CBR led formation of a broad coalition called the California Business for Education Excellence (CBEE) in 1988. It included the state chamber of commerce, manufacturers' association, taxpayer association, technology network, and several other business associations; it was financed by Hewlett-Packard, IBM, Pacific Bell, and Boeing among other corporations. The stated objectives of CBEE emphasized accountability and choice (CBEE, 1998).

California is America's epitome of a direct democracy; through the initiative process, voters may directly set educational policy. For example, by proposition 98 in 1988, voters required that at least 40% of all General Fund revenues had to support K-12 education. In 1995, voters approved a class-size reduction initiative, which provided incentives for lowering class sizes in the early elementary grades to 21 students (see Jepsen & Rivkin, 2002). Perhaps the single-most important impact on education funding was accomplished through the initiative process, when in 1978 voters approved the Jarvis-Gann property tax limitation amendment to the state constitution. Many pundits claim that this initiative was chiefly responsible for the decline in achievement of California's schools. At the least, it brought per capita K-12 education spending in California from considerably above the national median to well below it.

This complex set of actors taxes the coherence of the state's education reform process, at a time when reform seems needed because California students perform well below the national norms. In the estimate of Terry Moe (2003), a leading critic of public school education in the United States, it was the "horrible performance" of California schools that put education reform at the top of the state's public agenda (p. 105).

**Table 9.1. Ethnic Group Enrollment in 2003-04**

| Ethnic Group | Enrollment | Percent |
|---|---|---|
| American Indian or Alaskan | 52,706 | 0.8 |
| Asian | 504,537 | 8.0 |
| Pacific Islander | 39,744 | 0.6 |
| Filipino | 160,400 | 2.5 |
| Hispanic | 2,898,115 | 46.0 |
| African American | 510,613 | 8.1 |
| White | 2,046,422 | 32.5 |
| Multiple or no response | 86,237 | 1.4 |
| Total | 6,298,774 | 100 |

*Source:* California Department of Education (http://www.cde.ca.gov/ds/sd/cb/sums03.asp).

California's public school system is also the largest and probably the most diverse in the United States. In 2006, about 6.4 million students enrolled in 9,690 schools in 994 school districts or other local educational agencies (LEAs). Private schools numbered 3,700 in this year. The composition of the school population is an inexact match of the state's population as a whole, as seen in Table 9.1.

Non-Hispanic Caucasians are only one-third of the student population, yet they are the plurality of state residents. The Latino population is considerably younger than the non-Hispanic White population and comprises nearly half of the student population. African Americans too are a somewhat larger part of the student population than their component of state residents as a whole. Dropout rates for these ethnic minorities, as well as for the American Indian, Alaska Native, and Pacific Islander student population are twice as high as they are for non-Hispanic Caucasians.

These ethnic minorities are more likely than non-Hispanic Caucasians and Asians to be socioeconomically disadvantaged. Too, the recent immigrant population is more likely to be of limited English proficiency (LEP). California has the largest nonnative English speaking population of the American states (42.3% as compared to 19.4% nationally [U.S. Census Bureau, 2006]). About one quarter of all public school students are English language learners, and this presents serious challenges to improvement of schooling. For example, Betts and Danenberg (2002) point out that non-LEP students scored higher than LEP students at each grade in late 1990s testing of mathematics and reading. In their estimation, variation of students' ability in the English language is a more serious problem than funding inequities across schools (Betts & Danenberg, 2002, p. 2).

## THE CALIFORNIA ASSESSMENT
## AND ACCOUNTABILITY SYSTEM BEFORE 2002

California has been sporadic in the development of statewide assessment and accountability systems. In 1972, the state implemented the California Assessment Program, which used a system of matrix tests, measuring the average performance of students at the school level. The matrix sampling method did not produce scores for individual students, but provided assessments of performance in subjects at the school level; information from these assessments was published by many newspapers. This assessment system became the casualty of political rivalry between the governor, Republican George Deukmeijian, and the state superintendent of public instruction, Bill Honig (who supported it), and the governor vetoed continuation of the assessment (Kirst, 2002).

The first systematic census of students was not undertaken until 1991. This was the California Learning Assessment System (CLAS) developed under the direction of Honig; it consisted of a series of norm-referenced tests and student portfolios, and included open-ended questions to students such as "What are your feelings about this poem?" (Kirst, 2002, p. 3) Teachers liked the creative nature of this system, but conservative parents objected strongly to the history and literacy tests, believing that a number of the prompts used in the system were excessively personal, political, or violent, and that the tests threatened students' values and privacy. Representatives of concerned parents sought access to the test questions, but the education department, concerned about confidentiality of the tests, denied them access. The parents then took the issue to court, which acknowledged parents' right to have their children opt out of the tests (Hess, 2003; also see Honig & Alexander, 1996). This led the state to cancel the CLAS project in 1994, and each district was on its own with respect to selecting tests for assessment purposes.

The catalyst for development of the state accountability system was the administration of the National Assessment of Educational Progress (NAEP) examination in reading to California students in 1994. The results shocked state policymakers, for California's students tied for last place with Louisiana among the 37 participating states (Kirst, 2002).[1] In 1996 the legislature adopted a requirement for a statewide assessment, to be given in 1998. The new assessment regime was called the California Standardized Testing and Reporting (STAR) program, and at the outset it relied on a single test, the Stanford 9, a nationally norm-referenced achievement test (see Betts & Danenberg, 2002). School districts administered the Stanford 9 to all students in Grades 2 through 11, with the exception of those special education students whose individual education plans (IEPs) exempted them. The adoption of the STAR program and succeeding accountability measures reflected agreement on the part of a broad-scale non-partisan political coalition.

Simultaneously, California developed a series of content standards for the different grade levels. In late 1997, the state board had adopted content standards in language arts and mathematics. By the following year, standards in science and the social studies were completed. In 2001, content standards for the visual and performing arts were finished (Betts & Danenberg, 2002). Because the Stanford 9 was not matched to state content standards, in 1999 the state developed additional items to augment the STAR program.

With these accountability elements as a basis, in 1999 the state legislature enacted SB 1552, called the Public Schools Accountability Act (PSAA). Discussion in the legislature at the time focused on the poor academic performance of California's students and the increasing public outcry for school improvement; the legislation passed with a bipartisan majority. There was consensus that the state needed accurate information on performance of students and schools in order to hold educators accountable (Kirst, 2002). Significantly, the governor then was Gray Davis, a Democrat, and he was a leading advocate of accountability in the state's schools. The coalition of business organizations (CBEE) supported PSAA strongly; opposition of the education unions to this large-scale reform was muted. As noted above, the CTA objected to bonus payments for teachers in high-performing schools because of its likely adverse impacts on teacher morale, but education unions did not formally object to the accountability system. Indeed, it was difficult for teachers' organizations to stand in opposition to a reform promising to improve schooling for all youth and supported by large majorities in the legislature.

The PSAA had three components: (1) the Academic Performance Index (API), (2) the Immediate Intervention/Underperforming Schools Program (II/USP), and (3) the High Achieving/Improving Schools (HA/IS) program, which incorporated a special governor's performance award program. The API is used summarily to evaluate school performance on the STAR including its augmented elements. The II/USP has sanctions and assistance for low-performing schools, while the HA/IS program rewards high performing schools (Consortium for Policy Research in Education, 2000). As we shall see, fiscal problems have impaired both assistance and rewards parts of the accountability system (see Sandham, 1999, 2001).

The API is a ranking system for schools, and approximately 60% of its value is based on students' performance on standardized tests. Initially, its sole basis was the norm-referenced Stanford 9 test, and this test, in the opinion of critics, has been a major driver of the system.[2] Additional measures included some criterion-referenced tests which were developed to augment the STAR, and later other elements were added such as a high school exit examination, graduation rates, and daily attendance rates (Betts & Danenberg, 2002). The API formula is complex because of its several qualifications and sub-group analyses. For example, students enrolled in districts for less than 1 year are excluded; and only comprehensive schools at the high school, middle school, and elementary level with more than 100 students are included. Further, "numerically significant ethnic and socioeconomically disadvantaged subgroups" are identified in order to measure their progress (Betts & Danenberg, 2002, p. 131).

As a ranking system, the API established targets for school improvement (but not for students). The state specified an annual growth target for schools of 5% annually, based on the 1999 baseline score of the school. These targets might be varied by the state board at the top and bottom with a particular focus on low-performing schools, as they had the greatest room for improvement. Schools are grouped into categories having similar characteristics (including LEP and SES among other variables) and then sorted into deciles for comparative purposes. Betts and Danenberg (2003) note that "By focusing on improvement in test scores instead of the absolute level of performance for each subgroup, the California approach is intended to level the playing field for schools serving different student populations" (p. 163).

The second leg of the accountability system is the II/USP, which has both sanctions and benefits for schools. Schools landing in the bottom half of API rankings are eligible for financial assistance, conditional on their developing a reform action plan (in collaboration with a state-approved external evaluator) and implementing it over 2 years. The first assistance grants ($50,000/school) were issued in 1999 with $200 per student in the implementation year. The PSAA provided sanctions for schools in the intervention program. Within the first year, the affected districts were to hold public hearings to discuss initial progress. If the school failed to meet API growth targets within 2 years, a sliding scale of sanctions was imposed extending to state takeover of the school (Betts & Danenberg, 2003).

The third leg of the accountability system in California provides rewards for schools meeting or exceeding growth targets and for teachers and school staff. One component is the Governor's Performance Award Program (GPAP), which provides rewards of up to $150/pupil. Amendments to PSAA legislation in 2000 provided employee and staff performance incentives, and these rewards ranged up to $25,000 in a few cases (Betts & Danenberg, 2002). Nonmonetary awards and certificates are part of this program as well, insuring public commendation for high-performing schools.

Finally, accountability for students is determined through a state high school exit exam, given first in 2003-04 (but counting only for the class of 2006 and later classes). Students failing to pass this proficiency exam (which may be retaken) are denied high school diplomas. In addition, a second, older test, the Golden State Exam, recognizes students for outstanding academic achievement and is one of the bases for award of scholarships to college under the Governor's Scholarship Programs (Betts & Danenberg, 2002).

Altogether, the California PSAA, based on earlier statewide testing and content standards requirements, has all the elements of an articulated (but not necessarily integrated) accountability system.

## INITIAL IMPACT OF THE CALIFORNIA ACCOUNTABILITY SYSTEM

Passage of the No Child Left Behind Act (NCLB) by the U.S. Congress in late 2001 came at an untoward time for California, as its own assessment and accountability system was new and had been in the implementation process for less than 3 years. Several analyses have been made of performance during the first years of the state's accountability system. We treat specifically evaluations of the intervention program, assessment of student learning, and evaluation of charter schools.

### Initial Assessment of State Intervention Programs

The California Department of Education undertook an analysis of the first year in school reform planning of 430 low-performing schools eligible for assistance under the state's II/USP program. Two funding sources supported the reform efforts: state funds to hire an external evaluator and assist in developing a school action plan, and federal funds under the Comprehensive School Reform Demonstration (CSRD) program. The schools applied for assistance and all had scores in deciles 1 through 5, constituting almost 13% of schools in the bottom half of achievement as determined through the API. More than one third of the students in the schools were LEP, nearly two thirds were Title I students, and more than 70% were of low socioeconomic status (Just et al., 2001). While the state's report includes observations on both state-funded and CSRD improvement planning efforts in four areas, we summarize the former only, because the sample of schools is large enough to draw preliminary conclusions on this stage of intervention.

First, the schools tended to find that external evaluators—most of whom were retired educators—were useful and effective in initiating the reform planning process. They responded well to input from parents/community members, collaborated closely with the school, fulfilled terms of their contracts, and charged reasonable fees. In a minority of cases, there were mismatches of backgrounds of evaluators with schools, and some evaluators lacked experience of accountability requirements (Just et al., 2001).

Second, although survey data from principals indicated that initiation and implementation of planning activities went well, site visits revealed that reform was difficult to initiate given the uncertainty concerning process and planned outcomes, the short time period (three months) for preparation of planning documents, and potentially tense relationships between evaluator and school community. Some one third of the schools were reluctant to accept the new process; of the cooperative relationships, more were passive than active (Just et al., 2001).

Third, most districts were not actively involved in the school-level planning process. In some cases, the districts had "volunteered" schools without their knowledge, which created staff resistance to the planning process. Although principals reported that districts were involved, site visits demonstrated that schools were usually on their own in developing action plans. Finally, site visits revealed problems with "buy-in" to the planning process, confused expectations as to who would be responsible for implementing action plans, and limited awareness of the sanctions for schools failing to improve under the state's accountability system (Just et al., 2001, pp. 7-8).

This state study suggested considerable variance between the objectives of intervention and both familiarity and acceptance of them by school staff. Since the 1980s, California has gained a reputation for highly centralized school administration, and the accountability system itself reinforces state powers over both districts and schools. Indeed, districts are largely left out of the school improvement process. Yet the study was done during the first year of implementation, and may have reflected the normal start-up difficulties of a new system.

Other studies of state intervention suggest that California moderated its provisions from strong pressure on failing schools to support for them. Instead of applying severe sanctions, the state education department was most effective in identifying barriers to performance and offering suggestions, a practice adopted by other "first-generation" accountability systems (see Mintrop & Trujillo, 2004, p. 10).

## Initial Assessment of Low-Performing Schools

A well-designed study by Betts and Danenberg compares performance of California students over 3 years, immediately upon the adoption of the state assessment program (the years tested are 1997-98 through the 1999-2000 academic years), with a special emphasis on LEP students who present perhaps the greatest challenge to effective schooling in California.

Betts and Danenberg (2002) found that the largest absolute gain, which was statistically significant, during the 3-year period was for LEP students scoring above the 25th percentile of national norms. They note that math achievement in particular rose significantly. Further, when comparing students at the 25th percentile to those at the 75th percentile over the same time period, they found that the distribution of test scores was compressed: "Students who were the furthest behind national norms have improved more quickly than students who were initially above national norms" (p. 139). While there did not appear to be significant differences between growth rates in percentages of students at or above the 75th percentile of national norms, the percentage point increase of students above the 25th and 50th percentiles in bottom-performing schools was twice that of top-performing schools. Of course the poor performing schools had greater room for improvement, and the results might have been expected. Yet Betts and Danenberg (2002) attribute the gains to testing and accountability. And the results withstood several tests to ascertain whether there might have been a normal regression to the mean.

Betts and Danenberg also considered the myriad factors which might account for differences in school performance. They found no significant difference between bottom- and top-performing schools with respect to the levels of college-preparatory and advanced placement course offerings. They discovered no difference in the class size of elementary and middle schools across the levels of school performance. Nor did they find significant differences in drop-out rates, which ran at about 25-30% over the period tested. (The rate posted by the authors is nearly twice that published by the California Department of Education, or 12% [Betts, 2003].)[3]

There were differences between low and high performing schools with respect to income levels, as expected. High-performing schools had lower numbers of students receiving free or reduced-price lunches (the primary indicator of socio-economic status in schools research). They also had teachers who had more years' experience teaching and more credentials for teaching (Betts & Danenberg, 2002). Yet, while the academic gap between low- and high-performing schools was narrowing, teacher resources for low-performing schools were declining relatively and absolutely, particularly with respect to teacher preparation. The authors hypothesize that this may be related to the state's accountability system:

> Therefore it seems plausible that teacher mobility between schools and perhaps different exit rates from the teaching profession across schools are the driving forces behind the increase in resource inequality. One possibility is that the accountability system, with its sanctions for bottom-performing schools, has discouraged highly educated and experienced teachers from moving to, or staying at, such schools. Another possibility is that the class size reduction initiated in 1996 in elementary schools has lured highly qualified elementary teachers from low-performing schools to high-performing schools. (Betts & Danenberg, 2002, 162)

This study was initiated before the full implementation of the new accountability system in California, and increases in scores, particularly of students in low-performing schools, may reflect increased familiarity with test items and not substantive gains. (During the period of study, the same Stanford 9 tests were used, and teachers had become familiar with them.) The study is criticized on other grounds as well. For example, Rothman (2002) comments that the lack of coherence in California's education policy makes it impossible to attribute changes in school performance to the new accountability system (p. 182). On the other hand, Hauser (2002) faults Betts and Danenberg for omitting study of the null hypothesis: that "test scores are normally distributed with constant variance, but possibly changing means within each grade level and group of schools" (p. 192). Moreover, absence of information about the way in which the accountability system is implemented at the school and classroom level makes it impossible to rule out other factors.

## Initial Assessment Results From Charter Schools

California has about 570 charter schools, serving nearly 200,000 students, and these schools will be of increasing importance as placement targets for parents seeking alternatives to schools failing to make adequate yearly progress ("NCLB Accountability," 2005). A recent study by Slovacek, Kunnan, and Kim (2002) examines a sample of charter schools serving low-SES students, measuring their gains on the API as compared to noncharter schools. The study incorporated a longitudinal statistical analysis of test data from the years 1999, 2000, and 2001, comparing a sample of 6,520 noncharter schools with 93 charter schools.

When comparing mean API scores across the two groups of schools, charter school students did not perform as well as the students in noncharter schools. However, when taking into account the number of students participating in the Free or Reduced Lunch Program (again, in schools research, this is the standard measure of student SES), and comparing the two school groups based on comparable participation rates, the charter school students out-performed students from noncharter schools (Slovacek et al., 2002).

Slovacek et al. concluded that "California charter schools are doing a better job of improving the academic performance ... of California's most at-risk students, those who are low-income, than non-charter California public schools" (p. ii). However, this is a preliminary study, and it does not account fully for the interrelationships of SES, limited English proficiency, and student mobility as well as experience and credentials—all of which may have bearing on student achievement. The authors also raise the issue of charter school funding, claiming that charter schools cost 15 to 20% less on average than noncharter public schools.

The costs of charter schools, and their accountability, are now under review in California. The state legislature included an increase in the block grants for charters, from $300 per pupil to $500 per pupil in the 2007-08 school year, which raised concerns in some districts that schools would have a monetary incentive to convert to charters. Also, the misuse of state and federal funds by a large, multi-campus network charter with more than 11,000 students caused the state to increase fiscal oversight and accountability (Hendrie, 2005). Mark Kushner, the chairman of the state board of education's advisory commission on charter schools and the CEO of San Francisco-based Leadership Public Schools says that in California "Too many charters are not performing well." The schools deserve support, he remarked, but not endless patience ("NCLB Accountability," 2005).

## RESPONSE OF CALIFORNIA TO NCLB REQUIREMENTS

NCLB raised immediate questions about the assessment and accountability regime used in the state, and its adequacy under terms of NCLB, as well as the bar to be set for the determination of annual measurable objectives (AMO) under the federal legislation. NCLB specified a different form of intervention, specifically the ability of students to transfer from low-performing schools (thereby increasing parental involvement), an option not then available in California. Also, NCLB raised questions about how California would insure that its teaching force, at 305,000 and the nation's largest, would meet the "highly qualified" requirements of the act.

NCLB prompted many significant changes in state policies and local school practices, which involved the diverse array of education policy actors (EdSource, 2004). We review changes in assessment series, accountability measures, intervention, and preparation of teachers.

## Assessment

The primary assessment measure under the PSAA had been the Stanford 9, a norm-referenced test. It had been augmented by several criterion-referenced questions, but the match with the state standards was still inexact. For this reason, the state developed three new assessments, which were directly based on California's curriculum content standards (recognized as some of the most rigorous content standards in the nation).

The first and most widely used assessment is the California Standards Test (CST), which is used in measuring API for English-language arts, mathematics, social studies, and science in Grades 2 through 11 (in the computation of Adequate Yearly Progress [AYP], only Grades 2 through 8 are tested). The state did not develop standards-based tests for certain grade spans. For students with significant cognitive disabilities who are unable to take the CST, even with modifications, the state developed the California Alternate Performance Assessment (CAPA). Finally, the California High School Exit Examination (CAHSEE) was used to comply with NCLB requirements for testing at least once in high school, but these results do not constitute part of the STAR program and are not included in API. The state uses a national norm-referenced test, the California Achievement Tests, Sixth edition (CAT/6 Survey), which is part of API but not used to measure AYP (California Department of Education [CDE], 2005a).

An example of the assessment challenge NCLB presented is seen in the treatment of English-language learners. These students perform far less well than other student subgroups, often by as much as 20 to 30 percentage points on tests. One measurement difficulty is that LEP tests measure both achievement and language ability. A second is that once students attain language proficiency, they usually are removed from the subgroup, which puts downward pressure on LEP test scores already worsened by new LEP students who typically are low-achieving (Abedi & Dietel, 2004).

## Accountability Measures

NCLB establishes four criteria to determine whether a school has met AYP:

- Participation rate of 95% or greater for the state test results used to establish the percentage of students at the proficient level or above for AYP;

- Percentage of students who score proficient or above in English-language arts (ELA) and mathematics as compared to Annual Measurable Objectives (AMOs);
- Growth in the API of at least one point OR a minimum 2005 API Growth score of 590;
- A graduation rate of at least 82.9 OR improvement in the graduation rate of at least 0.1 OR improvement in the graduation rate average over 2 years of at least 0.2.

The participation rate and graduation rate requirements for California are identical to those for the other states, however determination of AYP and API growth rates varies. With respect to AYP, states had the option of front-loading the requirement (asking for steeper proficiency rates early on), back-loading the requirement (waiting until later in implementation to require steeper proficiency rates), or evening out the annual rate over the 12-year period of implementation from 2002 to 2014.

California back loaded the requirement. Some 13.6% of students in 2003-04 had to test at the proficient level in English/language arts, while 16% had to test proficiently in math. In 2004-05, the targets increased by 10.8% in language arts and 10.5% in math. From 2007-08, the targets will increase annually by 10.8% in language arts and 10.5% in math until the 100% goal is reached in 2013-14.

A critical report of this AYP determination notes:

> Using targets based on aggregate average scores of groups of students … provides a temptation for states to focus their immediate attention on students performing just below the proficiency bar rather than the lowest performing students. It is easier to push students performing just below proficiency over that bar, thereby allowing the state to meet its annual proficiency target goal. (Izumi & Yan, 2004, p. 2)

The California solution to setting the bar has the effect of focusing attention on students near the proficient level, and delaying attention to the students performing least well. By the time attention shifts to these students, it may be too late to help them attain proficiency. This then will be an incentive for the state to lower its definition of proficiency, which is precisely what the state's Legislative Analyst's Office recommended in 2004 (Izumi & Yan, 2004).

A second difference in the use of accountability measures pertains to how API is employed in federal target criteria. Under state requirements, a school must increase its API score by 5% of the difference between the school API and 800 (the scale begins at 200) OR maintain a score of 800 or above. Under federal requirements, a school or local education agency must have a minimum API of 590 OR have at least one point growth in the school wide API in addition to the other federal AYP targets (CDE, 2005a). As we shall see below, proficiency is easier to attain under state than federal requirements. This creates an accountability system with two parallel tracks.

The nature of API itself has been studied as part of the state's response to NCLB requirements. In the Budget Act of 2000-01, the legislature asked for an independent analysis of API, to determine whether it should include other factors in addition to use of student scores from STAR, and how it compared to techniques used in other states. The analysis was done by CREDO, a nonpartisan research group at the Hoover Institution of Stanford University.

CREDO examined 32 additional factors that might be included within API, for example class size, college entrance test results, number of computers in a school, number of support personnel, parent/community satisfaction, retention rate, student attendance rate, and teacher mobility (Fletcher & Raymond, 2002). The research team eliminated three factors because of lack of data in California. Twenty of the factors were at best moderately related to student achievement; the remaining nine were strongly associated with student outcomes. However, the variables lacked robustness: they displayed insufficient variation in values of the variable, consistency problems in data collection or calculation, or biases distorting the measurement (Fletcher & Raymond, 2002).

Finally, CREDO considered how student test data were aggregated to produce school scores, by comparing the method used in California to that used in other states. California has used a "static measure" of schools, which is also known as a "status model." Test data are compiled from all eligible students at one point in time, to form a single school score. Such a model does not make it possible to eliminate the influence of year-to-year changes in student body composition or grade-to-grade changes in instructional design or teacher quality. The plurality of states uses the status model. A slight improvement to this model, used in states including Alaska, Florida, Louisiana, and Wisconsin, examines changes in grade level performance across years. Called a "cross-sectional" model, it factors out shifts in instructional design or teachers across grades. A third model focuses on student change; it follows the same students from year to year, and thus isolates the effects of changes in student body composition, teacher differences and instructional design shifts across grades. Such a "change" or "value-added" model is used in a small number of states including North Carolina and Massachusetts (Fletcher & Raymond, 2002, pp. 46-47).

CREDO recommended that California move toward a change model that would improve the performance of API. However, this would require an ability to take into account student mobility across districts and the creation of student identifiers that could be used statewide (Fletcher & Raymond, 2002). To the present, these recommendations have not been adopted.

## Intervention

Although under the PSAA, California offered a series of carrots and sticks as sanctions to improve school performance, NCLB imposed additional requirements. In the third year of failing to attain AYP (the 2005-06 academic year), the local education agency (usually a school district) was required to provide choice to attend another school in the district (or county) that was not under program improvement status, and to pay for transportation costs. This posed serious difficulties for California, given the large number of LEAs and schools likely to have failed to meet AYP at that point. Also, the school improvement process designed under NCLB did not match the II/USP intervention strategy of California's accountability system, which was based on individual schools (Alan, 2004). Nor did California's pre-2004 intervention programs seem to work. A 2003 study found that given the large increase in standards-based tests in California, the II/USP interventions had a "negligible" effect (O'Day & Bittner, 2003, p. xi).

California used the Tennessee accountability model to determine which of its districts did not meet federal standards. This model labeled LEAs in need of improvement if they failed to attain federal achievement goals or AYP for two consecutive years in a subgroup or subject across all grade spans. Too, as mentioned, the state's threshold for low-income students on state standardized tests was lower, and under the combined methods few districts—just 14—met the needs-improvement criterion (Davis & Sack, 2005). If the state had followed federal rules exactly, nearly 310 of California's 1,000 school districts might have been found in need of improvement. For these reasons among others, the state department of education conducted negotiations with the U.S. Department of Education (USDOE), and sought a compromise with USDOE on its interpretation of the federal requirements. The agreement between the state and the department brought the number of districts needing improvement to 184, and postponed until the 2005-06 school year the first year for district improvement plans. Jack O'Connell, the state's superintendent of public instruction, commented: "This is a compromise from a very inflexible federal department and their one-size, overly prescriptive approach to public education" (Davis & Sack, 2005, p. ).

At its March 2005 meeting, the California Board of Education revised the NCLB requirements chart for local education agencies (LEAs). For the first 2 years, entry to the program improvement category was restricted to LEAs both failing to make AYP and failing to meet AYP grade span criteria. Then, for those LEAs in years 3-4 (school improvement), the California board differentiated year 3 as a period for intensive planning and year 4 as a time for plan implementation. In year 5 of corrective action, the board changed somewhat the corrective actions required:

- defer programmatic funds or reduce administrative funds,
- institute new curriculum and professional development for staff,
- replace LEA staff,
- remove individual schools from jurisdiction of LEA and arrange for governance,
- appoint trustee in place of superintendent and school board,
- abolish or restructure LEA (CDE, 2005a, p. 89).

The revision puts off student transfers until the fifth year and also delays the onset of restructuring of schools. Too, it voids the requirement of lengthening the school day or year. Accompanying these changes was development of another intervention strategy, a School Assistance and Intervention Team (SAIT), applicable after 2 years of poor performance. The focus of SAIT is on bringing standards-based coherence to remedial actions for failing schools (Evers & Izumi, 2005).

Scholars focusing on state implementation of NCLB requirements have found that states falling behind in meeting AYP, such as California, are more likely to offer technical assistance, professional development, and planning assistance for troubled schools instead of imposing tougher sanctions, such as restructuring. For example, Julian R. Betts, a UC San Diego economist, charges that "NCLB choice is clearly at risk of becoming irrelevant to student achievement statewide.... The reason is simple: Nobody is participating" (Olson, 2006, p. 19).

The overall effect of the negotiated revisions is to delay further implementation of corrective and restructuring provisions of NCLB for LEAs and soften intervention into schools.

Meanwhile, citizen activists have begun protesting California school districts' failure to enforce the choice provisions of NCLB. In 2006, lawyers representing two conservative groups (the Alliance for School Choice and the Coalition on Urban Renewal and Education) filed administrative complaints with USDOE against the Los Angeles United and Compton Unified School Districts. They alleged that the districts had not adequately notified parents of their school choice rights, and they had not provided sufficient options for children attending schools defined as in need of improvement under NCLB. The complaint mentioned that only 527 of 250,000 eligible students (in a district of 760,000 students in the Los Angeles district) were able to make a transfer, and no students in the Compton district (for the reason that all middle and high schools failed to make AYP in 2004-05) were able to transfer (Hoff, 2006a). Although education secretary Spellings has threatened to withhold NCLB funding from districts that fail to implement school choice provisions (Hoff, 2006b), USDOE has not done so to the present (late 2006). Yet the department has approved waivers to allow districts to offer tutoring and other academic services, which reverses the order required under NCLB. The choice provision is among the most difficult to implement in most states.

## Teacher Preparation

The improvement of teacher quality under terms of NCLB is a challenging issue in California. Recent statistics indicate that more than one-third of middle school math teachers did not major in either math or math education in college. (Typically, middle school teachers may hold certification for elementary *or* secondary schools; and elementary school teachers do not need subject matter certification as they teach all subjects.) Further, one-third of teacher candidates failed the state's subject matter test for teachers. A very high number of teachers in the state's lowest performing schools—an estimated 20 to 50%—teach under state waivers, emergency teaching permits, or a credential allowing teachers to enter the classroom without subject-matter preparation (Keller, 2003).

The problem lies not only with new teachers but with veteran educators, who currently may but are not required to establish subject matter competence through testing. Veteran teachers also can demonstrate subject-matter competence by having a degree in that field or by accumulating points in a system recognizing activities in the subject area. For example, teachers can accumulate up to half the needed points by teaching classes in the subject area. They can gain points through "leadership and service to the profession in the assigned area," by having their colleagues observe their classroom work, and even by "establishing and communicating learning goals for all students" (Izumi & Yan, 2004, p. 3). Some of these activities may show evidence of or improve the quality of teaching, but others appear to be unrelated to that end.

An additional difficulty with teacher quality, discussed earlier, is the lack in alignment of the most highly qualified and credentialed teachers with the schools most in need of improvement. Although governors and the legislature in the last decade have sought to increase salaries for entry-level teachers[4] and provide other incentives to attract them to work in low-performing schools, the proposals have been overly broad. In 2000 the Legislative Analyst's Office reported that incentives for teacher recruitment were not targeted to schools most needing them (California, Office of the Legislative Analyst, 2000). Available research indicates that serious problems in teacher preparation are concentrated in about 20% of the state's public schools (Dawson & Billingsley, 2000). A related issue of alignment, often mentioned in conservative critiques of the state's education establishment, is the imbalance between teachers and nonteaching personnel. For example, in the 1998-99 school year, there were 10,000 more support staff, janitors, school counselors, and other professionals than certificated teachers. Paraprofessionals command a large slice of the educational pie, draining resources from teachers.

A third issue and repeated source of controversy concerning school improvement in California is the inflexibility of state laws and regulations, and the expansion in scope of the Educational Employment Relations (collective bargaining) Act of 1975. The California education code, at 9,000 pages in length, directs instructional practices in schools, the textbooks to be used in classrooms, and details concerning professional development activities for teachers. Contractual provisions influence class-size reduction, assignment of instructors, and peer review of instruction (Howell, 1999).

These and other flaws in addressing the requirement that teachers be highly qualified led the National Council for Teacher Quality to give California the grade of "F" in its evaluation of state teacher-quality improvement systems (Howell, 1999). The state's response was threefold. In 2001 the legislature approved a Teacher Quality Index, but then Governor Gray Davis vetoed the bill because of fiscal concerns. In 2003 a bipartisan and bicameral committee of the legislature proposed a prohibition on license waivers and emergency permits by 2005 as part of a 20-year education master plan. Although major elements of the master plan were scuttled because of the state's financial troubles, the prohibition was enacted (Keller, 2003; see also Galley, 2003). Third, as discussed below, teachers' salaries in California have become more competitive. Yet at the first hearing of the NCLB Commission in California, Gavin Payne, CDE's chief deputy superintendent commented "If Congress and the federal government want better results (in raising teacher quality standards), they must be willing to pay for their expectations" (Jacobson, 2006). He recommended additional hiring incentives such as college loan forgiveness and signing bonuses provided at local, state, and federal levels.

## INITIAL RESULTS OF NCLB IN CALIFORNIA (2003-2006)

Because California changed the test series after the implementation of NCLB, it is difficult to ascertain whether the state has made large improvements in school performance since the development of its accountability system in 1998-99. Yet by 2006, the state had aggregated 4 years' of data on school performance under NCLB, and this permits analysis of initial results. We consider first the rates in attainment of AYP for different ethnic and special groups, in English-language arts and mathematics under state tests. Next, we look at student performance on the NAEP since 1996/1998. Then, we turn to different rates of high school graduation. Finally, we examine the number of schools placed on program improvement status over 5 years.

Table 9.2 compares achievement rates of large student population groups from 2004 to 2006.

The computational formula for API does not trace student change over time, and thus the table presents snapshots of groups of students, some of whom do not appear in all groups, at different points in time. Nevertheless, we can discern slight improvement in proficiency rates, for all groups, and in both reading and mathematics. For example, English language arts scores rose from 35% proficient in 2004 to 42% proficient in 2006; math proficiency scores rose from 34% in 2004 to 40% in 2006.

**Table 9.2. Percentage Proficient in English and Math, 2004-06**

| Groups | Eng04 | Math04 | Eng05 | Math05 | Eng06 | Math06 |
|---|---|---|---|---|---|---|
| All Students | 35 | 34 | 40 | 38 | 42 | 40 |
| African American | 23 | 19 | 27 | 23 | 29 | 24 |
| Am. Ind./Ak. Native | 31 | 28 | 36 | 32 | 37 | 35 |
| Asian | 56 | 60 | 62 | 65 | 64 | 67 |
| Filipino | 50 | 45 | 55 | 50 | 58 | 54 |
| Hispanic or Latino | 21 | 23 | 25 | 27 | 27 | 30 |
| Pacific Islander | 31 | 31 | 36 | 35 | 39 | 38 |
| White (non-Hispanic) | 54 | 46 | 58 | 51 | 60 | 53 |
| Econ. disadvantaged | 21 | 25 | 25 | 29 | 27 | 30 |
| Students w/ disabilities | 10 | 13 | 11 | 15 | 13 | 16 |
| English Learners | 10 | 20 | 12 | 24 | 14 | 25 |

*Soure:* Adapted by author from California Department of Education, State Reports, 2004, 2005, 2006 Accountability Progress Reports; retrieved on February 19, 2007 from http://www.cde.ca.gov/ta/tg/sr/documents/yr06rel89summ.pdf

The gaps between ethnic subgroups as compared to White students continued, at roughly the same rate, during these 3 years of testing; they did not narrow (nor did they increase).[5] Scores of economically disadvantaged students improved, but the gap with other students remained the same. Although scores of students with disabilities increased somewhat (for example, in English language arts, from 21 to 27% and in math from 25 to 30%), the gap between these students and non-disabled White students increased significantly. In 2004 the gap in English was 34%; in 2006 it was 47%. This was the case for English language learners as well. The gap widened somewhat in mathematics (from 26 to 28%, over the 3 years); in English it widened from 34% in 2004 to 46% in 2006.[6] However, growth in AYP from year to year has been slow on a statewide basis. Following state accountability rules, from 2003 to 2004 growth was just 9 API points; from 2004 to 2005 API increased by 20 points. In neither year did the state make AYP by federal accountability rules, and the targets were low.

Shortly after release of the 2006 API scores, the National Center for Research on Evaluation, Standards, and Student Testing (CRESST) released its analysis of California's progress in accountability. Authors Goldschmidt, Boscardin, and Linn (2006) discussed growth in scores, continuing gaps among subgroups, and methodological difficulties in the assessment system. The authors indicated that overall, California schools demonstrated an 11 point or 1.6% improvement over the previous year, notwithstanding the fact that fewer schools (52%) met growth targets in 2006 than in 2005. However, they cautioned observers about the leveling-off phenomenon on virtually any test:

> The longer an accountability system is in place, the smaller the gains. California may have reached that plateau, which usually happens between the 3rd and 7th year of an accountability program. STAR (the main component of the state assessment system) began in the1997/1998 school-year and the API was passed into legislation in 1999. (p. 1)

Second, Goldschmidt et al. noted continued progress of subgroups on the tests. However, as we have noted, they emphasized the substantial size of the achievement gap among subgroups: "For example, English Learners (over 32 % of students included in the current API growth report) scored about 80 points lower in the overall comparison. The achievement gap is as high as 96 points in Grades 9 through 11 for ELs" (p. 2) They questioned whether school growth targets were appropriately aligned, and "whether API scores accurately reflect the performance of student subgroups and corresponding performance gaps" (p. 2).

In a related but broader methodological critique, Goldschmidt et al. question whether API scores identify good schools, whether the improvement in student scores validly represents achievement growth, and whether they are sufficient as a guide to a state's progress under the NCLB accountability model. On this point, the authors suggest that many schools with good API scores, which currently meet NCLB targets, will not meet the final proficiency targets in 2013-14 (p. 3).

The third author of the CRESST report, Robert Linn (former president of the American Educational Research Association) has made these comments previously, with respect to NCLB nationally. He recommends developing a common definition of proficient achievement to be used by all states and considering student achievement growth (as opposed to fixed achievement status). An innovation he proposes based on the experience of California as well as many other states is that performance targets be made more realistic (his phrase is that there needs to be "an existence proof": evidence that the goal does not exceed a target previously achieved by the highest performing school) (Linn, 2005, p. 3).

As noted previously, California's computation of AYP based on API produces a proficiency score that is higher than that recorded through the National Assessment of Educational Progress (NAEP). For example, the NAEP rate for Californian fourth graders scoring at or above proficient in 2003 was 21, compared to the state test score of 39 (and California was the 46th state in rank order). For eighth graders the NAEP score was 22 and the state test score 30 (with California ranked 40th). Rankings in mathematics were slightly better. The NAEP score for fourth graders was 25, compared to the state test score of 45 (a difference of 20, with California rank-ordered 40th). The NAEP score for eighth graders was 22, compared to the state score of 30 (a difference of 8, with California ranked thirty-eighth of the American states) (*Quality Counts*, 2005). In all comparisons, California, over the 2 years, remains in the bottom quartile of states nationally.

Policy Analysis for California Education (PACE), a policy institute affiliated with UC Berkeley and Davis, questions the validity of reported gains in California (and other states) based on state tests. PACE contends that state gain scores are exaggerated because of "overly easy" exams. One report author, UC Berkeley education professor Bruce Fuller, says "Parents and policymakers and journalists should not trust state test-score results. They should place them alongside national test-score results" (Cavanag, 2006, p. 19). We follow this advice by examining NAEP scores for California students on the NAEP from the period corresponding to the start of state testing (1997-98) to 2005), as seen in Table 9.3.

Comparing the 2 years (2003, 2005) during which NCLB has been implemented in California with earlier years (1996/1998, 2000), one notes no change of student proficiency in reading, but significant changes in math. Scores of students' reading proficiency in 1998 are virtually iden-

**Table 9.3.   California Students' Proficiency on NAEP, 1996-2005**

| Grade Year | Math04 | Eng04 | Eng08 | Math08 |
|---|---|---|---|---|
| 1996 | 11% | | | 17% |
| 1998 | | 20% | 21% | |
| 2000 | 13% | 21% | 20% | 17% |
| 2003 | 25% | 21% | 22% | 22% |
| 2005 | 28% | 21% | 21% | 22% |

*Source:*   Adapted by the author from National Center for Education Statistics, State Profile (http://nces.ed.gov/nationsreportcard/states/profile.asp).

tical to those of students in 2005. However, fourth grade math scores increase from 11% in 1996 to 28% in 2005, more than doubling; eighth grade math scores increase by 5%, from 17% in 1996 to 22% in 2005. Although authors of the PACE study (Cavanagh, 2006) noted that states made stronger average annual gains in reading before NCLB took effect in 2002, the California NAEP data do not support this. Again, reading scores (as based on a sample of students) were flat, but there were significant gains in mathematics.

High school achievement rates show a similar pattern of slight improvement. In 2002, only 33% of California high school students took upper-level math courses (compared to the national average of 48%), and just 18% took upper-level science courses (the national rate was 31%). The state graduation rate this year was 67%, compared to the national rate of 71%. Rates of Caucasians (non-Hispanic), Blacks, and Latinos were 76, 59, and 54 respectively, compared to the national breakdown of 78, 56, and 52% (*Quality Counts*, 2005), so the gap is somewhat wider nationally.

Initially, California's High School Exit Examination (CAHSEE) was to have taken effect in 2004, but was delayed 2 years until 2006. Students are tested for knowledge of 8th grade math and 10th grade English, and can pass the tests by answering little more than half the questions correctly. Students who have not met the requirement by the tenth grade have five chances to retake the test. To the present (late 2006), passage rates for students in the class of 2006 have been higher than expected. In August 2005 the superintendent of public instruction, Jack O'Connell, announced that the passage rate had exceeded projections: 88% had passed both English-language arts and mathematics portions of the test. Yet, while all subgroups of students made progress, gaps between Asian and Caucasian (non-Latino) students on the one hand and Latino, African American, LEP, and special education students remained (CDE,

**Table 9.4.  2005-06 Title I Program Improvement Status**

| Year | Advance* | Remain** | Total*** |
|---|---|---|---|
| Year 1 | 303 | 97 | 400 |
| Year 2 | 473 | 65 | 538 |
| Year 3 | 388 | 17 | 407 |
| Year 4 | 133 | 19 | 154 |
| Year 5 | 237 | 10 | 247 |
| Total | 1,534 | 212 | 1,746 |

*"Advance" means the number of schools or LEAs that moved into PI or the number that moved from the prior year of PI implementation.
**"Remain" represents the number of schools or LEAs that did not change the year of PI implementation from 2004-05 to 2005-06.
***"Total" represents the number of schools in PI and each year of implementation.
*Source:*  California Department of Education, 2005-06 Title I PI Status Statewide Summary. Retrieved February 19, 2007 from:  http://www.cde.ca.gov/ta/ac/ay/tistatesum05.asp

2005b). News of this gap prompted a legislative response to lower the bar, by giving school districts the authority to use alternative performance assessments to award diplomas to students failing to pass CAHSEE (Yan, 2005). The state average high school graduation rate in 2006 was 71%, slightly above the national average of 70% in this year (and an improvement over the graduation rate of 2000-03, by 2.7%) (*Quality Counts*, 2007).

Finally, more than one third of California's schools have failed to make AYP under NCLB rules. In 2002-03, some 3,200 schools failed to attain AYP, and 925 schools were identified as low-performing. The following year, in 2003-04, some 3,213 schools failed to attain AYP, and 1,626 were identified as low-performing (CDE, 2005c; see also *Quality Counts*, 2005). In the 2005-06 school year, 44% of all schools failed to make AYP. Table 9.4 presents data on the statewide program improvement status of Title I schools in 2005-06:

This table indicates that some schools have left the PI status as a consequence of school improvement plan activity, among other factors; however, somewhat more than half of the schools placed on improvement status remain there in 2006. Schools in the fifth year are scheduled for restructuring in the 2006-07 academic year.

## PROSPECTS FOR ATTAINMENT OF NCLB GOALS BY 2014

*Education Week*'s *Quality Counts* national survey gives California reasonable marks for its assessment and accountability system. It comments "The state is one of six that have clear and specific standards at the elementary, middle, and high school levels for English, mathematics, science, and social studies/history." This gives it a grade of "B+." In the 2007 edition, *Quality Counts* evaluated state education alignment policies. California ranked 11th of the states, a ranking that recognized the match of school policies with preparation of students for the economy and the workforce; the match to postsecondary education was less good (especially with respect to alignment of high school courses and the high school assessment system to the postsecondary system). *Quality Counts* also examined state activity in the area of standards, assessments, and accountability. Here, California ranked 14th (2007).

The Fordham Foundation's review of content standards in English and mathematics gave California "A" grades in 2005. The report calls language arts standards "clear, specific, and measurable and (they) address all areas of the English language arts and reading well and comprehensively" (Stotsky, 2005, p. 33) The math report notes:

> California's standards are excellent in every respect. The language is crystal clear, important topics are given priority, and key connections between different skills and tasks are explicitly addressed. (Klein, 2005, p. 42)

California's efforts to improve teacher quality rank at a "B–" in *Quality Counts*, but then the rankings drop. The state school climate is graded "C," because of high rates of student absenteeism, tardiness, and physical conflicts in the classroom. (Indeed, a federal audit chided California in 2005 for failing to implement NCLB's policy on educational choice for students in unsafe schools [Robelen, 2005].) In resource equity, California stands at the middle of states, yet some analysts, such as Betts and Danenberg (2001) argue that "Compared to SES, school resources appear to play a modest role in determining variations in student achievement" (p. 56).

California was at the low-end for per-pupil spending in 2001-02, ranking 44th among the 50 states. Then the state spent $6,659 per pupil, about $1,000 less than the national average of $7,734 (*Quality Counts* 2005). Because of Proposition 98 and economic growth, the state has made a partial rebound in this area. In 2003-04, per student spending for education, at $9,324, ranked 23rd in the nation (U.S. Census Bureau, 2007). Certainly, most observers (and virtually all teachers) would agree that higher spending on education would help California improve its schools. Higher entry-level teacher salaries (in 2002-03 the average for beginning teachers was $34,805, ranking fifth nationally) may help attract qualified teachers. But the state would need to provide significantly larger incentives to attract highly qualified teachers to the areas of greatest need. As mentioned, the least qualified and credentialed teachers are found in the lowest-performing schools. California stands apart from the other states in the very high percentage of LEP students (25%) and students who are socioeconomically disadvantaged (19%). It seems apparent that without an infusion of highly qualified teachers to assist these student populations, that little fundamental change in achievement will occur.

The California economy has been on a "roller coaster ride" in the last decade (Korey, 2006, p. CA-1). From a surplus position at the turn of the century, the state encountered an energy crisis, which turned into a budget deficit, worsened by the national economic slowdown after 9/11. Budget woes were a major factor driving Gray Davis out of office in 2003. Then, in 2004 the state entered another period of solid growth. In this year, 71% of California voters approved Proposition 58, the Balanced Budget Act, an attempt to prohibit bonds designed to fund budget deficits (Korey, 2005). In short, while slight increases to K-12 education funding occur in good budget years (such as FY 07), it appears unlikely that California schools will receive a significantly larger infusion of economic resources that would help school reform efforts.

One could argue that obstacles to school improvement efforts in California are as much political as economic. We have noted above that educational leadership in the state is divided. Even when governor and legislature are of the same party, they compete as often as they cooperate on educational issues (see Myres, 1999). And even if governor, legislature, superintendent of public instruction, and state school board are unified, they face the prospect of citizen groups, which historically have taken ample advantage of the state's initiative process to write laws and influence funding for state schools. Among these citizen groups are conservatives and liberals, representatives of minorities and every variety of special interest group. The lack of a unified and centralized political structure in the state also permits business associations as well as teachers' unions (Posnick-Goodwin, 2006) to influence educational outcomes, particularly when they believe they have not been involved in school governance.

The national political context became especially important to California following the 2006 midterm elections. San Francisco's Nancy Pelosi became the first female Speaker of the Democratic-majority House of Representatives. Representative George Miller, a contributing author of NCLB, became chair of the Education & Labor committee, which will play the key role in re-authorization of NCLB. As a supporter of NCLB, Miller also has been critical of the Bush administration, alleging it has underfunded the act. In the Senate, Barbara Boxer will serve as chief deputy whip and also head of the Environment and Public Works committee. She too has been a supporter of NCLB and advocate of increased federal funding for it. A joint interest of the California congressional delegation will be increased federal spending in the state. In the first three-quarters of the Bush administration, California received only 78 cents for every dollar it sent in taxes to Washington, DC (see, Klein, 2006; Steinhauer, 2006; and Hoff, 2006c). A greater share of the federal revenue pie would enable the state to allocate a larger percentage of its general fund to K-12 education.

Like other states, California will not meet the inspirational goals of NCLB. Yet the act has focused attention on the basics of reading and math in the state, and directed attention to the large achievement gaps needing to be closed. As Goldschmidt et al. note: "Our analysis and experience with other state accountability systems leads us to conclude that the API and STAR have successfully pushed California schools to improve learning for many of its students" (2006, p. 4). However, much remains to be done to improve inputs, such as teacher quality and intervention strategies, which doubtless will require new resources and continued coalition-building. The largest challenge California education faces is that one-quarter of the students are English language learners, and the number continues to grow.

## NOTES

1.  Kirst notes that the 1994 federal Title I reforms, which required states to develop a three-legged accountability system (academic standards, tests tied to the standards, and a combination of assistance and sanctions for low-performing schools) had almost no impact in stimulating California into action.

2.  Kirst calls Stanford 9 "the tail that wagged the accountability dog." See Kirst (2002, p. 2).

3.  Betts and Danenberg (2002) note, respecting the difference in dropout rates: "The state has not adopted a longitudinal database that tracks students as they move between schools, leave the state, or in the case of immigrants reverse migrate to their country of origin" (p. 153).

4.  California's average salary for instructional staff in 2001-02 was $53,870, third highest in the nation. See American Legislative Exchange Council, *Report Card on American Education* (2004).

5.  An analysis conducted by Associated Press in 2006 reported that many schools nationwide were escaping accountability for the progress of racial or ethnic subgroups under NCLB. According to the study, "the achievement scores of more than 400,000 minority students in California are not being counted by their racial or ethnic categories at the school level when determining AYP results" See Olson and Jacobson (2006), Analysis finds minority NCLB scores widely excluded, *Education Week, 25 (33)*, 5.

6.  The USDOE denied California's request to waive the NCLB requirements on testing kindergartners and first graders with limited English skills in reading and writing. The state has tested LEP students in listening and

speaking skills. See Zehr, (2005, p. 18). In another compliance issue, the office of the inspector general of DOE found that the California department of education and some school districts had not made required test accommodations for LEP students. See "U.S. Cites" (2005).

## REFERENCES

Abedi, J., & Dietel, R. (2004, Winter). *Challenges in the No Child Left Behind act for English language learners* (CRESST Policy Brief, no. 7). Los Angeles, CA: UCLA, Center for the Study of Education.

Alan, R. (2004, September 15). NCLB law's focus turns to districts: states must identify lagging systems. *Education Week*, pp. 1, 17.

American Legislative Exchange Council. (2004, September). *Report card of American education: A state-by-state analysis, 1981-2003*. Washington, DC: Author

Barone, M., & Cohen, R. E. (2005). *The almanac of American politics, 2006*. Washington, DC: National Journal Group.

Bateman, D. M., & Lascher, E. L., Jr. (2000). California. In *Proceedings—Roundtable: State budgeting in the 13 western states*. Salt Lake City, UT: Center for Public Policy & Administration.

Betts, J. R. (2003). *A critical path analysis of California's K-12 sector*. Irvine, CA: California Council on Science and Technology.

Betts, J. R., & Danenberg, A. (2001). An assessment of resources and student achievement. In J. Sonstelle & P. Richardson (Eds.), *School finance and California's master plan for education* (pp. 47-79). San Francisco: Public Policy Institute of California.

Betts, J. R., & Danenberg, A. (2002). School accountability in California: An early evaluation. In D. Ravitch (ed.), *Brookings Papers on Education Policy, 2002* (pp. 123-81). Washington, DC: The Brookings Institution.

Betts, J. R., & Danenberg, A. (2003). The effects of accountability in California. In P. E. Peterson & M. R. West (Eds.), *No Child Left Behind? The politics and practice of school accountability* (pp. 197-214). Washington, DC: The Brookings Institution.

California Business for Education Excellence. (1998, December 16). *California business leaders join forces to pursue education reform agenda* (Press release). Sacramento, CA. Retrieved February 20, 2007, from http://caltx.org/commend/cbee.htm

California Department of Education. (2005a, August). *Overview of the 2005 accountability progress report*. Sacramento, CA: Author.

California Department of Education. (2005b, August 15). News release.

California Department of Education. (2005c, September). *2005-06 Title I PI status statewide summary*. Sacramento, CA: Author.

California, Office of the Governor (1999). *California state budget highlights 1999-2000* (News release). Sacramento, CA.

California, Office of the Legislative Analyst. (2000, February 17). *Analysis of the 2000-01 budget bill, teacher quality and supply*. Sacramento, CA.

Cavanagh, S. (2006, July 12). California study questions validity of gains under NCLB. *Education Week, 25*(42), 19.

Consortium for Policy Research in Education. (2000). *Assessment and accountability in the fifty states: 1999-2000, California*. Madison, WI: Author.

Davis, M., & Sack, J. (2005, March 16). California, U.S. Department of Education strike deal on NCLB rules. *Education Week, 24*(27), 6.

Dawson, T. C,. & Billingsley, K. L. (2000, September). *Unsatisfactory performance*. San Francisco, CA: Pacific Research Institute for Public Policy.

EdSource. (2004, January). *No Child Left Behind in California? The impact of the federal NCLB so far*. Palo Alto, CA: Author.

Emery, K. (2002). *The business roundtable and systemic reform: How corporate-engineered high-stakes testing has eliminated community participation in developing educational goals and policies*. Unpublished doctoral dissertation, University of California, Davis.

Evers, W. M., & Izumi, L. T. (2005). Fixing failing schools in California. In J. Chubb (Ed.), *Within our reach: How America can educate every child* (pp. 113-40). Lanham, MD: Rowman & Littlefield.

Fletcher, S., & Raymond, M. (2002, April). *The future of California's academic performance index*. Stanford, CA: Hoover Institution, CREDO.

Galley, M. (2003, August 6). Many teachers missing "highly qualified" mark. *Education Week, 22*(43), 30, 32.

Goldschmidt, P., Boscardin, C. K., & Linn, R. (2006, September 4). *CRESST analysis of California accountability progress report*. Los Angeles: UCLA Center for the Study of Evaluation, CRESST.

Hauser, R. (2002). Comment. In D. Ravitch (Ed.), *Brookings Papers on education policy, 2002* (pp. 181-98). Washington, DC: The Brookings Institution.

Hendrie, C. (2005, October 12). Legislation tightens fiscal oversight of California charters. *Education Week, 25*(7), 18.

Hess, F. (2003). "Refining or retreating? High-stakes accountability in the states. In P. E. Peterson & M. R West (Eds.), *No Child Left Behind? The politics and practice of school accountability* (pp. 55-79). Washington, DC: Brookings Institution.

Hoff, D. (2006a, March 29). Complaint targets NCLB transfers in Calif. *Education Week, 25*(29), 5.

Hoff, D. (2006b, September 20). Groups press for enforcement on NCLB choice option. *Education Week, 26*(4), 28, 30.

Hoff, D. (2006c, November 15). Democratic majority to put education policy on agenda. *Education Week, 26*(12), 26-27.

Honig, B., & Alexander, F. (1996). Re-writing the tests: Lessons from the California state assessment system. In $95^{th}$ *NSSE Yearbook, part I* (pp. 1433-1465). Chicago: University of Chicago Press.

Howell, P. (1999, March). Collective bargaining: Explaining California's system. *EdSource*, pp. 1-8.

Izumi, L. T., & Yan, X. C. (2004, December). *California 2005: Reform agenda, education studies*. San Francisco, CA: Pacific Research Institute, Policy Briefing.

Jacobson, L. (2006, April 19). NCLB commission starts gathering testimony. *Education Week, 25*(32), 28.

Jepsen, C., & Rivkin, S. (2002). *Class size reduction, teacher quality, and academic achievement in California public elementary schools.* San Francisco, CA: Public Policy Institute of California.

Just, A. E., Boese, L. E., Burkhardt, R., Carstens, L. J., Devine, M., & Gaffney, T. (2001, May). *Public school accountability (1999-2000; research summary).* Sacramento, CA: California Department of Education.

Keller, B. (2003, February 12). Legislation would strengthen teaching requirements in California. *Education Week,* p. 22.

Kirst, M. W. (2002, Summer). Swing state. *Education Next,* pp. 1-8.

Klein, D. (2005). *The state of the state math standards.* Washington, DC: Fordham Foundation.

Klein, A. (2006, September 27). Political shift could temper NCLB resolve. *Education Week, 26*(5), 24-5.

Korey, J. (2004). California. In *Proceedings—Roundtable: State budgeting in the 13 western states.* Salt Lake City, UT: Center for Public Policy & Administration.

Korey, J. (2005). California. In *Proceedings—Roundtable: State budgeting in the 13 western states.* Salt Lake City, UT: Center for Public Policy & Administration.

Korey, J. (2006). California. In *Proceedings—Roundtable: State budgeting in the 13 western states.* Salt Lake City, UT: Center for Public Policy & Administration.

Linn, R. L. (2005, Summer). *Fixing the NCLB accountability system.* Los Angeles: UCLA, Center for the Study of Evaluation, CRESST Policy Brief 8.

Mintrop, H., & Trujillo, T. (2004). *Corrective action in low-performing schools.* Los Angeles, CA: University of California at Los Angeles, National Center for Research and Evaluation, Standards, and Student Testing.

Moe, T. M. (2003). Politics, control, and the future of school accountability. In P. E. Peterson & M. R. West (Eds.), *No child Left Behind? The politics and practice of school accountability* (pp. 80-106). Washington, DC: Brookings Institution.

Myres, J. W. (1999, June 9). Why reforms won't work in California. *Education Week.*

NCLB accountability seen as opportunity for Calif. charters. (2005, February 2). *Education Week,* pp. 21, 24.

O'Day, J,. & Bittner, C. (2003, June 20). *Evaluation study of the immediate intervention/underperforming schools program and the high achieving improving schools program of the public schools accountability act of 1999.* Sacramento, CA: California Department of Education, report.

Olson, L. (2006, December 6). U.S. urged to rethink NCLB "tools." *Education Week, 26*(14), 1, 19.

Olson, L., & Jacobson, L. (2006). Analysis finds minority NCLB scores widely excluded. *Education Week, 25*(33), 5.

Posnick-Goodwin, S. (2006). Punitive law fails to get results. *California Educator.* Retrieved February 21, 2007 from: http://www.cta.org/media/publications/educator/archives/2006/200609_feat_1.htm

*Quality Counts.* (2005). No small change. *Education Week.* Retrieved November 19, 2005, from http://www.edweek.org/ew/qc/2005/tables/17achieve-tlc.html

*Quality Counts.* (2007). From cradle to career: Connecting American education from birth through adulthood. *Education Week.* Retrieved January 13, 2007, from www.edweek.org/go/qc07

Robelen, E. W. (2005, April 6). Audit faults Calif. districts on unsafe-schools data. *Education Week, 24*(30), 18.

Rothman, R. (2002). Comment. In D. Ravitch (Ed.), *Brookings papers on education policy, 2002* (pp. 181-184). Washington, DC: The Brookings Institution.

Sandham, J. L. (1999, September 22). Struggling Calif. schools get a shot in the arm. *Education Week, 19*(3), 14.

Sandham, J. L. (2001, January 24). Calif. test-based bonus plan gets off to rocky start. *Education Week, 20*(19), 1, 20.

Slovacek, D. P., Kunnan, A. J., & Kim, H-J (2002, March). *California charter schools serving low-SES students: An analysis of the academic performance index.* Los Angeles, CA: California State University, Charter College of Education.

Sokolow, A. D. (1997). California. In *Proceedings—Roundtable: State budgeting in the 13 western states.* Salt Lake City, UT: Center for Public Policy & Administration.

Steinhauer, J. (2006, November 13). The 2006 election; with changes on Capitol Hill, California is set to assert new clout. *New York Times,* p. A31.

Stotsky, S. (2005, February). *The state of state English standards.* Washington, DC: Fordham Foundation.

U.S. Census Bureau. (2006). *Percent of people 5 years and over who speak a language other than English at home: 2005.* Retrieved February 28, 2007, from http://factfinder.census.gov/servlet/GRTTable?_bm=y&-_box_head_nbr=R1601&-ds_name=ACS_2005_EST_G00_&-lang=en&-format=US-30&-CONTEXT=grt

U.S. Census Bureau. (2007). *Public education finance,* table 11 (2004). Retrieved February 28, 2007, from http://ftp2.census.gov/govs/school/04f33pub.pdf

U.S. cites problems in California testing. (2005, November 9). *Education Week,* p. 9.

Yan, X. C. (2005, October 7). Educational excellence: Why lowering the bar on the California high school exit exam will not raise results. *Sacramento Union,* p. 14.

Zehr, M. A. (2005, May 18). Calif. NCLB waiver denied. *Education Week,* p. 18.

CHAPTER 10

---

# ALASKA

---

## INTRODUCTION

We introduce first the social, economic, and political environment for
education reform in Alaska, and then turn to a discussion of education
policy makers and student characteristics, followed by a discussion of
Alaska's two school systems.

### State Socioeconomic and Political Characteristics

Alaska is America's largest state in land area at 378 million acres. If the
map of Alaska were superimposed on that of the 48-contiguous states, it
would stretch from the west to the east coast, and from the Gulf Coast in
the south to the Great Lakes in the North. Yet the state is America's third
most sparsely populated, having just 663,661 residents in 2006 (U.S. Census, 2007).

Most Alaskans, about two thirds, are Caucasians. The most significant
ethnic minority group—socially, culturally, economically, and politically—
comprises about 16% of the population and is Alaska Native. "Native" is
the term preferred by the aboriginal residents of Alaska, who may be
Yupik or Inupiat Eskimos, Aleuts, or Indians. They have lived in the state
"since time immemorial" and at least for 30,000 years. Most of Alaska's
Natives had limited contact with the Russians who colonized Alaska in the

*Education Reform in the American States*
pp. 255–281
Copyright © 2008 by Information Age Publishing
All rights of reproduction in any form reserved.

eighteenth century and with Americans who purchased the territory in 1867, until the twentieth century. Unlike Indians in what Alaskans call the "Lower-48" states, most Natives have remained close to their original sites of residence, and many are still engaged in traditional subsistence pursuits of hunting, fishing, and gathering.

Alaska's other ethnic minorities include African Americans (3.7%), Asians (4.6%), and Latinos (5.1%), with the remainder of the state's population split among two or more races or other groups (U.S. Census, 2007). A large number of the non-Native minority Alaskans as well as many Caucasians came to Alaska in the military and retired in the state.

Economically, Alaska is among America's richest states because of its natural resource wealth. Even before statehood in 1959, Alaska had developed an oil industry on the Kenai Peninsula. The discovery of the western hemisphere's largest oil field at Prudhoe Bay in 1968 spurred economic growth and modernization, and until oil prices fell in the mid-1980s, Alaska had the highest per capita income (and highest teachers' salaries) in the nation. In 2006, oil still contributes from 65 to 80% of the state's General Fund revenue. A second unique feature of the Alaska economy is the state's Permanent Fund (PF), established by voters in an amendment to the state constitution of 1976. In late 2006, the principal of the PF reached $33 billion, and voters (and their instructed representatives) have been reluctant to allocate earnings of the PF to any purpose other than an annual dividend payment to the state's residents.

The largest single private employer in the state is the fishing industry, followed by tourism. A number of Alaska's cities, such as Fairbanks, Juneau, and Nome, were founded in the Alaska gold rush, and hard rock mining remains an important part of the state's economy. New industries, such as the air freight business, and an expansion in wholesale and retail sales contribute jobs to the economy. However, the chief mainstay of the economy beyond oil and gas is government. About 10% of the resident population works in the military at the state's large army, air force, and naval installations. Because the federal government owns more than 60% of the state's lands and has a trusteeship responsibility for Alaska's Native population, the federal civilian workforce is large. On a per capita basis, Alaska spends more on state government services (including education) than any other state, and the state and local government workforces are large as well. Altogether, government employees comprise about 27% of the state workforce.

Since the late 1960s, Alaskans have voted Republican in national elections at a higher rate than residents in most of the other American states. In the 2000 election, George W. Bush received 59% of the vote making Alaska a "red" state, and his vote total increased to 61% in 2004 (Barone & Cohen, 2005). The state's congressional delegation has been Republican since 1980; even after Senator Frank Murkowski won the governorship in 2002 and deeded his senate seat to daughter Lisa, the seat remained Republican in the 2004 election. Alaska began its course in the union as a Democratic state, and then for more than 10 years, coalitions ran the state legislature; but in the 1994 elections, Republicans established majorities in both houses, which they retained to the 2006 election (after which Republicans, with a slight majority in the state senate, formed a coalition with Democrats). Only the governorship is competitive consistently, with Democrats holding the office as often as Republicans. In recent years, however, this has been possible only when the Republican party has been split between its social and economic conservative wings. The most recent Democratic governor was Tony Knowles, serving from 1994 to 2002; in the November 2006 elections, voters chose Republican Sarah Palin, who became Alaska's first female (and at 42 its youngest) governor.

## The State Educational System

Education policymakers in Alaska are few in number as compared to the other American states. The state has a "model constitution," which created both strong and streamlined executive, legislative, and judicial institutions of government. The governor and lieutenant governor are Alaska's only statewide-elected officials. The governor appoints members of the state board of education, who set education policy and recommend candidates for the commissioner of education, one of whom is selected by the governor. Thus the governor can be said to have more to do with education policy than his peers in the other states, and since the late 1980s Alaska's governors, whether Democratic or Republican, have developed important initiatives in education.

Alaska's strong legislature has education committees in both houses, and since the mid-1990s has focused much attention on schooling. As we note throughout, Alaska's politics are regional, with political fault lines separating the most populous south-central region (centering on the state's largest city, Anchorage), from the Interior (with a headquarters in Fairbanks), southeast Alaska (focusing on Juneau), and the far-flung rural (also called "bush") regions of the state. While the inter-governmental lobby of teachers' unions (NEA-Alaska with a membership of nearly 8,000 is one of the state's most powerful unions), school boards, the state school boards association, and administrators often forms a united front on education issues—particularly to promote increases in education funding and school construction—this interest competes with both regional rivalries and partisan alignment. Despite the Republican cast of contemporary state politics, most public sector employees are unionized. Alaska is not a right-to-work state, and teachers have finality in bargaining with school districts.

Alaska's school system consists of 521 schools in 53 school districts, and a total of 134,364 students in 2005-06. There are about 85 private schools (with an enrollment of 4,200 students),[1] mostly sectarian, and 23 charter schools. Alaska has slightly more than 8,000 public school teachers. The ethnic composition of Alaska's public school population is: American Indian/Alaska Native—26%; Asian/Pacific Islander—6.5%; Black—4.7%; Latino—3.9%; and White (non-Latino)—58.9% (National Center for Education Statistics [NCES], 2005).

Ethnic minorities are a larger part of the school-age population than in the resident population of the state; particularly notable is the 26% of students who are Alaska Natives. Minority students compose the largest part of "children in poverty" who are 12% of the student population; students with disabilities are 13.5%; and LEP (limited English proficiency) students are 12.2%. About 27% of Alaska's students are eligible for free or reduced fee lunches, the standard indicator of low-income status. Most of the Alaska Native student population lives in rural areas of the state, in school systems quite different from those of urban Alaska.

## Two School Systems

The dissimilarities between rural and urban schools are significant enough to be characterized as two separate systems.[2] Until the late 1970s, most rural schools were administered and operated differently than schools in Alaska's cities. They were either Bureau of Indian Affairs' (BIA) schools or under control of the territorial and then the state-operated school system (see Darnell, 1972), a condition which lasted until the closure of the latter system in 1976 and the termination or transfer of BIA schools to the state, completed by 1982. Rural schools today are far smaller than urban schools. About 40% of Alaska's schools have 100 or fewer students; about one quarter enroll 50 or fewer students; and 16% have fewer than 25 students (Olson, 2003). Most rural schools with the exception of those in regional hubs, such as Bethel, fit into these categories. Rural schools remain distinctive from urban schools in governance, finance, curriculum, staff, and outcomes.

Urban schools belong to municipal or borough (a strong county-type regional government) school districts. Although independent with respect to selection of superintendent, recruitment of teachers and school staff, establishment of curricula, and development of policies for student behavior, the urban schools are checked financially (for operating and capital budgets) by the relevant local government unit. Some rural schools operate as city school districts in first-class cities (meaning the most powerful municipal decision-making units, e.g., Nenana, Galena, Dillingham), or as borough school districts (e.g., North Slope, Northwest Arctic, Yakutat). Most, however, are governed by one of the 19 Regional Educational Attendance Area (REAA) boards. These legislatively-created school districts—products of the rural school decentralization act of 1975—are autonomous. They report directly to the state Department of Education and Early Development (DEED) without the interference of local government bodies.

The financial plans of most rural schools differ from those in urban areas too. The REAAs receive 100% of their funding from state and federal governments. They have no taxation powers, and may receive no local contributions to education (as there is no local tax base, in most cases). The rural city and borough school districts receive contributions from local governments, but these are unlikely to be as large (reaching to 35% of their budgets) or as directly based on property taxation as the contributions from urban local governments.

There is a clash of perceptions concerning the funding of urban and rural Alaska schools. Urban legislators and school leaders contend that their schools are short-changed because urban taxpayers must contribute to the costs of education while rural residents do not. Also, they argue that the funding formulas benefit rural more than urban schools. Rural legislators and school leaders on the other hand, contend that rural schools receive insufficient funds and are discriminated against in the state's funding formulas. Rural educators also argue that rural schools are more costly to operate than are urban schools because they are remote and isolated and because they lack any economies of scale. Their maintenance and administrative costs are significantly higher than those of urban schools.

The state's foundation formula always has attempted to compromise rural and urban interests. It requires both a local contribution from urban schools and limits the size of that contribution in order to reduce statewide disparity in education funding. In the mid-1990s the school foundation formula was revised significantly, and the rebalancing seemed to favor urban schools (see Berman, 2001; and Alaska, Office of the Governor, 2001).

The *Quality Counts 2005* report card for Alaska gives the state a "C+" for resources equity. It praises the state for reducing inequities in state and local funding based on local property wealth. Then it faults the state's ranking as last in the nation for the "coefficient of variation"—which examines the spending per pupil across districts. Alaska's spending ranged from $3,930 at the bottom to $20,150 at the top[3] in the 2001-02 school year. The expenditure per pupil in 2001-02 was $9,406, ranking ninth highest in the nation (American Legislative Exchange Council,

2004). These figures are weighted for regional cost differences and student needs. Overall, the state's funding formula brings advantages to poor rural districts that require more resources because of large numbers of special needs students.

The curricula of rural schools are different from those in urban settings. They lack the variety of programs and courses that students expect to find in any American school. For example, they are unlikely to offer any foreign language (but may offer Native language training in early grades); they cannot offer specialized middle and high school courses in English, mathematics, the sciences or the social sciences. Art or music instruction, if offered, most likely is provided by an itinerant teacher from the district office. There are no opportunities for band, orchestra, and of course, no high school football program. (In fact, basketball is the sport of choice in rural Alaska, and the gym is the center not only of school but also community life.) In some of the smaller rural schools, those with under 30 students, there may be no defined "courses" in the high school curriculum at all; instead, instructors will teach students in multi-grade classrooms on an individualized study basis.

Neither urban nor rural schools have many Native teachers (about 5% of the total teaching force statewide), notwithstanding the size of the Native student population (McDowell Group, 2005). Also of importance, rural schools have less veteran teaching staffs than urban schools, due to high turnover rates. A survey of a random sample of teachers in 2003 indicated that 56% of rural teachers had been in their schools 4 years or less, as compared to 44% of urban teachers. Some 75% of rural principals had held their posts 4 years or less, as compared to 55% of urban principals (McBeath, Reyes, & Ehrlander, 2006).

Most telling is the difference in length of time the educators had lived in Alaska. Nearly half (46%) of rural teachers had lived in the state 10 years or less, compared to 18% of urban teachers; over half (52%) of rural principals had been in Alaska 10 years or less, as compared to 15% of urban principals (McBeath et al., pp. 7-8). In short, not only have educators in rural schools been in their positions a shorter time than their counterparts in urban Alaska, they have been in the state an even shorter period relatively. We note below the extent to which these urban-rural differences are reflected in rates of student achievement.

## THE ALASKA ASSESSMENT AND
## ACCOUNTABILITY SYSTEM BEFORE 2002

During its first 2 decades as a state (1959-79), Alaska brought its school districts into the state constitution's new and integrated local government system and then decentralized rural schooling through the establishment of state-funded rural districts. Because the state school system, like that in many states, was highly decentralized, and the state education department was quite small, most action in the 1980s developed in the state's largest districts, and particularly in Anchorage and Fairbanks. Regional and local school leaders echoed themes from the national reform movement after publication of *A Nation at Risk* in 1983 by focusing on an "excellence in education" program and then "outcomes-based education." Significantly, Democratic Governor Steve Cowper in 1988 proposed an "education endowment fund," to be located within the state's Permanent Fund, and to be used to fund education into the future. The idea went nowhere as critics labeled it a "raid on the Permanent Fund," which over time would greatly diminish permanent fund dividends.

Prior to the 1990s, the only accountability system in effect pertained to Title I schools (more than half of the schools in the state, including 36% of all students), which were measured annually on norm-referenced tests, initially the ITBS and then more recently the CAT/5 series. Although DEED had compliance responsibilities for all public schools, its small staff was sufficient to handle only egregious cases of non-compliance with education regulations. The department encouraged schools to seek accreditation, conducting a self-study following a template provided by the department or by applying to the Northwest Association of Schools and Colleges. By the late 1990s, only 27% of Alaska's schools were accredited. Alaska is one of only two western states without a mandated accreditation system (Consortium for Policy Research in Education [CPRE], 2000).

Systematic reform in Alaska schooling began with the election of Wally Hickel as governor in 1990. Hickel was a long-term Republican who had served as governor from 1966 to 1968, when he joined President Nixon's cabinet as Secretary of the Interior. He had been on the gubernatorial ballot for the primary or general election in each state election since 1974, and in 1990 ran a third-party campaign as candidate of the Alaska Independence Party, winning with a plurality of the vote. Upon taking office, he replaced the entire state board of education, appointed a new education commissioner, and directed them to develop a plan to improve Alaska's system of public schools (Alaska Department of Education & Early Development [DEED], 2002). In 1991 the governor appointed a blue ribbon commission of 21 prominent Alaskans, who identified 10 broad areas of educational need and asked the governor and state board of education to invite 100 Alaskans, both outside and inside the state's education system, to make recommendations in each area. This reform effort was called Alaska 2000 (AK2K).

In 1992, the state board approved AK2K recommendations, including developing student academic standards. It adopted a regulation (4 Alaska Administrative Code 04.030) of goals for schools, to provide students with "a working knowledge of English, mathematics, science, geography, history, skills for a healthy life, government and citizenship, fine arts, technology and world languages." In the following year, the state board's Standards and Assessment Oversight Committee recommended the development of content standards in these 10 core subject areas. Standards in English/language arts, mathematics, science, history, geography, government and health were crafted, distributed for public review, and adopted in 1994, taking effect the following year. However, little work was done during the Hickel administration to match standards with assessments. The state then used the Iowa Test of Basic Skills (ITBS) in selected grade levels, a norm-referenced test that did not match the standards under development.

In 1994, Democrat Tony Knowles was elected to Alaska's governorship. He too replaced the state board and appointed a new commissioner, but his administration accepted most of the work done during the previous administration. Knowles was elected with enthusiastic support of the state's major teachers' union, NEA-Alaska, and he filled seats on education boards and commissions with those sympathetic to the status quo. His new education commissioner renamed AK2K the Alaska Quality Schools Initiative (QSI), and broadened it to include standards for teachers, school excellence, and partnership networks with business and communities. Knowles held two education summits during his terms in office, in 1996 and 2000, but his administration proceeded slowly on the development of an accountability system. For this reason, the Republican legislature seized the initiative.

In 1997, the legislature adopted the "Secondary Pupil Competency Testing" statute to establish Alaska's first high-stakes test. The education department contracted with CTB/McGraw-Hill to craft the High School Graduation Qualifying Examination (HSGQE), requiring that students pass its three sections (reading comprehension, mathematics, and writing) in order to receive a high school diploma (DEED, 2002). The legislature did not consider alternate diplomas, and included special education students under the testing umbrella (but allowed them "accommodations" in the administration of the test). Students failing all three parts of the test would receive certificates of attendance, but students had multiple opportunities to take the test. The effective date of this requirement was January 2002, later extended by the legislature to 2004 (see Olson, 2001).

The chief architect of the HSGQE was Representative Con Bunde (R-Anchorage), a retired speech professor of the Anchorage Community College whose spouse was a school teacher. Bunde envisioned the HSGQE as an accountability measure. Responding to the author's questions in 2001, he pointed out these concerns with the status quo:

There had been a universal concern from the business community. They couldn't hire functionally literate kids—they needed to supply them with a remedial education.... [W]hat does the high school diploma mean? Is it minimum competency or is it an attendance certificate? (personal communication, May 16, 2001)

Governor Knowles signed the competency testing legislation "reluctantly," (given bipartisan support, the legislature likely would have overridden a veto), and then promised to propose a complete accountability system in the following legislative session. The program emphasized development of student performance standards in reading, writing, and mathematics and benchmark examinations. The six elements of the accountability system included:

- **Academic Standards**—A mandate for the state board to adopt academic standards in reading, writing and math for four age groups;
- **Alaska Benchmark Examinations**—assessments of students in the third, sixth, and eighth grades, beginning in spring 2000;
- **Developmental Profile**—to be prepared for all entering kindergarten and first grade students;
- **QSI Grants**—additional funding for school districts to adopt standards, provide intervention services for low-performing students, and focus instruction in a results-based system; the grants later became part of the school funding program;
- **School Accountability Designations**—Based on students' test scores and other performance indicators, the state board was required to develop an annual system of rating schools by 2002 (later delayed to 2004-05) as distinguished, successful, deficient, and in crisis;
- **School Report Cards**—An annual report to communities and the state, beginning in 2000, and drawing upon assessments, parent and community involvement, and attendance, retention, drop-out, and graduation rates.[4]

In the next 2 years, work on performance standards was completed (DEED, 2000). The state contracted with McGraw-Hill to produce both the HSGQE and Alaska Benchmark exams, based on state standards, and committees of Alaska educators evaluated the alignment of items with state standards, test bias, and fairness. Also, cut scores were developed for the HSGQE and Alaska Benchmark exams. Most of the implementation work, however, fell into the orbit of school districts, which needed to match curricula to the new state standards, develop intervention programs for low-performing students, and increase staff development and school communication activities to spread information about the state's high stakes testing regime.

## INITIAL IMPACT OF THE ALASKA ACCOUNTABILITY SYSTEM

In spring 2000 the HSGQE and Benchmarks were administered for the first time. Table 10.1 presents proficiency scores on the Benchmarks for students in Grades 3, 6, and 8 for this year, with results from 2001 and 2002.

In this cross-sectional comparison, scores for third grade students show improvement from 2000 to 2002. For the other grades, scores improved only in writing for sixth graders, and then only slightly. In general, the test results revealed deficiencies in writing for third grade students, and in mathematics for eighth graders; yet because the test items matched state standards (and committees of educators developed cut scores based on their conceptions of proficiency), we cannot make comparisons to national norms. Nevertheless, these initial results confirmed expectations as to differences of performance levels among population subgroupings. For example, proficiency rates on the eighth grade reading Benchmarks for 2002 showed this range: White (91.4%), American Indian (80.7), Hispanic (80.5), Asian-Pacific Islander (77.9), Black (69.3) and Alaska Native (58.3) (DEED, 2002b). The achievement difference between Caucasian and Alaska Native students amounted to 35.1%. The gap between minority students and Caucasians did not narrow from 2000 to 2002. In each of the

**Table 10.1.   Percentage Proficiency on Benchmarks, 2000-02**

| Grade | Year | Reading | Writing | Mathematics |
|---|---|---|---|---|
| Third | 2000 | 72.5 % | 48.8% | 65.0% |
|  | 2001 | 71.2% | 53.5% | 66.3% |
|  | 2002 | 74.6% | 58.0% | 70.8% |
| Sixth | 2000 | 69.9% | 72.2% | 62.2% |
|  | 2001 | 69.4% | 73.0% | 62.9% |
|  | 2002 | 69.8% | 75.5% | 63.9% |
| Eighth | 2000 | 83.2% | 67.5% | 39.0% |
|  | 2001 | 82.5% | 67.9% | 39.5% |
|  | 2002 | 81.6% | 66.3% | 40.2% |

*Source:* Adapted by the author from DEED, Spring 2002 Benchmarks: Total Numbers and Percentages of Students Scoring Above and Below Proficiency, 7/22/02, p. 1.

**Table 10.2.   Percentage Proficiency, 8th Grade Students, 2002**

| Category* | Reading | Writing | Mathematics |
|---|---|---|---|
| Low income | 62.6% | 43.4% | 20.8% |
| LEP | 47.5 | 31.9 | 11.9 |
| Migrant | 56.8 | 40.5 | 25.9 |
| Disabled | 47.0 | 18.2 | 7.8 |
| Gifted | 99.5 | 99.0 | 94.6 |

*Low income students are those receiving free or reduced price lunches; limited English proficient students are those whose first or dominant language is not English; disabled students are those served under the Individuals with Disabilities Education Act or the Vocational Rehabilitation Act.

*Source:* DEED, Spring 2002 Benchmarks, Grade 8, 7/22/02, p. 7.

test areas and for all 3 years, Alaska Native students scored at the bottom of the subgroups. Table 10.2 continues this analysis by presenting data on special population students for the spring 2002 Grade 8 Benchmarks.

Membership within these subgroupings is not evenly distributed across ethnic groups. Indeed, a majority of students in the low income and LEP,[5] and a sizable number of students in special education groups are Alaska Natives attending schools in rural areas of the state. These scores are from 57 to 77% of the mean in reading, 27 to 65% in writing, and 19 to 64% in mathematics. Students in these special groups are clustered in Title I schools, and when in 2002 the state reviewed performance of students under the Improving America's Schools Act of 1994, which required demonstration of adequate yearly progress, the vast majority of the schools were rural with a Native majority student population. Of the 50 schools not demonstrating AYP in year 1, only 3 were in urban areas. All 9 schools in first year school improvement status were bush schools, as were the 8 schools in second year improvement status (McLain, 2002).

In a memorandum to policy makers and education leaders at the 2001 release of testing data, DEED Commissioner Shirley Holloway stated:

> The data I am releasing today will cause deep soul searching in Alaska. The analysis shows a deep divide in student achievement among ethnic groups. White students score higher than other ethnic groups, much higher on average than Native students. Why is this so? What steps do we need to take to shrink this divide?... It is vital that our data-driven debate be free of political and personal agendas and is focused on students. (DEED, 2002).

Results from the 3 years' administration of the HSGQE did not differ substantially with respect to performance of ethnic groups and special population subgroupings. These results cannot be compared easily to the Benchmarks, for two reasons. First, the state did not disaggregate scores by grade level. Second, mathematics curricula of most high schools had not yet been aligned to standards for the first HSGQE given in spring 2000. In effect, students were being tested on content that they had not yet received in the classroom. Also, the Alaska educators who composed the cut-score committee believed in the need to establish high standards in mathematics (Dr. Nicholas Stayrook, personal communication, December 7, 2005). As a result, a majority of students failed to demonstrate proficiency in mathematics. Subsequently, the HSGQE was refocused, and tests given in 2002 and later years do not compare with those of 2000 and 2001.

Alaska's funding for education as well as other state government services had remained flat for most of the 1990s, a time of relatively low oil prices and declining reserves in the state's several rainy day accounts. The Knowles administration was unable to raise the floor of the school foundation funding formula to account for increases in inflation, as he confronted a fiscally conservative Republican legislative majority. As mentioned, he was able to gain support for temporary QSI funding to implement the state's new accountability system. In late 2000, the governor appointed an education funding task force to recommend a 5-year funding plan to fulfill QSI goals and improve schooling. The legislature did then increase the basic student allocation by a small amount and continued a new Learning Opportunity Grants program to assist low-performing schools.

Initial testing results also focused attention on Alaska's difficulty in attracting and retaining teachers, particularly for its small rural schools. At DEED's request, the legislature in 2001 allowed the department to issue preliminary teacher certificates to new teachers from outside Alaska who held baccalaureate degrees. It allowed the department to issue revocable teacher certificates to teachers whose certificates had expired before they had completed renewal requirements. And it allowed schools districts with teacher shortages to employ qualified retired teachers, without their losing retirement pay. Finally, the legislature created a limited teacher certificate for "subject-matter experts," if they could demonstrate expertise and held baccalaureate degrees. Then, in 2002, the legislature provided low interest loans for teacher housing in small communities through the Alaska Housing Finance Corporation.

## RESPONSE OF ALASKA TO NCLB REQUIREMENTS

When in late 2001 the Congress adopted President Bush's No Child Left Behind (NCLB) legislation, Alaska was struggling through implementation of its own accountability system. NCLB instantly called into question the state's method of assessing students, its accountability provisions, and the qualifications of its teachers and paraprofessionals. The state responded in these areas and also encouraged a new model of instruction to aid improvement in small rural schools.

## Changing Assessments and Determining AYP

NCLB requires testing of students from Grades 3 through 10 in English/language arts and mathematics, but the Alaska Benchmarks covered only Grades 3, 6, and 8, augmented by CAT/5 tests for grade four students in Title I schools. Before NCLB became law, the state board of education adopted regulations expanding testing to grades four, five, seven, and nine, and opted for the TerraNova norm-referenced test series (also produced by McGraw-Hill). This gave the state cross-sectional coverage of the required grades, but use of two different tests, one norm- and the other criterion-referenced, made it difficult to examine improvement of individual students or even classes as a whole as they passed through the school system.

In 2004, DEED, under a new gubernatorial administration, replaced the Benchmarks and TerraNova assessments with a single testing system, the Standards Based Assessment (SBA). It was used the first time in spring 2005. The SBA was based on Alaska grade-level expectations (GLEs) and met federal and state requirements.[6] However, its adoption makes it difficult to compare assessment results under NCLB before 2005 with those in ensuing years.

Prior to the passage of NCLB, Alaska had used adequate yearly progress (AYP) only for Title I schools. The new federal legislation required that AYP determinations include all students and all schools, in order to allow differentiation of ethnic, ability, and economic groupings on a statewide basis so that achievement gaps could be narrowed. The basis for AYP determination is the state's annual measurable objectives (AMO) in English/language arts and mathematics. In Alaska, the AMO in language arts started relatively high, at 64.03% and then ratcheted up gradually and in intervals of about 6%. The pattern is: 2001-04, 64.03%; 2004-07, 71.48%; 2007-10, 77.18%, 2010-11, 82.88%, 2011-12, 88.58%, 2012-13, 94.28%; and 2013-14, 100%. In mathematics, the ascent is steeper, because initial AMOs are lower: 2001-04, 54.86%; 2004-07, 57.61%; 2007-10, 66.09%; 2010-11, 74.57%; 2011-12, 83.05%; 2012-13, 91.53%; and 2013-14, 100% (DEED, 2005a).

As has been the case in many states, the Alaska education department elected to focus on those students relatively close to meeting proficiency, and to delay until the final 4 years the truly difficult work of raising proficiency levels of the lowest-performing students. Too, the state has taken liberal advantage of the "safe harbor" provision, and this effectively allows school districts, and particularly those in rural areas, to postpone interventions needed for subgroups with low achievement rates. In 2005 for example, 45 Alaska schools met AYP through the safe harbor provision.[7]

## Accountability Provisions

The state accountability legislation of 1998 included sanctions for students—failure to receive a high school diploma if they did not pass the HSGQE—but it contained no sanctions, either positive or negative, for schools and school districts. NCLB requires Title I schools to provide choice for students if their school fails to demonstrate AYP in the second year of placement in improvement status, and schools have implemented choice in accordance with regulations (school choice was not required for districts in the second year of improvement status). To the present, Alaska has not developed a system of choice for students in low-performing schools. *Quality Counts 2005* gives Alaska a low score on choice and autonomy because "The state charter school law is rated weak by the Center for Education Reform, and the state does not have an open-enrollment program" (p. 18).

Although legislators in Alaska have introduced proposals to provide vouchers for students to attend better schools, no such proposal has been adopted by either house. The state has a relatively closed enrollment policy for students seeking to change school districts; and most districts restrict enrollment in schools to students from different attendance areas. Alaska has just 23 charter schools, with a student enrollment of about 5,000 students, but the charter school law is considered weak. Thus, legislatively and administratively, Alaska offers very little choice outside of private school education, home schooling, and both state and district correspondence programs. Yet the home schooling and district correspondence programs enroll a large number of students for a sparsely populated state.

The practical problems in providing choice for students, particularly in rural areas of the state, are perhaps insuperable due to sheer geography. With few exceptions, rural districts do not have private schools, and no rural district has a charter school. The largest number of small rural schools is found in Alaska's villages, typically with an elementary or a K-12 small school. If that school does not meet AYP for successive years, students would have to be transported away from their homes, at considerable social and economic cost. For these reasons the state has sought delays and exceptions in the choice provisions of NCLB, and USDOE has allowed the state to provide Supplemental Educational Services to students from rural schools failing to meet AYP in lieu of school choice (see DEED, 2006).

Other issues of accountability concerned calculation of test participation rates and inclusion of students with disabilities or LEP students in AYP decisions. In 2003, some 65 Alaska schools failed to make AYP because they missed targets for students with disabilities. Under a waiver from USDOE, in 2004 Alaska publicly reported results when schools tested as few as five students with disabilities or LEP students; however, such schools were not required to meet annual performance targets for such groups if they had fewer than 40 children. This change resulted in the exclusion of about 85% of state schools from having to meet AYP targets for special education students, an increase of 20% from the previous year (Olson, 2004).

## Teacher Quality

NCLB requires that teachers demonstrate that they are highly qualified by 2005-06. The federal legislation also requires that paraprofessionals be highly qualified as well. Both requirements pose difficult challenges to America's largest state, with proportionately the largest number of rural schools (see Northwest Regional Educational Laboratory, 2003).

In general, most Alaska schools have the same difficulties attracting and retaining teachers as schools in the other states. For example, in the early twenty-first century, there is a national sellers' market for special education teachers and secondary math and science teachers. Yet about one third of Alaska's schools face chronic teacher shortages. These schools are in remote areas of the interior, western, and northern Alaska, with very high costs of living. Such school districts have turnover rates of from 30 to 50% annually, and as a recent study by McDiarmid, Larson, and Hill (2002) points out, "Districts with the highest turnover have the highest cost per student, the lowest household incomes, the least experienced teachers, and the largest Native populations" (p. 4). The new legislation to subsidize construction of teachers' housing in rural areas, and general increases in education funding,[8] may ameliorate these difficulties, but they will not eliminate them any time soon.

Meanwhile, the state has been slow to develop effective programs to improve teacher quality. Indeed, the 2005 issue of *Quality Counts* gives Alaska a grade of "D–" for this endeavor, largely because "prospective teachers must only pass a basic-skills test to earn their initial license" (p. 19) The need for improvement is mammoth as so many of Alaska's rural teachers operate in small schools where they must teach several subjects.

In the 2005-06 school year, some 35.8% of the total core classes in Alaska were not taught by highly qualified teachers (DEED, 2006, p. 52). The state accepts advanced certification or credentialing (through national board certification), baccalaureate majors or graduate degrees in content areas, or passing scores on Praxis content-area examinations. In addition to hiring subject-matter experts enrolled in teacher prep programs, the state developed an "alternative procedure" for becoming highly qualified in regulation (4 AAC 04.212).

Two new state programs may help address the problem of preparing highly qualified teachers. In the 2004-05 school year, the state initiated a statewide mentoring program, advertised as the first of its kind in the nation (but modeled after the one in UC Santa Barbara). Some 22 experienced teachers, each receiving release-time from her/his district, mentored 350 first- and second-year teachers in 37 school districts across the state. The project is a collaborative venture among the DEED, the University of Alaska system, and school districts. Each mentor teacher is paired with from 12 to 19 beginning teachers, whom he or she meets weekly by phone, monthly in person, and regularly by e-mail (DEED, 2005b). One can hope that this program will help reduce teacher turnover in the state as well as increase teacher quality.

A second attempt to improve teacher qualifications is a recent change in state teacher certification, moving it in the direction of a standards-based system. In June 2005 the State Board of Education adopted a new three-level system, consisting of initial, professional, and master certification. The "initial" level includes all teachers holding provisional, temporary, preliminary, reemployment, or subject-matter limited certificates (and thus enable them to meet "highly qualified" rules under NCLB), and will be good for 3 years. New teachers with a BA degree, who have passed a competency exam such as the Praxis I, and completed or enrolled in an approved teacher prep program will be issued the "initial" level certificate. The second level or "professional" certification requires completion of the teacher prep program and passage of a content area examination, and, after 2006, passage of two performance reviews. The third level or "master" certificate is available for teachers having achieved national board certification or who have completed two performance reviews with the required score. The certificate will be valid for 10 years (Sampson, 2005; see also DEED, 2005c). This new system increases somewhat the rigor in teacher certification or recertification.

The final issue of teacher quality concerns paraprofessionals—primarily teachers' aides and other instructional support staff. NCLB requires that paraprofessionals (over 2,000 statewide) have high school diplomas and have completed 2 years of higher education or attained an associate's degree or undergone state or local assessment. The last option currently is available in the form of the HELP assessment and an observation checklist, but is not available in most rural districts of the state. The pool of qualified paraprofessionals in Alaska cities is as large as it is in most other states, but in rural areas of the state, paraprofessionals qualified under NCLB definitions are a minority. Yet, they play extremely important roles, for at least two reasons: (1) usually they are long-term members of the community, while most teachers are transient; (2) usually they are Alaska Natives and can familiarize teachers with the Native community as they translate community norms to non-Native teachers; and (3) in many rural schools, they provide much of the direct instruction to students even when a certified teacher is in the classroom.

## Development of a Model for Rural School Success?

The implementation of the state's accountability system and particularly the administration of the HSGQE in 2000, followed by administration of additional NCLB requirements in the early twenty-first century, affected all schools in Alaska, but targets were harder to reach for low-performing schools in rural Alaska than for urban schools. We discuss the most organized response to assessment and accountability system requirements, the Alaska Quality Schools Coalition, and then briefly mention responses in other rural schools.

The Quality Schools Coalition formed in 1999 and today has 18 members: 15 school districts, a charter school, one urban district's alternative school, and a tribal council (McBeath & Reyes, 2004). The school districts all are located in rural Alaska. The coalition is based on the experience of Chugach School District, a small district in southcentral Alaska enrolling about 215 students in 5 schools with a headquarters in Anchorage. In 1995-96 Chugach initiated an "Onwards to Excellence" program that incorporated standards-based, systematic reform. The coalition brings districts into partnership with the Staff Development Network and the Bill and Melinda Gates Foundation. The Gates Foundation supplied a multimillion dollar grant to coalition schools for the period October 2000 to September 2005.

Member districts and schools agree to observe these seven elements of the Quality Schools Model: shared vision, leadership, standards, appropriate instructional strategy, assessments tied to standards, reporting student progress, and sustainability/continuous improvement (Alaska Quality Schools Coalition, 2004). The coalition sponsors 3-day fall, winter, and spring Quality Schools Symposia, and a week-long summer Quality Schools Institute. One of its objectives is to have 30-days of staff development activities annually.

The Quality Schools Model (also called *Continuous Progress* or the *Chugach Model*) requires extensive restructuring of schooling and individualized instruction for each student. It began in the Chugach District with the articulation of performance standards in 10 content areas, and then the complete alignment of the curriculum to these standards (2004). In each of the content areas, levels or phases were established, with assessments given to determine whether students had mastered the standards. Because within one classroom students might be working at two or three different levels, the quality schools model typically eliminates traditional grades. The Chugach District received a waiver from the state education department, allowing it to forgo traditional Carnegie units, or credits, as high school graduation requirements in lieu of its performance standards. The assessments are a combination of "skills-based, self, analytical, and contextual." They generate an abundance of information on students' progress, which is made available to parents in the form of a standards report card. The accounting aspects of the quality schools model are time-consuming for teachers, which explains partly the resistance of educators to this version of educational reform.

The Chugach model predates NCLB and benefits from its attention to standards, assessment, and accountability. It claims a record of success in raising achievement levels in rural, small schools, a record which was instrumental in vaunting its superintendent to the commissionership of education in Alaska in 2003. Yet the Chugach District has been criticized for the way it aggregated data in reporting student scores to the state education department, and for the construct it employed in educational change (Jester, 2002). Moreover, during the 4 years when the state used consistent assessments (2000-04), there was little change in scores of the Chugach District.

The Chugach Model is perhaps too radical a version of education reform for most of Alaska's rural schools. Nevertheless, research on rural school adaptation to Alaska's assessment and accountability system discovered a pattern in the response of high-achieving schools that were not part of the Quality Schools Coalition. They had made eight common changes in curriculum and instruction (McBeath & Reyes, 2004):

- **Focus on the core.** High-achieving rural schools focused attention of students on the core areas of reading, writing, and mathematics. They de-emphasized areas such as science and social studies, not yet covered on state assessments, or used non-core areas opportunistically for the assistance they might provide students in meeting expectations in core areas.

- **Curricular alignment.** Schools had completely aligned their curricula in English/language arts and mathematics to state standards.

They selected textbooks based on how well they matched the standards, and the same logic applied to the use of special instructional approaches.

- **Concentration of instructional time.** At the elementary level, most schools had blocked out common times for language arts and mathematics instruction, usually in the morning. They attempted to prohibit pull-outs during this period.

- **Intervention to aid instruction.** In addition to special education programs, the schools invested in specialized intervention programs to aid instruction in core areas, such as development of phonemic awareness and models of technical writing.

- **Preparation for assessments.** Most of the schools used their summer schools and before/after school tutoring programs to help prepare students to do well on state assessments.

- **Diagnostic use of assessment results.** Teachers paid attention to results of Benchmark and TerraNova results, and those of the HSGQE, and used them in ascertaining strengths and weaknesses of classroom instruction. Districts used test results as subjects of in-services for teachers.

- **Monitoring staff.** Teachers' use (or failure to use) standards in instruction was not part of the formal evaluation instrument; nor did any of the instruments evaluate teachers based on their students' test scores. Yet school administrators emphasized the importance of using standards, and found ways to remind teachers if they found them unresponsive.

- **Mentoring new teachers.** In most high-achieving schools, new teachers were paired with veterans in the same teaching area, although the system might be informal.

Use of these elements helped teachers and school staff meet the requirements of the state accountability system and NCLB.

## INITIAL RESULTS OF NCLB IN ALASKA (2003-2006)

Although the state tested all Grades from 3 to 10 at the outset in implementation of NCLB, Table 10.3 presents information on the Benchmarks alone, for comparative purposes.

Comparing Table 10.1 to Table 10.3, we note a slight improvement in scores across the three grade levels and three testing areas after 2002, keeping in mind that we are comparing different classes of students cross-sectionally, at different points in time. Overall, the gains from 2003 to

**Table 10.3.   Percentage Proficiency on Benchmarks, 2003-06**

| Grade | Year | Reading | Writing | Mathematics |
|-------|------|---------|---------|-------------|
| Third | 2003 | 73.9% | 59.8% | 71.8% |
|       | 2004 | 73.8% | 58.8% | 72.2% |
|       | 2005* | 79.1% | 74.8% | 75.5% |
|       | 2006 | | | |
| Sixth | 2003 | 69.8% | 75.0% | 64.3% |
|       | 2004 | 70.2% | 76.2% | 64.6% |
|       | 2005* | 75.9% | 71.5% | 64.9% |
|       | 2006 | | | |
| Eighth | 2003 | 67.9% | 73.6% | 63.8% |
|        | 2004 | 67.8% | 76.3% | 63.8% |
|        | 2005* | 80.3% | 73.7% | 62.1% |
|        | 2006 | | | |

*Note that the 2005 results are based on a new state test, the Standards Based Assessment, which also had new cut scores for proficiency and cannot be compared easily to 2003-04 results, based on state Benchmarks.
*Source:* DEED, Spring 2004 Benchmarks, and Spring 2005 Standards Based Assessment, retrieved 8/25/04 and 11/15/05.

2006 are greater than those from 2002 to 2004, but it must be kept in mind that the 2005-06 test series was different from that used in the previous 5 years, and there are problems in interpreting the data. (A focus on the 2 years, 2005 and 2006, when the same test series was used, shows improvement in scores only for eighth grade students.) Two areas stand out in a comparison of Tables 10.1 and 10.3. First, eighth grade scores in reading appeared to decline by more than 15% in 2003 and 2004, from their levels in years 2000, 2001, and 2002. Then, they jumped back to previous levels in the new test series (in 2005 and 2006). Second, eighth grade scores in mathematics increased by more than 20% in years 2003 through 2006, when compared to their levels in the three previous years. This may be a consequence of refocusing of test questions, curriculum, or test preparation.[9]

The NCLB requires each state to test its fourth and eighth grade students on the National Assessment of Education Progress (NAEP), the gold standard of assessment nationally. The percentage of Alaska students proficient in reading at the fourth and eighth grades in 2003-05 is 28 and 27% respectively; the percentage of students proficient in mathematics at the fourth and eighth grades is 30%. This compares with an average proficiency on the fourth grade TerraNovas in 2003 and 2004 of 74% in reading and 72% in mathematics, and on the eighth grade Benchmark of 68% in reading and 64% in math. Like most of the other states, Alaska students score more than twice as high on the state assessments than on the national criterion-referenced test.[10] The state Department of Education and Early Development claims that Alaska students score about as well as most other U.S. students on the NAEP; indeed, Alaska is 26th of the 50 states, exactly at the median.

We pointed out the disparity in test scores of ethnic student groupings on the eighth grade reading Benchmark of 2002. Two years further into the implementation of the high stakes testing regime, in 2004, the eighth grade Benchmarks showed this distribution of proficiency levels: Caucasians, 80.3%; American Indians, 66.7%; Latinos, 61.2%; Asian-Pacific islanders, 58.9%; Blacks, 55.2%; and Alaska Natives, 41.7% (DEED, 2004, p. 79). The divide between top and bottom groups in 2004 was 38.6%, as compared to 33.1% in 2002—a widening of the achievement gap.

In October 2005, Governor Murkowski, addressing the Alaska Federation of Natives convention, remarked that the state had made significant progress in improving educational outcomes for Alaska Native students (*Anchorage Daily News*, 2005). The commissioner of education repeated the governor's observation in appearances throughout the state. Both viewpoints were based on 2005 results of the Alaska Standards-Based Assessments, used first in spring 2005. They showed increases (although quite small in eighth grade math) for Alaska Natives, but the results were inconsistent with two other test series used by the state. The TerraNova-CAT for grades five and seven showed declines in performance from 2004 to 2005. The NAEP showed slight changes from 2003 to 2005, none of which was statistically significant. DEED officials believe the new tests measure Alaska standards better than the other assessments, but Alaska's chief assessments expert argues that the state "altered the content of the tests as well as lowered the cut score that is used to identify proficient students" (Stayrook, 2005). The governor and commissioner appear to have politicized the state assessment system.

Table 10.4 presents information comparable to that of Table 10.3, for the 2004 eighth grade Benchmark.

Scores of low income students dropped in reading, but increased significantly in writing and mathematics. LEP students' scores declined in reading and writing, but improved significantly in math. Scores of migrant students declined in reading yet increased in writing and math. Scores of disabled students declined in all subject test areas. Of course, this was a different group of students than tested in 2002. Nonetheless, the decline in reading scores and rise in math scores for these special subgroupings are noteworthy.

**Table 10.4.   Percentage Proficiency, 8th Grade Students, 2005-06**

| | Reading | | Writing | | Mathematics | |
|---|---|---|---|---|---|---|
| Category | 2005 | 2006 | 2005 | 2006 | 2005 | 2006 |
| Low Income | 48.0% | | 60.5% | | 45.2% | |
| LEP | 32.3% | | 52.4% | | 36.4% | |
| Migrant | 43.7% | | 59.7% | | 47.9% | |
| Disabled | 25.2% | | 30.8% | | 20.3% | |

Source:   DEED, Spring 2004 Benchmarks, Grade 8, retrieved 8/25/04.

Results from administration of the HSGQE in 2003 to 2006 (the same test was used in all 4 years) show little change from those reported for 2000-2002, with the exception of mathematics, due to a refocusing of the exam in this area, and a resetting of the cut scores for all three tests. Too, differences in percentage proficiency continued between Caucasian, non-Latino and ethnic minority populations, with the greatest gaps on the reading examination in 2006 (White students scoring at 85.5% proficient and Alaska Natives at 51.3% proficient). The HSGQE requirement gives students five opportunities to retake portions of the exam they have not passed before the date of graduation (and multiple opportunities after their senior high school year). The spring 2004 graduation was the first directly linked to the HSGQE, and the majority of students did receive diplomas, some 63% of all students. The highest rates of non-graduation, as expected, were in small, rural schools, with only 33% of Alaska Natives graduating (Center on Education Policy, 2005). The 2006 graduation rates showed the same trend lines: Caucasians, 68%; Asians, 60%; Latinos, 54%, Blacks, 49%; and Alaska Natives, 45% (DEED, 2006).

Finally, in 2006, the state released information on the performance status of schools under NCLB. In 2003, 289 schools (or 58% of all schools) met AYP, and the percentage remained the same the following year. In 2005, 292 schools (59%) met AYP, the same number as met the target in 2006 (DEED, 2006). Overall, nearly 40% of Alaska schools did not meet AYP.

Roger Sampson, Commissioner of Education, cautioned Alaskans to be circumspect in evaluating the performance status of schools: "It is very difficult for a school to make AYP. There's one way to make AYP and 31 ways of not making it. In fact, 69 schools met AYP targets in all (but one) categories, and missed AYP in only one category" (DEED, 2005d). The commissioner commented that nearly half of the schools missing AYP failed in "two or fewer of the 31 categories." Putting a positive spin on state testing results, the commissioner said: "(M)any schools made substantial improvements in student achievement over the past 2 years, but did not meet AYP yet. Nevertheless, the progress these schools have made is remarkable" (DEED, 2005d, p. 1).

Alaska's accountability system does not include sanctions for non-Title I schools. The Title I schools failing to make AYP proceed from Level 1 to Level 5; schools leave the list subject to sanctions (Level 2 and higher) only if they meet AYP for two consecutive years, a condition that applies to 39 of the 192 schools at Level 2 or higher in 2005-06 (DEED, 2006, p. 49).

## PROSPECTS FOR ATTAINMENT OF NCLB GOALS BY 2014

Alaska is a relatively late entrant to state educational assessment and accountability. It has a strong tradition of local control of schooling, a small department of education, and a wide gulf between urban and rural schools. By late 2006, Alaska has had just 7 years' experience with this type of education reform, three under state auspices and the last four under joint federal/state requirements.

In general, Alaska students probably have received more benefits than endured costs under the high stakes testing regime. Educators have had to specify the standards they believe students should meet, align curricula to the standards, develop methods to help low-attaining students, and monitor student performance. The emphasis on basic skills has focused instruction.

Yet there is evidence that the state has not done its homework in establishing a credible regime of standards, assessments, and accountability. The Fordham Foundation gave Alaska's content and performance standards low marks ("Ds"). The English standards are "unclear in purpose," poorly matched to grade levels, and use "non-literary" more than literary categories (Stotsky, 2005, pp. 29-30). Math standards rely on calculators too early and extensively, over-emphasize manipulatives, and slight mathematical reasoning (Klein, 2005). Previously, we pointed out that the state changed its assessment system without a justifiable reason in 2004-05, making it difficult to compare results over time, especially for subgroups. And Alaska's accountability system receives low marks from *Quality Counts*, because it lacks sanctions for schools failing to meet AYP unless they operate under Title I rules. The state also does not reward schools that have made exemplary progress. *Quality Counts 2007* rates Alaska's policies aligning education from "cradle to career" as 20th of the 50 states. Alaska's policy activity in the areas of standards, assessments, and accountability earns it a rank of 39 (pp. 3, 5). Fordham's (2007) most recent evaluation opines that the state's laissez-faire approach to standards makes them "among the worst in the nation" (p. 4).

During the first phase in implementation of the high stakes testing and accountability regime, Alaska spent less money on schooling than the average state. High oil prices in the early twenty-first century have made it possible for the state to significantly increase school funding in FY2006 and FY 2007 (McBeath, 2006, in press). This may make it possible for school districts to increase teacher salaries, as they search for ways, especially in rural Alaska, to attract and retain highly qualified teachers.

With increased funding, efforts to improve teacher preparation, and more programmatic interventions to assist low-performing students, the state may lift achievement levels of most identified subgroups by 2014. However, the gulf between student achievement rates in urban and rural schools referred to throughout this chapter will not be easy to bridge, and certainly will not close by the conclusion of the 12-year NCLB experiment. This challenge is more daunting than that faced by most states, and to address it will require greater reforms than enacted in Alaska to date.

## NOTES

1.  The state education department notes that its count of private school enrollment "does not reflect the entire Religious and Other Private Schools population for Alaska. This only reflects the schools that have sent in forms required for exempt status which is recognized by complying with Alaska Statute (AS) 14.45.100-14.45.130." Retrieved November 26, 2005, from http://www.eed.state.ak.us/stats

2.  This section is drawn from McBeath and Reyes (in press). See also Covey, Hill, Lind, and Oldaker (1999, pp. 118-23).

3.  Throwing off the *Quality Counts* calculation is the extremely high contribution of two local governments—the North Slope Borough (home of Prudhoe Bay) and the city of Valdez (home of the marine terminal from which Alaska's oil is shipped to the Lower-48 states)—to school budgets. The state exempts the two districts from its disparity calculations, but *Quality Counts* has not.

4.  AS 14.03.120 (education planning; reports). Dr. Nicholas Stayrook, former director of program planning and evaluation of the Fairbanks North Star Borough School District comments that this statute was adopted in 1990 and amended several times thereafter. The statute requires creation of both a school report card to the public and a district report card to the public, annually. It was on the books well before QSI, but the QSI used it as a component of the new state reform effort.

5.  Approximately 30% of the LEP students are also migrants to the state and living in Alaska cities; most, however, are Alaska Native students from villages where the Native language remains dominant.

6. USDOE never determined that the previous assessment system did not meet NCLB requirements. Dr. Nicholas Stayrook notes: "It was the *opinion* of the current commissioner and assessment director that the previous assessment system did not meet federal requirements, and they used their opinion as the justification for replacing the system. The previous administration's plan was to augment the CAT/6 with additional test questions to align the test measures with state GLEs" (personal communication, December 13, 2005)

7. NCLB regulations provide an alternate method for schools failing to meet AMO if the school or subgroup shows improvement by having a 10% reduction in the percent not proficient from previous year performance data or falls within the lower bound of a 75% confidence interval or a 10% reduction in percent not proficient from the previous year. Dr. Nicholas Stayrook notes that in addition to the safe harbor provisions, Alaska also has used a confidence interval approach to meeting the AMOs. This approach allowed schools with low percent proficiency and small numbers of students to meet the AMO by falling within the 99% confidence interval. In fact, schools with only 29% proficiency in language arts and just 10 students met the AMO of 64%. In math, a school with 10 students only needed 19% proficiency to meet the AMO.

8. Although Alaska ranked first in average teacher salary in the 1980s, by 2000-01 the state had dropped to ninth, with average pay of $48,123. Taking into account Alaska's high cost of living, the state's ranking is about 32nd among the American states. See *Quality Counts* (2003).

9. Dr. Nicholas Stayrook notes that this is also a consequence of resetting the cut scores for proficiency for eighth grade students in 2003. The state established cut scores on the CAT/6 in 2003 using an equipercentile equating model based on the sixth grade 2002 student performance. This set cut scores on the CAT/6 scale score that were comparable to the cut scores used on the sixth grade benchmark test. During this cut score setting process, the state also reset the cut scores on the eighth grde tests to make them more comparable to the sixth grade cut scores.

10. For this reason, USDOE Secretary Margaret Spellings urged observers to compare the percentage of students performing at the proficiency level on state tests with the percentage of students performing at the "basic" level on NAEP. Performance at the basic level, by fourth graders in reading (2003) was 58%; in math, 77%; by eighth graders (2003) in reading the basic figure was 70%, and the math figure also 70%. Indeed, the gap narrows if the basic level is used, but this level indicates only "partial mastery of prerequisite knowledge and skills." See also Dillon (2005).

## REFERENCES

Alaska, Department of Education and Early Development. (2000, February). *Alaska standards: Content and performance standards for Alaska students.* Juneau, AK: Author.

Alaska, Department of Education and Early Development. (2002, June). *History of Alaska school reform: 19091-2002.* Juneau, AK: Author.

Alaska, Department of Education and Early Development. (2004, August). *Spring 2004 benchmarks, grade 8, scoring above and below proficiency by race/ethnicity.* Juneau, AK: Author.

Alaska, Department of Education and Early Development. (2005a, August). *Alaska accountability: adequate yearly progress.* Juneau, AK: Author.

Alaska, Department of Education and Early Development. (2005b, May 20). *Alaska initiates statewide teacher mentoring program* (Press release). Juneau, AK: Author.

Alaska, Department of Education and Early Development. (2005c, August 12). *Education department releases statewide school performance status* (News release). Juneau, AK: Author.

Alaska, Department of Education and Early Development. (2006). *Report card to the public.* Juneau, AK: Author.

Alaska, Office of the Governor (2001). *A+: A strategy for year two funding.* Juneau, AK: Education funding Task Force.

Alaska Quality Schools Coalition. (2004). *Reinventing schools.* Retrieved September 3, 2004, from www.reinventingschools.org/aqsc.php

American Legislative Exchange Council. (2004). *Report card on American education.* Washington, DC: Author.

*Anchorage Daily News.* (2005, October 23).

Barone, M., & Cohen, R. E. (2005). *The almanac of American politics.* Washington, DC: The National Journal Group.

Berman, M. (2001). Alaska. In *Public school finance programs for the United States and Canada: 1998-99.* Washington, DC: National Center for Education Statistics.

Center on Education Policy. (2005, August). *States try harder, but gaps persist.* Washington, DC: Author.

Chugach School District. (2004). Retrieved September 2, 2004, from http://www.chugachschools.com/standards_based_system/shared_vision/index.html

Consortium for Policy Research in Education. (2000, June). *Assessment and accountability in the fifty states: 1999-2000, Alaska.* Madison, WI: Author.

Covey, J., Hill, F., Lind, M. & Oldaker, L. (1999). Education: Continuing urban-rural tension. In C. Thomas (Ed.), *Alaska public policy issues* (pp. 118-23). Juneau, AK: Denali Press.

Darnell, F. (Ed.). (1972). Systems of education for the Alaska Native population. In *Education in the north* (pp. 293-324). Fairbanks: University of Alaska Press.

Dillon, S. (2005, November 26). Students ace state tests, but earn D's from U.S. *New York Times*, p. A1.

Fordham Institute. (2007). The Fordham report 2006: How well are states educating our neediest children? Retrieved February 22, 2007, from http://www.edexcellence.net/institute/publication/publication.cfm?id=363&pubsubid=1401

Jester, T. E. (2002). Healing the "unhealthy Native": Encounters with standards-based education in rural Alaska. *Journal of American Indian Education, 42*(3), 1-21.

Klein, D. (2005). *The state of state math standards.* Washington, DC: Fordham Foundation.

McBeath, J. (2006). Alaska's FY 06 budget process. In *Proceedings—roundtable: Budgeting in the 13 western states*. Salt Lake City, UT: Center for Policy and Administration.

McBeath, J. (in press). Alaska. In *Proceedings—roundtable: Budgeting in the 13 Western states*. Salt Lake City, UT: Center for Policy and Administration.

McBeath, J., & Reyes, M. (2004, September). *High performing rural schools: Responses to high stakes testing in Alaska*. Fairbanks: University of Alaska Fairbanks, The Alaska Schools Research Fund.

McBeath, J., & Reyes, M. (in press). Testing, testing, testing: Rural and urban responses to Alaska's high stakes assessment regime. *Northern Review*.

McBeath, J., Reyes, M., & Ehrlander, M. (2006, August). *School adaptation to high stakes testing in Alsaska*. Fairbanks: University of Alaska Fairbanks, The Alaska Schools Research Fund.

McDiarmid, G. W., Larson, E., & Hill, A. (2002). *Retaining quality teachers for Alaska*. Anchorage, AK: University of Alaska Anchorage, Institute of Social and Economic Research.

McDowell Group. (2005). *Alaska Native K-12 education indicators, 2004, final report*. Anchorage, AK.

McLain, E. (2002, December 3). 2002/2003 Adequate yearly progress (AYP) and school improvement status (letter from deputy commissioner to members of state board of education). Juneau, AK.

National Center for Education Statistics. (2005). *Alaska state profile*. Retrieved November 23, 2005, from http://nces.ed.gov/nationsreportcard/states/profile .asp

Northwest Regional Educational Laboratory. (2003, June). *Challenges and opportunities of NCLB for small, rural, and isolated schools*. Portland, OR: Author.

Olson, L. (2001, January 24). States adjust high-stakes testing plans. *Education Week, 20*(19), 1, 18.

Olson, L. (2003, February 19). Small schools pose big challenges. *Education Week, 23*(42), 22.

Olson, L. (2004, July 14). States dicker over changes to AYP plans. *Education Week, 23*(43), 1, 22.

*Quality Counts*. (2003). The teacher gap: Alaska. *Education Week*. Retrieved November 23, 2005, from http://counts.edweek.org/sreports/qc03/templates/state .cfm?slug-17qcak.h22

*Quality Counts*. (2005). Report card: Alaska. *Education Week*. Retrieved November 23, 2005, from http://counts.edweek.org/sreports/qc05

*Qualitiy Counts*. (2007). From cradle to career: Alaska. *Education Week*. Retrieved February 10, 2007, from http://www.edweek.org/go/qc07

Sampson, R. (2005, September 27). *New three level teacher certification system* (Memorandum #2006-05). Juneau, AK.

Stayrook, N. (2005, December 9). *Comparison of state assessments to NAEP and TerraNova results* (Memorandum to school board members). Fairbanks, AK.

Stotsky, S. (2005). *The state of state ENGLISH standards*. Washington, DC: Fordham Foundation.

U.S. Census Bureau. (2007). *State & county quick facts: Alaska*. Retrieved February 23, 2007, from http://quickfacts.census.gov/qfd/states/02000.html

# CHAPTER 11

# CONCLUSIONS

We conclude the volume with a summary of findings from each of the nine state studies. Then we examine the dimensions that seem to describe the initiation of education reform in the states, the impact of the No Child Left Behind (NCLB) federal reform legislation, and variation in effects across the states.

## SUMMARY

*Massachusetts* has been a leader in the standards-based reform movement. The efforts began in the 1980s with leaders from the business sector advocating for accountability in education to prepare students better to meet the needs of the economy and the commonwealth. The Massachusetts Education Reform Act (MERA) of 1993 passed with broad bipartisan support and backing from education leadership and business. MERA called for academic standards with aligned assessments and improvements to instruction. It also fundamentally revised the funding of public education to increase substantially the state's contribution and to insure much greater equity among school districts. Massachusetts' achievement levels were among the highest in the nation, and the Bay State's students' scores rose with each round of the Massachusetts Comprehensive Assessment System (MCAS) and National Assessment of Educational Progress (NAEP) tests. The most vocal opponents of education reform have been the teach-

*Education Reform in the American States*
pp. 283–296
Copyright © 2008 by Information Age Publishing

ers' union, the Massachusetts Teachers' Association, and high achieving students and their parents who resent what they consider excess time spent on unchallenging work. The leadership of Republican governors, of the Democratic legislature, and of the relatively insulated state Board of Education have kept education reform moving ahead in the face of this relatively narrow opposition. The greatest challenge to the state in meeting the demands of NCLB will be raising achievement levels of Massachusetts' poor and minority students who enter school with significant educational deficits. The state is on the verge of beginning a pilot program that will increase time in school in order to meet the educational needs of these children.

Once America's most populous state, with the largest number of K-12 students, in 2006 *New York* ranks third. New York City, however, remains America's premier city. The city is diverse ethnically, racially, and socioeconomically, and school achievement gaps are pronounced. New York led other states in the establishment of an high school exit examination. As part of comprehensive accountability reforms in the mid-1990s, the Regents' Examination became a high stakes test. A second distinctive aspect of education reform in New York was decentralization of education to community boards of New York City in the late 1960s. New York's assessment and accountability system won national acclaim before enactment of NCLB and appeared to be working to raise student performance based on assessments done from 1999 to 2002. Passage of NCLB hit New York at an awkward time, and the state sought delay of implementation in order to cover all grades from three to eight, measure subgroup performance, and insure that all teachers of core subjects were highly qualified. Initial testing results after NCLB indicate very modest initial success. Serious problems remain in providing equitable funding to New York City students, improving teacher qualifications, and implementing consistent standards.

*Virginia,* too, has been a leader in the standards-based reform movement. Republican Governor George Allen initiated the reform, having run on an education platform in 1994 that called attention to Virginia students' poor achievement levels. The process of developing the commonwealth's Standards of Learning and Standards of (school) Accreditation was highly contentious, but the results were praiseworthy, and Virginia's standards have been used as a model in many states. After initial tests administered in 1998 showed dismal results, the state implemented several programs to render assistance to students and to school personnel to improve student learning. Then test scores improved. Yet, Virginia's response to NCLB has been ambivalent. While the state had a model accountability system in place well before implementation of NCLB, Virginia's system had not called for disaggregation of students' scores by race and socioeconomic status. When this was done and Virginia faced the onerous task of raising all subgroups to proficiency under NCLB, the state raised loud objections. Like other states, Virginia will have to respond much more aggressively and apply greater resources and innovation to meet the needs of low-performing students and schools if it is to meet the 2012-14 targets for NCLB.

*North Carolina's* approach to education reform has been exemplary in a number of ways. The state launched its ABCs of Public Education in 1996 following a decade-long process that united the business sector and political and education leaders behind the call for accountability to improve the state's public education program and to boost the economy. The state won acclaim for having the largest gains in the nation on the NAEP in the 1990s. This success engendered even greater resolve to become a national leader in education, and in the late 1990s, Governor Jim Hunt (D) challenged the state to become "First in Education in 2010." Governor Mike Easley (D) endorsed his predecessor's goal, and given the synergistic efforts of the business sector, higher education, public education, and political leadership, the state is poised to succeed in its quest. North Carolina embraced the principles of NCLB, integrated its ABCs with the national accountability system, and has met every challenge with increased vigor and commitment to investing the resources necessary to meeting the educational needs of all its students. North Carolina has much work to do to meet its own and NCLB's goals, especially in terms of raising achievement levels of its poor and minority students. However, the leadership from within the various sectors that launched the education reform and has steadfastly pursued commitment to the state's youth has been nothing short of inspirational.

*Florida's* progress in the educational accountability movement has been supported by a strong coalition of business interests, a Republican legislature, and a popular Republican governor, Jeb Bush. These groups and the public in general have shown strong support for school choice. The state had early charter school legislation, perhaps the reason that the number of charter schools grew from five in 1996 to 222 in 2002. The state had a comprehensive and effective assessment plan prior to NCLB that provided both rewards and sanctions to schools based on student performance. The governor recently signed new legislation that will provide school vouchers for a universal pre-K program for 4-year-olds. Florida has a healthy "booming" economy. There has been a small but steady increase in student performance after NCLB. However, improvement in math scores lags behind for students across all grade levels. In 2003, fourth graders in Florida were the only group in the nation to show improved performance in reading on the NAEP. The state has a large minority population. In 2005, the state attempted to gain approval from the USDOE for a "Provisional AYP" plan that would have allowed some of the best schools in the state to escape not meeting AYP based on the performance of students in special subgroups (poor, minority). Secretary Spellings rejected the state's plan.

*Texas* has been a national leader in education reform. The Texas economy is generally healthy; the state lost its reliance on oil in the 1980s when it diversified its economy. Regardless, there is a large disparity between rich and poor, and the state appears as a study of contrasts in many other ways. Texas has a history of segregated schools and a public school system that until the 1980s was not very effective in educating its most vulnerable citizens. Today, Texas has an over 60% minority student population. Of these, nearly 40% qualify for free lunches. The state has a growing and increasingly politicized and educated Latino population, which generally supports social change. Pressure for improving schools came in the early 1980s led by the Perot Commission representing the business sector. Texas had a relatively comprehensive assessment plan prior to NCLB, which showed impressive early student performance results (on both the state tests and the NAEP) that many believe served as the model for NCLB. Much of the progress in education appears to have been prompted by results of a series of lawsuits. NCLB requirements seem to have further fine-tuned the system but also created another layer of bureaucracy at the Texas Education Agency. According to the NAEP, Texas needs to improve on rewarding schools for improved student performance, on fixing the pesky problem of unequal financing of schools, and on requiring a set of content specific courses for teachers.

*Michigan's* fortunes long have been married to those of the auto industry, and with the decline of the latter the state is undergoing a re-examination of expectations. The state is considered progressive based on its liberal and generous social policies. There has been strong opposition to the use of public funds for school vouchers, but there appears to be strong support for school choice from the state legislature and business groups, some of which have organized to provide private voucher support for poor children. Michigan's system of standards, assessments, and accountability has evolved over a period of 40 years, in a pattern of fits and starts. NCLB brought about some tightening and centralization of the system overall. By 2006, the state had aligned assessments to state standards in the core content areas at every grade level, and the state board had adopted rigorous new standards for high schools. The state faces challenges related to teacher quality, low-performing schools, and resource equity. Between 2003 and 2006, there were particularly wide discrepancies between state and national scores on student performance. Scores on state tests indicated progressive improvement and a slight narrowing of the achievement gap for some subgroups, but NAEP scores reflected little change. The restructuring of the Michigan economy in the last three decades has helped focus public attention on the need to prepare students for a competitive future.

*California* is America's largest state in population and the most diverse demographically; it has large populations of super-rich and the very poor. Once highly regarded for the quality of its schools, California's education system deteriorated because of resource limitations (especially the 1978 tax revolt curbing rises in property taxes) and increase of ethnic/racial and socioeconomic diversity. At the state's first participation in NAEP tests in 1994, California students tied for last with Louisiana, and this spurred the state to develop an assessment and accountability system called the Public School Accountability Act (PSAA) in 1998, with clearly marked rewards and sanctions. Preliminary analysis of school efforts under the state's system revealed a narrowing of the gap between low- and high-performing schools. When NCLB was enacted in 2002, California had barely completed implementation of its own accountability system, and had to enlarge its assessments, develop standard accountability measures, revise its interventions for failing schools, and launch new efforts to prepare teachers whose qualification rates were among the lowest in the nation. Tests of California students in the three years following NCLB implementation indicate very slight improvement in proficiency rates and slow growth in AYP from year to year, and more than one third of California's schools have failed to make AYP under NCLB rules. Most attention has focused on the need to increase fiscal resources to support K-12 education reform. We also note that obstacles to reform may be as much political as economic.

Finally, *Alaska* is America's third most sparsely populated state but the largest territorially. Its population includes the largest percentage of aboriginal residents—16%—who form a majority in most rural areas of the state. Today, rural Native schools are distinctive from urban schools in governance, finance, curriculum, staff, and outcomes. Alaska began to develop statewide standards and matching assessments only in the mid-1990s and in 1997, under business and conservative Republican legislative pressure, adopted a high stakes competency test for high school students. Its accountability system lacked sanctions or rewards for schools, however, and did not include all students in lower and middle-school grades. Preliminary analyses of the system showed large achievement gaps among ethnic groups, with most Alaska Natives in rural schools performing at the bottom. NCLB entered Alaska education while the state was struggling to implement its own system. NCLB required changes in state assessments, development of a choice system for students in poorly performing schools, and effective programs to improve teacher quality. An additional response to state and NCLB requirements was the development of the Quality Schools Model, an effort that initially was funded externally, representing an extensive and significant restructuring of schooling for small rural schools. Analysis of NCLB's impact on Alaska schooling shows little improvement of scores in reading, writing, and math from 2002 to 2006. Increased funding to low-performing schools (40% did not make AYP in 2003-06) may assist in bridging the serious achievement gaps. Yet the geography of the state, low population density in many regions, high teacher attrition, high rural living costs, and cultural differences between Alaska Natives and non-Natives: all are significant barriers to school improvement.

## DIMENSIONS OF CHANGE

Our observation of education reform at the state level, through relatively detailed investigations of standards-based reform in nine states, leads to conclusions regarding the dimensions of change. Six questions prompt the search for patterns: (1) What factors were most important (both internal and exogenous) in the development of state accountability systems before NCLB? (2) How much variation was there in state systems at the time in enactment of NCLB? (3) What impact did NCLB have on the different state systems of accountability? (4) What variation was there in resistance to reform at the state level? (5) What challenges remain to effective implementation of NCLB? And 6) How efficacious has this episode of educational reform been? We explore each in turn.

### Factors Influencing Development of State Accountability Systems

Most of the states we have introduced had assessment and accountability systems in place before the enactment of NCLB in January 2002. Although they did not follow identical paths toward education reform, the state-level processes expressed several common elements. In each of the pioneering states, the formation of a broad-scale coalition was either led or supported by pressure from business associations and alliances. For example, the California Business Roundtable was especially active in that state and formed an alliance with other associations to promote school reform. Business groups responded positively to the challenge presented by *A Nation at Risk* in 1983, by their own experience in the marketplace, and by changes in the global economy. Their campaigns for reform emphasized lack of workforce preparation of high school graduates as well as the impact of uneven school performance on national competitiveness. In a few instances, such as the Texas reform efforts of H. Ross Perot in the mid-1980s, business leaders also were policy entrepreneurs who sought to develop political capital through the successful orchestration of change.

Education reform is an attractive area for policy entrepreneurs. Education increasingly interests voters as it rises on the agenda of public issues (see McGuinn, 2006, p. 200), inspires their protective interests, and allows policy entrepreneurs to reach beyond partisan confines to form a majority in support of change. Several of the states we studied had policy entrepreneurs who led campaigns to improve choice for students and parents, and in particular who championed school vouchers.

An old generalization in the literature on educational change is that reforms flow more frequently from Democratic governors and legislatures than from Republicans. Our studies did not demonstrate this to be the case. Governors in most of the nine states played reform roles, but Democrats were no more likely than Republicans to lead change efforts. Too, Republican legislatures, such as that in Alaska, were as often in the lead as were Democratic ones. In most states, electoral dynamics figures in major reform efforts (see Wong & Shen, 2002). Because the NCLB reform effort focuses on responsibility and accountability, which long have been emphases of the national Republican Party, partisan differences of governors and legislatures have been less salient. (As Peterson remarks, in education "the party of local control has become the party of the federal mandate" [2003, p. 29].) Finally, gubernatorial leadership of reform was balanced in a few of the states with strong leadership by the state department of education. This latter organization is more insulated from political pressures in all states except those which elect a superintendent of public instruction (just three in our sample of states), and thus may not benefit as greatly from tides of reform generally.

Exogenous factors also affected the reform process in the states. First, the early reform states, such as Texas, transmitted reform ideas to other states in a classic process of horizontal diffusion. Diffusion occurred mostly in the South initially, an area with the poorest education results of any region, and then spread to states in other regions. Transmitters of reform included not only the state's public officials—governor and legislature—but also groups in the expanded issue network of educational politics (see Cibulka, 2001) such as business associations, policy entrepreneurs, educational consultants, religious groups, and even the firms, such as McGraw-Hill, which developed assessments and textbooks to match state-level reforms.

A second important exogenous source of change was national, and illustrates vertical diffusion. All states were implicated by the Clinton administration's revision of the ESEA, which required states to develop content and performance standards, but not all states followed the request. Some states, such as Alaska, took advantage of the federal call for standards-based education; other states, such as California and Michigan, virtually ignored it. Other national agents of change included the Education Commission of the States, the Council of Chief State School Officers, and policy and research organizations focusing on accountability—for example, the Consortium for Policy Research in Education and the Fordham Foundation.

## Variation in State Systems Before Enactment of NCLB

Nearly all the American states had elements of assessment and accountability systems before 2002, but they varied significantly in comprehensiveness and quality of standards and assessments, agents held responsible, rewards for high performance and sanctions for failure. Each of the nine states we have surveyed had an assessment system, and in most the assessments were aligned to content and performance standards. None of the states in our sample tested students each year from Grades 3 to 8; and none tested the same students as they progressed up the educational ladder instead of different cohorts of students.

Just one-third of the states we investigated held students responsible through denying high school diplomas if they failed to pass competency examinations. And as noted above, states were likely to delay the effective date of accountability for students beyond that originally planned. Only a few states, notably Texas, initially held teachers accountable through requiring them to pass competency examinations. More of the states had developed accountability provisions for low-performing schools; typically these allowed schools long periods, up to five years, to meet state expectations. Most of the states provided assistance for students who attended failing schools, but choice was limited by availability of charter schools (or state vouchers for students to attend private schools) as well as regulatory flexibility permitting students to cross district lines and pay for their transportation. In few cases we examined, were institutions beyond students, teachers, and schools held responsible—for example, school districts or the state education agency.

States differed too in the systems of rewards and punishments developed to spur improved school performance. Sanctions were more likely to be used than rewards, but some states such as Florida provided both.

## Impact of NCLB on State Accountability Systems

To most observers, the enactment of NCLB represented the most sweeping national reform of education in the United States since the adoption of the Elementary and Secondary Education Act in 1965 and an even more intrusive federal role in education. Others believe it to be a natural evolution of federal K-12 education policy and not an abrupt change from the past. All commentators agree, however, that NCLB is an example of vertical diffusion of education reform, with mandates from the federal government to the states for the purpose of attaining federal objectives.

Although most states had elements of accountability systems before NCLB, they were not uniform, and NCLB has introduced greater similarity in state systems. For example, state assessments must be aligned to standards and the assessments must test all children in Grades 3 through 8 and once in high school. However, states determine their own standards, and they select their own assessments.

One of the greatest differences between NCLB requirements and those of the state systems is the mandate that student scores be disaggregated by racial/ethnic group as well as LEP, disability, and poverty status. NCLB did not require that students be held accountable, and as a result some states have high stakes exit exams (high school competency examinations) and others do not. The unit held accountable is the individual school, which is required to demonstrate proficiency of all students and student subgroupings, based on 95% attendance, by 2014.

States had great latitude in determining what level of proficiency satisfied Adequate Yearly Progress (AYP), because each state selected the assessments based on which proficiency was measured and its level. Some states established even steps on the ladder toward 100% proficiency in 2014; others allowed baby steps in early years and then required giant steps in the last 3-4 years (perhaps in the belief that by then the reform spirit would have waned and NCLB amended into nothingness). In nearly every case study, we have pointed out the difference between proficiency rates on state assessments and those on the NAEP, the national measure that now all states are required to use under NCLB. It is important to keep in mind that state assessments are a census of all students at grade level; the NAEP tests a sample of students in all states.

NCLB mandated that states provide meaningful choice to students in failing schools, but the U.S. Department of Education (USDOE) has allowed postponements and liberal waivers to this requirement (for example, supplying tutoring services to students in failing schools or districts). NCLB also required that failing schools be sanctioned, but it is too early to determine the impact that this requirement will have in tightening sanctions at the state level or encouraging school restructuring, because 2005-06 is the first year of imposition for the restructuring requirement.

## Resistance to Reform at the State Level

To reform K-12 education requires establishment of a majority coalition and its continued attention to consolidation of reform over time. It is not difficult initially to form a majority coalition to improve education, because in general most citizens support an increase of standards and achievement levels of students, which benefits most students and society at large. What is difficult is to sustain the reform momentum over time. This is because those who bear the costs of education reform—primarily public school teachers—as Wilson (1980) points out, have a strong and obvious incentive to organize in opposition to change. Education reformers, on the other hand, find it difficult to hold their coalition together, given that the benefits to reform are so widely dispersed and seem to provide no clear incentives for beneficiaries to counter systematic opposition from those, such as teachers and school administrators, with vested interests to protect.

We have provided some evidence of teacher resistance to reform in each of the nine states surveyed. We distinguished right-to-work states, on the one hand, from those in which teachers have free rights to organize and the state enforces collective bargaining agreements between teachers' unions and school districts, on the other. In right-to-work states, teacher resistance has been muted; in the other states, teachers unions have spoken out and mobilized against state accountability systems, and in some cases filed suit against accountability laws and regulations in state and federal court. In this regard, NEA has played a more hostile role than AFT (see Koppich, 2005).

In a few case studies we also pointed out opposition to accountability reforms on the part of upper-income parents and some education researchers who believe that accountability systems, with their emphasis on "drill and kill" among other practices designed to help students achieve on assessments, have dumbed down schooling so that it no longer challenges youth (see Kornhaber, 2004). In several states for example Texas and Florida, organizations representing minority youth, such as the NAACP and (in Texas) MALDEF, also opposed the seemingly more rigorous requirements of accountability legislation for minority than majority youth, believing it punished students instead of holding the system accountable.

Teachers and minorities are represented by the Democratic Party in the United States today; certainly in several state legislatures and in the U.S. Congress, it is the Democratic Party that has been on point with attacks on NCLB (although in some states, such as Virginia, opposition comes from both political parties). Already, several bills have been introduced in the Congress to amend NCLB, none of which has yet moved to the floor for discussion and debate. NCLB is scheduled for reauthorization in 2007, and hearings under the NCLB Commissions have already begun. Concentrated opposition to its provisions may weaken the majority bipartisan coalition in its support. As Hess (2003) noted in his study of education reform, there is likely to be pressure to relax NCLB's rules and deadlines for moving all children to academic proficiency.

Economic and social conservatives, most of whom are Republicans, have used the choice provisions of NCLB to attempt to increase the number of charter schools and to promote use of school vouchers. Indeed, several states have strengthened charter school provisions, and the number of charter schools has doubled since 2001, correlating with the implementation of NCLB. To the present, however, supporters of school vouchers have not seen their development in all or even most states. Florida stands apart from most states in this respect.

## Challenges to Effective Implementation of NCLB

We can identify four areas in implementation of NCLB in the states that present continuing challenges: sufficiency of financial resources to support reform; improvement of teacher quality, particularly in poverty areas of high minority enrollment; assistance to students of limited English proficiency (LEP); and the "race to the bottom" of states in dealing with other subgroupings of students (ethnic/racial, students with disabilities, and socioeconomically disadvantaged students).

Opponents to educational reform and especially NCLB have called it an "unfunded mandate," arguing that the federal government has not allocated sufficient funds to assist states in meeting national objectives. ESEA funding increased for the first 2 years in implementation of NCLB, but then leveled off, and indeed states have had to increase education funding to meet requirements. While critics of the critics state that the United States already spends more on K-12 education per capita than any other nation, the problems NCLB is designed to solve—chiefly the gap in student achievement of racial, income, and disability subgroupings—will require greater resources than currently dedicated to the task. For example, North Carolina won praise for turning around the first 15 low-performing schools it identified by dispatching super teams of master teachers and administrators to work closely with schools. Yet to provide similar assistance to hundreds of schools exceeds this state's capability. We noted the difficulty that school improvement efforts imposed on several states during the economic recession of 2001-02.

Second, the requirement that teachers of core subject areas be "highly qualified," has not been satisfactorily addressed in all states. Permissive federal rules allow states to develop their own definitions and tests of what highly qualified means. As we noted in discussing California, teachers could use a variety of methods to demonstrate their qualifications, reducing uniformity nationwide. And, in some states, charter schools are not required to abide by this regulation. Furthermore, this new requirement coincides with a national teacher shortage. States now compete with one another for a shrinking pool of qualified teacher applicants. Yet the least tractable problem is assigning teachers to areas of greatest need—poverty regions with high concentrations of minority youth—and retaining qualified teachers in those districts. Few of the states we examined had changed regulations and improved resources so that schools and districts in greatest need could enlarge the applicant pool and reduce mobility of those teachers. A small sign of hope is that some states such as Alaska, Florida, and Texas have implemented mentoring programs for new teachers.

Third, unlike the other subgroupings, which seem likely to either remain constant in size and percentage or grow only slightly, students of limited English proficiency are increasing in tandem with the increase of the American immigrant population. Four of the states we reviewed—California, Texas, Florida, and New York—have growing numbers of LEP students. While it may be possible for these states to bring LEP students to proficiency levels within 5-6 years, this begs the question of how proficiency problems will be addressed for students entering the United States from 2006-7 to 2013-14.

Fourth, we noted the extent to which NCLB encouraged some states to develop the lowest possible proficiency levels and insofar as possible to reduce their accounting for subgroupings by increasing the minimum subgroup size required for their reporting under NCLB accountability requirements (see Kane & Staiger, 2003). This is the most direct challenge to successful implementation of NCLB in the states, and it reflects the fundamental compromise that enabled passage of the legislation.

## Efficacy of Educational Reform Through Accountability

In each of our case studies, we compared the results of the state accountability system before enactment of NCLB with that after the fact. In the states having well-established assessment and accountability systems, such as Virginia, North Carolina, Florida, and Texas, early results of the state system were impressive, even when measured by NAEP in addition to the states' assessments. This apparent success of the education reform fortified advocates and diminished criticism by opponents.

We note a correlation between support for NCLB and degree of student improvement on the state's own accountability system before the enactment of NCLB. Strong support for national accountability legislation is seen today in North Carolina, Texas, and Florida, all three of which experienced significant rises in student test scores. (Opposition from Virginia, which also demonstrated increases in test scores [but after dismal initial test results], is more difficult to explain.)

Because NCLB applies to each of the 50 states and the District of Columbia, it is not possible to design tests showing the impact it has had on state accountability systems. We cannot establish control and experimental groups, varying by whether states fall under state accountability rules, federal, both, or neither. And NCLB has been in effect only four years as of this writing, too short a period to measure the effectiveness of reform. Thus we cannot answer the large question about the efficacy of federal education reform through uniform assessment and accountability requirements.

In the individual chapters, we have not been sanguine in our estimates of the states' abilities to reach proficiency for all students under NCLB rules. Although the 2014 goal is inspirational, virtually every education specialist believes it is unattainable. In concluding our argument in this chapter, we have pointed to the significant obstacles to the attainment of national objectives by 2014. Yet what strikes most interest and is illustrated throughout this study is the way in which the federal government adopted reforms to education initiated by several of the states, and the way in which states, in turn, transformed federal objectives as they began to implement the mandates. If nothing else, the large-scale education reform that is NCLB demonstrates the continued resilience of America's federal system of government and policy implementation. States negotiated with USDOE for waivers to the most onerous requirements, and the agency was flexible (especially under Secretary Spellings), without losing sight of the chief goals (see Fast & Erpenbach, 2004; Manna, 2007).

If nothing else, the large-scale education reform that is NCLB demonstrates the continued resilience of America's federal system of government and policy implementation. NCLB has not centralized educational federalism in the United States, because as Manna notes "federal officials are still fundamentally quite weak when it comes to leveraging changes in the nation's schools" (2007, p. 135). Instead, as a number of commentators (especially McGuinn, 2006) emphasize, NCLB has moved K-12 education concerns toward formation of a new regime, while individual states, as pointed out in this volume, have chipped away at the edifice.

## REFERENCES

Cibulka, J. G. (2001, January/March). The changing role of interest groups in education: Nationalization and the new politics of education productivity. *Educational Policy, 15*(1), 12-40.

Fast, E. F., & Erpenbach, W. J. (2004). *Revisiting statewide accountability under NCLB.* Washington, DC: Council of State Chief School Officers.

Hess, F. (2003). Refining or retreating? High stakes accountability in the states. In P. E. Peterson & M. West (Eds.), *No Child Left Behind? The politics and practice of school accountability* (pp. 55-79). Washington, DC: The Brookings Institution.

Kane, T. J., & Staiger, D. O. (2003). Unintended consequences of racial subgroup rules. In P. E. Peterson & M. R. West (Eds.), *No Child Left Behind? The politics and practice of school accountability* (pp. 152-76). Washington, DC: The Brookings Institution.

Koppich, J. E. (2005). A tale of two approaches—the AFT, the NEA, and NCLB. *Peabody Journal of Education, 80*(2), 120-37.

Kornhaber, M. (2004, January/March). Appropriate and inappropriate forms of testing, assessment, and accountability. *Educational Policy, 18*(1), 45-70.

Manna, P. (2007). *School's in: Federalism and the national education agenda.* Washington, DC: Georgetown University Press.

McGuinn, P. (2006). *No Child Left Behind and the transformation of federal education policy, 1965-2005.* Lawrence: University Press of Kansas.

Peterson, P. (2003). The changing politics of federalism: In *Evolving federalism: The intergovernmental balance of power in America and Europe.* Syracuse, NY: Maxwell School of Syracuse University.

Wilson, J. Q. (1980). *The politics of regulation.* New York: Basic Books.

Wong, K. K., & Shen, F. X. (2002). Politics of state-led reform in education: Market competition and electoral dynamics. *Educational Policy, 16*(1), 161-192.

# ABOUT THE AUTHORS

**Jerry McBeath** has been professor of political science at the University of Alaska Fairbanks since 1976. He earned BA and MA degrees at the University of Chicago (1963, 1964) and a PhD in political science at the University of California at Berkeley (1970). His other teaching positions include stints at Rutgers College, the City University of New York, and Fulbright positions at the National Chengchi University in Taiwan and the China Foreign Affairs University in Beijing, China. Research relevant to this study includes studies of education, political socialization, and development in Taiwan and China, educational organization in rural areas of Alaska and the United States, the politics of education in the American states, and education reform in postindustrialized countries. From 1986 to 1995 he was an elected member of the Fairbanks Board of Education. McBeath contributes the chapters on New York, California, and Alaska.

**Maria Elena Reyes** has been associate professor in the College of Education at the University of Texas Pan American in the Rio Grande Valley since the fall of 2006. She earned a BA degree in English and sociology from the University of Texas at Pan-American and a MEd in secondary education from Sul Ross University. For nearly ten years, she was a high school English teacher for the Eagle Pass School District. In 1991 she earned her doctorate in curriculum and instruction at the University of Texas, and then, at the university, she developed and implemented the Hispanic Mother-Daughter Program to serve educational needs of children in Latino families, work which earned her a national award. From 1996 to 2006, Dr. Reyes taught in the School of Education at UAF where she directed the secondary teacher education program, developed distance-delivered education courses for teachers, paraprofessionals, and secondary students in rural schools, supervised technology and education programs serving rural school districts, and taught in the graduate program. Research relevant to this study includes studies of standards-based education in the American states, gender and racial/ethnic disparities in education, and determinants of success for minority student populations. Reyes contributed the chapters on Texas, Florida, and Michigan.

**Mary Frank Ehrlander** has been assistant professor of history and co-director of northern studies at the University of Alaska Fairbanks since 2001. She earned BA and MA degrees (in political science and northern studies) at UAF, and an MA and PhD in government at the University of Virginia in 1999. For 4 years, she taught social studies at Austin Lathrop High School in Fairbanks. Research relevant to this study includes the history of desegregation in American schools and the inability of courts to effect the equal educational opportunity promised in *Brown v. Board of Education* (published as *Equal Educational Opportunity: Brown's Elusive Mandate*) as well as other public education issues. Ehrlander contributed the chapters on Massachusetts, North Carolina, and Virginia.

The authors collaborated in crafting the introduction and conclusion to the volume.

# INDEX

CPSIA information can be obtained at www.ICGtesting.com
Printed in the USA
LVOW01s1049270713

344777LV00001B/32/P